Research
&
Evaluation

in Recreation, Parks &
Leisure Studies

SECOND EDITION

Research & Evaluation

in Recreation, Parks & Leisure Studies

SECOND EDITION

Richard Kraus
Temple University

Lawrence R. Allen
Clemson University

Gorsuch Scarisbrick, Publishers
Scottsdale, Arizona

Publisher:	Gay L. Pauley
Editor:	A. Colette Kelly
Developmental Editor:	Katie E. Bradford
Consulting Editor:	Robert W. Douglass
Production Editor:	Eric Kingsbury
Cover Design:	Kevin Kall
Typesetting:	Andrea Reider

Gorsuch Scarisbrick, Publishers
8233 Via Paseo del Norte, Suite F-400
Scottsdale, AZ 85258

10 9 8 7 6 5 4 3 2 1

ISBN 0-89787-632-6

Library of Congress Cataloging-in-Publication Data

Kraus, Richard G.
    Research & evaluation in recreation, parks & leisure studies /
by Richard Kraus, Lawrence R. Allen. — 2nd ed.
      p. cm.
    Rev. ed. of: Research and evaluation in recreation, parks, and leisure
studies. 1987.
    Includes bibliographical references and index.
    ISBN 0-89787-632-6
    1. Recreation—Research. 2. Recreation—Evaluation. 3. Leisure—
Research. 4. Leisure— Evaluation. I. Allen, Lawrence, 1948–   .
II. Kraus, Richard G. Research and evaluation in recreation, parks, and
leisure studies. III. Title.
GV14.5.K72 1997
790'.072—dc20   96-18709
                                                                   CIP

Brief Contents

Contents

3 Basic Concepts and Language of Research and Evaluation   27

4 Professional Applications of Research and Evaluation   41

5 Experimental Research Designs   53

12 Selecting Subjects for Research: The Sampling Process   155

13 Implementing the Study: The Data-Gathering Process   171

14 Data Organization and Descriptive Statistics   193

15 Overview of Inferential Statistics   227

16 Evaluation as a Professional Function   253

Preface

Over the past two decades, research and evaluation have emerged as increasingly important areas of concern for professionals and educators in the field of recreation, parks, and leisure studies and services.

A primary reason for this trend has been the need to strengthen the theoretical base and professional image of the field by developing a body of specialized knowledge gained through sound research. Beyond this, many leisure-service managers have become heavily dependent on data-based planning and marketing methods in public, voluntary, armed forces, commercial, and therapeutic recreation agencies. As a result, college and university leisure-service curricula now include specialized courses in research and evaluation, and national professional organizations in the United States and Canada regularly sponsor research symposia and assist in the publication of scholarly research reports.

Although some specialized texts on recreation and parks evaluation methods have been published, professors teaching research courses have generally relied on books describing educational, social, or behavioral science research. In writing the first edition of this text, our intention was to provide a source that combined research and evaluation principles and methods and that emphasized the types of studies most relevant to recreation, parks, and leisure concerns. Our conviction was that research and evaluation were closely linked processes and that students in this field should be exposed to both within a single course structure. Beyond this, our purpose was to familiarize readers with the role of systematic inquiry in leisure studies and services, to give them an overview of current research findings on a broad range of topics, and to stimulate their future interest and involvement in research and evaluation.

In preparing the second edition, our purposes have remained the same—to present both research and evaluation as vital elements in the higher education of recreation and parks professionals and to provide both a theoretical framework and practical guidelines for conducting research and evaluation.

This edition has been heavily updated in terms of the studies cited, the inclusion of citations from both the specialized and the general research literature, and current applications in leisure-service programs. Greater emphasis has been given to the actual conduct of research and evaluation studies, including the selection of problem areas, the design of instruments, and the use of a variety of investigative techniques.

Several new chapters have been added, including chapters on the types of research methodologies, such as experimental, descriptive, and historical. This edition also includes new chapters on the role of measurement, sampling procedures, and qualitative or naturalistic research designs. The chapters on evaluation emphasize the benefits-based approach that has gained prominence in numerous national meetings as well as in recreation and parks publications.

Despite these revisions, the book is unchanged in that it continues to steer a middle course between approaching research and evaluation from a conceptual perspective and presenting them as practical tools essential to successful programming and effective agency management.

Throughout this revision, our effort has been to integrate research and evaluation as closely as possible, presenting evaluation as a special purpose and subset of the overall research process.

We recognize that in many universities research and evaluation are taught separately. Evaluation courses are offered at the undergraduate level, and research courses are required for graduate students to equip them to carry out thesis, project, or dissertation assignments. Based on this reality, instructors may need to use this book in different ways. Chapters 1–4 discuss the professional role, concepts, and language of research and evaluation. Chapters 5–8 cover research design and the different types of research methodologies. Chapters 9–13 describe the process of developing and conducting research studies. Chapters 14 and 15 cover descriptive and inferential statistics, which are likely to be of particular interest in graduate courses dealing with research methodology. Chapters 16–19 deal primarily with evaluation study designs and instruments.

As previously noted, instructors may tailor the use of the text to the special purposes of the courses they are teaching and to the interests and aptitudes of their students. It should be clearly understood: This book is an *introduction* to the field of research and evaluation. No single textbook or course, whether undergraduate or graduate, can equip future professionals to become full-fledged researchers or evaluation specialists. Instead, the process of gaining such specialized skills is gradual and cumulative, comprised of taking additional courses and conducting simple studies or assisting on more complex ones, and extends over a period of time. Some students may develop a fuller interest in research and evaluation, to the point that it becomes a major element in their professional lives; others will remain essentially consumers of study findings. In either case, a broad awareness of research and evaluation purposes and methods that is supported by an awareness of knowledge gained from ongoing investigations will benefit both practitioners and the field itself.

Because it is difficult to learn about research by simply reading about it, this text includes several features designed to promote an experiential and participative approach to exploring its contents. Depending on their content, chapters may include any of the following: (1) suggested questions for class discussion or essay examinations; (2) problem-solving exercises to be undertaken by small groups of students within the classroom setting; and (3) other assignments or tasks to be undertaken by individuals or small groups of students outside the classroom and then shared with the class.

When used together, these activities constitute a potential workshop for learning how to design and conduct research and evaluation studies. The workshop could include both hypothetical and simulated tasks, the actual preparation of instruments and/or study proposals, or the conducting of small-scale surveys or other investigations in the field.

Obviously, there are too many such assignments for all students to be involved in all types of applied learning activities directly. All students may certainly be involved in the discussion of suggested issues or chapter-related questions. In addition, in most courses it would be feasible to have each student undertake approximately three tasks or other individual or group projects during a semester—some to be submitted directly to the instructor and others to be reported to the class at large. These might be viewed and analyzed by other students so that they become shared learning experiences.

As in the first edition, we have combed the literature widely, including texts by other authorities in research and evaluation methods and journals like the *Journal of Leisure Research, Journal of Park and Recreation Administration, Therapeutic Recreation Journal, Leisure Sciences, Leisure Studies,* and the *Journal of Applied Recreation Research.*

Books by educators in the leisure-service field, such as Lynn Barnett-Morris, B. L. Driver, Patricia Farrell and Herberta Lundegren, Karla Henderson, Marjorie Malkin and Christine Howe, and Carol Peterson and Scott Gunn, were consulted. John Shank and Catherine Coyle of Temple University were helpful in obtaining materials on therapeutic recreation research. We have cited too many researchers in the leisure-service field to mention them all here, but they are included in the "Author Index." Numerous practitioners in both the United States and Canada also contributed useful materials. John "Pat" Harden of the U.S. Navy and Carl Clark of Sunnyvale, California, were particularly helpful. We wish also to express our gratitude to Joseph Arave, of the University of Utah, for reviewing the manuscript and providing valuable suggestions and feedback.

It is not possible to credit all sources in detail. However, we express our deep gratitude to them and to other educators and researchers who have contributed to the development of scientific inquiry in recreation, parks, and leisure studies and services.

The final product, of course, is our own. We hope that it proves useful to faculty members, students, and practitioners throughout the field and for years to come. Without question, providing valid documentation of the role and positive outcomes of organized leisure-service programs will continue to be a high-level priority for all professionals in the field. The purpose of this text is to contribute to this important effort.

Systematic Inquiry in Leisure Studies and Services: Research and Evaluation

Research is best understood as an extension of the scientific method which provides a more rigorous approach to seeking solutions to specific problems. The scientific method is not the private domain of the scientist or the researcher . . . . In assessment, evaluation, and decision making, research is the only way to make rational choices between alternative practices, to validate improvements, and to build a stable foundation of effective practices as a safeguard against faddish but inferior innovations. This type of research is an activity in which every future-oriented leisure-service professional should engage . . . .[1]

Evaluation research—*sometimes called* program evaluation—*refers to a research purpose rather than a specific research method. Its special purpose is to evaluate the impact of social interventions such as new teaching methods, innovations in parole, and a wide variety of such programs. Many methods—surveys, experiments, and so on—can be used in evaluation research.[2]*

INTRODUCTION

This chapter discusses the meaning and importance of research and evaluation in fields such as recreation, parks, and leisure services, where it is necessary both to develop a sound theoretical base and to demonstrate the positive outcomes of programs and services.

The terms *research* and *evaluation* are defined in this chapter, which also shows their relationship and then presents an overview of their past development in the field, with emphasis on the role of professional societies and the growing number of higher education curricula offering leisure studies. The chapter concludes by pointing out the need to develop more effective links between researchers and recreation and park practitioners and by outlining the desired goals of courses in research and evaluation for students in this field who hope to become successful professionals.

THE MEANING AND IMPORTANCE OF RESEARCH AND EVALUATION

As this text will show in detail, research and evaluation are critically important in all areas of social service and, indeed, in a wide range of professions and business operations. They are particularly important in fields such as recreation, parks, and leisure services, where there is a vital need to develop a sound theoretical base for providing programs and to demonstrate the positive outcomes and benefits of participation.

Before presenting the specific functions of research and evaluation in the leisure-service field, however, it is necessary to define precisely what these two terms mean.

The terms *research* and *evaluation* are closely connected and often describe similar processes. In fact, evaluation should be regarded as a subset of research, using the full range of investigative techniques employed in research. Both research and evaluation are forms of systematic inquiry. In contrast to casual or haphazard observation, opinion, or the use of scattered evidence to draw conclusions, research and evaluation must be purposeful and carefully directed. They employ scientifically designed data-gathering methods, supplemented by study controls and data-analysis methods, to test selected hypotheses, provide important insights, or document the effectiveness of professional services or interventions. As does research, evaluation may attempt to identify relationships among variables in leisure- or recreation-related situations. However, there are certain differences between research and evaluation, as the following section demonstrates.

Research

There are many different conceptions of the meaning of the term *research.* If you were to ask a dozen different scholars or scientists to define it, you might well receive a dozen different replies—some lofty and complex, others more casual and down-to-earth. One approach is to use the definition found in an authoritative literary source. *Research* is defined in *Merriam-Webster's Collegiate Dictionary* as:

> Studious inquiry or examination; . . . investigation or experimentation aimed at the discovery and interpretation of facts, revision of accepted theories or laws in the light of new facts, or practical application of such new or revised theories or laws.[3]

Beyond this general statement, scientific research is considered controlled, purposeful, and systematic investigation of natural or social phenomena within a theoretical framework, in order to test hypotheses about the relationships among such phenomena. Research may vary in form. It may involve observational studies, mailed surveys, historical investigations, laboratory experiments, and numerous other types of designs or data-gathering procedures.

At one level, research may simply observe and report *what is,* in an organized way. At another level, it may be concerned with developing theories that explain the *how* and *why* of things or that show how various phenomena are related or cause certain outcomes. Research may deal with the past, the present, or the future and may be carried out in real or in artificial settings. It may involve an unobtrusive, "hands-off" approach in which the researcher seeks to be as invisible as possible, or it may introduce various factors or environmental conditions which affect the behavior of participants.

Whatever its dimensions, the ultimate purpose of research in recreation, parks, and leisure studies is to provide a solid base of knowledge and theory, both to the field at large and to individual practitioners.

Evaluation

The term *evaluation* is defined in Webster as the "process or result of evaluating." The verb *evaluate* means "to ascertain the value or amount of; to appraise carefully; to express numerically."

Evaluation has commonly been thought of as a means of documenting an agency's worth by providing evidence of its positive contribution to society or other desirable outcomes it has achieved. Within varied types of community organizations, evaluation is used to determine the success of programs in meeting their stated objectives. It may also seek to assess the quality of agencies or programs, based on professionally accepted standards or criteria used to judge such agencies. In addition to examining overall agencies or programs, evaluation may also measure the effectiveness or quality of component elements, such as administrative policies and practices, personnel, or facilities.

Increasingly, the phrase *evaluation research* has come into professional use. Chadwick, Bahr, and Albrecht point out that evaluation research is of relatively recent origin—a development of the social action programs initiated by government in the 1960s and 1970s. At that time, evaluation became a key element in the creation of Planning, Programming, and Budgeting Systems (PPBS) and was widely used in the review of government-supported programs. They write:

> Evaluation research is generally considered to be applied rather than basic research. . . . [It] is a general term that refers to a wide variety of research activities. Within the past 25 years evaluation research has come of age and there is now a vast published and unpublished literature on the topic.

Several professional journals are devoted to evaluation, an annual review publishes the latest trends and research, and the study and practice of evaluation research have become a specialty in sociology, psychology, education, and economics.[4]

Relationship Between Research and Evaluation

As stated earlier, evaluation is actually a form of research in that it relies on the use of valid, carefully designed data-gathering instruments and procedures to acquire information and arrive at conclusions. It differs from research in terms of its scope and purposes. Whereas research is primarily concerned with the discovery or production of knowledge, evaluation seeks to use that knowledge in meaningful ways. Thus, evaluation typically has practical or applied purposes. It usually relies on empirical evidence—data that can be directly observed and measured. It deals with real situations or conditions in the present or recent past. It is concerned with the effectiveness or professional quality of agencies, programs, procedures, personnel, or similar elements. For example, an evaluation study might focus directly on the impact or value of a recreation program designed to reduce the aggressive behavior of youth in an at-risk environment.

In contrast, research is extremely varied in its purposes and methods. It may deal with both theoretical and practical concerns and often is intended to test hypotheses that may have either immediate or long-term purposes. Some research studies may not appear to have a result that has immediate utility. These studies are considered more basic in orientation and provide a foundation for applied research studies. For example, an interesting research task associated with the study of a recreation program designed to reduce the aggressive behavior of youth might be to analyze the communication style used in the program or to analyze the family backgrounds of the youth in the at-risk environment. Although the knowledge gained would not have immediate utility in terms of reducing aggressive behavior, it might ultimately be of value in planning future agency programs.

CONTRIBUTION OF RESEARCH AND EVALUATION TO LEISURE SERVICES

Any social institution or field of human service that seeks to gain public respect or to be regarded as a legitimate profession must advance its body of specialized knowledge through scientifically valid research and evaluation. These procedures serve both to document the actual benefits and outcomes derived from the field and to develop more effective policies and procedures. They also provide a theoretical base for the field, by formulating basic principles or concepts that support professional practices.

In the field of medicine, for example, research is constantly being conducted to identify the causes of disease and to develop new solutions in terms of environmental controls, medicines, or other treatment procedures to combat illness and maintain individual and community health and well-being.

In the business world, research and evaluation lead to new products or improved methods of marketing them, to fuller understanding of consumer needs and attitudes, or to more effective personnel management or financial investment strategies.

Psychologists extensively explore the nature of personality, psychopathology and mental health, learning processes, and family relationships. Within specialized areas of professional practice such as counseling, theoretical research is directly linked to work in the field in a two-way process. Tracey writes:

> . . . principles learned from theory and more basic scientific study apply in the "real" world [while the] contribution of principles gleaned from practice apply to theory and basic science.[5]

Just as those in other areas of professional practice have gained maturity and respect through scientific validation of their methods and results, recreation, park, and leisure-service professionals *must* conduct meaningful research and evaluation studies if they are to justify *their* efforts, document *their* outcomes, and compete within the total spectrum of governmental and human-service programs today.

OVERVIEW OF PAST RESEARCH AND EVALUATION PRACTICES

In the past, it was frequently stated that the recreation and leisure-studies field lacked a body of significant research literature. However, there has been a steady increase in the number and variety of studies in this field and in the publication of research journals and reports. The following section offers a brief review of research trends in recreation, parks, and leisure studies.

During the nineteenth century, a number of authorities examined the nature of play activities in both animal and human societies. Such writers as Karl Groos, Herbert Spencer, G. Stanley Hall, and others formulated several theories of play behavior. These theories were based on the systematic observation of play and constituted an early form of empirical research in this field. For the first time, play and recreation were perceived as significant aspects of life that deserved careful scholarly attention.

In the late nineteenth century, the social historian Thorstein Veblen carried out an extensive historical and sociological study of leisure in the lives of the wealthy that profoundly influenced our understanding of the relationship between leisure and social class.

Early Twentieth-Century Studies of Recreation and Leisure

During the first three decades of the twentieth century, several forms of research into recreation, play, and leisure were initiated: (a) With the establishment of community recreation and park systems throughout the United States, there were a number of nationwide studies of facilities, programs, and personnel that documented progress in this field; (b) a number of psychologists examined the role of play in the lives of children and documented its value; and (c) with growing concern about leisure as a social problem, many cities and social welfare organizations conducted surveys that focused on the problem of poorly utilized free time, including juvenile delinquency and gang activity, as a means of gaining support for organized recreation programs for youth in American communities.

Depression and Post–World War II Period

During the 1930s and 1940s, more comprehensive and solidly based studies of recreation, parks, and leisure services began to appear. Lebert H. Weir, for example, did an extensive, detailed survey of recreation and park systems in European nations. George Lundberg, Mirra Komarovsky, and other social scientists carried out studies of the leisure behaviors and values of different age groups, occupational groups, and social classes. Studies carried out by the National Recreation Association provided a continuing profile of the expanding recreation and park agencies in American communities. Some social scientists, such as Gunnar Myrdal, examined the role of recreation in the lives of American blacks. Other sociologists included leisure as an important element in community life, in their studies of prototypical American cities like "Elmtown" and "Middletown."

Research in Outdoor Recreation: The ORRRC Report

In 1962, the 26-volume report of the Outdoor Recreation Resources Review Commission provided a comprehensive picture of the nation's forests, wilderness, water-based resources, and overall park and open-space needs. This study stimulated a wave of national concern in this field and led to legislation that assisted open-space acquisition, the protection or restoration of wild rivers and trails, and substantial funding of outdoor recreation planning studies by federal and state agencies.

At that time, considerable federal assistance was given to research studies dealing with open space, parks, and other wilderness or environmental issues. Substantial assistance was also given to research dealing with the needs of special populations, including persons with mental or physical disabilities and elderly individuals.

The National Recreation and Park Association and other professional societies developed evaluation standards and guidelines for the operation of recreation and park agencies, for the certification of personnel, for the accreditation of college and university curricula, and for other similar purposes. A number of research quarterlies were founded in the period following the 1960s, including the *Journal of Leisure Research, Leisure Sciences, Leisure Studies,* the *Therapeutic Recreation Journal,* the *Journal of Park and Recreation Administration,* and such Canadian journals as the *Journal of Applied Recreation Research.*

EFFECT OF HIGHER EDUCATION EXPANSION

With the expansion of higher education in recreation, parks, and leisure studies, growing numbers of graduate students did research leading to master's theses and doctoral dissertations. Annual research conferences and symposia were held, either independently or attached to major meetings of professional organizations. Drawing on the theories and models that were being developed in other academic disciplines, researchers began to investigate a range of issues with contemporary priority, such as the influence of gender or race on leisure values and behavior, outcomes of recreational involvement, constraints and barriers to participation, and varied management, planning, and policy-related concerns.

Extensive compilations of the findings of research done during the latter half of the twentieth century may be found in several sources, including: (1) the 1987 *Literature Review of the President's Commission on Americans Outdoors,*[6] dealing with such varied themes as trends and demand, values and benefits of outdoor recreation, natural resources management, special populations, tourism, urban recreation, and financing; and (2) Barnett's text, *Research About Leisure: Past, Present, and Future,*[7] which deals broadly with the history and philosophy of leisure and recreation and with the management and evaluation of leisure programs, including such specialized fields as tourism and commercial recreation.

A CURRENT ISSUE:
THE RESEARCHER-PRACTITIONER GAP

Given the advanced nature of research today, investigators have listed more than 25 distinct types of research designs that are being used to assess the social and environmental impacts of government programs—including highly technical and specialized data-gathering methods.

In the recreation, parks, and leisure-service field, such complex and scholarly studies often deal with issues that have little apparent meaning for practitioners who are concerned with the realistic task of providing facilities and programs to meet public needs. As a result, Mobley suggests that a significant gap has developed between researchers and professionals in recreation and park agencies. Too often, he states, college and university professors carry out studies that use agencies and participants as sources of data, without giving practitioners the opportunity to become meaningfully involved in the process. Often their reports are not intelligible to readers who lack research expertise and are rarely read by practitioners.[8]

In a keynote presentation made at a research symposium of the Ontario, Canada, Research Council on Leisure, Goodale warned that highly theoretical research runs the risk of having little relevance for practitioners who instead want and need credible evidence that will help them create or defend positions. Realistically, he writes:

> We should understand that policy and decision makers need syntheses more than analyses, that for them knowledge is a means rather than an end, that readily defensible grounds are preferred to those conceptually and methodologically pristine, and that what is right must be shaped by what is feasible and palatable. . . . In short, if we are serious about bridging gaps between research, policy and practice, we have to understand that policy and practice, in the public sector at least, are shot through and through with political and bureaucratic imperatives.[9]

Goodale concludes that there needs to be more systematic sharing of information between the two groups regarding their research interests, needs, and capabilities. Students in recreation, parks and leisure studies curricula who are the professionals of tomorrow must become literate with respect to research and evaluation principles and methods—not only to improve their own professional competence but to strengthen the field at large.

Such expertise is critically important for professional-level personnel in all types of government, business, educational, and social agencies today. Basic skills in research and evaluation are essential for individuals who may be assigned roles as members of research staffs or project teams or who may be asked to write proposals or conduct program evaluations.

Even those who are not planning to become researchers as such must gain a basic knowledge of the most widely used research designs and methods or models of evaluation. In the modern era we are all "consumers" of research results and must be able to judge the adequacy of the methods by which they have been obtained.

The ability to read research reports intelligently and to be able to interpret and discuss their findings and conclusions is of greater importance today than ever before. Because of economic constraints in government and all social-service agencies, there is growing pressure on leisure-service practitioners to justify their programs in concrete, believable terms. As a result, in the early and mid-1990s, a number of special reports in journals and textbooks have focused on the proven outcomes of recreation services.[10] Efficacy research is a vital aspect of the field, and benefits-driven or outcomes-oriented evaluation projects have increasingly been recognized as important management tools.

LINKAGE OF RESEARCH AND EVALUATION IN HIGHER EDUCATION CURRICULA

In many college and university curricula in recreation, parks, and leisure studies, research and evaluation are arbitrarily separated in course work. Evaluation is taught primarily on the undergraduate level, and research tends to be presented as a graduate course requirement. Ideally, however, the two subjects should be taught in an integrated way, since they are both forms of systematic inquiry that are important to leisure-service practitioners on all levels and share many common elements. This text therefore covers both subjects, with the assumption that undergraduate course work will be at an introductory level, with greater emphasis on applied, practical uses of research and evaluation, and that graduate courses will be more theoretical or basic in nature.

What important understandings or skills should leisure-studies students gain from an introductory course in research and evaluation? They include the following:

1. Through appropriate course experiences, assignments, and readings, students should gain a feeling of enthusiasm about research and evaluation and a degree of confidence in terms of using them as professional tools. While they *cannot* become expert researchers by taking a single course, they *can* gain a beginning understanding of research concepts and methodology and develop skill in formatting research problems and proposals. They can also learn to develop evaluation instruments and to analyze descriptive data.

2. They should develop the habit of *reading the current literature* in recreation, parks, and leisure studies. This means that they can identify useful journals and can understand research articles at an appropriate level of complexity. They should also be exposed to literature retrieval methods and techniques for carrying out computer searches, using available reference sources and similar tools.

3. They should recognize and respect the potential *contribution of research and evaluation* in terms of (a) developing the field's status by providing a body of scholarly knowledge and theory and (b) improving their own job performance and enhancing their own career development by gaining useful professional skills in this area.

4. They should develop the capacity for *critical thinking,* through which they view research findings cautiously and accept claims or statements of outcomes only on the basis of sound evidence. One of the key purposes of research and evaluation is to dispel unrealistic claims and platitudes that are carelessly used to support and justify the field. These strategies must be

replaced by accountability and solid documentation that command respect from other professionals, public officials, and members of the public at large.

It should be emphasized again that a single course on either the undergraduate or graduate level will *not* equip students to become full-fledged, capable researchers or evaluators. To expect this would be wishful thinking. Instead, those who expect to engage seriously in either form of inquiry should take additional, more advanced courses in research methods and statistics, should undertake simple study projects as part of other courses, and should gain experience, if possible, as assistants within larger, organized studies. The purpose of an introductory course in research and evaluation—and of this text—is to provide the groundwork for such personal and professional development.

SUMMARY

This chapter defines the terms *research* and *evaluation,* showing their similarities and differences and their relationship to planning as a professional function. It stresses that all forms of human enterprise or societal organization rely heavily on research to advance knowledge and improve professional practice.

The chapter presents an overview of the past development of scientific inquiry in recreation, parks, and leisure studies and emphasizes their importance in the preparation of capable practitioners. It argues that the two forms of inquiry—research and evaluation—should not be arbitrarily separated in course work and textbooks, but should be explored by students in an integrated way. In concluding the chapter, it should be stressed that research and evaluation are *not* mystical, abstruse, or dull areas of learning and professional practice. Instead, they can and should be highly interesting and challenging areas in undergraduate and graduate leisure-service curricula, leading to increased competence and career success.

QUESTIONS AND ACTIVITIES

1. Compare *research* and *evaluation.* Define each term and show their similarities, in terms of common purposes and methods, and their differences, as described in this chapter.

2. Why is it essential for a field such as recreation, parks, and leisure studies and services to have a body of specialized knowledge that is based on carefully designed research studies? What recent societal trends have made this all the more essential?

3. Mobley and Goodale describe the gap that has developed between professional practitioners and scholarly researchers in the recreation, park, and leisure-service field. What is the cause of this gap? What can be done about it?

4. What are the desired outcomes of a course in research and evaluation in the leisure-service field, in terms of personal understanding and professional competence?

ENDNOTES

1. Tony A. Mobley, "Practitioner, Researcher—A Team," *Parks and Recreation* (April 1980): 40.
2. Earl Babbie, *The Practice of Social Research* (Belmont, CA: Wadsworth, 1992): 346.
3. *Merriam Webster's Collegiate Dictionary,* Tenth Edition (Springfield, MA: Merriam-Webster, Inc., 1994): 995.
4. Bruce Chadwick, Howard Bahr, and Stan Albrecht, *Social Science Research Methods* (Englewood Cliffs, NJ: Prentice-Hall, 1984): 282–83.
5. Terence Tracey, in C. Edward Watkins, Jr., and Lawrence Schneider, *Research in Counseling* (Hillsdale, NJ: L. Erlbaum Associates, 1991): 3.
6. *President's Commission on Americans Outdoors: A Literature Review* (Washington, DC: U.S. Government Printing Office, 1987).
7. Lynn Barnett, *Research About Leisure: Past, Present, and Future* (Champaign, IL: Sagamore Publishing Co., 1994).
8. Mobley, "Practitioner, Researcher," 41, 72.
9. Tom Goodale, "Bridging the Gap Between Research, Practice and Policy," *Journal of Applied Recreation Research* 16, no. 3 (1991): 175.
10. See for example: B. L. Driver, Perry Brown, and George Peterson, eds., *Benefits of Leisure* (State College, PA: Venture Publishing, 1991) and *The Benefits of Parks and Recreation: A Catalogue* (Gloucester, Ontario, Can.: Parks and Recreation Federation of Ontario, 1992).

The Scientific Method: Ways of Knowing

Scientific method is a set of procedures that allows us to generate information of high quality and to check the worth of what we have been told by others. . . . One hallmark of scientific method is that it is self-correcting. Properly applied, scientific procedures will expose weaknesses in information gathered in earlier research and suggest new research to deal with these weaknesses. Scientists "believe" something only on a provisional basis. . . . Behaving like a scientist means fighting a continuing battle against the inclination to be dogmatic about what we "know."[1]

INTRODUCTION

This chapter clarifies some of the fundamental assumptions and processes that underlie both research and evaluation. Since both are forms of systematic inquiry intended to gather meaningful knowledge, it begins by discussing the nature and sources of knowledge and the ways in which we can accurately perceive and understand reality.

It then describes the scientific method in terms of its intention and its component steps, including the use of inductive and deductive reasoning and investigative steps. In concluding, the chapter identifies two influential approaches to scientific inquiry—the *positivistic* (heavily based on *quantitative* methods) and *naturalistic* (linked to *qualitative*) approaches—and shows how they are reflected in research studies today, particularly within the social and behavioral sciences and in fields such as leisure studies.

THE NATURE OF SYSTEMATIC INQUIRY

Typically, most of us ask many questions each day and seek answers to them. As part of this inquiry, we may carry out random observations and collect information—usually on a casual basis. Often we make judgments about the meaning of what we have observed on the basis of "common sense," or what appears to be the case to us. While this does represent an informal sort of research, it is not an example of systematic inquiry.

Instead, systematic inquiry—as exemplified in the scientific method—implies that there must be a deliberate, purposeful, and organized effort to gain knowledge. The purposes of the investigation are clearly stated and understood, and the sources of information are selected so that the data they yield will be representative and accurate. The data-gathering instrument or procedure is carefully designed and applied to ensure that the findings are as correct as possible. The researcher must not arrive at conclusions on the basis of inadequate evidence or possibly biased sources.

Beyond these points, systematic inquiry in the form of research and evaluation often seeks information that provides more than just a superficial description of what exists. Instead, it is often concerned with understanding *why* things occur as they do, what the *relationship* is between various factors or study elements, and whether given behaviors or outcomes can be accurately predicted, given certain circumstances. When carried out on this level, research can be used to develop fundamental principles or theories that provide fuller understanding of human or societal processes and that can be used to improve agency functions.

Ways of Knowing

The term *knowing* refers to the cognitive process and to intellectual or mental awareness of a fact or condition. Typically, we are apt to say, "I *know* this is the case," or "I *know* how to carry out a particular activity." But how *do* we come to know something or *think* we know it? There are several sources of knowledge that we may draw on.

Tradition

This describes the kind of knowledge or belief that may have been handed down from past generations or that has been an accepted custom or behavioral practice. For example, we tend to hold a number of beliefs because our parents or other older relatives believed them—often through superstition, folklore, or other inherited attitudes. While they may have a degree of validity, as in the case of much folk medicine or herbal remedies, often they are inaccurate or misleading.

Similarly, many of our customs in society tend to be based on handed-down tradition. For example, Mason and Bramble point out that in the United States most children begin formal education at the age of six. When this practice is questioned, they write:

> . . . the response is usually that six has always been regarded as the best age to begin formal education. When traditions are valid, they are depend-

able sources of knowledge. However, traditions based on false beliefs will result in faulty knowledge.[2]

Tradition exerts an extremely powerful influence on our thinking. Indeed, Kerlinger describes it under the heading of *tenacity,* writing:

> Here men hold firmly to the truth, the truth that they know to be true because they hold firmly to it, because they have always known it to be true. Frequent repetition of such "truths" seems to enhance their validity. People often cling to their beliefs in the face of clearly conflicting facts.[3]

Authority

Another common source of accepted knowledge is the advice or judgment of so-called experts, who are recognized authorities in a given field. For example, people who have had an advanced level of technical training in a relevant area often are called as expert witnesses to give testimony in civil or criminal trials.

Despite their expertise, however, such experts may disagree; it is not at all unusual to have one psychiatrist or psychologist claim that a defendant is seriously mentally ill, while another authority claims that this is not the case. Such disagreement may occur because authorities use different sources of data or interpret them differently. They may also be influenced by different belief systems or by a conscious or unconscious bias in favor of the side they represent.

While agreeing that relying on the wisdom of authorities has advantages—as a quick and simple way to learn something—Neuman points out that it also has its limitations. He writes:

> It is easy to overestimate the expertise of other people. You may assume that they are right when they are not. Authorities may speak on fields they know little about; they can be plain wrong. An expert in one area may try to use his or her authority in an unrelated area. . . . History is full of past experts whom we now see as being misinformed.[4]

Beyond the testimony of experts, Neuman points out that television shows, movies, and newspaper and magazine articles are important sources of information about past and contemporary events. However, because of editorial restrictions, time limitations, or the need to sensationalize or frame stories within socially acceptable contexts, they may often serve to perpetuate "media myths" that do not reflect social reality.

Personal experience

One's own personal experience, or knowledge based on direct observation, would appear to be an excellent source of knowledge. However, this can be misleading if it is based on partial evidence or incomplete sources of information.

For example, it would not be uncommon to hear the comment, "I really don't believe that smoking causes lung cancer, because my grandfather smoked all his life, and lived until he was 90." Often racial or ethnic stereotypes are based on very limited kinds of knowledge or contact with individuals of a particular ethnic background. Personal experience is also fallible in that, for purely physical reasons or environmental factors that distort our perceptions, we may not interpret correctly what we see or hear. Beyond this, we often tend to screen out input that does not agree with our existing biases or value systems.

Babbie points out that much human observation tends to be casual and incomplete because it is not based on a conscious effort to record phenomena accurately. Often it is based on highly selective examples that are then overgeneralized to suggest patterns of behavior that are inaccurate.[5]

Documentation

Another frequently used source of knowledge is documentation, or use of the extensive information that society amasses each year and stores in economic reports, court records, census statistics, and similar sources. While documentation is valuable in many areas of public activity, it is only as good as the methods used to obtain it. Selective reporting or inadequate controls over data-gathering methods may lead to misleading information. For example, for a number of years a national sports organization published figures that portrayed the number of children, youth, and adults who took part regularly in major team or individual sports and games. However, their chief sources for these figures were special-interest organizations or trade associations which were heavily involved in promoting each of these sports activities. Often they either did not know the actual numbers who took part in a given activity because there was no accurate way to find out, or they presented inflated estimates of annual participation because of an understandable desire to make their own activity "look good." In either case, the knowledge that was presented through such documentation was clearly inaccurate. Depending on the sources used, therefore, documentation may or may not represent a valid means of gathering knowledge.

Scientific method

Clearly, systematic inquiry that makes use of the scientific method is the most trustworthy source of knowledge available today. Through it, purposeful and unbiased investigations are carried out to gather information and interpret it accurately. The element of subjective, personal judgment is eliminated, insofar as possible, with a fundamental purpose of the inquiry being to determine the "why" of things, rather than simply the "what."

However, as later sections of this text will show, even scientific inquiry may be limited, in terms of the methods it uses or its ability to analyze data meaningfully. It may also be influenced by political, religious, or other pressures or controls. As an example, for several decades, Soviet scientists had a view of the influence of genetic or environmental factors on human development and the nature of mental illness that was distinctly different from that of Western scientists. Soviet scientists were required to follow a party line on such matters. In a number of other cases, major anthropological or medical findings that had been reported by presumably reputable scientists have later been revealed as fraudulent—based on deliberately distorted reporting and interpretation of data.

Thus, even scientific inquiry may yield distorted findings. However, of the several sources of knowledge cited here, it clearly offers the most valid source of accurate knowledge and understanding. Within the recreation, parks, and leisure-studies field, while we may recognize value in tradition, authority, or other sources of knowledge, we must accept that the most reputable and respected approach to developing a body of valid information is through research based on the scientific method.

The scientific method has been described as a "controlled extension of common sense," implying that there is nothing magical or mysterious about it. However, it differs from "common sense" in several important respects.

First, as Neuman points out, science is a social institution, intended to produce knowledge. It evolved during the so-called Age of Reason or Enlightenment in Europe during the seventeenth and eighteenth centuries, which gave birth to a wave of new thinking, including

> . . . a faith in logical reasoning, an emphasis on experiences in the material world, a belief in human progress, and a questioning of traditional religious authority. It began with the study of the natural world and spread to the study of social life.[6]

SCIENCE DEFINED

Mason and Bramble write:

> . . . a parsimonious definition of *science* is that it is the systematic development and organization of a body of knowledge. The material is organized to provide structure by which phenomena can be explained. By phenomena, we mean facts or events which can be observed. Thus, Sir Isaac Newton . . . was able to integrate observations (about falling objects) into a universal explanation in the form of a mathematical relationship . . . a good example of the content of the physical sciences. The behavioral and social sciences have not yet been able to develop explanatory relationships that are quite so elegant in their simplicity.[7]

Today, scientists are obligated to communicate their findings and conclusions clearly, along with the methods used to reach them. Scientific investigation is typically based on the application of technology—a set of accepted procedures for gathering and verifying data. Ultimately, science must be viewed as a unified activity involving three elements: knowledge, technique and social context, and the scientific community.

Typically, science makes use of theoretical structures and concepts as a basis for explaining events; it applies them regularly and submits them to repeated tests. This is done through the systematic, controlled testing of theories and hypotheses. Kerlinger points out that the scientific method has a characteristic that no other approach to gaining knowledge has: self-correction. He writes:

> There are built-in checks all along the way to scientific knowledge. These checks are so conceived and used that they control and verify scientific activities and conclusions to the end of attaining dependable knowledge. Even if a hypothesis seems to be supported in an experiment, the scientist will test alternative plausible hypotheses that, if also supported, may cast doubt on the first hypothesis. Scientists do not accept statements as true, even though the evidence at first looks promising. They insist on testing them.[8]

Another important difference between science and common sense is that, while the layperson is only casually interested in the relationships among different phenomena, the scientific researcher sees them as a primary focus of her investigations. Within the classical approach to formal scientific research—known as the *positivistic approach*—scientists believe that all phenomena are subject to certain basic laws that can be explored and defined and that adhere to the following underlying assumptions.

Nature of Reality

This assumption holds that the world is real and knowable and that all human or social phenomena can be explored and logically explained. Thus, supernatural elements such as magic or other metaphysical explanations cannot be accepted as the cause of such events or conditions.

Related to this assumption is the principle of determinism—that nothing in the world occurs totally by chance or accident or in a purely spontaneous way. Instead, every phenomenon has a *cause,* although we may not be able at present to explain such unusual happenings as demonstrations of extrasensory perception or other mystical forms of human performance.

Concepts of Natural Kinds or Classes

This assumption holds that all kinds of elements—including people, animals, events, social conditions, communities, and programs—can be classified in appropriate groupings according to their shared characteristics or other common factors.

Thus, instead of having to deal with great numbers of totally dissimilar or random events or subjects, researchers are able to classify the subjects of their investigations into typologies or models. To illustrate, instead of accepting the idea that people have thousands of reasons for taking part in recreation, the researcher seeks to identify a limited number—perhaps fifteen or twenty—key motivations that would include all possible reasons. Linked to the first principle that events are not purely random and unrelated, but tend to stem from specific causes, this assumption argues that they tend to follow common or typical patterns that may be identified and predicted by researchers.

Principle of Constancy

This assumption holds that conditions in nature or in human society tend to be relatively constant, until their equilibrium is upset by intrusive factors of some sort. These disruptions bring about certain changes or outcomes that can be logically explained; in other words, this is the principle of *causality,* in which given factors or circumstances tend to cause the same effects consistently.

This principle emerged first within the physical sciences, such as chemistry, biology, or physics, in which all elements or phenomena could be precisely measured and in which causal relationships could be confidently identified as scientific laws. Emile Durkheim, a pioneer sociologist, argued that the same approach could be applied to human behavior and social institutions. Bailey writes:

> He [Durkheim] said that social phenomena are orderly and can be generalized . . . just as physical phenomena follow physical laws. In Durkheim's view . . . there was little difference between physical and natural science and social science except for subject matter. The logic of inquiry was essentially the same.[9]

This approach to inquiry is often called *logical positivism.* It suggests that sociologists or other social scientists should use the methods of natural science, such as experimentation, to examine and explain social behavior. It was illustrated in the views of Alfred North Whitehead, a leading philosopher of science, who believed that all life is part of a comprehensive "order of things," governed by basic laws and principles. This order, he concluded, must combine carefully gathered or observed facts (the basis of empirical research) with theories based on the "weaving of general principles," which tie the facts together.

The scientific attitude does not claim omniscience. Scientists recognize that error is possible and that their findings are therefore tentative and subject to possible revision. Scientific theories are refutable, and others may challenge them by carrying out similar studies or advancing competitive theories.

Despite such reservations, the positivistic approach is widely used in research studies today, and much of this text's content is based on it. It should also be noted, however, that another type of scientific inquiry, generally referred to as *naturalistic* or *qualitative* research, is becoming more widely used in the social and behavioral sciences and is discussed fully later in this text (see pages 97–104).

INDUCTIVE AND DEDUCTIVE REASONING

Generally, the scientific method is considered to be based on two distinctive types of reasoning and analysis: *inductive* and *deductive.*

Inductive Reasoning

This approach moves from the specific to the general, by using logical analysis of individual cases or occurrences to develop a broad explanatory theory or generalization. To illustrate, one might examine the recreative behavior of senior citizens.

First, we observe Mrs. Jones, who is a senior citizen. We note that she plays Bingo frequently. Based on this knowledge, we conclude that all senior citizens play Bingo—an example of the inductive process of moving from specific facts to broad generalizations. Of course, one must question the wisdom of drawing such conclusions from only one observation. With added observations of senior centers, we might note that a considerable number of elderly persons play Bingo and might feel more comfortable about our conclusions. Regardless of the number of senior citizens we observe, however, we can never be sure that our general statement is absolutely true. With a substantial number of observations, and with parallel study of other age groups, we would probably instead come to the conclusion that Bingo is a favorite activity of older persons and is more popular in this age group than in any other.

Stated abstractly, inductive reasoning is summed up in the following sentence: "These *specific* forms of behavior which have been seen to occur provide support for the following *general* theory."

Deductive Reasoning

This approach is exactly the reverse, moving from the general to the specific. It involves using a general theory or model of behavior or causal relationships to develop inferences or predictions about a specific case.

Using the illustration of senior citizens and Bingo playing, one might start with the general statement that most senior citizens enjoy Bingo. Determining that Mrs. Jones is a senior citizen, one would therefore conclude that she plays Bingo—or that, if it were introduced, she would take part in it and enjoy it. This is actually the process used in much of the recreation programming carried on in senior centers.

Deduction is basically a matter of logical reasoning. It is illustrated by Aristotle's famous syllogism (a logical scheme or analysis of a formal argument, consisting of three propositions called respectively the *major premise,* the *minor premise,* and the *conclusion*): "If men are mammals, and mammals are mortal, then men are mortal."

Stated as a formula, "If *a* equals *b,* and *b* equals *c,* then we must deduce that *a* equals *c.*"

Such reasoning must be carefully applied and has logical validity only if the premises are correct. Both types of reasoning are found in social and behavioral research. For example, when researchers develop hypotheses that they intend to test through experimentation based on a theory, they are using deductive reasoning. In contrast, when they initially observe natural phenomena, using simple descriptive methods of data gathering to formulate theories, they are using inductive reasoning.

THE SCIENTIFIC METHOD

Often the scientific method is described as a three-step process that makes use of both inductive and deductive reasoning, as follows.

Induction

This consists of observing natural or social phenomena and then generating a preliminary theory or tentative explanation that is consistent with the observed facts and explains them and their relationship.

Deduction

From this preliminary theory, one "deduces" what the logical consequences or outcomes will be if exactly the same circumstances or conditions prevail in another setting or at another time. Customarily, this is presented in the form of one or more hypotheses, which are definitive statements or predictions of what will be found when the study is completed (see pages 30–31).

Verification

This is the testing stage, in which the hypotheses are tested under controlled conditions to determine whether the presumed consequences do occur or the predicted relationships can be found. Based on this process, the researcher arrives at conclusions that are justified by the evidence and that lead to accepting, rejecting, or modifying the hypothesis. He may also continue to develop new theories or hypotheses based on the study findings. This process of articulating new theories or generalizations from specific observations moves us back into the inductive phase, with the research process often becoming a continuous alternation of deduction, induction, deduction, and so on. Other researchers may also replicate the study in different settings to determine whether the findings are confirmed and whether the study has been a valid one with generalizable conclusions.

If fully accepted, the conclusions may become accepted as actual scientific laws. This is more common in the physical or natural sciences, where it is possible to maintain a high degree of rigor and obtain proof that is very convincing. It is less common in the social or behavioral sciences, where it is extremely difficult to control and predict human behavior or to control the variables that influence it within the societal setting.

As it has just been described, the *positivistic* approach to scientific research (also known as the *rational/empirical* or *logical/empirical* approach) is based on the assumption that the purpose of science is to discover the fixed natural laws that govern the universe, in order to be able to predict and control a wide range of natural and social phenomena. Essentially, it is based on objective, empirical data gathering, which seeks to reduce all study elements to their key components and which depends heavily on quantitative forms of measurement and analysis.

THE NATURALISTIC PERSPECTIVE

As the social and behavioral sciences developed during the twentieth century, however, a new approach to scientific research emerged: the *naturalistic* (also known as *interpretive* or *phenomenological*) perspective. This approach differs sharply from the positivistic perspective in that it assumes that knowledge is the outcome or consequence of human activity, rather than an entity that is out there to be discovered. Bullock writes:

> Knowledge is a human construction which by definition is never certifiable as ultimately true. Rather, it is always changing and forever problematic. Therefore, the *naturalistic* perspective [argues] that realities (not reality) exist in the form of multiple mental constructions that are socially and experientially based, local and specific, and dependent for their form and content on the persons who hold them.[10]

Within this framework, objectivity is not always useful or even desirable for the investigator. Instead, subjectivity is sought, in the sense that the subjective experience of the researcher helps her understand the realities under study.

COMPARISON OF POSITIVISTIC
AND NATURALISTIC APPROACHES

Karla Henderson sums up the differences between positivistic and naturalistic (which she calls *interpretive*) research approaches:

Followers of positivism make the assumptions that reality is:

1. External, separated, categorized, and isolated into independent parts which form a whole.
2. Approached through deduction and *a priori* (preestablished) theory.
3. Based on mechanistic processes that focus on [complete] understanding of a particular phenomenon and rational cause-and-effect.
4. Objective and value-free.

These assumptions differ sharply from the naturalistic view, which holds that reality is characterized by:

1. Multiple realities, relationships, connectedness, wholeness and inclusiveness.
2. An emphasis on induction and grounded (emerging within a context) theory.
3. Organic (contextual) processes that focus on meaning.
4. Subjectivity and perspectivity.[11]

Proponents of the naturalistic approach to science argue that men and women are not inanimate objects acted upon by outside forces; instead, they are purposeful, goal-seeking creatures capable of free will and individual choice. Thus, research dealing with people or with social groups must take into account the effect of different environments, changing circumstances, and individual needs—as well as the factor of chance that affects human behavior. It seeks to "get inside" the subjects of research and see the world from their perspective.

Based on these different views, many naturalistic investigators do not adhere to the traditional model of scientific research, in terms of reliance on inductive and deductive reasoning and the statistical testing of formal hypotheses. Instead, they may use research methods that are broader and more diverse than those found in the positivistic approach. Observational researchers such as anthropologists, ethnologists, or sociologists tend to rely heavily on verbal descriptions and analyses and usually do not seek to develop general scientific laws. Instead, they focus on the unique situational meaning and interpretation of social phenomena in particular settings. Although most social research is empirical, other ways of gathering knowledge may be useful in dealing with such phenomena as recreation, play, and leisure. Selltiz and associates write:

> Many religions, for example, identify revelation (a special, nonempirical, individual way of finding things out) as a source of knowledge. Intuition, visions, and reflective thought are all nonempirical strategies for acquiring knowledge about the social and physical worlds. . . .[12]

Philosophical and critical research and other forms of conceptual analysis may also be useful in developing a diversified approach to investigations of leisure and its meaning in society. Such techniques will help to enrich our understanding of this total phenomenon in ways that purely empirical, statistically based research cannot.

These contrasting approaches to research will become clearer in later chapters in this text. Clearly, both types of investigations are useful in recreation, parks, and leisure-studies research, and both are described in detail throughout this text.

SUMMARY

This chapter describes the nature of scientific inquiry, which is at the heart of both research and evaluation. It reviews several ways of knowing, including reliance on traditional beliefs, authority figures or experts, personal experience and observation, documentation from printed sources, and scientific inquiry.

The scientific method is reviewed, including several fundamental assumptions about the nature of reality that have been used to undergird it. Inductive and deductive reasoning are explained and placed within the context of the classical model of scientific research. In the final section of the chapter, the positivistic approach to science is discussed and contrasted with the newer naturalistic or interpretive perspective. The relevance of these two approaches to research in recreation, parks, and leisure studies will be made clearer in later discussions of quantitative and qualitative research methods.

QUESTIONS AND ACTIVITIES

1. Identify several *ways of knowing* that are described in the chapter and show how they may apply to public attitudes or understandings about recreation and leisure. Make your explanations as concrete as possible.

2. How do the *inductive* and *deductive* approaches to theory building fit into the process of scientific inquiry? Develop several illustrations of possible research questions in recreation, parks, and leisure services and show how they might be approached inductively and deductively.

3. The following is an individual or small-group assignment to be done by students and presented to the class: Select two or more articles from one of the recognized leisure-studies journals. Describe them, indicating whether they represent positivistic or naturalistic approaches to research and support your decision by showing the research methods they use.

ENDNOTES

1. Carol Saslow, *Basic Research Methods* (New York: Random House, 1982): 3.
2. Emanuel Mason and William Bramble, *Understanding and Conducting Research* (New York: McGraw-Hill, 1977): 4.

3. Fred Kerlinger, *Foundations of Behavioral Research* (New York: Holt, Rinehart and Winston, 1973): 6.

4. W. Lawrence Neuman, *Social Research Methods: Qualitative and Quantitative Methods* (Boston: Allyn and Bacon, 1994): 2.

5. Earl Babbie, *The Practice of Social Research* (Belmont, CA: Wadsworth Publishing Co., 1992): 22.

6. Neuman, *Social Research Methods,* 5.

7. Mason and Bramble, *Understanding and Conducting Research,* 2.

8. Kerlinger, *Foundations of Behavioral Research,* 6.

9. Kenneth Bailey, *Methods of Social Research* (New York: The Free Press, 1982): 5.

10. Charles Bullock, in Marjorie Malkin and Christine Howe, eds., *Research in Therapeutic Recreation: Concepts and Methods* (State College, PA: Venture Publishing, 1993): 27–29.

11. Karla Henderson, *Dimensions of Choice: A Qualitative Approach to Recreation, Parks, and Leisure Research* (State College, PA: Venture Publishing, 1991).

12. Claire Selltiz, Lawrence Wrightsman, and Stuart Cook, *Research Methods in Social Relations* (New York: Holt, Rinehart and Winston, 1976): 16.

Basic Concepts and Language of Research and Evaluation

Before beginning to do your own research, or even to read intelligently about research done by others, it is necessary to learn some of the language of scientific method. This language may seem dry at times, but it ensures that communication about research is clear and unambiguous. Once you can use it fluently, it will aid you both in planning your own research and in assessing the research efforts of others as possible sources of information for your own decisions.[1]

INTRODUCTION

Having examined the essential nature of systematic inquiry and the scientific method in the preceding chapters, we now turn to a more direct exploration of the key concepts and principles that underlie the research and evaluation process. This chapter presents several terms that are commonly used in the development of research proposals and the reporting of their findings—simply described as the "language of research." It then goes more fully into contrasting research styles and approaches, briefly describes the most common types of research and evaluation designs, and discusses the researcher's role and needed qualities.

PURPOSES OF RESEARCH

First, it is necessary to identify the fundamental goals or purposes of research. Babbie suggests that these fall under three major headings: exploration, description, and explanation.[2]

Exploration consists of a preliminary probing of a topic or problem area that is new to the investigator or about which little systematic study has been done. Its purpose may be to satisfy the investigator's curiosity, to determine the feasibility of more comprehensive or systematic study, and to test the research methods.

Description involves gathering comprehensive and accurate data regarding a topic or a research problem. As this text will show, research must be based on clearly stated study purposes and use appropriate sampling, data-gathering, and analytical or interpretive procedures.

Explanation seeks to determine why events or situations occur as they do. It may seek evidence of causal relationship, in which one element is clearly shown to affect or influence another, or may at a minimum show correlation—meaning some degree of relationship between or among different study elements. This last purpose of research is an important contributor to theory-building and may enable one to draw conclusions that predict program outcomes or the effects of agency policies.

PURPOSES OF EVALUATION

In contrast, as Chapter 1 points out, the purposes of evaluation are more narrowly defined: (1) to measure the *effectiveness* of recreation, parks, and leisure-service agencies and programs in terms of meeting their stated goals and objectives; and (2) to measure the *quality* of their performance in other terms, such as their adherence to professionally accepted principles of standards of operation. Because evaluation is generally regarded as a subset or specific purpose of research as a broader process, the bulk of this chapter will focus on the concepts and language of research.

THE LANGUAGE OF RESEARCH

Research proposals and reports customarily use certain words in specific, technical ways. Although defining all these terms in this chapter is not possible, a number of the most important ones are discussed here, and others are defined in later chapters.

Concepts

Basically, a concept is an idea. It is an intellectual representation of some aspect of reality but is not tangible or concrete. Instead it is a term or symbol that helps us understand the nature of various phenomena or describe them in useful ways.

Concepts do not represent material objects as such, but may describe aspects of them. For example, concepts such as "liquidity," "weight," or "density" are essentially abstract ideas, although they refer to physical characteristics of objects or substances and can be measured.

Other concepts such as "brotherhood," "patriotism," or "religion" describe social values or behavioral patterns. They can also be measured, although they are clearly abstract. Both "leisure" and "recreation" are concepts in a broad sense, although they may be made more tangible or visible in the form of acts of participation, physical resources for play, or spending patterns, which can all be measured. An important task in research is to *operationalize* abstract concepts by translating them into concrete phenomena that can be observed and studied descriptively.

Constructs

The term *construct* is used to describe a concept that has been deliberately invented or adopted for scientific or research purposes. For example, the term "intelligence" is normally viewed as a concept, based on the observation of behavior that shows varying degrees of problem-solving or coping ability. However, as a construct, scientists use the idea of intelligence in two ways: (1) as a way of explaining or understanding behavior and (2) as an element that is so defined and specified that it can be observed and measured. In the latter case, intelligence has become a construct that is useful in scientific research.

To illustrate the difference between concepts and constructs in recreation-related terms, one might use the idea of "recreation demand." As a *concept,* recreation demand might be described as the degree of interest and/or participation in a specific type of leisure activity. As a *construct,* recreation demand might be defined as the quantity of specific recreation opportunities engaged in by a given population group in a certain location during a specific period of time.

Theories

A theory is a generalization or series of generalizations on a theme, through which we seek to describe or explain some phenomena in a systematic and logical way. Often it is used to clarify relationships between research elements or to predict outcomes that will occur.

Theories can range from relatively simple generalizations to much more complex formulation of ideas. They help to provide a framework for research by giving a systematic picture of the elements that are being studied, showing how they influence or interact with each other in logical ways. Within the scientific method, the word "theory" may be used in several ways: (a) inductive theory, based on observed facts with essentially an unconfirmed statement; (b) functional theory, or "best guess," which is really a working statement that is a preliminary tool of a research plan that is being developed; or (c) deductive theory, to be confirmed or tested by systematic observation under controlled conditions.

The term *grounded theory,* made popular in recent decades, refers to theories that stem from observation of various aspects of social life, leading to preliminary statements of perceived patterns of behavior—which, in turn, are subjected to new waves of observation and revised statements over time. Essentially, grounded theory is a form of inductive theory construction.

Theories may be used to assist research by identifying or summarizing relevant facts, classifying phenomena into logical groups or classes, formulating explanations of relationships, predicting facts or happenings, and showing the need for further research. When they are based on very impressive, consistent evidence, theories may be described as *laws* or *principles*.

Laws

Laws are defined as universal generalizations about classes or groups of facts, such as the law of gravity. Laws must be applicable in all circumstances, rather than accidental patterns found within a particular environment; they must be proven beyond doubt. Some laws that have been presented in recent years that deal with human behavior or the world of business, such as Parkinson's Law or Murphy's Law, are not actual laws. Instead, they represent humorous or satirical views that are often based on observed behavior, but tend to be exaggerated or overgeneralized statements.

Hypotheses

Hypotheses (plural form for the word "hypothesis") are statements or predictions of relationships that are believed to exist between two or more variables. They represent concrete, declarative statements of these anticipated relationships, based on a theory. The key variables in the theory are operationally defined and placed within a research context so that it is possible to measure accurately whether the expected relationship occurs.

Hypothesis statements must therefore contain two or more variables that are measurable or potentially measurable, and they must specify how they are related. Customarily, hypotheses take two forms in research proposals.

Working hypotheses

These are general statements of the relationship that is believed to exist between two or more study variables. Working hypotheses contain the researcher's expectation regarding this relationship and cannot be tested as such because they are not stated in a manner that lends itself to measurement. Customarily, they are stated in a positive or affirmative form.

Statistical hypotheses

These are more precise statements of the working hypotheses, put into operational terms that permit testing and statistical analysis. Usually, statistical hypotheses are stated in the "null" or "negative" form, which indicates that the *opposite* of the working hypotheses will be found and that *no* significant relationship will be proved to exist between the key variables in the study.

If the null hypothesis is accepted or confirmed, the working hypothesis has been rejected. If, on the other hand, the null hypothesis is rejected, the working hypothesis has been proved to be correct.

Hypotheses may also be categorized as "directional" or "nondirectional." A directional hypothesis might state that there would be a statistically significant difference in the camping behaviors of two groups of research subjects and would predict the nature or direction of the difference—for example, that one group would participate more frequently in aquatic activities. A nondirectional hypothesis would predict that there would be a difference but would not state *which* group would be involved more frequently.

Models and Paradigms

A model is a theoretical abstraction or depiction of a given process or set of relationships. It identifies the major elements of the subject or system under investigation and shows how they are believed to relate to each other or how a process occurs over a period of time. Models often take a visual form and may involve charts or constructions showing the sequence of events occurring in a process.

In such fields as government or social service, models may be used to show the interplay of community groups or how social change occurs. Models may either deal with real phenomena, such as the work schedules and productivity of park maintenance personnel, or with more abstract concepts, such as the therapeutic uses of play.

The words "models" and "theories" are sometimes used interchangeably, in the sense that a set of propositions relevant to one section of a field may be expressed as a theory or, in more concrete and operational terms, as a model.

Paradigms are sometimes described as being similar to models in that they serve as a means of conceptualizing research. A paradigm might represent the perspective of the researcher toward the problem being studied and might be illustrated through a flow chart or other visual scheme that shows the steps of research or the relationships among variables.

In a broader sense, the term *paradigm* refers to a perspective or frame of reference for viewing the social world or some other subject of investigation, consisting of a set of concepts and assumptions held by the researcher.

Often, there may be a number of different, conflicting paradigms within a scholarly discipline or area of research. Since each paradigm is likely to have its own set of concepts or jargon and since scholars may also differ in the research problems they consider important, this may lead to difficulty in carrying out effective and cooperative research efforts within a field.

Over the past several years, paradigms have been widely referred to in the research literature. Paradigms represent much more than an abstract term.

Whether one is a practitioner, researcher, student, or teacher, one's paradigm of leisure and its role in human society is likely to sharply influence one's thinking and behavior.

Variables

A variable is an element or characteristic of the subject being studied through research; it may take different values or forms for different observable units. Examples of variables might include different types of participants or characteristics of participants (such as age, sex, or educational level); different categories of recreational participation; settings for participation; leadership styles or behavioral outcomes. There are two types of variables—those that have a fixed nature, such as different types of local government (city, town, village, county), and those that vary on some measure, such as quantity, intensity, or frequency. For example, this second type of variable might be the amount of time a person participates in a recreation experience or the income of an individual. Although such variables can take on any value and are not normally assigned to categories, they might be arbitrarily assigned to units on a scale, such as "high," "middle," or "low."

In addition, research variables may also be classified as either *independent, dependent,* or *intervening* variables.

Independent variables

These are factors or elements in an experiment or other empirical research study which, in the researcher's view, influence other variables or cause certain effects. Although they are called independent, they may be introduced deliberately or manipulated by the researcher to test their influence.

For example, in an experiment that seeks to determine the best methods of preventing vandalism in a recreation center, if three methods are used (such as expelling youth gangs from the center, hiring guards to supervise the areas, or seeking to work out the problem through group discussion and an attempt to change the values of those responsible), each of these methods represents an independent variable.

Dependent variables

These are factors or elements in a study which are caused or influenced *by* independent variables. In the example just given, the vandalism rates in the recreation centers where the three methods of preventing vandalism were applied constitute the dependent variable. Simply stated, the variable that causes change or influences the other variable is called the independent variable; the variable that is affected by the other is the dependent variable.

Intervening variables

A third type of variable is referred to as *intervening* or *extraneous;* these are elements or factors in a study over which researchers may have little control and which may contaminate or distort the results of a study. For example, fluctuating weather conditions or short-term economic factors might influence the results of a study of recreation participation and be beyond the ability of the researcher to control. Such factors are sometimes referred to as *uncontrolled* variables or, when they create confusion or misleading effects in a study, as *confounding* variables.

As much as possible, researchers must seek to keep the possible influence of such intervening variables to a minimum. Variables may be compared to *constants,* which are study elements that are held constant (kept the same) for all observable units within the study. To illustrate, in an experiment which seeks to measure the effects of fees and charges on recreation program participation, variables might be the different levels of fees and charges (independent) and the actual rate or frequency of participation (dependent). Constants might be the kinds of activities or the sponsoring organizations, which are kept the same for all research units.

Parameters

Parameters are somewhat similar to variables or constants, in that they refer to elements or characteristics of a study. The term has two specific applications:

1. A *parameter* is an element of a study that remains unchanged throughout the course of research. It refers to the important dimensions or characteristics of the *population* that is being studied or to the process that is being carried on. For example, quantitative factors, such as the numbers of subjects, their age, or length of involvement that are descriptive of the entire study population, are referred to as parameters of the study.

2. In a related meaning, a *parameter* is a property or characteristic of the entire universe that is determined or measured through research. In contrast, a *statistic* is a characteristic obtained from a *sample* of the population, which therefore represents an estimate of an actual parameter.

Data

Another commonly used research term is *data.* This is the plural form of the Latin word *datum* and is usually defined as information derived from the observation of one or more variables. It may take the form of numerical or qualitative ratings or descriptions or other kinds of information about the variables observed. Data are gathered through observation, interviews, the use of survey forms or questionnaires, the perusal of records, psychological or physiological testing, or numerous other procedures.

The gathering of data is a central task in most research studies involving the process of measurement. Customarily, this implies comparisons of some kinds: for example, whether the participation rate in a water-play park has gone up or down or whether people engage in certain activities more or less frequently as they age.

Data may be gathered in a host of ways. Physical scientists may use scientific instruments, while social scientists may use opinion scales, survey questionnaires, or tally sheets that scrutinize and record behavior. Babbie comments that there is an almost limitless variety of measurement techniques available for gathering data in social research. "The only limit, really," he concludes, "is your imagination." At the same time, the task of correctly identifying and measuring data in a research study or evaluation project is demanding and often difficult.

CONTRASTING FRAMEWORKS FOR RESEARCH

As Chapter 2 points out, there are two contrasting approaches to scientific research: the *positivistic* and *naturalistic* perspectives. These two models of investigation are based on fundamentally different views of the world and are reflected in different research emphases and methods. Beyond them, there are other contrasting frameworks that help shape the design and process of research studies.

Applied and Basic Research Emphases

An important distinction is frequently made between *applied* and *basic* research approaches. Applied research involves studies carried out for clearly practical purposes—either to find immediate solutions to real problems or to develop sound policies or administrative strategies.

By contrast, basic research (often referred to as *pure* or *theoretical* research) has as its primary purpose the search for knowledge for its own sake, rather than because of any practical value it might have. As its name suggests, basic research is concerned with fundamental understandings and with the development of concepts or theories that underlie leisure participation. Typically, its function in the leisure-service field might be to identify and explain such phenomena as play motivations or constraints or to clarify value systems or patterns of involvement as influenced by economic, gender, or racial factors.

Saslow argues that research in any academic area or professional discipline should include both basic and applied studies in order to solve immediate, practical problems and to make major breakthroughs that can lead to expanded new bodies of knowledge and large-scale policy shifts.[3] In addition, there is increasing awareness that the distinction between applied and basic research is often arbitrary and that many studies may have both practical and theoretical elements.

Obtrusive and Nonobtrusive Research

Another contrast in research approaches involves the degree to which researchers impinge on the lives of those they study. In one approach, the investigator might actually manipulate study subjects or their environment and thus affect their behavior. This is called *obtrusive* research. Any experimental study in which the researcher deliberately introduces conditions or environmental stimuli that influence participants is an example of such manipulation. For example, a research study in which three styles of leadership are used with groups, to determine their effects, would be a form of obtrusive research.

Studies that are carefully designed to record only what is happening in a natural way and that seek to avoid influencing subjects in the slightest way are considered forms of *nonobtrusive* research. In such investigations, the researchers should not be seen or should be as inconspicuous as possible; they must also avoid altering environmental conditions that might influence the behavior of study subjects.

Research Settings: Field or Laboratory

A similar contrast may be drawn with respect to the settings in which research is conducted. In so-called *field* studies, the research is done in actual, established settings, such as existing agencies, leisure settings, classrooms, or other places that are not deliberately formed for purposes of research.

Laboratory research refers to studies that are carried out in an artificial or specially created environment. For example, special facilities may be used to explore the influence of different types of toys, equipment, or other factors on children's play. Often, such artificial settings are designed so that they appear to be real to the participants; however, they may contain special viewing facilities, hidden recording devices, or other equipment that would not be available in a natural, field setting.

Time Frame of Research: Past, Present, and Future

Research may be carried on within varied time frames. Obviously, it may explore and interpret the past, as in historical studies of colonial life or the establishment of the recreation and park movement. Most research deals with the present or recent past, as we examine the nature of present-day recreation participation or the operation of contemporary leisure-service agencies and programs.

Research may also be used to predict the future, based on projections of past or present trends or on the use of Delphi planning techniques, in which groups of experts go through a sequence of blending their perceptions of the future. Research may be fixed in time, in the sense that it analyzes what is happening at a given moment, or it may extend over a lengthy period of time through longitudinal studies that examine programs or other subjects at fixed intervals. In contrast, evaluation studies usually deal only with the present or the very recent past.

Quantitative or Qualitative Approaches

A final distinction that is widely made with respect to contrasting research designs involves quantitative and qualitative study approaches. As described earlier, quantitative research tends to adhere to the positivistic approach to scientific investigation and to seek numerical kinds of data that can be analyzed statistically to test study hypotheses. In contrast, qualitative research, which is linked to the naturalistic approach and which is described in fuller detail in Chapter 8, deals with elements that cannot as readily be precisely measured or put into numeric terms.

Quantitative research has tended to be more highly regarded than qualitative methods in varied scholarly disciplines, in part because this has been the approved method of investigation in the physical and natural sciences. However, a strong case can be made that, in such an individualistic and diversified field as recreation and leisure, there ought to be a place for research of a more deeply probing, intuitive, or philosophical nature.

DIFFERING RESEARCH DESIGNS

Beyond these contrasts in the overall framework of research, there are other distinct contrasts in terms of research design and purpose. In the past, it was considered that research should be grouped under three major headings: *historical, descriptive,* and *experimental.* Best wrote:

> Practically all studies fall under one, or a combination, of these types.
>
> 1. *Historical research* describes *what was.* The process involves investigating, recording, analyzing, and interpreting the events of the past. . . .
> 2. *Descriptive research* describes *what is.* It involves the description, recording, analysis, and interpretation of conditions that exist. . . .
> 3. *Experimental research* describes *what will be* when certain variables are carefully controlled or manipulated. . . .[4]

However, there are numerous other specialized forms of research design, including varied subtypes within each of the major headings. Descriptive research, for example, might include surveys, case studies, and longitudinal, cross-sectional, and comparative methods, to name only a few. Each major kind of research design is described in the chapters that follow, with illustrations showing how it applies to recreation, parks, and leisure studies.

ROLE OF THE RESEARCHER

A final important element in any understanding of the scientific inquiry process involves the researcher. First, it should be clearly understood that it must *not* be the researcher's purpose to *prove* that something is true. Frequently, when students are asked the purpose of a study proposal they are offering as a course assignment, their reply will be, "It is to *show* that, etc., etc." This response suggests a degree of bias or preconviction that might lead to distortion of the truth. Instead, the purpose should be to discover the real facts—whether they involve testing a hypothesis, identifying correlations among variables, or measuring participation outcomes.

To accomplish this, it is generally accepted that the researcher should possess such qualities as expertise in the field being investigated, objectivity, thoroughness and rigor, and high ethical standards.

Expertise

Customarily, it is expected that the investigator be knowledgeable in the area being studied. This does not mean that she must be a leading authority in the field, but rather that she has a high level of competence in the subject and sufficient command of the methods that will be used to investigate it. At the same time, there have been dramatic examples of individuals who have made important contributions to contemporary thinking who have not been technically qualified in given fields through specialized degrees or other professional background.

Researchers often improve their expertise while conducting a study and examining other work that has been done in the area. In addition, researchers often do successive studies within a particular area of research and thus gradually gain greater competence and reputation within the area.

Objectivity

Normally, it is expected that the researcher be objective and lack bias or preconviction in a given area. The researcher is expected not to seek to prove a case, to deceive, or to exclude or distort evidence. This is a critical concern, in that researchers obviously stand to gain from successful research or from findings that benefit their own organizations or professional groups. Too often, the press reports studies that have been manipulated within such areas as medical research, political affairs, or marketing surveys. When such shortcuts or deliberate distortions are discovered, they inevitably damage the public's confidence in scientific research and can destroy the careers of those responsible for presenting inaccurate findings.

In recent years the principle that researchers must be objective and dispassionate in their investigations has been challenged by proponents of qualitative research approaches. In field studies of an anthropological or sociological nature, for example, researchers may enter deeply into the lives of the individuals or groups they are studying. In such situations, they are likely to play a much more subjective role in their analyses and conclusions.

Thoroughness and Rigorous Process

Even when the researcher's intentions are honest, study findings must be questioned when they rely on inadequate or irresponsible investigation, with casual observation or follow-up of subjects, the use of inexact data-gathering instruments, or poor sampling procedures. Studies must be designed so that the entire process is as rigorous as possible.

As later chapters will show, within the research process it is essential that all data-gathering or analytical procedures be carefully controlled and that all records and documents related to studies be held for a period of time after publication in order to respond to questions or challenges that may be raised.

Ethics and Concern for Subjects

Apart from the need for honesty and careful research procedures, other ethical considerations today include the need to avoid possible dangers or negative effects for subjects. In the past, many research studies have resulted in harmful outcomes for participants. Today, all study proposals that involve human subjects, particularly in experimental research projects where they may be manipulated to the extent that psychological or physical harm may occur, must normally be reviewed and given clearance by a "human-subjects" review committee. Still other ethical considerations may involve the need for confidentiality in research reporting; usually subjects who participate in surveys, for example, are assured anonymity.

Particularly in experimental studies in therapeutic recreation service, the issue of having subjects in control groups who do *not* receive special treatment that might be helpful to them must be considered from an ethical perspective. Other ethical concerns may involve the need for "full disclosure" of study purposes and procedures to participants or the adherence to appropriate professional guidelines in terms of acknowledging coauthorships in the publication of study findings (see page 320).

THE CHALLENGE OF RESEARCH

When carried out according to high scientific standards, research represents a challenging conceptual task. It also demands the ability to manage a mix of investigative processes within what is often a complicated administrative operation. The best research also demonstrates solid scholarly ability, imagination, and excellent writing skills.

Research is often circular, building on what has been explored in earlier studies and leading to new theories, investigations, and findings. It is revealing to trace research in a given field through professional or scholarly journals over a period of years, showing how various theories have been developed and disseminated and how knowledge proliferates and becomes more refined within separate special areas of the overall field. Often, a number of scholars within a profession may be working on the same general problem, communicating with each other through publication and thus cooperating in the advancement of a professional body of knowledge.

For those who carry out truly innovative or ground-breaking research, the task is almost like reading a complicated mystery or detective novel, with painstaking, patient efforts to gather evidence, test solutions, and finally to come out with the "truth."

Although some scientists who conduct research may regard it simply as a job or a professional responsibility, others consider it a uniquely satisfying and rewarding craft. In a famous essay, "On Intellectual Craftsmanship," C. Wright Mills began with the words, "To the individual social scientist who feels himself a part of the classic tradition, social science is the practice of a craft." Other authors have suggested that scientists are as completely involved in their work as creative artists or poets. Often, researchers are described as individuals who must possess a very special kind of intuitive imagination, linked with practical skills of study organization, data-gathering, and analysis.

Certainly, for both practitioners and scholars within the overall field of recreation, parks, and leisure studies, probing investigations into the "how" and "why" of human involvement in varied forms of leisure activity or into the process of managing recreation and park programs should constitute an absorbing and challenging pursuit. The nature of such studies will be shown in fuller detail in the chapters that follow, beginning with Chapter 4, which demonstrates the specific values of research and evaluation in recreation, parks, and leisure studies.

SUMMARY

Research is a process that uses a special language of terms and symbols. Among the most important terms are these: concepts, constructs, theories, and laws; hypotheses, models, and paradigms; variables, parameters, and data. Apart from the positivistic/naturalistic and quantitative/qualitative contrasts, most research today in the social sciences or fields such as recreation, parks, and leisure studies may be classified under two broad headings: applied and basic.

Other contrasts in research design include the use of obtrusive and nonobtrusive methods, field or laboratory settings, and varying time frames for study, such as the past, present, and future. Finally, the role of the researcher as scientist, administrator, and craftsperson involves ethical concerns that should govern study procedures.

QUESTIONS AND ACTIVITIES

1. Search one of the journals cited in later chapters or listed on page 323. From it extract one or more articles that make use of such terms as *theory, paradigm, hypothesis,* or *variable.* Briefly outline the study's purpose, and show how each of these terms is being used, with specific illustrations from the article(s).

2. Develop a simple question regarding a problem or an issue related to recreation, parks, or leisure studies or services. Without attempting to develop a full research proposal, indicate the possible *theories, paradigms, hypotheses, variables,* or other special research terms that might be used in studying this problem or issue.

3. Select one or more research articles in the professional literature. After reading it, determine where it belongs with respect to the following possible contrasting frameworks for research: *applied* or *basic; obtrusive* or *nonobtrusive; field* or *laboratory* setting; *time frame* (past, present, or future); and *quantitative* or *qualitative* study approaches.

ENDNOTES

1. Carol Saslow, *Basic Research Methods* (New York: Random House, 1982): 29.
2. Earl Babbie, *The Practice of Social Research* (Belmont, CA: Wadsworth Publishing Co., 1992): 90–92.
3. Saslow, *Basic Research Methods,* 24–25.
4. John W. Best, *Research in Education* (Englewood Cliffs, NJ: Prentice-Hall, 1981): 25.

Professional Applications of Research and Evaluation

Research underpins all of these criteria [of profession-
alism] . . . A body of validated knowledge on which the
profession is based requires codification of research find-
ings from a variety of sources as well as research results
from studies geared to recreation programs or leadership
problems. This last criterion calls for a social policy con-
cern on the part of the profession which again requires
research methods for an explanation of the causes and
consequences of such social problems. Research then
becomes a major vehicle in professionalizing recreation.[1]

INTRODUCTION

This chapter begins by discussing the general role of research and evaluation within the recreation, park, and leisure-service field, with emphasis on the current pressure for documentation and accountability in agency operations and community planning for leisure service. It examines the traditional separation of research into applied and basic categories and shows how many studies today include both kinds of emphases. To provide a fuller picture of scientific investigation in recreation, parks, and leisure studies today, a number of reports of research studies in the field are then identified.

GENERAL ROLE OF SCIENTIFIC INQUIRY IN THE LEISURE-SERVICE FIELD

The most important contribution of research and evaluation to the overall field of recreation, parks, and leisure studies is that they provide a body of contemporary scholarship based on scientific investigation. This is essential if the field is to be recognized as a significant professional discipline, comparable to other specialized areas of human service or social management.

There are a number of specific needs in the field of recreation, parks, and leisure services that can be met through systematic, carefully designed research and evaluation studies. They include the following:

1. The need to improve, test, or apply new professional techniques and practices in order to upgrade leadership and management operations in various areas of leisure service, including programming, facilities development, and fiscal management.

2. The need to understand the leisure experience, its motivations, structure, and consequences. Linked to this is the need to identify and measure the leisure needs and wishes of clients, patients, or other population groups in institutions or communities as a basis for developing policies and programs designed to serve them more effectively.

3. The need to be able to measure the specific outcomes and values of organized recreation and park service and experiences in order to provide convincing documentation and support for the field. Related to this is the need to measure the quality of agencies or programs in order to provide an intelligent basis for decision making or policy formulation.

In a sense, each of the preceding functions is related to the overall task of planning, managing, and marketing recreation programs and services. Beyond these values, research may also contribute to society's understanding of recreation and leisure as important aspects of community life and personal well-being.

EMPHASIS ON ACCOUNTABILITY AND DOCUMENTATION

Underlying the functions of research and evaluation that have just been described is the need to document the effectiveness and value of recreation agencies and programs. *This is particularly crucial in the case of governmental agencies or nonprofit, voluntary organizations that rely on public support in the form of appropriated tax funds or monetary contributions that support program efforts.* Over the past two decades, financial pressures in an era of austerity have resulted in budget cutbacks in many settings and the increasing demand that all such social-service agencies justify their existence in convincing terms.

As a result, it has become absolutely essential today that leisure-service practitioners and researchers join together to carry out scientifically sound studies that document the important outcomes of recreation, parks, and leisure-service programs. Through such efforts, a number of publications have described the benefits of organized recreation service, and major professional conferences and symposiums have focused on the need to extend research into new areas of leisure-service outcomes.

Ellis and Witt point out that in the past the evaluation of recreation programs tended to be "biased, self-serving and ultimately misleading." Today, they argue, such evidence will not suffice. Instead:

> . . . evaluation by design is a necessity. No longer will intuitive judgments suffice. The best proof possible is needed so that what is said to be done is really being done. There is a need for ammunition to fight to save park, recreation, and leisure services from the tax cutter's axe. It is also essen-

tial to fulfill the responsibility to spend tax dollars in the most efficient and effective way possible.[2]

Program accountability—the degree to which varied types of leisure-service agencies achieve their stated goals and objectives, thus justifying their financial support—is a primary focus of evaluation research. Too often, we have measured program effectiveness only in terms of attendance or fiscal returns. Given the severe social problems that face many communities today that have direct implications for recreation, park, and leisure-service programs, it is absolutely essential that accountability in social "impact" terms be a key focus of evaluation in public-agency settings.

Similarly, in therapeutic, voluntary agency, armed forces, or campus recreation programs, there is the same need to demonstrate accountability in terms of meeting specific agency objectives or mission goals.

Even in commercial recreation or private membership organizations, which do not justify themselves in terms of community needs or social outcomes, there is strong pressure to demonstrate effective performance.

It should be stressed that research and evaluation must *not* be expected to provide automatic justifications for one's program. They must be carried out in an objective, unbiased, and totally honest fashion; when they are, they may well yield negative findings, rather than positive outcomes. Like all forms of research, evaluation does not seek to "prove" a case. Instead, it gathers evidence and makes judgments as objectively as possible—not only to determine whether programs have been successful, but also to improve them as they are being carried on or in future planning and implementation.

RESEARCH EMPHASIS: APPLIED OR BASIC

As Chapter 3 points out, research studies that are directed to practical ends and outcomes are usually designated as applied research. They may range from the routine evaluation of programs or management techniques to determine their effectiveness, to experimental studies designed to measure recreation's effectiveness in achieving important personal or community goals. Problems related to environmental protection, the reduction of social deviancy, the improvement of personal health, or the strengthening of family life might all be appropriate subjects for such research.

In contrast, basic research has as its primary purpose the accumulation of knowledge and the development of theories for their own sake, rather than because of their direct usefulness. Such studies attempt to identify and explain phenomena and the relationships among them in order to develop a stronger theoretical base for leisure-service delivery.

Later in this chapter, it is pointed out that many research studies may be based on both applied and basic approaches. At this stage, however, it is helpful to look at the kinds of problems that are typically examined under these two contrasting approaches.

Examples of Applied Research

The following section presents examples of different types of applied research studies in recreation, parks, and leisure services. Four areas of concern are identified: (1) recreation programs and services and their outcomes; (2) professional development in recreation and parks; (3) design, development, and maintenance of areas and facilities; and (4) management functions, problems, and trends. In each case, several typical research topics are presented.

1. Recreation Programs, Services, and Outcomes
   a. Surveys of program practices and trends, within a community or region, a given type of agency, or other setting. Such studies might deal with program activities, participation levels, economic factors, areas and facilities, or other elements.
   b. Feasibility studies, which are intended to determine whether it is necessary to develop a particular type of facility or program and whether it can be economically justified; these studies may examine the potential audience or market for the project, competitive facilities or programs in the area, potential revenues to be derived, possible environmental impacts, and similar elements.
   c. Participant needs assessments are studies that measure the felt or expressed leisure needs and interests of individuals or groups and other factors related to time, cost, and levels of participation. Needs assessment may also be carried out in a prescriptive manner, in which the programmer makes her independent assessment of the individual's needs based on observation of functional performance and other background information.
   d. Studies of program outcomes or benefits, either in general terms or by measuring success in achieving stated objectives. These studies may be conducted in several ways: (1) through self-reported satisfactions and reported benefits; (2) through observation of performance and behavioral change; or (3) through measurement of other factors, such as changes in absenteeism or the accident rate in a company-sponsored recreation program.
   e. Examination of a program or an agency based on published performance guidelines or standards or on accreditation standards and criteria.
2. Professionalism in Leisure Service
   a. Surveys of personnel at work in the field: for example, surveys of numbers of professional employees in public recreation and park agencies in a given state; their salaries, job titles, and descriptions; and working conditions and qualifications or standards for employment.
   b. Competency-based studies, which systematically analyze the specific job skills needed for successful performance in a given type of position or area of professional service.

c. Studies of college and university curricula in recreation, parks, and leisure studies, including degree options and curriculum trends, number and background of faculty members, enrollment statistics, and accreditation processes.

d. Role of professional societies in promoting public awareness of the leisure-service field, improving professional performance, unifying the field, supporting needed legislation, sponsoring research, and similar functions.

e. Research into staff productivity, using systematic cost-benefit analysis or other techniques to evaluate performance.

3. Recreation and Park Areas and Facilities

a. Planning studies which include inventories of parks, playgrounds, aquatic, sport, and other specialized facilities. Might include classification of facilities as to type and purpose, linked to projections of future needs and short- and long-range priority ratings for acquisition and development.

b. Experimentation with different types of facilities to determine their effectiveness in attracting participants, promoting specific types of play, or minimizing accidents or other undesirable incidents.

c. Studies of the environmental impact of recreation on forest areas or other outdoor resources. Examples might include the effect of off-road vehicles on vegetation and wildlife, or boating and related water activities on reservoir water quality.

d. Studies concerned with access to recreation facilities for persons with disabilities, including both indoor and outdoor settings. May deal with application of guidelines for ramps, doorways, lavatories, and other modified facility elements or with the design of special types of facilities to encourage participation by the disabled.

4. Management Problems and Trends

a. Research in fiscal practices, including trends in budgetary allocations, use of fees and charges, leasing and concession arrangements, use of gift catalogs, grants and subsidies, subcontracting of recreation functions, and similar topics.

b. Studies of vandalism, crime, and related management problems in recreation and park settings, including methods used to deal with them. Linked to this area, studies related to risk management, accident prevention, health, and safety.

c. Analysis of community relations and cosponsorship practice involving synergetic relationships with other community agencies or businesses.

d. Examination of new or emerging managerial approaches, including marketing methods, systems-planning techniques, participative management emphases, and similar topics.

New management theories dealing with TQM (total quality management), "customer-" or "benefits-driven" approaches, "just-in-time" programming, concepts of "continuous improvement" or "flattened" management structures are all appropriate subjects for applied research.

At the simplest level, such studies may simply provide a descriptive report of the factual findings of the research. When this is done, using tables and charts or other convenient forms of summarization, the process represents a somewhat superficial or mechanical form of research. At a more advanced level, they may seek to test hypotheses and build models that explain relationships and cause-and-effect sequences. In either case, the intention of the researcher is to gather information or arrive at conclusions that will be directly useful to practitioners. Such results will obviously be more valuable if they have broad applications to the overall leisure-service field, rather than just to the agency that conducted the study or to the specific setting that was examined.

Examples of Basic Research

In contrast, so-called basic research studies are primarily concerned with developing or testing concepts and theories and tend to make use of investigative and analytical techniques that are found in the social and behavioral sciences, such as psychology, sociology, anthropology, or economics. Their purpose essentially is to examine recreation and leisure as social phenomena, to clarify their meanings and implied values, and to relate them to the broader societal context.

Twelve examples of the kinds of subjects dealt with under this broad heading follow. The list is by no means exhaustive; many other theoretical research subjects are discussed each year at national research symposiums.

1. Philosophical or conceptual analyses of play, recreation, and leisure in society; typically, they might involve defining the term or concept, examining its historical roots, and suggesting contemporary applications or changes in public perceptions of it.

2. Examination of the influence of such socioeconomic or demographic variables as social class, racial or ethnic identification, occupation, or educational background on leisure attitudes and behavior.

3. Studies of personality patterns in relation to recreational interests and involvement.

4. Historical studies of specific types of leisure activity (sports, performing arts, gambling, etc.) in different eras or of changing attitudes toward recreation and leisure.

5. Anthropological analysis of play and ritual in tribal cultures or of the social impact of tourism on undeveloped countries.

6. Esthetic or critical examinations of creative/cultural forms of expression, such as the fine and performing arts, as examples of leisure activity.

7. Relationship between sex or gender and one's leisure values and choices; study of recreational involvement as an aspect of family life or marriage.

8. Measurement of quality and beauty of outdoor environments as factors in wilderness-related planning and management policies.

9. Analysis of changing professional roles; for example, extension of therapeutic recreation specialists' functions into advocacy, community education, counseling, facilitating and referring clients, and similar responsibilities.

10. Typologies of leisure behaviors in relation to fundamental patterns of motivation and psychosocial needs of participants.

11. Leisure behavior patterns of special populations, such as persons with physical or mental disabilities.

12. Differences in values and positions with respect to public policy between different groups or recreation participants; for example, contrasting environmental attitudes and leisure values of cross-country skiers and snowmobile club members or of canoers and speedboat enthusiasts.

NEED FOR MIDDLE GROUND IN RESEARCH EMPHASIS

Applied studies tend to be sponsored by leisure-service agencies, government departments, or professional societies. They are usually reported in professional newsletters, magazines that have a broad appeal in the field, or separately published research monographs or reports. When statistics are reported, they are usually fairly simple and presented through charts or tables that are readily comprehensible to a lay audience.

In contrast, theoretical research is more complex in the questions that it asks and the investigative methods used. Often it is carried out by specialists in such fields as psychology, sociology, or economics—or by recreation and park educators who have had training in these disciplines. Usually, the research reports are technical and are presented in scholarly journals with limited readerships.

There is growing awareness today that the division between applied and basic forms of research is somewhat arbitrary and that many studies have both kinds of elements. Often, studies that are primarily conceptual in nature may have important implications for practitioners. For example, analysis of motivations for participation may lead to the more effective design of recreation programs. Similarly, research for practical reasons may also yield findings that help to build a theoretical framework for the analysis of leisure behavior or trends. Therefore, it makes sense to visualize a continuum which ranges from very simple, practical studies at one end of the spectrum to highly theoretical research at the other end.

In the middle of this range, there is a substantial amount of research that is mixed in both purpose and method. Such studies have both practical and theoretical value. What is important is that they are carefully designed and carried out with true scientific rigor. To conduct such research, it is essential that practitioners and research specialists work closely together in jointly conducted studies. Therefore, fuller emphasis should be given to research studies that occupy the middle ground and are both academically respectable and clearly relevant to the concerns of recreation agencies and practitioners.

MAJOR THEMES IN CURRENT RESEARCH

To illustrate the wide range of subjects investigated by recreation, parks, and leisure-service researchers today, the concluding section of this chapter lists studies dealing with a number of themes of major concern for practitioners and educators in this field.

Although the majority of entries deal with a specific research theme and summarize a *single* investigative effort, some are essays that synthesize several *different* research studies on a given topic.

Philosophical and Historical Analyses of Recreation and Leisure

Among the most clearly theoretical examples of leisure research are numerous essays and reports that deal with conceptual models of leisure, with philosophical interpretations of its meaning or with historical discussions of its past. Examples include:

Gerald S. Fain, "Moral Life of the Leisure Scientist," *Abstracts of the 1990 NRPA Leisure Research Symposium* (October 1990): 4.

L. H. Haggard and D. W. Williams, "Identity Affirmation Through Leisure Activities: Leisure Symbols of the Self," *Journal of Leisure Research* (2nd quarter 1990): 1–8.

Kevin D. Lyons and Diane M. Samdahl, "The Fallacy of Freedom: The Preoccupation with Individualism and Freedom in American Leisure Research," *Abstracts from the 1993 NRPA Leisure Research Symposium* (October 1993): 40.

Charles Sylvester, "The Ethics of Play, Leisure and Recreation in the Twentieth Century, 1900–1983," *Leisure Sciences* (1990): 173–88.

Social and Economic Trends Affecting Leisure

Numerous studies examine the social and economic trends of the recent past that have affected leisure sponsorship and involvement or that project future trends. These tend to focus on governmental recreation and park agencies and on outdoor recreation facilities and programs. Examples include:

John C. Bergstrom and H. Ken Cordell, "An Analysis of the Demand for and Value of Outdoor Recreation in the United States," *Journal of Leisure Research* 23, no. 1 (1991): 67–86.

David Scott, "Time Scarcity and Its Implications for Leisure Behavior and Leisure Delivery," *Journal of Park and Recreation Administration* 11, no. 3 (1993): 51–59.

Ellen Weissinger and William D. Murphy, "A Survey of Fiscal Conditions in Small-Town Public Recreation Departments from 1987 to 1991," *Journal of Park and Recreation Administration* 11, no. 3 (1993): 61–70.

Leisure Values, Motivations, and Constraints

Many scholarly studies of leisure focus on the values that individuals attribute to it and their motivations for leisure participation. Linked to such research studies have been investigations of the barriers and constraints that limit participation for many individuals. Examples include:

Alan W. Ewert, "Why Do We All Have a Good Time: Trip Outcome and Motivations for Participation," *Abstracts from the 1993 NRPA Leisure Research Symposium* (October 1993): 73.

Ronald E. McCarville and Bryan J. A. Smale, "Perceived Constraints to Leisure Participation Within Five Activity Domains," *Journal of Park and Recreation Administration* 11, no. 2 (1993): 40–59.

Francis A. McGuire and Joseph T. O'Leary, "The Implications of Leisure Constraint Research for the Delivery of Leisure Services," *Journal of Park and Recreation Administration* 10, no. 2 (1992): 31–40.

John W. Lounsbury and Jeffrey R. Polik, "Leisure Needs and Vacation Satisfaction," *Leisure Sciences* 14 (1992): 105–19.

Demographic Factors Affecting Participation

Numerous studies that examine the racial or ethnic identification of participants or their gender reflect a growing concern about such issues in American education and public life. Other demographic influences on leisure include age, family status, and degree of disability. Entire issues of professional journals have been devoted to these concerns, which are illustrated very selectively in the following studies. Examples include:

Maria T. Allison, "Nature of Leisure Activities Among the Chinese-American Elderly," *Leisure Sciences* 15 (1993): 309–19.

Patricia Bolla, Don Dawson, and George Karlis, "Serving the Multicultural Community: Directions for Leisure Service Providers," *Journal of Applied Recreation Research* 16, no. 2 (1991): 116–31.

Valeria Freysinger, "Leisure with Children: What It Means to Mothers and Fathers," *Abstracts from the 1993 NRPA Leisure Research Symposium* (October 1993): 2.

Myron F. Floyd, James H. Gramann, and Rogelio Saenz, "Ethnic Factors and the Use of Public Outdoor Recreation Areas: The Case of Mexican Americans," *Leisure Sciences* 15 (1993): 83–98.

Karla A. Henderson and M. Deborah Bialeschki, "A Sense of Entitlement to Leisure as Constraint and Empowerment for Women," *Leisure Sciences* 16, no. 1 (1991): 51–66.

Robert Madrigal, Mark E. Havitz, and Dennis R. Howard, "Married Couples' Involvement with Family Vacations," *Leisure Sciences* 14 (1992): 287–99.

Management Goals, Strategies, and Program Evaluation Studies

A considerable number of recent studies have examined the goals and management strategies of different types of recreation, park, and leisure-service agencies or have carried out detailed evaluations of their overall operations or of specific projects. Examples include:

Sam Lankford and Don DeGraaf, "Strengths, Weaknesses, Opportunities, and Threats in Morale, Welfare, and Recreation Organizations: Challenges of the 1990s," *Journal of Park and Recreation Administration* 10, no. 1 (1992): 31–45.

Steven Selin and Debbie Chavez, "Recreation Partnerships and the USDA Forest Service: Managers' Perceptions of the Impact of the National Recreation Strategy," *Journal of Park and Recreation Administration* 11, no. 1 (1993): 1–8.

Jerry J. Vaske, Maureen P. Donnelly, and Bradford N. Williamson, "Monitoring for Quality Control in State Park Management," *Journal of Park and Recreation Administration* 9, no. 2 (1991): 59–70.

Carlton Yoshioka, "Organizational Motives of Public, Nonprofit, and Commercial Leisure Service Agencies," *Journal of Applied Recreation Research* 15, no. 2 (1990): 59–70.

Fiscal Policies: Equity Issues and Pricing Structures

A critical aspect of recreation and park management today involves the marketing approach, the use of revenue sources, and policies governing the provision of recreation facilities and services to different segments of the public. Linked to this problem area are concerns about the pricing of fees and charges for public involvement, which has become an important focus of research. Examples include:

James E. Fletcher, Ronald A. Kaiser, and Susan Groger, "An Assessment of the Importance and Performance of Park Impact Fees in Funding Park and Recreation Infrastructure," *Journal of Park and Recreation Administration* 10, no. 3 (1992): 75–87.

Craig W. Kelsey and Steve Rubio, "Nonresident Pricing Structures of Municipal Parks and Recreation Agencies," *Journal of Park and Recreation Administration* 9, no. 2 (1991): 25–33.

Stephen D. Reiling, Hsiang-Tai Cheng, and Cheryl Trott, "Measuring the Discriminatory Impact Associated with Higher Recreational Fees," *Leisure Sciences* 14 (1992): 121–37.

Professional Development: Higher Education and Personnel Evaluation

Another major area of research interest has involved professional development in recreation, parks, and leisure services. Numerous studies examine the role of higher education programs of professional preparation, personnel management practices, and staff evaluation methods. Examples include:

Claude Cousineau and Patricia Bolla, "Leisure Studies Graduates and Their Careers: A Follow-up Study at the University of Ottawa," *Journal of Applied Recreation Research* 15, no. 1 (1989): 25–40.

Charles H. Hammersley, "Commercial Recreation in the Leisure Studies Curriculum," *Abstracts from the 1990 NRPA Leisure Research Symposium* (October 1990): 81.

Mark E. Havitz, G. David Twynam, and John M. DeLorenzo, "Importance-Performance Analysis as a Staff Evaluation Tool," *Journal of Park and Recreation Administration* 9, no.1 (1991): 43–53.

William R. McKinney and Carrie L. Chandler, "A Comparative Assessment of Duties Between Full-Time and Part-Time Recreation Leaders," *Journal of Park and Recreation Administration* 9, no. 1 (1991): 13–29.

Another major theme for current research studies in recreation, parks, and leisure studies involves measurement of the economic, social, and personal outcomes of recreation programming and involvement. This area of investigation is described in fuller detail in Chapter 18, which deals with efficacy studies in professional practice and the documentation of benefits as a justification of leisure-service programs.

The measurement of personal outcomes of leisure service is particularly relevant in the field of therapeutic recreation service, which is concerned with the psychosocial development or rehabilitation of people who have mental or physical disabilities or who have had serious illnesses or trauma. Beyond this need, it is critical that increased emphasis be given to measuring the effectiveness of organized recreation programs in confronting such serious social programs as youth violence, family breakdown, sexual promiscuity, gang warfare, and similar concerns. Practitioners and researchers must join forces in conducting scientifically sound studies that examine such issues.

SUMMARY

This chapter identifies several major purposes of research and evaluation in recreation, parks, and leisure studies, including a primary emphasis on developing accountability and documentation of recreation agencies and program outcomes. It discusses the widely accepted assumption that research should be categorized as either applied or basic and argues that these types represent the extreme points of a continuum, with many studies having both kinds of characteristics, within a "middle" ground.

Examples are given of the subjects of both types, with a listing of recently reported research studies dealing with several major themes. These have to do with both theoretical and practical approaches to the analysis of recreation and leisure, social and economic trends that affect sponsorship and participation, demographic influences, and recreation and park management goals and strategies. Having set the stage with this chapter's overview of the professional applications of research and evaluation, we are now ready to examine the major types of research designs that are used in the field today.

QUESTIONS AND ACTIVITIES

1. Identify and discuss the major areas presented in this chapter, in which the applied concerns of recreation and park programming and management are described. Of these areas, which do you feel are most critical as subjects for ongoing research?

2. In what ways can essentially "pure" or "theoretical" forms of research be designed so that they may have applied or practical outcomes? Using the examples cited in this chapter or similar ones found in research journals, show what some of the potential applied findings of such studies might be. If necessary, show how a given study might be redesigned or given an additional focus.

3. Comb the professional literature (journals and magazines) to identify several different research reports dealing with a similar theme or subject. Analyze the reports, showing how their findings contribute to a fuller understanding of the subject. If possible, by identifying studies that appear over a period of years on the same theme, show how knowledge in a given area progresses chronologically, with successive researchers building on the work of earlier investigators.

ENDNOTES

1. Genevieve Carter, "The Challenge of Research in Today's Society," in *Recreation Research: Report of a National Conference* (Washington, DC: American Association for Health, Physical Education and Recreation, and National Recreation and Park Association, 1966): 2.

2. Gary Ellis and Peter Witt, "Evaluation by Design," *Parks and Recreation* (February 1982): 40.

Experimental Research Designs

In an experiment researchers make changes in the envi-
ronment and observe what effect these changes have on
animal or human behavior. The researchers hope thereby
to establish a cause-effect relationship. . . . *Experimental*
research aims at providing an explanation of how some-
thing happens, improving our capacity to predict and
even to control future events.[1]

INTRODUCTION

We now move to a consideration of the most important types of research designs used in recreation, parks, and leisure studies. Of these, experimentation is the most widely used form of research in the physical and natural sciences. It has not been as accepted in recreation or other social-service fields because of the difficulty in maintaining the required controls. Nonetheless, experimentation has significant potential for testing possible causal relationships and should be seriously considered for use in leisure research.

NATURE OF EXPERIMENTAL RESEARCH

Experiments are essentially a form of obtrusive research. They involve *doing,* in the sense that the researcher structures actual situations and introduces or controls certain variables in order to measure their effect on each other. Simon points out that the crux of the experiment is that the investigator intentionally manipulates one or more independent variables:

> . . . . thus exposing various groups of subjects to the different variables (or to different amounts of the independent variables), and then observes the changes in the dependent variables. . . . The experimental groups are usually selected randomly, which further ensures that observed differences among groups really reflect differences in the independent variables.[2]

There are essentially three types of experiments, in terms of the settings and subjects they involve. The first is the *laboratory-based* study, in which the researcher can control the immediate physical and social environment by determining the number of subjects, their characteristics, and other conditions.

The second type involves *field* studies, conducted in actual social settings such as clubs, schools, hospitals, or prisons.

The third category involves *natural* experiments, in which the researcher cannot control the independent variable—which might involve such events as earthquakes, hurricanes, or riots—but does use instruments to measure both dependent and independent variables, obtaining baseline levels and then measuring changes that occur in the dependent variable.

Although laboratory settings permit the researcher to maintain rigorous controls over a study by eliminating or controlling extraneous influences (confounding variables), they have the weakness of being artificial and therefore run the risk of encouraging misleading or atypical kinds of responses among subjects.

Similarly, although field experiments offer a useful and realistic setting for research, it may be difficult to maintain continuity of study participants or control other extraneous events or factors that may influence the dependent variable. In general, natural experiments are unpredictable and are less frequently used in leisure-centered research than in other study fields, such as social psychology.

KEY ELEMENTS IN EXPERIMENTAL DESIGN

The essential elements in the classical type of experimental design include the following: (a) presentation of a formal hypothesis, in which the investigator states clearly the proposition that the research is intended to test; (b) random selection or formation of two or more types of groups of subjects, including "control" and "experimental" groups; (c) pretesting of both groups on measures of the quality or performance element that the study is investigating; (d) application of one or more experimental procedures or "interventions"; and (e) posttesting of both groups.

The following symbols are used to represent the elements in experimental research studies:

R   random selection of subjects

X   experimental variables or intervention (independent variable)

C   control group

E   experimental group

O   observation or test (dependent variable)

__   a line between levels indicates matched groups

To illustrate in a study design with matched (randomized) groups and a pre-posttest procedure, the following diagram describes the experiment's structure:

	Pretest	Treatment	Posttest
E(R)	O_1	X	O_2
C(R)	O_1		O_2

Beyond these elements, experiments may require a number of other st. which are described later in this text. They may include developing ope tional definitions for the variables that are to be measured or manipulatec the study, identifying types and degrees of intervention or applying indep dent variables, and selecting or creating instruments to use in measuring changes that occur as a result of the experimental process.

A major concern in all experimental research is the need to achieve a h degree of *validity*—the accuracy or truthfulness of study findings in meas ing what they purport to measure—and the extent to which the findings be generalized in other settings. These two aspects of validity are knowr *internal* and *external* validity (see pages 146–148). It is essential to sel research designs and to apply controls that will achieve the highest degree validity of both types, given the realistic limitations that study circumstar may impose.

Internal Validity

There are seven classes of extraneous variables that may affect the truthful-ness of study findings and that can be controlled by the type of experimental design that is chosen. They include:

1. Contemporary History: This refers to events occurring between the pre- and posttesting stages, in addition to experimental treatments or other interventions.
2. Maturation: Subjects actually mature biologically or psychologically or change in other ways that may affect results, regardless of the effects of the experimental treatment.
3. Pretesting Procedures: These may influence subjects by improving their skills or otherwise affecting their attitude or performance beyond the effect of the experimental treatment.
4. Instrumentation: Changes in testing instruments, raters, or observers may influence the responses of subjects.
5. Statistical Regression: When subjects are selected who have extreme scores, in subsequent testing there is a natural tendency for them to regress toward the scores of the larger population from which they were selected.
6. Selection: Varying responses by control and treatment groups may be due to inadequate selection procedures.
7. Experimental Mortality: The loss of subjects in experimental and control groups over a period of time may affect the findings of the study.

In addition to these separate factors, it is possible that two or more such conditions may interact to contribute to even greater loss of validity in experimental research findings.

External Validity

The generalizability or representativeness of findings may also be affected by the research design and the rigor with which it is carried out. Four factors affecting generalizability of results are:

1. Interaction effects of selection bias and experimental intervention; the results may be influenced to the degree that findings apply only to the specific study population.
2. Pretesting may cause a reaction to the study's experimental procedures that would not be found in subjects who are not pretested.
3. The presence of raters and/or experimental equipment and an artificial study setting may alter the normal response of subjects, apart from the actual effect of the intervention itself.
4. Multiple treatments may influence the subsequent response of subjects; it may not be possible to eliminate the effect of previous experimental interventions.

LEVELS OF EXPERIMENTAL DESIGN

There are several levels of experimental design, ranging from studies that are relatively simple and lack rigorous controls to more carefully structured approaches. Depending on situational factors—such as the ability to select experimental and control groups, carry out pre- and posttests as needed, and exclude extraneous or confounding variables—studies may take any of the following forms.

Preexperimental

Sometimes referred to as a one-shot case study, subjects are exposed to an experimental variable, and the effects are measured.

Example: In a playground or community center where there has been a rash of acts of vandalism, the recreation director posts a new set of rules and urges all participants to be on the lookout for vandals. If vandalism declines after several weeks, he or she concludes that this strategy was responsible for it. The data are gathered loosely, with no effort to exclude other variables or identify other possible causes of the change.

This design has virtually no internal or external validity.

	Treatment	Posttest
E	X	O_2

One Group Pretest, Posttest

This design is somewhat more structured, in that a single group of subjects is used, with careful measurement being done before applying the experimental treatment and again afterward.

Example: A group of disturbed adolescents in a community mental health center is observed, and a careful record is made of their behavior. New methods of group therapy or behavior-modification techniques are applied, and then the subjects are carefully observed again and their behavior recorded, to determine whether there has been change.

This design has minimal internal validity, controlling only for selection of subjects and experimental mortality. It has no external validity.

	Pretest	Treatment	Posttest
E	O_1	X	O_2

Two Groups, Nonrandom Selection, Pretest, Posttest

Here, two groups are used, with one (the control group) receiving no treatment or special considerations, and the other (the experimental group) receiving some type of intervention or special treatment. They are both given pretests and posttests, to determine possible changes. However, the groups have not been randomly selected.

Example: Select two playgrounds for the study. In one, the control playground, provide traditional playground equipment (such as slides, swings, a jungle gym, and a merry-go-round). In the other, the experimental playground, introduce a new set of innovative equipment (such as lumber, ropes, or other materials used in so-called "adventure" playgrounds). Measure the play behaviors of children in both settings, before and after the intervention.

This design has minimal internal validity, primarily because of the lack of random selection. However, it is somewhat better than the previous design because of the control playground. There is no external validity.

	Pretest	Treatment	Posttest
E	O_1	X	O_2
C	O_1		O_2

Two Groups, Random Selection, Pretest, Posttest

This is similar to the preceding design, except that both control and experimental groups are randomly selected from a larger population so that they are as alike as possible. Thus, any differences that appear in the posttest should be the result of the experimental variable, rather than possible differences between the two groups to start with. This is the design previously presented on page 55.

Example: This could involve the teaching of a sports skill with two or more groups of subjects who are randomly selected from a larger group or class of subjects. As a variation of totally random selection, group members might be deliberately paired to match such characteristics as age, sex, height and weight, or previous experience, to ensure that they are as equally matched as possible.

This is the classical type of experimental design and has good internal validity. There is some question, however, regarding the validity of results because of possible pretesting effects on the dependent variable. Nevertheless, randomization of the subjects allows generalization of the findings to the population from which the sample was selected and thus provides a degree of external validity. A variation of this approach is found in the following model.

Solomon Four-Group Design

This is a variation of true experimental design, in which four groups are used, but in which only two of them are given a pretest, because it is believed that the pretest may heighten the motivation of subjects or introduce key skills inappropriately and thus contaminate the study's findings.

Example: In a study of the effects of a leisure education program on recreation interests of physically disabled young adults, the design is:

Group A: Pre- and posttesting with leisure education intervention.
Group B: Pre- and posttesting without intervention.
Group C: Posttest only with intervention.
Group D: Posttest only without intervention.

This design has very strong internal and external validity, since the effect of pretesting can be accounted for.

	Pretest	Treatment	Posttest
$E_1(R)$	O_1	X	O_2
$C_1(R)$	O_1		O_2
$E_2(R)$		X	O_2
$C_2(R)$			O_2

MODIFIED STUDY DESIGNS

Recognizing the difficulty that researchers may encounter in maintaining high levels of both internal and external validity, it is important to use two-group, random selection, pretest-posttest study formats when possible and to control other extraneous variables that affect subjects and study outcomes. In many situations, however, it may not be possible to establish separate groups of equivalent subjects. In other cases, as in therapeutic recreation—an area that generally lends itself to experimentation—objections may be raised to withholding a form of service or treatment (the independent variable) from patients or clients who constitute control groups.

Many examples of research in recreation, parks, and leisure studies therefore do not adhere to the full classical model of experimentation, but instead use modified designs. These may include quasiexperimental, single subject, ex post facto, and action research projects.

Quasiexperimental Designs

These are studies carried on in natural or field settings where some, but not all, of the essential elements of experimental design may be maintained. The researcher is able to select the setting and to determine what variables are to be involved; however, it may not be possible to assign subjects randomly or to control for all of the extraneous variables.

For example, Coyle, Kinney, and Shank describe the use of pre-posttest research designs with nonequivalent groups. Instead of randomly assigning subjects to treatment and control groups, the researcher

> . . . uses intact groups (e.g., wings of a nursing home or patients from two different treatment teams). The most serious validity threat to this type of research design is selection. Hence, the [researcher] should try to use groups that are as similar as possible.[3]

Single-Subject Research

Single-subject designs are those in which one or several subjects are measured over time during the course of an experiment in which different interventions are applied, in terms of environmental changes, leisure counseling, or other activities or services. Although it is often classified as a form of qualitative research, single-subject research may also be considered a modified type of experimentation. Dattilo, Gast, and Schleien point out that this method is often used in therapeutic recreation programs, where it would be difficult to locate large, homogeneous groups from which to draw randomized control and experimental groups for between-group comparisons. They write that, in effect, each subject serves as his or her own control, with changes being measured over time. They stress that:

> Single-subject research requires careful identification and measurement of dependent variables (behaviors in need of treatment) that are influenced by the systematic application of independent variables (treatments).[4]

Although this approach is certainly more manageable than research that requires the establishment of separate, randomly selected groups that must maintain their membership over a period of time, it is obviously weaker in terms of external validity—that is, the ability to predict generalizable outcomes based on the experience of one or a few individual subjects.

Ex Post Facto Research

Another type of study that seeks to measure the effect of recreation programs or services is found in ex post facto research. This type of research examines events or processes that have taken place in the past (ex post facto means "after the fact"). An example of such research was carried out by Brown and Dodson, who examined the possible relationship between Boys' Club programming and juvenile delinquency rates in three areas of Louisville, Kentucky, over a period of several years. The areas were similar in several demographic respects, although they could not be exactly matched and their populations were obviously not randomly selected. The key finding was that in the one Louisville area where a Boy's Club had been built at an early point in the period that was examined, the juvenile delinquency rate declined steadily over an eight-year period. In the other two areas, the delinquency rate increased over the same period.[5]

While the obvious finding would appear to be that the Boys' Club represented an independent variable that was responsible for lowering the delinquency rate, the fact that the three areas had not been matched in all major respects and that it was not possible to control other social factors meant that the findings could only be tentatively suggested. In such investigations, it is not always possible to identify the exact direction of causality. For example, it is possible that a third factor—such as a stronger sense of civic responsibility or concern about youth, or more stable family structures in the area where the new club was built—was responsible both for the establishment of the Boys' Club and for the decline in delinquency during this period.

Action Research

A fourth form of experimentation that does not fit the classical model of experimental research involves so-called *action research*. This approach to the study of organizations and group dynamics began with the work of Kurt Lewin and his associates at the Center for Group Dynamics at the Massachusetts Institute of Technology and the Tavistock Institute of Human Relations in Great Britain. It used experiments in both laboratory and field settings that examined the nature of leadership, intergroup relations, communication, and group productivity.

Rather than rely on traditional experimental methods, action research seeks to engage both researchers and their subjects in a continuing process of creative discovery. Cunningham writes:

> The process . . . deals with conscious and unconscious data. It involves theorizing, experimenting, and implementing, being extremely rigorous with some steps, and very flexible with others. . . . Action research encourages the researcher to experience the problem as it evolves. This is the act of "engaging" in real-life problem-solving . . . in the universe where the problem is occurring.[6]

Although action research is not a traditional approach to research, it certainly involves a type of experimentation in that it tests the effectiveness of new and innovative work structures or group dynamics processes. However, it clearly differs from standard experimental research in that experimental and control variables are not identified, subjects are usually not selected and placed in randomized groups, and there is little attempt to control all the influences that might have an effect on study outcomes.

Action research is sometimes carried on under the rubric of *demonstration projects*. These are programs which seek to test new techniques or methods or to provide badly needed services in high-priority areas. Usually they receive special funding, and it is expected that they will be evaluated—although not with the degree of rigor found in true experimental studies.

Examples of demonstration projects might include efforts to mobilize volunteers to carry out needed park and playground rehabilitation tasks in their neighborhoods, or the application of special tutoring or substance-abuse programs in youth centers in inner-city neighborhoods. Such projects would rarely concern themselves with developing theoretical models or testing hypotheses, and their results cannot usually be regarded as generalizable to other settings.

STRENGTHS AND WEAKNESSES OF EXPERIMENTAL RESEARCH

Recognizing that experiments may be carried out at different levels of scientific rigor, as a generic type of research they have the following *advantages:*

1. Experimental research can be convenient to supervise, since it permits the investigator to control study conditions and operate the study on a time schedule of his or her own choosing. In addition, it is possible to select or impose variables that might not exist in clear-cut form, or at different desired levels, in ordinary life.

2. Experimental research may be less expensive to carry out than large-scale descriptive studies; typically, in other types of research, such as engineering, it is possible to test a small model under experimental stresses, rather than build a full-scale building, boat, or plane.

3. Experiments make it possible to confirm or reject hypotheses through statistical analyses in areas where descriptive methods cannot do this, because the experimenter is able to control the various elements affecting internal and external validity, whereas this cannot be done as easily in surveys or comparative studies.

4. Because experiments are sharply defined in terms of subjects and procedures, it is possible to replicate them exactly in other settings, to determine whether the findings will be exactly the same. When this happens, it shows

that the experiment has been valid and that it has generated theories that are broadly generalizable.

On the other hand, experimental research may have the following weaknesses or *disadvantages:*

1. Despite the statements regarding its relative convenience and inexpensiveness, experimental research may be very costly if it requires special environments, trained observers, or testing procedures.

2. Experimental research may suffer from a lack of reality and external validity in that it may not be possible to simulate recreational attitudes or behaviors in a laboratory setting or to establish needed controls in a field setting. To generalize from what happens in an artificial situation (as in the case of children playing in a special play laboratory) may not be applicable in natural settings, such as neighborhood playgrounds.

3. Because experiments are usually done with few subjects, findings may be misleading if these individuals are not representative of the larger population. In addition, because experimental research involves actually doing things to or with people or altering their life circumstances or experiences in some way, there is the risk that it might be regarded as hazardous or harmful from an ethical perspective.

EXAMPLES OF EXPERIMENTAL RESEARCH

In conclusion, it should be stressed that a limited number of experimental studies tend to be carried out each year in the field of recreation, parks, and leisure services. Although a number of such studies have been conducted in areas such as resource management, the majority of experiments have dealt with therapeutic recreation concerns—chiefly to determine the outcomes of specific forms of service with selected populations. Examples of two experimental studies in this area follow, illustrating different levels of randomization and control.

▼   *FOR EXAMPLE*

Mactavish and Searle conducted a study to measure the effect of a physical activity program designed to facilitate choice and responsibility on the perceptions of competence, locus of control, and self-esteem held by older men and women with mental retardation.[7] In the two-group, pre-test, posttest, experimental design, subjects were matched based on gender, age, past activity experience, and other variables and were randomly assigned to experimental and control groups. The experimental group took part in a five-week activity program that included a variety of familiar activities (stationary cycling, swimming, bowling, dancing, walking, and other fitness pursuits), with each individual choosing the activity. Results confirmed that experimental subjects made significant gains, compared with control group members, in the study variables of perceived competence, locus of control, and self-esteem.

Rawson and Barnett carried out an exploratory study investigating changes in children's anxiety while enrolled in a 10-day residential therapeutic camp program for male and female campers characterized by severe behavior and emotional problems.[8] The hypothesis was that the camp's program—which included behavior modification, modeling, high levels of personal reinforcement, and individual tutoring—would reduce levels of anxiety, which is regarded as closely linked to depression and other clinical concerns. Utilizing pre- and posttests, the study yielded statistically significant decreases in the subjects' anxiety.

These examples illustrate the tendency for experimental studies in therapeutic recreation to focus on psychosocial variables that can be measured through scientifically validated psychological tests. Clearly, there is a need for experiments that measure other kinds of empirical variables—such as the actual performance of subjects or the effectiveness of innovative management strategies or leadership techniques in achieving agency goals and objectives. Other types of study designs, such as descriptive and evaluative research studies, do focus on such research needs and are described in the chapters that follow.

SUMMARY

Experimental research—using randomized experimental and control groups and pre- and posttesting—is regarded as a valuable source of both theoretical and practical information in the field of leisure studies and services. This chapter describes its basic character, giving several levels of experimental design, and discusses internal and external validity and the advantages and disadvantages of experiments. Other forms of less rigorous experimentation—such as single-subject, quasiexperimental, ex post facto, and action research—are also described, with two concluding examples of the use of experiments in therapeutic recreation service.

QUESTIONS AND ACTIVITIES

1. Discuss the strengths and weaknesses of experimental research as they apply to the leisure-service field. What are some of the difficulties that prevent more experimental research from being done?

2. Subjects in the Rawson and Barnett study of the effects of a therapeutic short-term camping program were *not* randomly assigned to experimental and control groups. Instead, the entire group of 147 boys and girls enrolled in successive 10-day camping sessions was monitored for

changes during the experience. What concerns might this raise, in terms of measuring causal relationships in the study?

3. Discuss the kinds of research problems that might be suitable for action research or demonstration projects. Small groups of students may be assigned the task of briefly outlining different action research studies to investigate problems that would not lend themselves to traditional experimental research.

ENDNOTES

1. Carol Saslow, *Basic Research Methods* (New York: Random House, 1982): 26.
2. Julian L. Simon, *Basic Research Methods in Social Sciences: The Art of Empirical Investigation* (New York: Random House, 1978): 146–47.
3. Catherine Coyle, W. B. Kinney, and John Shank, in Marjorie Malkin and Christine Howe, eds., *Research in Therapeutic Recreation: Concepts and Methods* (State College, PA: Venture Publishing, 1993): 220–22.
4. John Dattilo, David Gast, and Stuart Schleien, "Implementation of Single-Subject Designs in Therapeutic Recreation Research," in Marjorie Malkin and Christine Howe, eds., *Research in Therapeutic Recreation: Concepts and Methods* (State College, PA: Venture Publishing, 1993): 182–83.
5. Roscoe Brown, Jr., and Dan Dodson, "The Effectiveness of a Boys' Club in Reducing Delinquency," *Annals of American Academy of Political Science* (March 1959): 47–52.
6. J. Barton Cunningham, *Action Research and Organizational Development* (Westport, CT: Praeger, 1993): 4–5.
7. Jennifer Mactavish and Mark Searle, "Older Individuals with Mental Retardation and the Effect of a Physical Activity Intervention on Selected Social Psychological Variables," *Therapeutic Recreation Journal* (1st quarter 1992): 38–47.
8. Harve Rawson and Thomas Barnett, "Changes in Children's Manifest Anxiety in a Therapeutic Short-Term Camping Experience: An Exploratory Study," *Therapeutic Recreation Journal* (1st quarter 1993): 22–32.

6

Descriptive Research Methods

Survey research is one of the most common forms of research engaged in by educational researchers. It involves researchers asking a large group of people questions about a particular topic or issue. This asking of questions, as related to the issue of interest, is called a survey, and it can be done in a number of ways—face-to-face with individuals or groups, by mail, or by telephone. Each method has its advantages and disadvantages, but obtaining answers from a large group of people to a set of carefully designed and administered questions lies at the heart of survey research.[1]

INTRODUCTION

We now move to a consideration of several forms of descriptive research—studies that are intended to gather information about a variety of subjects without influencing them or affecting the conditions of the situation in any way. Of all types of descriptive research in applied fields such as recreation, parks, and leisure studies, the most common form over the past several decades has been the survey. However, several other types of research, including case studies, longitudinal, comparative, and correlational methods, are also important forms of descriptive research and are described in this chapter.

ROLE OF DESCRIPTIVE RESEARCH

As earlier chapters point out, the primary purpose of descriptive research is to gather data that will lead to an accurate picture of a given phenomenon in contemporary life. Although those involved in descriptive research may make direct contact with subjects or respondents, through interviews or mailed surveys or through intensive observation in field studies, they strive to avoid altering study variables or environmental conditions in any way. They may be limited to a quantitative or narrative reporting of their findings, but they may also seek to probe more deeply to uncover relationships among variables.

SURVEY RESEARCH

In the past, the term *survey* was often used to describe a large-scale case study of a community, in terms of the agencies providing leisure facilities and services, the patterns of participation of various population groups, and other factors useful in developing park proposals or other planning recommendations.

Today, the word *survey* implies a broad study of normative (typical) conditions within a given population or set of subjects. Often it involves the examination of a cross-section of people and their values, beliefs, or behaviors. However, it may also deal with the study of agencies and their policies and programs or with social conditions, facilities, higher education curricula, professional development, and numerous other subjects.

Surveys usually gather data from many subjects at a given time and are concerned with drawing a picture of the entire group rather than profiles of individuals. Although their purpose is primarily descriptive, they may also be used to develop new models or theories that explain the relationships observed or that suggest appropriate agency policies or management strategies.

Typical Subjects of Survey Research

Research journals or compilations of symposium abstracts in the leisure-studies field typically include a high proportion of study reports that are based on surveys. They may deal with any of the following kinds of concerns.

Public attitudes and opinions

Mailed questionnaires or directly administered opinion polls may be used to determine the attitude of members of the public with respect to their leisure needs and interests, their view of present recreation opportunities in the community, their position with respect to policies or problems faced by municipal government, their willingness to pay expanded fees and charges for recreational involvement, and similar concerns. They may also explore participants' motivations or levels of satisfaction derived from recreation.

Patterns of participation

Numerous surveys are carried out each year to measure the extent of participation in varied activities, such as sports, outdoor recreation, the arts, travel, or similar activities. Such surveys may be done through questionnaires on a local, state, regional, or national level or may involve studies of representative sites, such as state or national parks, selected cities, or similar settings. They may also examine such issues as the extent of spending on given activities, the nature of family participation, modes of travel used to get to recreation settings, or a comparison of motivations for participation with the satisfactions derived from them.

Surveys of facilities

Trends in the development of different types of facilities, such as art centers or water play parks, may be examined. Whether or not facilities have been made accessible to the physically disabled, the environmental impact of recreation on outdoor settings, where and how people camp in federal or state parks, or safety factors in wilderness or mountainous areas may all be examined.

Surveys may also examine potential public interest in different types of facilities, as part of feasibility studies conducted to determine whether new recreation enterprises would be profitable. Thus, they provide a valuable tool within the overall "marketing" process.

Management practices

Studies may also deal with management policies and practices in terms of staffing arrangements, policy development, sources of fiscal support, marketing methods, public and community relations, liability and negligence suits, cosponsorship of programs with other agencies, and similar issues. Recreation and park administrators in varied types of agencies—including private, commercial, armed forces, and therapeutic—may be queried regarding their values and goals; their relations with commissions, boards, and trustees; their philosophies of personnel management; and similar issues.

Advantages of Survey Research

Surveys constitute a major portion of the research that is carried on by social scientists or by specialists in a wide range of organizations serving public needs. They are regularly used to gather information about voters' attitudes about issues and candidates, religious beliefs and practices, consumer preferences, child-rearing beliefs, sexual behavior, and a host of other subjects.

They have several distinct advantages as a form of scientific inquiry: (1) It would be difficult to gather information from a large group of respondents by any other means; (2) they permit the collection of data from many respondents in short periods of time and at relatively low cost; (3) through careful sampling of respondents, they can be used to generalize findings to apply to substantially larger populations; and (4) it generally is relatively easy to get respondents to cooperate, particularly if the survey process is simple, brief, and on a subject of interest to them.

Disadvantages of Surveys

On the negative side, surveys too often are carried out with weak sampling methods or controls and may lend themselves to biased interpretation of findings or to misleading presentation of statistical data. This is particularly true of surveys carried out for political purposes or to promote commercial products. Another weakness of surveys is that

> ... it is virtually impossible to test for cause- effect relationships with survey methods. As a tool for causal analysis or for careful testing of theory, then, the survey is weak when compared with the experiment. In addition, the depth of information that one is able to obtain is usually not nearly so great as is the case with participant observation.[2]

In the past, surveys in the fields of education or human services were often criticized because they tended to lack careful, systematic procedures or because of the proliferation of studies on relatively trivial and unimportant subjects. However, well-done surveys can meet high professional standards and provide knowledge that cannot be obtained in other ways. Often, they may provide the first level of information about a subject that then points the way to later, in-depth analyses.

Types of Surveys

Most surveys involve either direct or indirect contact with a group of selected respondents. Direct contact usually takes the form of interviews.

Interviews

Simply defined, the interview is

> ... a two-person conversation, initiated by the interviewer for the specific purpose of obtaining research-relevant information, and focused by him on content specified by research objectives of systematic description, prediction, or explanation.[3]

Interviews may be conducted face to face or by telephone and may vary in their degree of formal structure. Although interviewers usually use schedules that contain the questions they intend to ask in a prescribed sequence, the actual method may range from highly formal presentation of the questions, with respondents asked to select answers from predetermined choices, to less structured approaches in which interviewers feel free to use open-end questions (see page 175) and follow up on interesting leads.

Despite their widespread use in social science research, marketing, and political polls, interview surveys have been criticized on several points. These may include nonrepresentative selection of subjects or the unwillingness of a substantial number of subjects to cooperate, as well as their providing responses that include misinformation because of lack of direct knowledge, embarrassment, or the need to conceal one's personal views or past experience. Responses often are influenced by the subject's perception of the interviewer and by the possible dissimilarity between the subject and interviewer in terms of race, gender, social class, or similar factors.

Questionnaire

Customarily, these are printed questionnaires that are carefully designed to cover key issues or problem areas in a logical sequence and to use either open-end or closed-end questions to elicit the fullest and most meaningful response. Usually, questionnaires are accompanied by a series of preprinted categorical responses; in some cases they have computer scanning sheets that permit automatic computerized tabulation. Some questions may ask respondents to simply reply yes or no; others may ask for choices from a checklist or from a series of graduated responses ranging from total agreement or support to total disagreement.

Since most survey questionnaires ask for a number of personal identification items—such as age, gender, marital status, place of residence, or occupation—they lend themselves to analysis that shows how different subgroups within the larger population respond to given questions. Analysis of such variables may lend itself to consumer or participant profiling from various perspectives, including age, socioeconomic, ethnic, or other demographic perspectives.

Although surveys have generally been regarded as a relatively simple form of inquiry, the development of questionnaires and the conduct of interviews are complex tasks (see Chapter 13). Saslow writes:

> Deciding how to word questions, which questions to include on a questionnaire, what answers should be allowed, and how to summarize the answers requires technical training in questionnaire design. . . . [In conducting interviews] you may want to maintain a conversational atmosphere yet fit all the standard questions into the discussion. Doing this well requires not only a good memory for both questions and answers but also a lot of supervised practice.[4]

The use of written questionnaires presupposes the literacy of respondents—that they are able to read and understand the questionnaire and follow directions correctly. In some cases, interview and questionnaire techniques may be combined, as in situations where a group of subjects may be assembled to fill out the survey and where the interview director may go over the questionnaire directions with them before they then fill out the forms individually.

At the same time, it is essential that interviewers not give respondents cues as to appropriate or desired responses or attempt to shape their replies in any way. In some cases, the questions themselves may constitute a form of preliminary brainwashing. So-called loaded questions are often found in supposedly neutral surveys. For example, political parties may send out questionnaires that characterize the policies or performance of opposing parties negatively and essentially ask for the support of their own candidates.

In other cases, surveys may be used as a form of recruitment—that is, making initial contact with individuals who may be asked to join an organization, make financial contributions, or serve in other ways. In such situations, they do not represent a form of research as much as they do an agency's promotional strategies.

Use of Surveys by Professional Organizations

Many professional organizations or associations in the recreation, parks, and leisure-service field survey their memberships to help determine appropriate policies and priorities or to measure their perception of the organization's effectiveness.

NRPA membership surveys

For example, the National Recreation and Parks Association conducted a Needs Assessment Survey in 1991, mailing questionnaires to more than 2,500 randomly selected members of the organization. Survey results indicated that the members felt that the organization should serve as a unifying agent within the overall leisure-service field. Among the reasons respondents cited for joining the organization were:

> To keep informed about current trends, through association publications and the magazine; to support the profession; to develop professional contacts; to continue their professional education; to build their reputation and credentials in the field; to learn about new career possibilities; to have a forum for ideas, and to be able to network with peers.[5]

Based on the findings of the Needs Assessment Survey, NRPA established a task force to follow through on its findings and recommendations. Branch/Sections and Regions of the organization joined in an effort to develop new special promotions to gain fuller public visibility for the recreation and park movement, to expand legislative efforts, and to expand communication among members through SCHOLE's electronic bulletin board (a service of NPRA). In another survey conducted for the National Recreation and Park Association, within the Midwest, Great Plains, and Rocky Mountain regions, strong support was given to comprehensive master planning and to public meetings and surveys as a means of developing more effective facilities and program planning and of enriching public support.[6]

Canadian fitness surveys

Government agencies, professional organizations, and colleges and universities frequently cooperate in the sponsorship of joint research studies on important leisure-related issues. For example, in Canada, the issue of national physical fitness was explored during the 1970s and 1980s by a number of major fitness surveys:

... the Canada Fitness Survey was one of the largest and most comprehensive surveys of its kind ever undertaken, anywhere. A sample of 13,500 households in 80 locations across Canada was identified to provide reliable population estimates at national and regional levels. . . . Household members were eligible to participate in the fitness testing if they were between 7 and 69 years of age and met conservative screening criteria.[7]

Fitness tests were carried out on 16,000 individuals, and 22,000 persons completed physical activity and lifestyle questionnaires as part of the overall survey. Published results of this Canadian survey focused on youth, girls and women, disabled and activity-limited persons, older populations, and regional and urban-rural differences in physical activity patterns and were useful in developing fitness norms and percentiles.

MACPARS report

In the United States, a comparable major study in the area of outdoor recreation was carried out as a cooperative effort of the Southeastern Forest Experiment Station of the USDA Forest Service, the Recreation Technical Assistance Office of the University of Georgia, and the National Recreation and Park Association, American Park and Recreation Society, and National Society for Park Resources. The report of this study, *Local Opportunities for Americans: Final Report of the Municipal and County Park and Recreation Study (MACPARS)*, presented data gathered from almost 1,350 recreation and park professionals surveyed throughout the United States, grouped within four major U.S. census regions and eight NRPA regions.[8]

The MACPARS report illustrated two levels of investigation and two kinds of data. Much of it had to do with quantitative analysis of study findings dealing with the nature of government jurisdictions providing recreation and park programs, sources and levels of funding, staffing practices, trends in the development of facilities and outdoor recreation areas, programming emphasis, and similar factors. However, a second level of study concern had to do with issues confronting recreation and park professionals in municipal and county agencies, essentially of a qualitative and subjective nature.

OTHER TYPES OF SURVEYS

Large-scale surveys such as those just described often result in substantial printed reports that are widely disseminated. They may include a variety of investigative techniques, including task-force meetings, conferences, and symposiums, along with the use of questionnaires. Most surveys, however, are carried out on a smaller scale, with a more sharply defined focus, and are reported chiefly in professional journals or at research symposiums.

Leisure Values, Motivations, and Outcomes

A significant body of survey research utilizing questionnaires deals with the values, motivations, and outcomes of leisure experiences reported by various types of program participants.

▼ *For Example*

Example 1. In a study of the relationships between leisure participation and satisfaction and perceived wellness, Ragheb surveyed 468 employees of 4 randomly selected private firms, using an instrument that measured participation in 8 categories of recreation: mass media, reading, social activities, outdoor activities, sports participation, attending sports events, cultural activities, and hobbies.[9] Perceived wellness was based on 5 components: physical, mental, emotional, social, and spiritual.

Example 2. McCormick, White, and McGuire conducted a study of the perceptions of parents of campers with mental retardation in terms of the benefits of summer camps for their sons and daughters.[10] Using a questionnaire listing 22 areas of potential benefits, responses were grouped under 6 headings, or "dimensions": social skills development, social competence, respite care, cognitive development, expressive developments, and physical competence. Overall, the most important benefit appeared to be social growth, along with feelings of self-worth, success, and joy and cognitive development.

Example 3. Fisher and Price studied the potential of tourism as a form of interaction among people of different nations and cultures to improve intercultural relations.[11] Data were obtained from a questionnaire distributed to passengers exiting the U.S. Customs area of a major airport, covering eight flights over a five-day period. The survey examined the degree of vacation satisfaction, extent of intercultural interaction, travel motivations, and attitude change and found a strong positive relationship between cultural interaction and vacation satisfaction.

Influence of Race, Ethnicity, and Gender on Leisure

As Chapter 4 points out, in recent years numerous research studies have examined the influence of demographic factors such as race, ethnicity, gender, or age on leisure values, interests, and participation. Many surveys have focused on such issues and have tended to treat subjects within a given population group in terms of simple descriptions of participation interests and involvement without differentiating among them.

▼ *For Example*

For example, in a study supported by California State Polytechnic University at Pomona, a randomly generated telephone survey of 200 Los Angeles residents explored their past visits to national forest sites, the activities they had taken part in, and those in which they expressed interest.[12] Findings included such statements as "Anglos were more likely to have tried picnicking, hiking, and swimming, while African Americans were least likely to have tried these activities," "Anglo and Hispanic Americans reported a greater desire to try natural history hikes," or "Hispanic and African Americans reported a greater desire to try shooting ranges."

In contrast, other studies have examined the influence of different types of forest environments or of the differences among ethnic subgroups. Carr and Williams used a self-administered, on-site survey at four locations in neighboring national forests in Southern California to explore the role of ethnicity in outdoor recreation involvement.[13] They found that different sites attracted specific groups of participants with different ethnic backgrounds, ranging from less acculturated Hispanic immigrants to mixed Anglos and Hispanics with longer generational tenure and higher levels of acculturation.

In terms of gender, numerous studies have recently examined the meaning of leisure for women, their psychological experience in it, and constraints to their enjoyment of leisure.

▼ *For Example*

For example, Bolla, Dawson, and Harrington surveyed more than 9,000 randomly selected women in 67 municipalities in the province of Ontario, Canada.[14] The definitions of leisure for respondents were grouped around such meanings as "self-gratification," "relaxation," "personal freedom," "free time," "activity," and "achievement." Beyond this, the most important subjective experiences in leisure for women were related to feelings of competence, security, playfulness, independence, serenity, freedom from guilt, femininity, and assertiveness. Constraints to participation were related to such factors as the pressure of family and work experiences, lack of time, money, or skill; fatigue; guilt; or the lack of appropriate programs or activities.

SURVEYS OF AGENCY PRACTICES

Although most social research surveys involve questioning human subjects about their values, behavior, experiences, or similar elements, in leisure studies the emphasis may be placed on using respondents as informants about agencies or professional practices. In some cases, it may not even be necessary to question subjects as such. Instead, one might do a survey of a recreation and park department's playgrounds, centers, pools, or other facilities simply by touring them and using a checklist or rating scale approach to record information about their volume of attendance, safety, maintenance, and supervisory conditions.

In many cases, surveys may be supplemented by the exploration of records and annual reports, by case studies, and by a number of other types of descriptive research methods, which are described in the following pages.

OTHER FORMS OF DESCRIPTIVE RESEARCH

Case Studies

In contrast to survey research, which examines a broad range of respondents or subjects to get an overall view of a given issue or research question, case studies have a much sharper focus. They usually involve a fuller or more detailed examination of a single entity, such as a person, a family, a neighborhood, an agency, or similar subject. They are concerned with gaining an in-depth picture of the subject within its environment, including all the forces that play on it. Mason and Bramble write:

> Case studies are basically intensive investigations. . . . In a sense, when a physician investigates the condition of a patient, he is performing a case study. The same can be said for the work of the psychologist, social worker, marriage counselor, efficiency expert, and school administrator when they investigate a specific person, group, institution, or school.[15]

Although case studies usually involve individuals or single clusters of subjects, their findings may be used to develop general theories that have broader applications. In this sense, they are a form of inductive theory development. For example, Piaget's theories of learning were based on case studies of children observed over a period of years, and Freud's experiences with individual clients led to the formulation of his broader concepts of psychoanalytic theory. Case studies may or may not make use of detailed statistical data and analysis. For example, the study of a large marina operation might include extensive quantitative data concerning use patterns, destinations of boaters, types of craft, income and expenses, and similar factors. Or it might involve a qualitative analysis of boating behavior or social groupings with little numeric content.

Case studies are likely to use several methods, including direct observation, interviews, review of records or other documents, testing procedures, and other techniques. In some case studies in which the researcher uses a model found in sociological and anthropological research, she may actually become part of a group or organization, or live in a given neighborhood, in order to observe it more fully.

▼ FOR EXAMPLE

Example 1. Some case studies in the recreation, parks, and leisure-studies field have involved detailed studies of professional projects or community groups. For example, Machlis and Harvey carried out an extensive study of the Visitor

Services Project of the National Park Service, gathering data at 45 different parks.[16] Their purpose was both to evaluate this program and to determine the potential values and uses of recreation research in general, within the overall park system, with implications for other leisure-service agencies.

Example 2. Another case study that focused on a social group rather than on a single subject was a study of the Greek community in Ottawa, Ontario, Canada. Karlis and Dawson sought to determine the nature and degree of involvement in Greek cultural activities by Ottawa residents of Greek background, including such factors as their religious affiliations, involvement with the Hellenic Community Association, recency of immigration, and varied elements of acculturation within the overall Canadian society.[17]

Comparative and Cross-Sectional Research

Comparative research is typically used in the social sciences to examine and compare groups with different national or ethnic origins, both to identify general laws or patterns of behavior that hold across different societies and to find similarities or differences among groups. They may be conducted locally or on a broader scale. Neuman writes:

> Comparative research helps a researcher identify aspects of social life that are general across units (e.g., cultures), as opposed to being limited to one unit alone. . . . The comparative orientation improves measurement and conceptualization. Concepts developed by researchers who conduct research across several social units or settings are less likely to only apply to a specific culture or setting. It is difficult for a researcher to detect hidden biases, assumptions, and values until she applies a concept in different cultures or groups.[18]

In the recreation, parks, and leisure-studies field, a number of different agencies or programs might be compared.

For example, recreation personnel requirements and practices in several different types of voluntary agencies might be compared. If a study simply gathered the facts and figures of revenue source practices among a large number of departments, it probably would be classified as a survey. If, however, the study did a set of profiles of several different agencies with respect to fees and charges, and then compared them based on a number of criteria or key points, it would be a comparative study.

In recreation, parks, and leisure studies, comparative research may be used either to study theoretical issues or applied, practice-oriented concerns. Several examples of possible research problems follow:

1. Analysis of the use of third-party payments (reimbursement for recreation services by insurance companies or government agencies) in therapeutic recreation agencies within several different regions of the country.

2. Comparison of the values promoted and coaching methods used in several areas of youth sport (for example: Little League baseball, Biddy Basketball, and youth soccer leagues).

3. Study of attitudes toward leisure or recreation participation patterns among members of four ethnic populations (Caucasian, African American, Asian, and Hispanic) within a particular state or region.

▼ FOR EXAMPLE

Both surveys and case-study methods may be used to conduct comparative research studies. For example, McKinney and Chandler carried out a systematic study comparing the duties of full-time and part-time recreation leaders.[19] Bolla, Dawson, and Karlis examined the social, cultural, and recreational infrastructure of six ethnic communities in Ottawa, using a case-study approach, to develop ways in which municipal recreation authorities could better serve a multicultural community.[20] Still other studies may be carried out to explore a general topic, but ultimately take the form of a comparative study. For example, Robertson, Heuberger, and Burdge examined the relationship between alcohol consumption and recreational use of natural settings, focusing on visitors to water-based recreation facilities. The primary thrust of their research was a comparison of "drinkers" and "nondrinkers" in terms of their recreational values and behaviors.[21]

Cross-sectional research is a related type of study design that also has the purpose of comparing two or more sets of subjects. In it, a single large system might be examined, with different elements or components in it compared with respect to given variables. For example, participation by different age groups in a community's public recreation program might be studied at one point in time to gain a picture of each group's current pattern of involvement, needs, special interests, and priority for service. It also can provide an indication of changes in leisure behavior or circumstances at different stages of the life-span by making it possible to examine given variables for all age groups at once, rather than wait for years to gather needed data through longitudinal research.

Causal-Comparative Research

One of the key purposes of much scholarly research is to determine whether causal relationships exist—in other words, whether one factor or set of variables can be proven reasonably to be the cause of another factor or variable. Unlike the experimental approach, in which the researcher deliberately manipulates one or more variables in order to measure the effect on other variables, in causal-comparative studies the researcher examines variables that already exist and—because it is a descriptive form of research—makes no attempt to change or influence them.

As an example, a researcher might seek to identify the causes of juvenile delinquency or of membership in youth gangs and might seek to test the hypothesis that gang members come from families lacking stable, two-parent family structures. By comparing the family backgrounds of adolescents who are or who are not members of youth gangs, the researcher would be in a position to state that there is statistically significant evidence that this hypothesis is confirmed—or that it is not. Fraenkel and Wallen sum up the nature of the approach:

> Causal-comparative research allows researchers to investigate the possibility of a causal relationship among variables that cannot, as in experimental research, be manipulated. In a causal-comparative study, two groups that are different on a particular variable are compared on another variable. . . . Since both the effect(s) and the alleged cause(s) have already occurred, and hence are studied in retrospect, causal-comparative research is also referred to sometimes as *ex post facto* . . . research.[22]

Correlational Research

This type of research is sometimes confused with causal-comparative research, and there are distinct similarities between the two. *Correlation* describes the degree of relationship between two or more sets of variables. For example, height and weight are likely to be *positively* correlated (as one variable increases, so does the other) in a class of junior high school students. This does not mean that the tallest child will always be the heaviest, the next tallest the next heaviest, and so on. However, it does mean that in general, taller children will tend to be heavier, and shorter children lighter. If two sets of variables are inversely correlated (that is, if subjects rank high on one variable they would be low on another and vice versa), their relationship would be described as *negatively* correlated.

Causal-comparative and correlational research studies have the same purpose: to explore contrasts and relationships between or among variables. Both may provide guidance for later experimental studies, although neither method permits the researcher to manipulate any of the variables involved. They differ from each other in that causal-comparative studies usually compare two or more groups of subjects, while correlational research usually investigates the relationship of two or more variables for a single set of subjects. Beyond this, causal-comparative research usually includes at least one categorical, non-quantitative variable (such as gender or national origin), and correlational studies typically investigate two or more quantitative variables.

Correlational analysis may be part of the data-analysis process in many survey research studies, although not the primary thrust of such surveys.

There are also studies that are carried out primarily to discover whether there *are* significant relationships between or among key variables. Examples of the methods used to determine the extent of correlation in either type of situation are found in Chapters 14 and 15.

Longitudinal Studies

These investigations are carried out over a designated period of time. Sometimes called "developmental research," longitudinal studies seek to measure changes that occur in individuals or groups of subjects—either in a natural, field situation or under controlled conditions.

There are several different forms of longitudinal research, including *trend, cohort,* and *panel* studies. In *trend* studies, different samples from a given population, which may change in its membership, are examined periodically to determine possible shifts on study variables. For example, the members of a state recreation and park society might be polled each year, with respect to their professional goals.

In *cohort* studies, a specific population that remains constant is studied over a period of time, with random samples being taken from this population at set intervals. For example, all children born in a given year might provide the cohort for a study of play activities from infancy through adolescence, with a sample drawn from the overall group chosen every two years. Although the school population might change, subjects would be chosen only from the original cohort.

In *panel* studies, a specific sample—the panel—is chosen at the outset of the study, and only these individuals are examined throughout the study process.

In addition to research done with human subjects, longitudinal studies may also examine programs, organizations, or settings for recreation. Often this type of study uses *time-series* observations, which gather data at regular intervals. For example, environmental conditions in a state forest or on an ocean beach might be examined regularly, using the same measuring instruments, with the results correlated to the volume or nature of recreational use over time or with measures that have been taken to protect the environment.

COMBINATION OF DESCRIPTIVE METHODS

In addition to using one type of research design exclusively, several different methods may be used in a single study. For example, in a marketing study of leisure needs and interests combined with an analysis of public recreation and park programs and policies in the city of Philadelphia, one author of this text employed several different techniques: (1) mailed questionnaires sent to a sample of adults drawn from voter registration lists; (2) interviews with participants of all ages at recreation sites; (3) meetings with community groups and recreation administrators; (4) surveys of recreation leaders; and (5) direct observation of selected playgrounds and centers. In addition, other non-public service providers were interviewed, and a special task force was formed to analyze current programming for physically and mentally disabled persons and to develop recommendations in this area. Historical records and annual reports were consulted to provide a background for the study, and census data were systematically analyzed to give a demographic picture of each of the recreation districts of Philadelphia.

Similarly, many other types of studies are likely to include more than one research technique. Not infrequently, a descriptive study may begin with a large-scale survey of individuals or agencies, followed by an in-depth investigation—through observations or interviews—of a sample of respondents to the survey.

SUMMARY

Surveys are a primary form of descriptive research, intended to gather information about a wide range of subjects through the use of questionnaires, either mailed or directly administered, or through in-person or telephone interviews. Typically, they are a relatively inexpensive means of learning the attitudes, values, or leisure behaviors of a cross-section of individuals or the policies, practices, or other significant aspects of recreation and park agencies and programs.

Although surveys have tended to be regarded as an inferior form of research when they were conducted with inadequate sampling procedures, poorly framed instruments, or weak research controls, they constitute an entirely respectable form of scientific inquiry when carried out with appropriate rigor. As such, they may not only provide a comprehensive picture of what is, in terms of varied aspects of recreation, parks, and leisure services, but may also yield valuable information with respect to interrelationships among variables that are being investigated. Thus, they may contribute to theory-building and may be helpful to the field in both conceptual and practical ways.

Several other types of descriptive research are also described in the chapter, including the case-study method, which involves intensive study of a single individual or smaller group of subjects, using varied methods. Comparative, causal-comparative, and cross-sectional studies, all of which serve to contrast different groups of participants, agencies, or other research subjects, are defined, with examples drawn from the current literature. Correlational research, which measures the relationship among different sets of variables, and longitudinal research, which measures change over a period of time, complete the chapter.

QUESTIONS AND ACTIVITIES

1. The most common research method used in recreation, parks, and leisure studies is descriptive research, particularly surveys. Why is this so? What are the strengths and weaknesses of this overall type of study as far as developing a comprehensive body of knowledge for the field is concerned?

2. The following assignment may be carried out by several small groups of students who develop plans that are then presented to their class for review and discussion. This chapter describes several types of descriptive research designs, including questionnaire surveys, interview surveys, case studies, comparative and cross-sectional research, causal-comparative and correlational studies, and longitudinal research. Which of these methods would you select to investigate the following issues or problems? In each, present a simple preliminary plan for selecting subjects and gathering needed data.

   a. The effectiveness of recreational programs serving young adults with mental retardation in a three-state area.

   b. The opinions of community residents with respect to increased fees and charges in public recreation and park facilities and programs in a major city.

   c. The employment and career-development patterns of graduates of recreation, park, and leisure-studies curricula in several state universities in the southeastern United States.

   d. The effectiveness of three youth-serving organizations (Police Athletic League, Boys' and Girls' Clubs, and selected public recreation youth centers) in reducing juvenile delinquency in a large metropolitan area.

   e. The television-watching habits of several major age groups (children, adolescents, adults, and senior citizens) in three types of communities: urban, suburban, and small town or village.

   f. The impact of off-road vehicles such as snowmobiles or mountain bikes on the environment in selected park areas.

ENDNOTES

1. Jack Fraenkel and Norman Wallen, *Research in Education* (New York: McGraw-Hill, 1993): 342.
2. Bruce Chadwick, Howard Bahr, and Stan Albrecht, *Social Science Research Methods* (Englewood Cliffs, NJ: Prentice-Hall, 1984): 101–2.
3. Ibid.
4. Carol Saslow, *Basic Research Methods* (New York: Random House, 1982): 14.
5. "Dateline," *Parks and Recreation* (Sept. 1992): 7.
6. "Dateline," *Parks and Recreation* (Feb. 1994): 7.

7. Blake Ferris, Russ Kisby, Cora Craig, and Fernand Landry, "Fitness Promotion and Research in Canada," *Journal of Physical Education, Recreation and Dance* (Sept. 1987): 27.

8. For summary of MACPARS Report, see "Changes in Park and Recreation Agency Operations Detailed in Survey," in "Dateline," *Parks and Recreation* (Mar. 1986): 6.

9. Mounir Ragheb, "Leisure and Perceived Wellness: A Field Investigation," *Leisure Sciences* 15, no. 1 (1993): 13–24.

10. Bryan McCormick, Charlie White, and Francis McGuire, "Parents' Perceptions of Benefits of Summer Camp for Campers with Mental Retardation," *Therapeutic Recreation Journal* (3rd quarter 1992): 27–37.

11. Robert Fisher and Linda Price, "International Pleasure Travel and Post-Vacation Cultural Attitude Change," *Journal of Leisure Research* 23, no. 3 (1991): 193–208.

12. Debbie Chavez, "Recreation Research Update: Ethnic Group Activities, A Survey of Los Angeles Residents," in *Recreation Research Update* (Riverside, CA: USDA Forest Service Research Station, Oct. 1992).

13. Deborah Carr and Daniel Williams, "Understanding the Role of Ethnicity in Outdoor Recreation Experiences," *Journal of Leisure Research* 25, no. 1 (1993): 22–38.

14. Pat Bolla, Don Dawson, and Maureen Harrington, "Women and Leisure: A Study of Meanings, Experiences, and Constraints," *Recreation Canada* 51, no. 2 (1993): 22–26.

15. Emanuel Mason and William Bramble, *Understanding and Conducting Research* (New York: McGraw-Hill, 1977): 34.

16. Gary Machlis and M. Jeannie Harvey, "The Adoption and Diffusion of Recreation Research Programs: A Study of the Visitor Services Project," *Journal of Park and Recreation Administration* 11, no. 1 (1993): 49–65.

17. George Karlis and Don Dawson, "Ethnic Maintenance and Recreation: A Case Study," *Journal of Applied Recreation Research* 15, no. 2 (1989–90): 85–100.

18. W. Lawrence Neuman, *Social Research Methods: Qualitative and Quantitative Approaches* (Boston: Allyn and Bacon, 1994): 388–89.

19. William McKinney and Carrie Chandler, "A Comparative Assessment of Duties Between Full-Time and Part-Time Recreation Leaders," *Journal of Park and Recreation Administration* (Spring 1991): 13–29.

20. Pat Bolla, Don Dawson, and George Karlis, "Serving the Multicultural Community: Directions for Leisure Service Providers," *Journal of Applied Recreation Research* 16, no. 2 (1991): 116–32.

21. Robert Robertson, Jody Heuberger, and Rabel Burdge, "Consumption of Alcoholic Beverages and Recreational Use of an Urban River Corridor: An Exploratory Study," *Abstracts from NRPA Leisure Research Symposium* (Oct. 1990): 32.

22. Fraenkel and Wallen, *Research in Education,* 392.

Documentary Research Methods

Historical research is the systematic collection and evaluation of data to describe, explain, and thereby understand actions or events that occurred sometime in the past. . . . some aspect of the past is studied, by perusing documents of the period, by examining relics, or by interviewing individuals who lived during the time. An attempt is then made to reconstruct what happened during that time as completely as possible, and (usually) to explain why it happened . . .[1]

INTRODUCTION

In addition to research designs that gather evidence directly from the words or actions of study subjects, there are several types of research methods that do not involve direct contact with subjects. Instead, they rely heavily on the analysis of past happenings, on documents, reports, and other forms of literature, and on demographic social indicators. Their primary purpose is to interpret information that has been gathered or published in order to arrive at new conceptual understandings of the past or present and to propose models that explain the forces involved in leisure behaviors or program sponsorship.

HISTORICAL RESEARCH

Historical research is concerned with an examination of the past—either distant or relatively recent. It seeks to develop a meaningful record of human achievement. Too often, history has been taught to schoolchildren in terms of political or military events, with required memorization of dates, the names of conquerors or rulers, and a dry recounting of major explorations and shifts in power. A better sort of approach to the study of history might be described as social history, concerned with the complex lives of people and societies, weaving together the intricate interaction of religion, government, daily living patterns, social customs, economic factors, and similar elements. Best makes the point clearly, in writing:

History . . . is not merely a list of chronological events, but a truthful integrated account of the relationships between persons, events, times, and places. We use history to understand the past, and to try to understand the present in light of past events and developments.[2]

Within the recreation, parks, and leisure-studies field, historians have examined such subjects as (1) the past development of various types of leisure pursuits or cultural interests; (2) the role of recreation and leisure in earlier civilizations or historical eras; (3) the development of parks in Europe and the United States; (4) the roots of the recreation movement during the Industrial Revolution; and (5) the development of professionalism in leisure service in the United States. By exploring such themes, historical research has contributed to a fuller understanding of how the present-day recreation and parks field developed. It is difficult to understand our contemporary situation with respect to the public image of the field, widely held attitudes about recreation and leisure, or issues like the place of ethnic or racial minority groups in recreation or the role of women and girls in this field, without full historical understanding.

Extending these purposes, Fraenkel and Wallen suggest five reasons that researchers in education or other human-service fields might undertake historical studies:

1. To make people aware of what has happened in the past so that they may learn from past failures and successes.
2. To learn how things were done in the past to see if they might be applicable to present-day problems.
3. To assist in prediction of future trends or events.
4. To test hypotheses concerning causes and effects.
5. To understand present-day practices and policies more fully.[3]

Uses of Primary and Secondary Sources

Historical research makes use of essentially two types of data: primary and secondary.

1. *Primary sources* are eyewitness accounts or first-hand reports of events and social trends, usually reported by actual observers or participants. They may take the form of letters, autobiographies, diaries, newspaper or magazine accounts, transcriptions of oral history, or similar sources. They may also make use of documents such as official records, charters, court decisions, contracts and deeds, films, and research reports, if they are demonstrably authentic in origin.

2. *Secondary sources* are second-hand accounts in which one person recounts what he has heard from others or in which primary sources have been translated or interpreted so that it is no longer the original informa-

tion that is being examined. Secondary sources are usually considered of limited value in historical research, although they may point out major developments in a field or help to direct other direct research efforts.

Authenticity of Data

How does the historical researcher determine the accuracy of the data she has uncovered? Two methods exist for evaluating historical evidence: external and internal criticism.

External criticism seeks to determine the genuineness of evidence and to establish its authenticity by analyzing such elements as handwriting or language usages; making physical or chemical tests of ink, paper, paint, wood, or other substances; or making sure that the sources are consistent with the knowledge and technology characteristic of the period in which the data were supposed to have originated.

Internal criticism examines the actual content of the document or other source material to judge whether it appears to be an accurate, unbiased account, based on other relevant evidence or what may be learned regarding the motives of the writer or individual being quoted. What was the experience of the individuals concerned? Did they have reasons for distorting or suppressing information? Can confirmation be obtained that they actually were on the spot as described and that they were able to make prompt records of the occurrences, or was the information reconstructed after a considerable period had gone by?

Often, it is necessary to examine data skeptically in terms of changing circumstances that may affect the meaning of recorded facts. For example, Saslow points out that in medicine the increased rate of diagnosis of a disease might mean that there actually was a change in the number of cases occurring or that there was improvement in diagnostic and recording procedures. Similarly, a historical study of delinquency might find that increases in the number of cases recorded over a period of time were significantly influenced by changing definitions of delinquency or by alterations in record-keeping procedures.[4]

Stages of Historical Research

The key steps in the process of carrying out historical research include the following:

Identify problem area

This is usually done by preliminary reading in the field, exploration of easily available sources, and the initial formulation of a research question or possible hypothesis to be explored.

Collect source materials

As indicated, these may include a wide range of possible sources, including primary sources wherever possible. Typically, minutes are better than newspaper accounts describing a meeting, and original copies are better than translations. In gathering source materials, every possible repository should be examined, including card catalogs, periodical indexes, encyclopedias, historical guides, visits to key locations, and often detectivelike tracking down of evidence that moves from source to source or person to person.

As an example, within the field of therapeutic recreation service, researchers might explore such sources as the major research journals (*Journal of Leisure Research, Leisure Sciences, Leisure Studies,* or *Therapeutic Recreation Journal*) or such specialized compilations as *Psychological Abstracts, Mental Retardation Abstracts,* or *Rehabilitation Literature.* They might also review research compilations that have been published over the past two decades by universities in collaboration with professional societies.

Each year, the National Recreation and Park Association publishes *Abstracts from the Symposium on Leisure Research* held at its annual Congress. The Ontario Research Council on Leisure has published similar abstracts from studies reported at its Congresses on Leisure Research. Finally, therapeutic recreation researchers should explore computer retrieval systems within the fields of education, medicine, and rehabilitation, such as the Educational Resources Information Center (ERIC) or the Medical Literature Analysis and Retrieval System (MEDLARS). Similar retrieval systems are available within other specialized areas of leisure-related research.

Evaluate and analyze data

Materials should be subjected to critical examination to determine their trustworthiness and importance. Both external and internal criticism should be applied to determine the authenticity of sources.

Is the material consistent with what has already been written or with other information that has been gathered in the study? At this stage, the data should be analyzed and placed within a sequential framework, based either on a chronological order or on a division of the subject into separate topical areas or themes.

Prepare historical report

All the material that has been gathered should be synthesized and developed in the form of a historical essay or report, with full citations of all sources used. Knowledge that has been developed at this point should be integrated, and historical explanations or theories may be more fully developed.

Historical research may be used as an introduction to other types of studies, in order to set the stage by providing relevant background information. It may also constitute a separate, independent study in its own right. Typically, when graduate students undertake historical research for theses or dissertations, they tend to suffer from the following weaknesses: (1) developing problems that are too broad; (2) relying excessively on secondary sources; (3) failure to establish the authenticity of data obtained; (4) poor logical analysis, based either on oversimplification of issues or overgeneralizing on the basis of limited evidence; and (5) inappropriate writing style, such as opinionated reporting or overly casual or flippant writing. Strong efforts should be made to overcome such weaknesses.

The Role of Historical Research in Leisure Studies

In the overall field of recreation, parks, and leisure studies, historical research may play a vital role in helping present-day students and practitioners understand the roots of this movement and dispel prejudices or misunderstandings about the past. For example, Henderson conducted a study of women who were active in the early decades of the recreation movement in the United States by examining minutes of the Playground Association of America and other influential organizations, as well as other publications of the period.[5] She found that, although many women had forcefully supported the need for expanded programming for youth and were active in establishing and staffing numerous pioneering recreation agencies, they tended to be ignored in later reviews of the period and were not recognized for their contributions.

Wesner points out that such historical research is all the more important if we are to take advantage of the memories of numerous individuals who contributed to the development of the recreation and park movement and who are still alive. He writes:

> . . . much work is still to be done. The need is urgent, for many legends and their contemporaries in the first half of the twentieth century are dying of old age, and few written records exist. Leisure studies practitioners and academics must recognize and appreciate this type of research.[6]

Historical-comparative research design

Just as those who do descriptive research, historical researchers frequently use comparative methods. Historians and sociologists have used them to study social change, social stratification, and social movements in relation to such areas as politics, religion, criminology, gender roles, and race relations.

In recreation, parks, and leisure studies, comparative studies may focus on such issues as the role of different professional organizations through time or the programs sponsored by different types of agencies, such as public, non-profit, or commercial.

Other historical approaches

Much historical research involves documentary analysis, as described later in this chapter. In recent years, however, many historical studies have made use of oral history, a technique involving the direct interviewing of people who have lived through an earlier period and who can provide a richness of detail through their recounting of personal experiences. For example, Henderson and Rannells carried out an extensive study of the past lives of Midwestern farm women, using the oral history approach.[7]

Another useful historical method involves "critical incident" techniques. This method blends both case-study and historical approaches. In it, the investigator identifies one or more events that appeared to provide a major stimulus to a field—an important new trend, a shift in public attitudes, or other significant outcomes. The critical incident method usually differs from history in that it avoids drawn-out studies that record events over a long time. Instead, it seeks to study short-term happenings with very intensive and varied methods in order to reveal the direct causes and effects of such incidents.

ARCHIVAL RESEARCH

A closely linked form of research that may deal with the past or the present consists of archival research. The term *archival* refers to public records or historic documents, which may include the annual reports of organizations, the minutes of meetings, legislative records, bylaws or charters, and similar materials.

Research in such sources may yield information of direct interest to recreation, parks, and leisure studies in terms of governmental actions, funding of recreational agencies, reports on social problems linked to leisure or environmental concerns, and similar issues. The 1962 Report of the Outdoor Recreation Resources Review Commission, for example, contained 26 volumes providing a detailed inventory of parks, forests, waterways, and other outdoor recreation resources throughout the United States, as well as threats to the environment and the leisure needs of citizens throughout the nation.[8] It drew from many other documentary sources and provided in itself a rich source of information for later researchers to use.

Similarly, the 1968 Report of the National Advisory Commission on Civil Disorder, the so-called Kerner Commission Report, provided a detailed analysis of the grievances held by African-American residents in urban ghettos throughout the United States that had led to destructive summer riots during the mid- and late 1960s. This report, which emphasized the lack of adequate recreation resources and programs for urban minorities as an important concern, was in itself an impressive example of the use of descriptive research in exploring contemporary social problems.[9]

Numerous documents published by government agencies provide information regarding participation and spending in varied forms of recreation, on organizations meeting social needs, on health conditions, on environmental trends, and similar issues. A prime example is the *Statistical Abstract of the United States,* published by the U.S. Department of Commerce, which annually reports hundreds of tables that detail information regarding varied aspects of leisure as an integral part of the nation's social, cultural, and economic life.

In 1991, Murdock, Backman, Hoque, and Ellis used population projection statistics drawn from the U.S. Bureau of the Census, the Department of the Interior, and other sources to develop a set of detailed demographic projections, with emphasis on ethnicity and age, to forecast outdoor recreation participation trends through the year 2025.[10] Similarly, Warnick carried out an analysis of domestic travel trends in the United States from 1979 to 1991, as influenced by generational trends reported by the U.S. Census Bureau.[11] This study provided important implications for the travel and tourism industry in terms of forecasting future marketing needs and strategies.

SOCIAL INDICATORS RESEARCH

Use of sources such as population projection statistics is part of what has been called "social indicators research." This is a relatively new technique that involves the monitoring and analysis of aggregated statistics that reflect both national trends and specific social changes affecting population groups.

By relating varied social indicators in a systematic way, it is possible to build models of social change, showing how different demographic, economic, and other factors relate and how changes in one sector of social life affect changes in others. As a specific example in the field of leisure studies, Christensen examined the use of social indicators in measuring the impact of a sustainable tourist industry on the quality of life in a host community.[12] In an even more specific example, Stubbles summarized the effects of newly legalized gambling in a small South Dakota town in terms of such social indicators as the loss of a number of businesses and an increase in traffic, noise, and various types of crimes.[13]

Clearly, research in recreation and leisure trends and needs on a large scale should make use of such social indicators to develop a macro view of the field's present and future needs. Increasingly, computer simulation methods are being used to identify the possible results of social intervention or public policy shifts, without having to encounter these results in real life.

BIBLIOGRAPHIC RESEARCH

Another form of systematic research, which is closely linked to archival and social indicators research, is bibliographic research. Actually, this is the type of study that most college students are familiar with; when they write course papers, their primary source of information is books and magazines on the subject. When bibliographic research is approached by professional researchers, however, searches must be much more comprehensive and systematic in terms of locating and summarizing past and present study reports.

Often called documentary research, this method involves careful analysis of the literature, including books, magazine or journal articles, research reports, and other records and documents within a given area. Its purpose may be to identify trends in public or scholarly interest or to analyze prevalent points of view or indeed to investigate any scholarly question or issue. Although it often involves studying a given period in the past, it would not be thought of as historical research, since it does not rely on the use of primary sources. In addition, its intention often is simply to study the literature itself as a reflection of scholarly and educational practices and approaches.

As indicated, documentary research consists of more than a casual skimming of the literature. Instead, it must involve a thorough search, usually probing computer listings with references from hundreds or thousands of relevant publications, with "keywords" providing access to all potentially important references. Such documentary studies today make frequent use of content analysis.

CONTENT ANALYSIS

This is a technique for gathering and analyzing the contents of written or visual materials, including articles, books, advertisements, speeches, films or videotapes, songs, photographs, works of art, or other cultural artifacts. The investigator searches for revealing words, meanings, symbols, themes, or other elements of communication that may provide meanings that lie below the surface or form patterns that suggest hypotheses for subsequent testing. Neuman writes:

> In content analysis, a researcher uses objective and systematic counting and recording procedures to produce a quantitative description of the symbolic content in a text. . . . [It] involves random sampling, precise measurement, and operational definitions for abstract constructs. Coding is used to turn aspects of content that represent variables into numbers. After a content analysis researcher gathers the data, he enters them into computers and analyzes them with statistics in the same way that an experimenter or survey researcher would.[14]

▼ *For Example*

In recreation, park, and leisure studies, some researchers have examined professional periodicals systematically to identify the subjects they have dealt with, the disciplines represented by those who have contributed articles, or other questions that might throw light on changing professional trends. For example, Voelkl, Austin, and Morris carried out an analysis of articles published in the *Therapeutic Recreation Journal* during the 1980s, which revealed a growth in the proportion of articles reporting actual research studies (as opposed to "think" pieces) and in the number of female authors.[15] Similarly, Busser and Valerius studied articles appearing in the *Journal of Park and Recreation Administration* between 1983 and 1993 to identify the subjects of articles, the research methods used, and the overall strengths and weaknesses of current management research.[16]

In contrast to this quantitative approach, other researchers may use a qualitative content analysis method, which seeks to interpret data in a more subjective or critical way. Instead of using statistical methods or charts and tables to reveal findings, the qualitative researcher probes for meanings or uses the principles found in such fields as literary criticism, psychology, anthropology, or political sciences to draw conclusions about the elements of content that have been identified.

▼ FOR EXAMPLE

Example 1. As an example, Lollar conducted a content analysis of advertisements promoting travel and tourism in two major magazines over a 75-year period in order to develop a typology of travel motivations of Americans during this period.[17] Hugh used content analysis of material drawn from four types of sources (economics publications, environmental publications, general publications, and congressional minutes and testimony) to identify current attitudes of Americans toward wilderness.[18]

Example 2. To explore the capacity of a developing country to sustain a growing tourist industry while minimizing its negative impacts, Russell and Hilton carried out an analysis of almost 300 news items on tourism in *The New Straits Times* in Malaysia.[19]

Rather than constitute a uniquely different form of research, content analysis is a technique that may be used in historical, archival, bibliography, and other types of documentary research. It may also be used as a tool in what has been called "secondary analysis," a term applying to the follow-up, more detailed analysis of research findings in a study or report by persons other than the original study team.

In many cases, a major survey or other quantitative study may be conducted covering a variety of related concerns, including recreation and leisure. Later researchers may return to the data reported for the overall study, drawing out materials specifically related to recreation and leisure and exploring or analyzing them in greater depth or from a different conceptual perspective.

Secondary Synthesis

In contrast to secondary analysis, which uses data from a single major source, *secondary synthesis* refers to journal articles that integrate the findings of numerous studies on a single theme. As Tom Goodale points out (see page 8), there is a significant need within the recreation, parks, and leisure-service field for syntheses that draw the essential meaning from separate analytical studies, which are often presented with highly technical statistics or conclusions.

▼ FOR EXAMPLE

Frequently, in the field of therapeutic recreation service, secondary syntheses focus on approaches to service for individuals with a particular form of disability or to outcomes of therapeutic programs. Sessoms, for example, reported the findings of a number of studies on the effects of organized camping on the self-concepts of children with physical disabilities.[20] MacNeil, in a similar synthesis, described the status of past, present, and future research dealing with leisure programs and services for older adults.[21] Within the broader area of the overall outcomes of leisure, many articles in professional journals have been devoted to secondary synthesis of a wide range of earlier research findings. For example, Andereck analyzed numerous research studies examining the impact of tourism and outdoor recreation on water resources, air quality, vegetation, and other elements of the physical environment. Like other studies of this type, Andereck's study pointed out the weaknesses in existing studies and suggested directions for future research.[22]

CRITICAL AND CONCEPTUAL RESEARCH

A final form of research consists of studies that deal primarily with ideas rather than with observed or empirical data. A number of recreation and leisure-studies educators such as J. L. Hemingway, Benjamin Hunnicutt, John Kelly, and Charles Sylvester, who have expertise in fields such as history, philosophy, and sociology, have presented conceptual or theoretical essays in leisure research journals in recent years.

Should their work be considered research as such? In the sense that it results from focused and organized inquiry and analysis and from the formulation of concepts and models of leisure values, behaviors, or social trends, it certainly is a form of basic research. Several examples of recently published papers of this general type follow.

▼ FOR EXAMPLE

Harper and Hultsman analyzed a major trend in American life—a shift toward the commodification of many aspects of cultural and social life and the rise of advertising as a major influence—as these changes have influenced the social meaning of leisure.[23] Sylvester explored the issue of leisure as a basic human right—through a variety of philosophical statements, charters or other governmental documents, and professional mission statements—with emphasis as its role in the lives of individuals with disability.[24] One example of studies that critique the writings of other major theorists is that of J. L. Hemingway, who reviewed the concepts of Jurgen Habermas, a contemporary social and political theorist, with respect to consumption, free time, and leisure—with emphasis on what Habermas regards as the degeneration of leisure into free time marked by the urge to consume play goods and services.[25]

Such studies use a variety of research methods or philosophical paradigms. In some cases, they may simply provoke thought or provide new insights. In others, they may stimulate the recognition of new priorities or effective strategies in areas of professional leisure-service practice. Halberg and Howe-Murphy make this case strongly, in describing the importance of having a personal philosophy for therapeutic recreation service practitioners:

> While some individuals may not be consciously aware of philosophy in their day-to-day practices, philosophy forms the very basis of what they do, both personally and professionally. . . . An awareness of the philosophical premises from which one operates and a strong philosophical professional foundation provide a basis for making decisions about professional activities, including the choice of professional organizations. In addition . . . other issues, such as recent contributions to the research literature from the social-psychological perspective of leisure, strengthen the importance of continuing the philosophical inquiry in our field.[26]

SUMMARY

This chapter deals with a variety of research methods that are unobtrusive in the sense that they do not deal directly with people involved with leisure, either through experimentation or observation. Instead, they tend to explore the past through historical studies or archival research or to explore the present through social indicators or documentary analysis. Techniques such as content analysis or secondary synthesis are reviewed. The chapter closes with an overview of conceptual, critical, and philosophical forms of research, with emphasis on their value in helping us understand the leisure phenomenon and their potential use in governmental or agency development of priorities and policymaking.

QUESTIONS AND ACTIVITIES

1. Recognizing that the study of history is often viewed by students as boring or irrelevant, what are the important reasons that justify historical

research in the field of recreation, parks, and leisure studies? Search for a historical report in one of the leisure journals that you find interesting or thought-provoking, and be prepared to summarize its subject, methodology, and findings in class.

2. Select one of the kinds of documentary research described in this chapter— such as archival research, content analysis, social indicators, or secondary synthesis. Be prepared to define this method and review for the class one article in a professional journal that illustrates its application.

ENDNOTES

1. Jack Fraenkel and Norman Wallen, *Research in Education* (New York: McGraw-Hill, 1993): 433.
2. John W. Best, *Research in Education* (Englewood Cliffs, NJ: Prentice-Hall, 1981): 131.
3. Fraenkel and Wallen, *Research in Education,* 443–44.
4. Carol Saslow, *Basic Research Methods* (New York: Random House, 1982): 17.
5. Karla Henderson, "Invisible Pioneers? The Impact of Women on the Recreation Movement," *Journal of Leisure Research* no. 2 (1993): 163–81.
6. Brad Wesner, "The Value of Historical Research," *Parks and Recreation* (Feb. 1994): 34.
7. K. Henderson and J. Rannells, "Farm Women and the Meaning of Work and Leisure: An Oral History Perspective," *Leisure Sciences* (1988): 46.
8. "Outdoor Recreation for America," *Report to the President and Congress by the Outdoor Recreation Resources Review Commission* (Washington, DC: U.S. Government Printing Office, 1968).
9. *Report of the National Advisory Commission on Civil Disorder* (New York: Bantam Books, 1968).
10. S. Murdock, K. Backman, M. N. Hoque, and D. Ellis, "The Implications of Change in Population Size and Composition on Future Participation in Outdoor Recreational Activities, *Journal of Leisure Research* 23, no. 3 (1991): 238–50.
11. Rodney Warnick, "U.S. Domestic Travel: Generational Trends in Travel," *Abstracts from NRPA Leisure Research Symposium* (Oct. 1993): 91.
12. Neal Christensen, "Sustainable Tourism and Quality of Life in the Host Community," *Abstracts from NRPA Leisure Research Symposium* (Oct. 1994): 81.
13. R. Stubbles, "A Question of Gambling," *Parks and Recreation* (April 1992): 64.
14. W. Lawrence Neuman, *Social Research Methods: Qualitative and Quantitative Approaches* (Boston: Allyn and Bacon, 1994): 262.
15. J. Voelkl, D. Austin, and C. Morris, "Analysis of Articles Published in the Therapeutic Recreation Journal During the 1980s," *Therapeutic Recreation Journal* (2d quarter 1992): 46–50.
16. James Busser and Louise Valerius, "A Decade of Management Research: 1983–1993," *Abstracts from NRPA Leisure Research Symposium* (Oct. 1993): 49.
17. Sam Lollar, A Typology of Travel Motivations," *Abstracts from NRPA Leisure Research Symposium* (Oct. 1990): 17.

18. Katherine Hugh, "Using Content Analysis to Explore Current Attitudes Toward Wilderness," *Abstracts from NRPA Leisure Research Symposium* (Oct. 1990): 65.

19. Ruth Russell and Karen Hilton, "Sustaining Tourism Growth: A Developing Country Case Study," *Abstracts from NRPA Leisure Research Symposium* (Oct. 1994): 76.

20. H. Douglas Sessoms, "Organized Camping and Its Effects on the Self-Concept of Physically Handicapped Children," *Therapeutic Recreation Journal* (1st quarter 1979): 39–43.

21. Richard MacNeil, "Leisure Programs and Services for Older Adults: Past, Present and Future Research," *Therapeutic Recreation Journal* (1st quarter 1988): 24–35.

22. Kathleen Andereck, "The Environmental Consequences of Tourism: A Review and Synthesis of Recent Research," *Abstracts from NRPA Leisure Research Symposium* (Oct. 1994): 83.

23. William Harper and John Hultsman, "Selling Leisure: Cultural Change and the Evolution of Advertising," *Abstracts from NRPA Leisure Research Symposium* (Oct. 1993): 42.

24. Charles Sylvester, "Therapeutic Recreation and the Right to Leisure," *Therapeutic Recreation Journal* (2d quarter 1992): 9–20.

25. J. L. Hemingway, "Emancipated Leisure: Habermas's Early Essays on Consumption, Free Time, and Leisure," *Abstracts from NRPA Leisure Research Symposium* (Oct. 1993): 39.

26. Kathleen Halberg and Roxanne Howe-Murphy, "The Dilemma of an Unresolved Philosophy in Therapeutic Recreation," *Therapeutic Recreation Journal* (3d quarter 1985): 11.

Qualitative Research Approaches

Typically qualitative methods yield large volumes of exceedingly rich data obtained from a limited number of individuals and whereas the quantitative approach necessitates standardised data collection, qualitative researchers exploit the context of data gathering to enhance the value of the data. Analysis of qualitative material is more explicitly interpretive, creative and personal than in quantitative analysis, which is not to say that it should not be equally systematic and careful.[1]

INTRODUCTION

Earlier chapters of this book described several forms of research that are essentially quantitative and that fit the traditional model of research, which originated in the physical and natural sciences. Several types of descriptive research, however, were identified as having been influenced by another model of systematic investigation that is particularly appropriate for social research—the qualitative research approach.

This chapter discusses the application of qualitative research methods today in recreation, parks, and leisure studies. It presents the underlying rationale and theoretical basis for qualitative research, as well as its methods, and contrasts them with quantitative research designs. It also discusses the strengths and weaknesses of qualitative research and illustrates its application in the leisure-service field.

MEANING OF QUALITATIVE RESEARCH

Chapters 2 and 3 point out that the positivistic view of the world, which has dominated traditional scientific thinking and research methods, was closely tied to a quantitative approach to gathering and analyzing data. Based on the assumption that all natural phenomena were subject to laws that could be identified and that systematic observation of their expression would be the most effective means of testing hypotheses and ultimately describing reality, the positivistic approach also came to dominate research in the social sciences.

However, a new paradigm—the naturalistic perspective—emerged during the twentieth century. This approach held that human behaviors and relationships were not as rigidly controlled by universal laws or predictable patterns as had been thought. It argued that the social sciences needed to be less mathematical and more subjective, more flexible, more intuitive.

The new approach, which expressed itself in the growing drive toward qualitative research, came to be widely used in fields such as psychology, sociology, and anthropology. It has been variously defined. A typical early description was:

> Qualitative methodology refers to those research strategies, such as participant observation, in-depth interviewing, total participation in the activity being investigated, field work, etc., which allow the researcher to obtain first hand knowledge about the empirical social world in question. Qualitative methodology allows the researcher to "get close to the data," thereby developing the analytical, conceptual, and categorical components of explanation from the data itself—rather than from the preconceived, rigidly structured and highly quantified techniques that pigeonhole . . . the operational definitions that the researcher has constructed.[2]

To understand this approach more fully, it is necessary to look at the underlying rationale of qualitative research, the methods used, their advantages and disadvantages, and finally their applicability to human-service fields such as recreation, parks, and leisure studies.

Today, the interpretive or naturalistic paradigm (the philosophical approach that underlies qualitative research) holds that, in order to investigate and understand phenomena for which no clear theoretical framework exists, it is necessary for researchers to attempt to understand the world as it is experienced by people in natural settings. In the field of therapeutic recreation, for example, Lee, Brock, Dattilo, and Kleiber point out that much research that professionals gather about living with disabilities is affected by an "outsider's perspective" that views disabled persons through the prism of their own scientific theories and research skills and that fails to understand the nature of disability as a lived experience.[3]

It therefore becomes necessary to describe social realities by observing not only the outward behavior of subjects, but also by seeking to comprehend their "inner events"—the subjective motives, feelings, and emotions of those being studied.

CHARACTERISTICS OF QUALITATIVE RESEARCH

Qualitative research may involve a variety of methods, including *case studies* that employ a number of investigative tools: *in-depth interviews* or *group interviews; participant observation,* which may extend over a period of time; *projective techniques,* to gather fuller information about subjects' feelings or views; and in some cases, *visual materials* such as photographs, documents, or other sources of information, to cross-check the hypotheses generated by observation.

Qualitative research typically is marked by several key elements:

1. It is carried out in natural settings, where people are living their real lives.

2. Data are collected in the form of words or pictures, rather than numbers, and may include field notes, videotapes, diaries, official records, and other data types that provide a rich picture of the subjects being studied.

3. It is concerned not only with what happens but how and why it happens—the nature of interpersonal relations, how people confront or respond to each other, their jokes, body language, and conversational gambits.

4. It requires trust and researcher integrity in that subjects must be assured that the researcher is being honest with them and will not exploit them or distort the meaning of their lives.

5. It is based on an inductive approach in which researchers do not begin with theoretical assumptions to be tested by observation, but rather with the need to see things from study participants' perspective and thus develop theory.

6. It demands checks in the form of detailed written notes and other types of documentation or evidence to confirm the researcher's conclusions.

Howe sums up the qualitative or naturalistic researcher's role in participant-observation studies:

> He or she looks, asks, listens, and to some degree participates. He or she plays a role in the unfolding of things, typically trying to be as unobtrusive and nonreactive as possible . . . However, recognizing that all research using human beings is intrusive to some degree and that some amount of contrivance is inherent in every research act . . . the naturalistic researcher records, describes, and interprets the influence of his or her intrusion on the experience being investigated.[4]

THE STEPS IN QUALITATIVE RESEARCH

The steps in qualitative research are similar to those found in other types of research. They involve the following:

1. Identifying the phenomenon to be studied, which may consist of groups of people and their interaction, customs, leisure behaviors, conflict situations, social change, or other problem areas that are significant enough to justify research. The durability of wooden park benches or physical causes of accidents on ski slopes, for example, would not be appropriate subjects for qualitative research; the behavior of bettors in a gambling casino or of wilderness recreationists on a white-water rafting trip might be.

2. Narrowing the overall problem or study area to yield research questions or issues that can provide meaningful kinds of data and that are "workable" in terms of logistical factors and the willingness of subjects to participate in the study. This need not always involve a formal agreement. In many observational studies, as in *Tally's Corner,* the detailed study of a group of African American men who "hang" regularly on a street corner,[5] the researcher simply becomes accepted gradually by group members over a period of time.

3. Gradually generating hypotheses over time, rather than initially formulating key theories to be tested. In this process, the researcher may discard some hypotheses, modify or sharpen others, and continue to formulate new ones. There is a continuous process of collecting and analyzing data, leading to the development of new theoretical explanations and hypotheses. This contrasts sharply with the quantitative research approach, in which both the hypotheses and the data-gathering process are sharply defined at the outset of the study.

4. Recording anecdotal and narrative observations in written notes or possibly in video or audio tapes.

5. Analyzing data by synthesizing the information gained from various sources and cross-checking it against other documents or sources, ultimately resulting in a detailed, comprehensive description of what has been learned. As personalities and patterns of group behavior become more evident, the researcher will arrive at a number of interpretations and conclusions. Throughout this process, numeric data may be used. Numeric data, however, would not be analyzed through inferential statistical procedures to test hypotheses, as in quantitative research studies.

6. Drawing conclusions throughout the course of a study, interpreting the behaviors observed, and noting patterns or relationships among study variables. As these continue to be refined and strengthened, they will be summarized in a final statement that presents them as significant findings of the study and relates them to other social theories or that presents models of social change, social structure, or even causal relationships that have appeared during the study.[6]

The findings of qualitative research may then be used to prompt further research, including quantitative studies that test hypotheses in a more formal way.

STRENGTHS AND WEAKNESSES OF QUALITATIVE RESEARCH

Qualitative research, as described in this chapter, is a growing trend in recreation and leisure studies, although most reports found in the literature rely on essentially quantitative approaches. What then are the strengths or advantages of qualitative research, and what are the weaknesses or disadvantages of this approach?

Clearly, observing behavior in its "natural" setting is a more realistic way of recording reality than research conducted in laboratory or in other artificially structured situations. Similarly, the researcher gains a richer and deeper experiential exposure to the subjects under study and is able to grasp their point of view and vision of the world. When the researcher is directly involved over time, his observations and impressions are grounded in real-life happenings, rather than limited by the need to quantify only those elements that can be numerically and sometimes arbitrarily measured. Beyond this, the qualitative approach is far more flexible in that it is not constricted by the need to develop matched groups of participants in the study or by the required use of validated instruments or measurement procedures.

On the other hand, a number of disadvantages or problems are connected with the qualitative research approach. Because it often involves intimate contact between the researcher and her subjects, there is the risk that the researcher may obtain and use revealing and potentially harmful data gained from the study without the knowledge or informed consent of the subjects. For example, following the publication of a 1970 study of homosexuals, the St. Louis Police Department demanded that the subjects who had been observed be identified so that they could be prosecuted for what was then illegal activity.

A second problem connected with qualitative research is that researchers who become part of groups may either deliberately or unconsciously influence their members in terms of values or actual behavior. Although investigators may attempt to remain neutral or limit their involvement, in some cases they may need to profess certain beliefs or engage in expected behaviors to gain and maintain membership in a group. Even when their identity as outside investigators is clearly known, their presence may influence group members who know that they are being observed.

Beyond this, because qualitative researchers are closely involved in real-life settings, they run the risk of criminal prosecution, health problems, or other negative outcomes if they are investigating fringe or antisocial groups:

> . . . drug or alcohol use accompanying participant observation may have lasting negative consequences for researchers. Similarly, participation in high emotional groups, such as a Satan worshipping cult or a charismatic Pentecostal sect, may affect a researcher's mental health. Sometimes participant observation may require the qualitative researcher to violate personal moral standards.[7]

Beyond such problems, other weaknesses of qualitative research include the following: (1) the risk that the study, because of its unstructured nature, will be so loose and flexible that its investigative techniques become random and unfocused and that no really significant findings are developed; and (2) if study findings are based on the observation of a limited number of subjects or groups that are not representative of a larger population, they may lack any degree of generalizability.

To overcome such weaknesses, it is essential that qualitative research designs strive to maintain a high level of reliability and validity and that issues of observer or researcher credibility be fully dealt with in study reports.

The tendency of board members, government officials, contributors or agency supporters, or the public at large is to want to see "hard" facts—epitomized by numbers that illustrate concrete, positive outcomes. Colorful anecdotes, narrative accounts of group experiences, details of individual interviews or case studies, or the subjective interpretations of qualitative researchers are not likely to be as convincing for them as statistics of attendance, improved health status, or social involvement.

Recognizing this problem, many qualitative researchers have used "triangulation" techniques—stated more broadly, *combined* qualitative and quantitative research methods—to overcome weaknesses in their studies.

TRIANGULATION AS A RESEARCH TECHNIQUE

The concept of triangulation involves combining different methodological designs and techniques to overcome possible weaknesses in data gathering or analysis. Thus, both qualitative research techniques involving field observation and subjective interpretation of events may be combined with quantitatively oriented gathering of numeric data and statistical analysis. This approach has several purposes: (1) to provide more sophisticated rigor to studies that otherwise might be questioned in terms of their validity or reliability; (2) to collect different kinds of data or information to provide a fully rounded picture of the research subjects or settings; and (3) to deal with the reality that multiple methods and theoretical approaches must be used in settings marked by varying personal values, conflicting social forces, or other psychological or sociological influences.

Walker suggests that there are essentially four kinds of basic triangulations that researchers may use:

1. collection of varied kinds of data and cross-checking with respect to time, place, person, and level of involvement or functioning;
2. use of multiple observers who examine the same phenomenon;
3. use of different theoretical perspectives with respect to the same group of subjects; and
4. methodological triangulation, in terms of use of instruments, study techniques, or methods of analysis.[8]

An example of triangulation in action is seen in a study of the effects of leisure education on the transition (from school to adult life) of students with mental retardation. In this study—by Bedini, Bullock, and Driscoll[9]—which evaluated a model program for adolescents with mental retardation in Wake County, North Carolina, such positivistic or quantitative research methods were used as pretests and posttests (including questionnaire surveys and interest inventories), along with random assignment of subjects to experimental and control groups. In addition, in-depth interviews were used to develop case studies of the lives of the students examined in the study. A number of statistical methods were used to analyze the data gathered, along with content analysis of progress notes and other observational techniques.

Most social researchers tend to use *either* quantitative or qualitative research methods and to reject other approaches. However, a growing number of researchers recognize that some questions cannot be adequately answered by one method alone. Henderson comments that each researcher must feel free to use the approaches suited to a particular problem or issue. Although her personal bias is toward qualitative research, she writes that she has used quantitative research methods in the past and will continue to do so when those methods are most appropriate for her research question. Her understanding of quantitative design and statistics has helped provide a fuller appreciation for the value of qualitative methods.

In some cases, investigators may begin by using quantitative measures to determine the dimensions and statistical relationships of study phenomena and then may move to qualitative approaches to illuminate or interpret their empirically determined findings. In other cases, exploratory qualitative methods may suggest certain theories or hypotheses, which can then be tested empirically through quantitative forms of measurement and analysis. In still other cases, both methods may be used simultaneously. Walker writes:

> Qualitative research is increasingly being used to complement quantifications during the principal phase of research. Often the two methods are used with different objectives. In evaluation research, for example, a distinction is made between impact and process analysis, the former using predominantly quantitative techniques, the latter qualitative ones. Impact analysis is concerned to measure, or predict, the outcomes of policy programmes. Process analysis is then used most frequently to determine why a particular programme was unsuccessful [or successful].[10]

Both forms of research may then be used to test and challenge, or to enrich and complement each other, depending in part on the purpose of the research effort and in part on the question being investigated. In concluding this section of the text dealing with an overall understanding of research purposes and approaches, it is essential to recognize that a wide range of investigative methods may be used in both research studies and program evaluation. The actual processes of research and evaluation, including the steps that are followed, and the principles and procedures that are involved are presented in following chapters.

SUMMARY

Although the most widely used forms of research in recreation, parks, and leisure studies have followed positivistic, quantitative study designs, there has been a growing trend toward the use of qualitative research methods. It is believed that these techniques are useful in exploring issues that do not lend themselves to numeric or statistical analysis, and that they provide both a different perspective and greater depth, particularly in understanding human values, motivations, and relationships.

Qualitative research is characterized by emphasis on field studies in natural settings, by the use of observational techniques, and by the gradual development of concepts or study conclusions, rather than by a deductive approach that seeks to test prestructured hypotheses. It is recognized that qualitative research may have certain weaknesses and risks, both in interpretation of findings and their ultimate believability, when hard-core evidence is needed. However, increasingly this approach's value is being recognized, and many researchers are now using both qualitative and quantitative methods in their studies.

QUESTIONS AND ACTIVITIES

1. What are the major differences between qualitative and quantitative research approaches? What are the major advantages of qualitative research in terms of the kinds of problems that might be studied?

2. Examine one or more leisure research journals to identify two or three articles that report qualitative research studies. Summarize these articles, with emphasis on the methodology used by researchers and the kinds of findings and conclusions that were reported.

3. Within a particular area of recreation specialization (such as public recreation and parks, commercial recreation, or therapeutic recreation), identify a specific problem or issue that would lend itself to qualitative study, and suggest a method of investigating it in a field setting.

ENDNOTES

1. Robert Walker, (ed.), *Applied Qualitative Research* (New York: Gower, 1985): 3.
2. W. J. Filstead, *cited in* Bruce Chadwick, Howard Bahr, and Stan Albrecht, *Social Science Research Methods* (Englewood Cliffs, NJ: Prentice-Hall, 1984): 206.
3. Younghill Lee, Stephen Brock, John Dattilo, and Douglas Kleiber, "Leisure and Adjustment to Spinal Cord Injury: Conceptual and Methodological Suggestions," *Therapeutic Recreation Journal* 27 (3d quarter 1993): 200–11.
4. Christine Howe, in Marjorie Malkin and Christine Howe, eds., *Research in Therapeutic Recreation: Concepts and Methods* (State College, PA: Venture Publishing, 1993): 236.
5. Elliot Liebow, *Tally's Corner: A Study of Negro Streetcorner Men* (Boston: Little, Brown, 1967).
6. Adapted from Jack Fraenkel and Norman Wallen, *Research in Education* (New York: McGraw-Hill, 1993): 381–84.
7. Chadwick, Bahr, Albrecht, *Social Science Research Methods,* 213.
8. Walker, *Applied Qualitative Research,* 15.
9. Leandra Bedini, Charles Bullock, and Linda Driscoll, "The Effects of Leisure Education on Factors Contributing to the Successful Transition of Students with Mental Retardation from School to Adult Life," *Therapeutic Recreation Journal* 27 (2d quarter 1993): 70–82.
10. Walker, *Applied Qualitative Research,* 22.

The Research Process: An Overview

*Before developing a specific research design, one must
first decide on the problem to be studied. There is no
shortage of researchable problems. . . . As a result, the
critical question to be answered at the outset is not
whether the project is interesting or feasible, but whether
it is* significant *enough to be worth doing at all. . . .
For this reason, people concerned with describing successful strategies of research often cite the early decisions
about what to do in a project as most critical.[1]*

INTRODUCTION

Developing a research proposal and carrying out an investigation successfully includes a number of major tasks:

- identifying an appropriate problem area and developing a clear statement
  of the proposed study's purposes or hypotheses
- formulating a detailed study plan or proposal for approval by a sponsoring committee or funding agency
- considering the possibility of collaborating with other individuals or
  agencies in the joint sponsorship and conduct of the study
- carrying out the actual investigation
- analyzing the data and preparing a final report for dissemination of the
  findings

This chapter begins by considering the possible reasons for undertaking a
research study, and examining the different kinds of sponsorship and the settings
in which research may be carried on. It deals with the process of identifying suitable problem areas for research and then outlines a six-step process that includes
the sequence of tasks normally undertaken by researchers in conducting studies.

MOTIVATIONS FOR DOING RESEARCH

Before undertaking any sort of research investigation, the would-be
researcher should take a hard look at his own motivations for carrying out a

study. Too often, research is done simply in response to a sort of personal challenge, somewhat like the mountaineer who explained his ascent of Mount Everest with the phrase, "Because it's there." Obviously, there should be better reasons for undertaking such a task.

Professional Commitment

A common reason for doing research is that one is required to do so, as in the case of a master's or doctoral student in a university graduate program in recreation, parks, and leisure studies.

It might also be a voluntary assignment, intended to fulfill requirements for the award of academic honors or to gather material useful in writing an article for a campus publication.

Similarly, one might be assigned to carry out a research study as part of one's ongoing work within a leisure-service agency. This would be particularly true of evaluation studies, since staff members who have had undergraduate or graduate course work in research and evaluation are likely to be assigned such tasks.

Intellectual Curiosity

Many other individuals undertake research because they are genuinely interested in a subject and seek to explore it in order to make a scholarly contribution to the field. Henderson comments that research invariably involves one's personal interests, which create a sense of motivation related to the research issue.[2] A practitioner might want to learn the broader implications of an issue or problem faced at work or to learn whether solutions have been found elsewhere.

Career Advancement

Research may do much to enhance one's professional reputation. Individuals—particularly college and university faculty members—who do research are often called upon to address conferences or to be part of special task forces or work groups that carry out investigations or make planning reports. If they write for publication, they become recognized as authorities in a given area and may be called upon to take consultant assignments. Ultimately, even for generalists in the field, research and evaluation may become an increasing part of their work assignments, and they may ultimately hold specialized positions as researchers.

TYPES OF SPONSORSHIP

Research studies may be carried out under several different types of sponsorship arrangements. These include the following:

University graduate programs. In graduate curricula in recreation, parks, and leisure studies, master's and doctoral candidates are normally required to write theses and dissertations, although in some master's curricula there may be optional choices of doing a project or taking a comprehensive examination.

In-house research projects. Many leisure-service agencies conduct research as part of their ongoing operations. These tend to be applied forms of research, such as needs assessment studies, feasibility studies to determine whether given programs or facilities should be initiated, personnel evaluation studies, management policy analysis, or similar ventures.

Specially funded studies. Research projects are often supported by special funding from outside sources or sponsors. Professional societies, as well as colleges and universities, may apply for grants from government agencies or foundations in order to carry out studies within a particular area of interest. Most foundations are known for having special areas of social concern and typically support grants in these areas. Similarly a number of government agencies fund research; numerous studies related to parks management, outdoor recreation, and related areas have been supported by the U.S. Department of Agriculture and the Department of the Interior. Typically, sponsoring agencies will advertise the fact that they intend to commission a research study in an area relevant to them and will request submissions from individuals or research agencies. Colleges and universities, as well as professional planning firms that respond to such RFPs (Requests for Proposals), must submit detailed proposals outlining their intended procedures, methods of analysis, team qualifications, preliminary budgets, and timetables for doing the research.

Independent research. Some research specialists conduct studies independently in areas of their own choice. Often, they are college or university professors, for whom scholarly productivity and publication are important priorities. In some cases, they may develop cooperative relationships with professional organizations or societies, which act as formal sponsors for their research.

KEY STEPS IN CARRYING OUT RESEARCH

The following section of this chapter describes six major steps that are typically followed in carrying out research studies—particularly within a scholarly or academic setting. In general, they would apply also to other types of research sponsors, although less emphasis might be given to exploring the literature or the formulation of theoretical concepts. They are summarized in Figure 9.1 and are suggested as guidelines for those entering the research field.

The first two of these steps, involving the selection of a problem area and the development of a problem statement and research questions and/or hypotheses, are discussed in the following sections of this chapter.

FIGURE 9.1   Six-Step Research Process

1. *Identify Broad Problem Area*
Explore different possibilities in terms of problem areas of personal and professional concern. Select an issue or problem that appears promising, and conduct preliminary search of the literature to (a) determine its significance, (b) identify the range and focus of past research efforts, and (c) consider possible study designs.

2. *Develop Problem Statement and Research Questions and/or Hypotheses*
Based on fuller literature reviews, interviews or other means of gathering preliminary information about the issue or problem, develop a problem statement that sharpens the focus of the intended study. Following this, prepare specific research questions or study purpose and, if appropriate, research hypotheses to be tested by the research.

3. *Prepare Study Plan and Proposal*
Develop a detailed operational plan for the study and a written proposal that includes the following elements:
  a. Based on the initial problem statement and study purposes or hypotheses, make decisions as to appropriate study type (experimental, case study, survey, etc.), and potential subjects, data-gathering procedures, methods of analysis, and similar tasks. Explore possibilities for collaboration with other agencies and needed funding, authorization, or other forms of cooperation.
  b. Develop a study plan that includes specific details of subjects and sampling procedures, key variables in the study that can be tested or observed empirically, identifying members of the study team and determining their functions and assignments, outlining a schedule for various phases of the study, and other research tasks. These are incorporated into a formal, written study plan or proposal following the format suggested in Chapter 10.
  c. Obtain approval for the study, based on the intended sponsorship arrangements. This step might consist of having a graduate thesis or dissertation committee review the proposal, in the case of a graduate research project in a college or university. In the case of a proposal that is submitted for funding to a foundation or other potential sponsor, or in response to a request for proposal, the plan might be examined in competition with other research proposals. In either case, it may be necessary to revise study goals and procedures or to negotiate terms of the research plan before it is approved.

4. *Conduct Research and Gather Data*
When the study plan has been approved, the research is carried out. Depending on the nature of the study, this might include the development of instruments, such as questionnaires or interview schedules for survey research, or the selection of experimental and control groups and intervention procedures for experimental studies. In the case of a historical study, it would involve the in-depth search for needed primary and secondary sources and the systematic recording of data. In a qualitative research study that included participant observation by a field investigator, it would include an intensive process of gaining access to subjects and the ongoing collection of information that is linked to the formulation of theoretical models.

5. *Data Analysis and Interpretation*
A key stage of the research process involves analyzing the data that have been gathered, interpreting them, and arriving at conclusions. In the case of positivistic, quantitative

(continued)

FIGURE 9.1   Continued.

studies, this will usually require statistical analysis (see Chapter 12) both to describe the study findings and to determine relationships among different variables, linked to the testing of research hypotheses. In naturalistic, qualitative research, statistics would not usually be a key part of data analysis. Instead, other analytical procedures that are carried out within appropriate theoretical frameworks would be used. At this stage, study findings would be concisely stated, interpreted, and used as the basis for discussion and research conclusions and recommendations.

6. *Prepare Research Report*
The final stage of research consists of the preparation of a study report, in a form suited to its academic, agency-centered, professional or other context. In addition to the written report which normally consists of a detailed, fairly lengthy document, briefer summaries of study purposes, procedures, and findings may be prepared for wider dissemination. Study findings of broader professional or public interest may also be publicized through journals and magazines, presentations at educational or research meetings, or even through news releases.

Identify Broad Problem Area

The initial stages of selecting research topics and formulating study questions are critical to the success of any research effort. Northrop sums up their importance:

> Again and again investigators have plunged into a subject matter, sending out questionnaires, gathering a tremendous amount of data, even performing experiments, only to come out at the end wondering what it all proves. . . . Others, noting the success of a given scientific method in one field, have carried this method hastily and uncritically into their own, only to end later in a similar disillusionment. All such experiences are a sign that the initiation of inquiry has been glossed over too hastily, without any appreciation of its importance or its difficulty.[3]

The broad problem area may be identified in a variety of ways. Initially, the researcher might begin by considering a number of topics within his field of interest, including those with which he has had direct experience as participant or practitioner or others that might have captured his imagination in course work or reading assignments.

The researcher might explore these possible topics through reading the professional literature, talking with other educators or professionals, visiting or observing the field, or attending conferences, workshops, or special seminars. Throughout this process, the researcher would begin to determine what has already been learned through research, which systematic forms of investigation are being carried out at present, and which kinds of issues or questions might justify new study efforts.

As the investigator begins to focus his interest on a more sharply defined problem and set of possible research questions, it is essential that several questions be answered, including the following:

1. Will the problem area under consideration be of interest both to the individual researcher and to some recognized segment of the community (the profession at large, public or nonprofit agencies, those within a specific scholarly discipline, college or university departments, or the public)?
2. Is it likely to be a significant study in that it will add to existing knowledge or contribute to professional practice in some meaningful way?
3. Will the topic be researchable in that it requires information that can be discovered or measured empirically, or that can be analyzed by known methods?
4. Will the study be administratively feasible in that it will be possible to carry it out within a reasonable time frame and with expenses that the researcher or study team can afford?
5. Will the problem area be one in which the investigator has special expertise and interest or in which he can readily develop the background, testing skills, or other competencies that will be needed?

Salkind emphasizes that it is particularly critical that a research problem be attractive to the would-be investigator. He writes:

> The selection of the problem you want to work on is terribly important for two reasons. First, research takes a good deal of time and energy and you want to be sure the problem you select interests you. You will work so hard throughout this project that even the most interesting project may at times become too much. Just think of what it would be like if you weren't interested! Second, the problem you select is only the first step in the research process. If this "goes well" the remaining steps . . . have a good chance of going well also.[4]

Gradually, the problem area is narrowed to a research topic that represents a fresh and significant line of inquiry and that can be summed up in a problem statement. The problem statement should delineate, as concisely as possible, the subject of the proposed research. It may begin with a background statement that describes in narrative or brief essay form the topic that is to be investigated and may then go on to define the specific purposes of the study, in terms of the questions that are to be explored or the hypotheses that will be tested.

Develop the Problem Statement

The problem statement serves two important functions. First, it compels the researcher to explain exactly what she wants to accomplish in the study. The problem statement should make quite explicit whether the research is intended to gather descriptive information, develop a classification system of phenomena, compare two or more agencies or systems, identify and test possible relationships among variables, or test a formally stated hypothesis.

Second, the problem statement usually serves as a key section in a research proposal. It may actually take two forms: (1) the introduction, a brief, carefully worded statement that presents the overall area of concern, arouses the reader's interest, and provides some general background information or indication of the problem area's significance and (2) a more explicit statement of the overall purpose and subpurposes of the study, or of the hypotheses to be investigated, along with a concise summary of the variables to be examined, including the nature of the population and settings that will be involved in the research.

Mason and Bramble suggest that problem statements should meet three important criteria: (1) They should explore relationships among different variables; (2) they should state the nature of the expected relationships clearly and precisely; and (3) they should suggest a method of researching the question or determining the exact nature of the relationship.[5] While some studies may not necessarily explore possible relationships—such as a descriptive study that seeks primarily to gather a broad sweep of knowledge and to organize findings into logical categories or classification systems—these criteria are applicable to most recreation, park, and leisure-studies research problems.

Identify Study Purposes

To clarify the precise focus of the study at this stage, it is necessary to identify one or more specific purposes of the research, either in broad descriptive terms or in the form of research questions or hypotheses that are to be tested.

Study purposes, as described in Chapter 10, are general statements that indicate the thrust of the intended research. Typically, they begin with statements of intention, such as: "to explore the impact of," "to measure the extent of," or possibly "to identify relationships among." In historical research, they might be stated in such phrases as "to trace the history of," "to examine the roots of," or "to analyze the forces that led to."

Develop Research Questions

These tend to be more specific and to outline the actual areas of inquiry that the proposed research might follow. For example, a master's thesis or a doctoral dissertation in the area of management problems and trends might identify such areas as the following: "participative management techniques," "total quality management," "the effects of fees and charges," "the advantages and disadvantages of privatization of recreation and park functions," or "the problem of lawsuits stemming from accidents in high-risk recreation programs." These problem areas may then be the basis for developing research questions that suggest significant potential topics. Several examples follow.

1. *Problem Area:* Participative management techniques.

   Possible Research Question: Are participative management techniques effective in terms of improving the motivation and on-the-job performance of employees?

2. *Problem Area:* The effects of fees and charges.

   Possible Research Question: What are the typical effects of fees and charges in recreation agencies?

3. *Problem Area:* The advantages and disadvantages of privatization.

   Possible Research Question: Does privatization (that is, the subcontracting of public agency functions to private or commercial firms) lead to greater efficiency and/or economy?

4. *Problem Area:* Growing number of lawsuits for accidents in high-risk recreation programs.

   Possible Research Question: Given the possibility of being sued for negligence, does it make sense to sponsor high-risk, adventure recreation programs?

Each of these questions represents a potentially useful subject for research in the leisure-service field. However, they tend to be much too general and need to be more precisely stated, if they are to serve as the basis for planning a research study.

To illustrate, a phrase like "what are the typical effects" lacks precision. What does the word "typical" mean? Similarly, a phrase like, "Does it make sense?" may be heard in informal conversation, but does not represent a precise or clear question that can be meaningfully answered.

Does the research question strike a proper balance between breadth and specificity? Often, beginning problem statements are far too broad and must be narrowed down to be researchable. However, it might also be a mistake to have a problem statement that is overly limited and that would therefore lack significance or generalizability.

To illustrate, the term, "the effects of fees and charges," might be rephrased to refer to three specific elements: (1) the effects on attendance and participation; (2) the effects on the income of an agency; and (3) the effects on the public's perception of the agency. At the same time, to deal only with the effects of fees and charges applied to a single event or type of program might be too narrow for a worthwhile study.

Similarly, in the fourth question, it would be helpful to know more specifically what types of agencies are being considered. For example, it might make sense for commercial organizations to undertake high-risk programs, but not for nonprofit, voluntary organizations.

If the problem area is a relatively new one and has not been investigated before, the question might be a simple or exploratory one. On the other hand, if considerable research has already been done on a subject, any new research question dealing with it should build on what has already been done and should examine a more specialized or in- depth aspect of the problem.

Develop Study Hypotheses

If the intention of the proposed study is to ask a research question or questions in such a way that they can be proven or disproven, it would be appropriate to develop one or more hypotheses at this point. A hypothesis may simply be defined as an "educated guess"—that is, an assumption on the part of the researcher with respect to the relationships that will be found to exist between or among variables in a study, including possible cause-and-effect relationships.

As shown in Chapter Three, hypotheses may be stated in different ways, as "working" or "statistical." Essentially, working hypotheses are presented as speculations or assumptions that the proposed research is expected to support. Statistical hypotheses are more precise, concrete predictions of expected relationships or outcomes—usually stated in the "null" or negative form—to be quantitatively proven or disproven. Some authorities use the phrase *research hypotheses* to describe hypotheses that are positively stated, in contrast to null hypotheses.

The majority of research studies that are reported in the professional literature in recreation, parks, and leisure studies do *not* rely on formally stated hypotheses. Of 50 articles reviewed in randomly selected issues of the *Journal of Leisure Research,* the *Therapeutic Recreation Journal,* and the *Journal of Recreation and Park Administration* published in the late 1980s and early 1990s, only three had formal hypotheses. The others tended to present research purposes, followed by research questions or other sharply defined study tasks.

SELECTION OF APPROPRIATE RESEARCH DESIGNS

At this point, it becomes necessary to think in terms of study designs and data-gathering techniques that will be most appropriate in terms of the purposes, research questions, or hypotheses that have been developed.

For example, if the study's purposes are to gather a broad picture of current practices or to identify prevalent leisure values and behavior patterns, descriptive research designs such as survey or cross-sectional analysis would be most suitable. If the research is intended to test cause-and-effect relationships, an experimental design will be most useful. Realistically, however, relatively few experimental research studies are reported in the social science literature. For example, Babbie points out that articles published in the *American Sociological Review* over a recent 14-year period were based predominantly on survey research.[6]

Henderson suggests a number of questions that should be asked to help researchers decide whether they should consider quantitative or qualitative research approaches. Several of these follow:

- Does the researcher desire to get close to study subjects and immersed in their experiences?
- Is the research question likely to change depending on the data that will be gathered?
- Does the researcher have a philosophical and methodological bias toward the interpretive paradigm and qualitative methods?[7]

Henderson suggests that if the answer to any of these questions is yes, qualitative methods should be seriously considered in formulating a research plan. At this stage, other important decisions must be made with respect to the subjects who will be involved, the population they will be drawn from, and the sampling procedures; the kinds of data gathering methods that will be used; the most appropriate methods of analysis; and the time frame in which the study would be carried on.

Based on the preliminary exploration that has been done, it is necessary to develop the actual instruments and procedures that will be used. This may include (1) establishing test conditions and making necessary arrangements or gaining permissions or approvals; (2) gathering preliminary data or exploring settings/systems that will be used in data-gathering; (3) operationalizing concepts by transforming each variable into an element that can be observed or tested empirically in the study; (4) developing, pilot-testing, and refining instruments that will be used in the study; and (5) identifying possible obstacles to be encountered or weaknesses in the research design and planning to overcome or avoid these.

As the thrust of the proposed research becomes more clearly defined, the researcher should ask herself questions such as:

1. Am I free of bias on this topic that might imperil my objectivity? If I do have some preconceived views—which would be normal in many problem areas—can I be scientifically objective in the design and conduct of the study?
2. Is the problem area one in which research will be helpful to my agency, institution, or program, or of value to other professionals? Will it be helpful to me in my career and professional development?
3. Does the problem meet the scope, significance, or other requirements of the institution I am affiliated with or the publication to which I would plan to submit a report?
4. Has similar research been done and, if so, is there justification for replicating it (repeating it in another setting or with different subjects to determine whether the findings will be repeated)? Or will my research effort extend or enrich the earlier line of investigation?

5. Can I obtain needed administrative support and cooperation to carry out the study successfully? Will access to needed subjects or other resources necessary for the study be available? Will it meet "human subjects protection" guidelines?

6. Can the concepts or variables included in the design that I am considering be made operational, in the sense that they can be identified and measured? Do instruments exist that can be used, or will it be necessary to create, test, and validate them, to carry out the study?

Customarily, the researcher will seek assistance in making such judgments or in developing detailed operational plans. If he is a graduate student planning to write a dissertation or a thesis, advice may be sought from faculty advisors or research seminar members or from other resource persons in the university. If the study is to be carried out as a joint venture, representatives of the collaborating agencies should be involved in making concrete plans.

OBTAINING APPROVAL FOR THE STUDY

At this point, formal approval must normally be obtained to carry out the study. If it is being done as a scholarly thesis or dissertation, usually a graduate faculty committee is selected to review and approve a detailed proposal or outline of the study (see Chapter 10). In many cases, this committee would have been formed at an earlier point, and its members would have assisted the student in developing her plan or might have met to consider earlier versions of the proposal. However, at this stage the committee must give official approval to the plan, which then serves as a contract which the researcher must live up to in doing the study.

If the research plan is being submitted as a response to an advertised "request for proposals," the individual researcher or team would prepare it according to the requirements or specifications of the organization that is prepared to fund the study. If it is being submitted to a government agency or foundation grants committee, or even if it is being carried out as an "in-house" research study by a recreation and park agency or a professional society, a similar process is normally followed.

In addition, the study may require permissions from those in charge of the setting where the work is to be done. The researcher may also need to obtain permission to proceed from a "human-subjects review" committee, and, if the study is to receive support from a professional society or to be cosponsored by other organizations, it will need to be reviewed and approved by them.

If the study being initiated is an evaluation study, it may not need to go through such procedures. However, normally agency administrators should be consulted to approve a plan for evaluation of programs, personnel, or other elements. And, while it is not necessary to gain the permission of staff members whose work is being reviewed, they should be fully briefed on the purposes of the study and involved as much as possible in the formulation of study instruments and the study's actual administration.

CONDUCTING RESEARCH AND ANALYZING DATA

As Figure 9.1 shows, later steps in the research process involve actually carrying out study procedures and analyzing and interpreting the data that will have been gathered. These stages of the investigation are described here briefly and in fuller detail in the chapters that follow.

It has sometimes been said that the most difficult and creative task in research is to identify a good subject and to develop a sound proposal and that the process of actually carrying out the research is relatively simple.

While there is some truth to this, the actual implementation of the study is critical. In gathering data, careful supervision must ensure that all conditions are uniform, that investigators or observers are carefully trained and objective in their work, that research instruments are reliable, that the recording of data is consistent and accurate, and that possible pitfalls to good research are noted and avoided.

If difficulties are encountered, it may be necessary to change original plans with respect to sampling procedures, timing of research steps, or similar elements. If changes are minor, they can normally be done without obtaining the approval of the advising committee or sponsoring group. If they are more serious, it is best to seek such approval rather than risk later challenges to the procedures followed.

In academic settings, if the changes in the study plan are fundamental, it might be necessary to reconvene the advising committee to consider and approve them. In the case of a study funded by an outside agency, periodic reports of study progress that are often required in such projects should include accurate statements of changes in research procedures.

From the very outset, the format of questions asked in questionnaire surveys or interviews or in other forms of data-gathering should be designed to permit efficient and convenient tabulation, analysis, and interpretation. As later chapters will show, even in interpretive studies relying heavily on observation and subjective analysis by the researcher, it is desirable to use systematic ways of recording verbal statements, forms of social behavior, or other study data.

Even while data gathering goes on, preliminary analysis of the data may be done. Sometimes questionnaires or other instruments may be changed during the course of a study as a result of such analysis. When all information has been gathered, the data are fully analyzed. Decisions regarding the research questions and/or hypotheses must be made and the results fully interpreted and discussed in relation to future research needs.

PREPARATION OF STUDY REPORTS

Every research study should conclude with a final report that summarizes its purpose and methodology and presents the findings, both in purely factual terms and also with interpretation of their meaning. Major conclusions are developed, and recommendations either for action or further study may be presented. Depending on the sponsorship of the study, the report may be a lengthy and scholarly one—as in a master's thesis or doctoral dissertation—or a brief, factual account for in-house review.

Research findings may also be published in professional journals, general magazines, or even through the major newspaper chains or press associations. Researchers may also disseminate their work through conferences and research symposia, lectures at colleges or universities, or other professional society meetings.

SUMMARY

Six major steps are involved in carrying out research: (1) identifying broad problem areas; (2) developing problem statements, research questions, and/or hypotheses; (3) preparing study plans and formal proposals that document the need for the research and outline study elements and procedures; (4) conducting the research; (5) analyzing and interpreting data; and (6) preparing final reports.

Before initiating a study, the researcher should examine his personal motivations or purposes for doing research, since they are likely to influence the choice of a research topic. It is also possible to undertake research under several different kinds of auspices, which may provide special kinds of support or assistance. Identifying a problem area is a key step in research; it may begin with a simple, casual question or point of curiosity, but must be transformed into a more detailed, analytical, and precise question that lends itself to systematic investigation. The researcher should ask a number of specific questions about the potential research topic, in terms of its significance and researchability, as well as her own interest in it and suitability for investigating the area. With fuller exploration and reworking, the research question is transformed into a detailed statement of the problem, and ultimately a convincing study proposal.

QUESTIONS AND ACTIVITIES

1. What are the key factors to be considered in selecting a problem area for possible investigation?
2. Probably the key step in developing a plan for a research study is the identification of specific, concrete research questions or hypotheses directed at the study of a broad problem area. What are some of the important qualities of such questions or hypotheses?

3. The class is divided into two teams, and each team into several sub-groups. Each subgroup then identifies and briefly describes a possible problem area in recreation, parks, and leisure studies. They then exchange written summaries of these problem areas with a subgroup in the other team. Each subgroup must develop a specific research question based on the problem area it has been given. Subgroups then report their results to the class for discussion.

4. Similar subgroups select research reports in professional journals. Reviewing these reports, paired subgroups attempt to identify three elements in them: (1) the overall problem area; (2) the statement of the specific issue or area of concern; and (3) the questions that the research seeks to answer or the hypotheses that are to be tested. They then compare their findings with those of the group with which they have been paired.

ENDNOTES

1. Bruce Chadwick, Howard Bahr, and Stan Albrecht, *Social Science Research Methods* (Englewood Cliffs, NJ: Prentice-Hall, 1984): 28.
2. Karla Henderson, *Dimensions of Choice: A Qualitative Approach to Recreation, Parks, and Leisure Research* (State College, PA: Venture Publishing, 1991): 102.
3. F. S. C. Northrop, cited in Claire Selltiz, Lawrence Wrightsman, and Stuart Cook, *Research Methods in Social Relations* (New York: Holt, Rinehart and Winston, 1976): 11.
4. Neil Salkind, *Exploring Research* (New York: Macmillan, 1991): 44.
5. Emanuel Mason and William Bramble, *Understanding and Conducting Research* (New York: McGraw-Hill, 1977): 59.
6. Earl Babbie, *The Practice of Social Research* (Belmont, CA: Wadsworth, 1992): 106.
7. Adapted from Henderson, *Dimensions of Choice,* 103.

Developing the
Research Proposal

The importance of the student's first formal proposal is measured by the fact that in most instances the decision to permit the student to embark on a thesis or dissertation is made solely on the basis of that document. The quality of the writing in the proposal is likely to be used by advisors as a basis for judging the clarity of thought that has preceded the study, the degree of facility with which it will be implemented if approved, and the skill of presentation the student will bring to reporting the results. In sum, the proposal is a document in which the student will reveal whether there is a reasonable hope that he can conduct any research project at all.[1]

. . . if you were interested in conducting a social science research project, it would be a good idea to prepare a research proposal for your own purposes, even if you weren't required to do so by your instructor or a funding agency. If you are going to invest your time and energy in such a project, you should do what you can to ensure a return on that investment.[2]

INTRODUCTION

A key step in the research process is to develop a research proposal. This represents a carefully designed and written plan for doing the research, including a clear statement of the problem and the purposes or hypotheses of the investigation, a review of the related literature, and a step-by-step outline of the methodology to be followed. Usually the proposal is submitted for review and approval by a faculty committee or other group before the researcher is authorized to conduct the study.

This chapter describes the process of preparing a research proposal, describing the key elements that they normally contain and offering a number of illustrations of how different sections may be phrased. It is intended as a general guideline, rather than as a precise model to be followed and is primarily concerned with academic research proposals for graduate theses, projects, or dissertations, although it also applies to other types of proposals.

ROLE OF THE PROPOSAL

Krathwohl describes the way in which many students tend to regard the research process. The typical novice in this field, he writes:

> . . . envisions the researcher as one who dreams up creative ideas, the needed resources miraculously appear, and the hero, in a state of eager anticipation, begins his investigation.[3]

The reality of course is that developing a proposal is a complex task, which may involve careful preparation and possibly a drawn-out series of presentations and revisions before the plan is finally approved. The preparation of a written proposal forces the researcher to face hard questions in advance and makes it possible to determine whether the proposed study is likely to be significant and whether the design for its investigation is appropriate to the problem being studied.

Locke and Spirduso point out that the completed research proposal in a college or university graduate program serves three functions: (1) it communicates the student's research plans to those who may give consultation and advice; (2) it serves as a detailed plan of action; and (3) it constitutes a bond of agreement, or contract, between the student and his or her advisors.[4] Similarly, in a proposal that is placed before a foundation or other funding agency for support, or that is submitted in a bid to carry out an advertised study, the proposal provides the basis for reviewing the researcher's intentions and judging the intended study.

As described in Chapter 9, a research proposal normally begins with the identification of a problem area, which in turn is refined or distilled into a specific research question. Following a thorough review of the literature, major decisions are made regarding the specific purposes or hypotheses of the research and the design that it will follow. Variables are identified, and the data-gathering procedures selected. All of these elements must be fitted into a proposal that presents a full and accurate picture of the researcher's intentions.

Although research proposals are normally expected to follow the guidelines just outlined, in some cases they may be less detailed in their statement of purposes, hypotheses, or procedures. For example, in qualitative research, Henderson suggests that some proposals may legitimately consist of loosely structured, flexible statements of study purposes and procedures. She argues that seeking the "perfect" research design in advance may cause unnecessary delay in undertaking an investigation, commenting:

> Probably the best advice is to make a decision about a topic and the methods and techniques that seem most appropriate and then "just do it. . . ."

It is important to get into the real world, begin to understand a phenomenon, and then decide how to proceed next. . . . Researchers do take risks and for many of us, that is what makes our research so exciting.[5]

Despite this view, most organizations that sponsor research studies *do* require formal and detailed proposals before approving their initiation.

FORMAT OF RESEARCH PROPOSALS

The authors of this text have done graduate study or served on the graduate faculties in recreation, park, and leisure-studies departments of nine well-known universities. In no two of them were the required formats of thesis or dissertation proposals exactly alike. However, they all tended to require that certain common elements appear in research proposals. While the names of these elements may vary from institution to institution, their essential functions are the same.

Key Elements in the Proposal

Typically, most academic research proposals contain three sections, or chapters, as they are often called. These chapters consist of the *Introduction,* the *Literature Review,* and the *Methodology.* They include the following subelements:

Chapter One: Introduction
1. Introduction
2. Statement of the Problem
3. Purposes and/or Hypotheses
4. Definitions of Terms
5. Limitations and Delimitations

Chapter Two: Literature Review
1. Summary and Discussion of Related Research
2. Implications of Literature Review for Proposed Study

Chapter Three: Methodology
1. Study Design
2. Study Variables: Subjects and Settings
3. Sampling Procedures
4. Data-Gathering Instruments and Procedures
5. Data-Analysis Plan
6. Study Timetable
7. Permissions and Human Subjects Approval

Manner of Presentation

The writing style of the proposal should be simple, matter-of-fact, and very clear and precise. Slang or overly light or humorous usages are to be avoided, as are excessively technical phrases or unnecessarily elaborate language. What is particularly important is that all statements are understandable and can be documented or supported and that they flow in a logical sequence in terms of conveying to the reader the purpose and methodology of the proposed research. The author of the proposal must be able to defend his plan before an examining committee—in terms of the need for the study, its conceptual framework, and the actual research process that is advanced.

It is essential that the physical appearance of the proposal be highly professional and attractive. Usually, it should be double-spaced and should either be neatly typed or computer-generated (different graduate faculties may specify the exact nature of the typing that may be required, and other details such as weight of paper, width of margins, nature of headings, and similar details). References and other format elements should follow specified style guidelines, which often are based on an approved publications style manual.[6] The proposal should be carefully proofread and free of all errors or handwritten corrections. Since it is a reflection of the researcher's scholarly capability and degree of motivation and effort, it should convey a very positive impression to the reviewer!

DETAILED DESCRIPTION OF PROPOSAL ELEMENTS

Title

The title should be fairly brief, but should contain a very clear indication of the major thrust of the proposed study or the key elements that are contained in the study. Normally, a study title would not be presented as a question or as a declarative statement. Instead, it usually takes the form of a descriptive caption, sometimes with a semicolon followed by an explanatory phrase or qualifying phrase. Examples of several titles which illustrate typical kinds of study headings follow:

Sex-Role Stereotypes and Evaluations of Administrative Performance by Municipal Recreation and Park Administrators

Imaginal Rehearsal Training: A Technique for Improving Simulation Training for Park Law Enforcement Officers

Data-Based Research in Therapeutic Recreation: State of the Art

Park and Recreation Directors' Perceptions of Organizational Goals

Social Interaction, Affect, and Leisure

The Effects of Direct and Indirect Competition on Children's State Anxiety

Systematic Observation of Use Levels, Campsite Selection, and Visitor Characteristics at a High Mountain Lake

The Publications Manual of the American Psychological Association presents guidelines for writing titles of published articles, which apply also to proposal titles:

> . . . avoid words that serve no useful purpose; they increase length and can mislead indexers. For example, the words *method* and *results* do not normally appear in a title, nor should such redundancies as "A Study of" or "An Experimental Investigation of" begin a title. Do not use abbreviations in a title . . . . The recommended length for a title is 12 to 15 words.[7]

Chapter One

The first major section of the proposal, Chapter One, is intended to provide a clear picture of the problem area, the specific research question or questions that the research is designed to investigate, and its actual purposes and/or hypotheses. In addition, it may clarify the terms used in the study by providing definitions and should indicate the ways in which the investigation is to be limited, either through the researcher's intention or for other reasons. It contains the following subsections:

Introduction

This is an opening statement of the problem and describes it briefly. It is almost like an abstract, which is the summary section (usually about 300 or 400 words) that appears in the beginning of many thesis or dissertation reports or articles in research journals. An article abstract, however, is usually presented in the *past* tense, since it describes work that *has* been done. Instead, the Introduction in a research proposal normally describes the problem area in the *present* tense and the proposed study plan—what *will* be done—in the *future* tense.

Within two or three pages, the proposal should give a concise picture of the area of investigation, the specific problem or research question under study, and the intended research strategy. After reading the Introduction, one should have a clear idea of the problem and the basic thrust of the research. An abridged example of an introduction intended to achieve these purposes follows:

> This study is concerned with the impact of selected off-road recreational vehicles on the natural environment in selected state parks in the midwest region of the United States. It seeks to measure the extent of damage caused by different types of vehicles and to learn both the factors related to more serious negative environmental impact and the effectiveness of different types of control procedures in limiting such negative impact.

The rapidly growing use of off-road vehicles such as snowmobiles or four-wheel-drive jeeps or dune buggies has been shown to have a serious environmental impact on different outdoor recreation environments. State and federal park officials have sought to develop policies and regulations to protect vegetation and wildlife from such incursions, while at the same time making it possible for those recreationists who enjoy the use of off-road vehicles to do so in appropriate settings.

This study will identify a sample of five park areas in each of the state park systems of four Midwestern states. They will include examples of different types of areas that have been described in classification systems like the Recreation Opportunity Spectrum, such as wilderness, primitive, natural, historic, and intensive-use areas.

Over a four-season period (fall, winter, spring, summer), the investigation will examine each of the selected parks through direct monitoring of park areas, measurement of physical forms of environmental damage, measurement of types and volume of off-road vehicle use, determination of park policies and restrictions regarding the use of vehicles, and the effectiveness of such policies and regulations.

Since a key function of the introduction is to show why the study needs to be done, many proposals include a subsection titled "Need for the Study" within the Introduction.

Statement of the problem

This section provides a more detailed discussion of the problem area, showing its dimensions or background more fully, summarizing its implications in terms of professional significance or theory development, and giving the reader a fuller understanding of what has been learned thus far by other researchers. Statistics may be cited, and the literature may be discussed briefly; there may also be a historical review, if appropriate. In developing the background, it is best to:

> . . . demonstrate the logical continuity between previous and present work. Develop the problem with enough breadth and clarity to make it generally understood by as wide a professional audience as possible. Do not let the goal of brevity mislead you into writing a statement intelligible only to the specialist.[8]

In discussing controversial issues, it is essential to avoid animosity or overly impassioned opinion statements. Instead, a simple statement that certain studies support one position and other studies support others is preferable to an extensive but inconclusive essay or a one-sided presentation of a partisan argument. When this section of the proposal emphasizes the theoretical background of the proposed study, it may be referred to as the Conceptual

Framework. It is important that this section not simply repeat the points covered in the introduction. Instead, it provides a fuller discussion and overview of the background of the problem and concludes with a concise statement of the research question or questions. For example, a problem statement based on the Introduction just presented would stress (1) the need to gain a comprehensive and systematic picture of the impact of off-road recreational vehicles on the environment and (2) the need to identify the measures that have been used to control such vehicles and to learn their degree of success.

Purposes and/or hypotheses

This section of the proposal presents a specific, detailed statement of the thrust of the intended research. At this stage, an important decision must be made with respect to the study: whether it is to test one or more hypotheses through statistical analysis. It is sometimes assumed that the *only* kind of worthwhile study is based on hypothesis testing, which is normally associated with experimental research. As shown earlier, however, a majority of published sociological articles in a recent period were based on survey studies. Similarly, it has been shown that 94 percent of all research studies reported in a recognized recreation research journal over a five-year period involved surveys, rather than other research designs.[9] Typically, relatively few surveys involve formal hypotheses.

Therefore, the proposal may simply contain a statement of purposes of the research. For example, in a study designed to determine the effect of increased fees and charges on certain population groups in public recreation and park programs within a designated region of the country, the following major purposes and related subpurposes might be advanced:

Purpose No. 1

To examine the impact of new and increased fees and charges on participation by selected special population groups in public recreation and park programs in the Delaware Valley region.

Subpurposes

a. To measure the impact of new and increased fees and charges on recreation participation in selected settings by the following population groups: (1) persons with physical or mental disabilities; (2) elderly persons; and (3) economically disadvantaged persons.

b. To determine the specific program areas or facilities (i.e., sports and games, arts and crafts, trip programs, adult classes, etc., or use of community centers, swimming pools, skating rinks, etc.) which have had the sharpest increase in fees and charges, and then to measure the specific rates of increased or decreased participation in each of these types of programs or facilities.

Purpose No. 2

To analyze management techniques employed in determining the level of fees and charges and the methods used in presenting them to the public, including possible "waiver" or "scholarship" arrangements with special populations.

Subpurposes

a. To identify any special measures which may have been taken to ensure that individuals are not excluded from participation, such as the use of special rates, discounts, fee waivers, "free" sessions or days, or work-exchange practices for individuals with disabilities, families on welfare, elderly persons, or other groups with special needs. Linked to this, to measure the degree of success of such practices in terms of participation by special populations.

b. To identify techniques that have been used effectively to increase revenues through fees and charges without negative public feedback or decline in participation and to develop a set of guidelines based on these practices. Linked to this subpurpose, to determine whether the public's perception and support of public recreation and park programs has been influenced by such fiscal practices and whether governmental support of leisure-service agencies has been affected by them as well.

Examples of hypotheses

Chapters 3 and 9 in this book define and describe the use of hypotheses. If the study proposal includes hypotheses, they might be formulated to test such assumptions as the following.

1. Working hypotheses
   a. Selected administrative policies or procedures may be useful in modifying the effect of excluding special populations from program participation because of increased fees and charges.
   b. Fees and charges may be successfully applied in certain types of communities, such as wealthy suburban townships or smaller communities, but may not be feasible in others, such as high-density central city areas.
2. Statistical hypotheses
   a. Participation by certain population groups will be significantly decreased by the imposition of new or higher fees, in contrast with other population groups or with past participation.
   b. The imposition of fees and charges will result in a significant increase in participation by some population groups.

In framing statistical hypotheses, the following guidelines are helpful. Normally, hypotheses have five key characteristics: (1) They should be stated in declarative form; (2) they should identify and describe a relationship between two or more variables; (3) they should be testable through empirical measurement that lends itself to statistical confirmation; (4) they should be so clearly stated that there is no ambiguity in the variables or the relationship that is being tested; and (5) they should lend themselves (particularly in the case of applied research) to developing a solution or outcome to a problem recognized as a key area of difficulty in the field.

Frequently, several hypotheses will be advanced to test a variety of possible relationships among study variables. For example, in a field investigation of the relationship between leisure participation and leisure satisfaction and perceived wellness, Ragheb tested the following hypotheses:

1. The more participation in leisure activities there is, the higher will be the perceived level of wellness.
2. Participation in leisure categories (i.e., mass media, reading, social activities, outdoor activities, sports activities, spectatorship, cultural activities, and hobbies) relates positively to perceived wellness and its five components.
3. Satisfaction gained from leisure is positively associated with perceived wellness.
4. There are positive relationships among leisure satisfaction components and perceived wellness components.
5. Perceived wellness is related positively to health satisfaction, family satisfaction, financial satisfaction, leisure satisfaction, and work satisfaction.[10]

In contrast to research or statistical hypotheses that predict positive relationships between two or more variables, the "null" hypothesis states essentially that no significant relationship will be found. Salkind offers several examples of typical null hypotheses:

1. There will be no difference in the average scores of ninth graders and the average scores of twelfth graders on the ABC memory test.
2. There is no relationship between the number of hours of study and the number of items correct on a spelling test.
3. There is no difference in voting patterns as a function of political party.
4. The brand of ice cream preferred is independent of the buyer's age, gender, and income.[11]

If the null hypothesis is rejected by study findings which demonstrate that relationships do exist, based on a level of statistical significance that rules out chance as a causative factor, the conclusion must be that the assumed relationships have been confirmed. Because of their reliance on statistical evidence, Salkind goes on to point out that most correlational, causal-comparative, and experimental studies use null hypotheses, while historical and descriptive studies usually do not.[12]

In addition to stating the purposes and/or hypotheses of the proposed study, this section may include a brief discussion of the rationale underlying these elements. Based on the preceding background section, it should be possible to make clear the logic behind each of the hypotheses or the way in which the purposes, when carried out, will contribute to fuller understanding of the study. This section may be made more explicit in the Literature Review section of the proposal.

Definitions of terms

This is a brief section consisting of a series of definitions of the key terms or concepts found in the study proposal. Since words like "recreation" or "leisure" may have various meanings, it is important to clarify the way they are being used in the proposal. Other words, which may be less familiar to the reader, may also require more precise definitions. The term "environmental quality," for example, may require a definition drawn from a governmental handbook, specifying exactly what it means and possibly even indicating levels of quality. Other terms like "professionalization," "mental retardation," "senility," or professional processes like "zero-based budgeting" or "orientation" may also require a clear definition.

Each definition should be as brief as possible, rather than a rambling discussion or essaylike presentation. The following distinction can be made between "operational" and "attribute" definitions:

> *Operational* definitions are to be distinguished from . . . *attribute* definitions, in which something is defined by saying what it *consists of.* For example, a crude attribute definition of a college might be "An organization containing faculty and students, teaching a variety of subjects beyond the high-school level." An operational definition of university might be "An organization found in *The World Almanac*'s listing of 'Colleges and Universities.'"[13]

Operational definitions differ sharply from dictionary definitions, which tend to rely on comparisons or synonyms, to give the meaning of a term or to help translate a word not known into words already known. In contrast, the operational definition provides a complete, independent understanding of the term. Usually it is best to draw definitions from widely accepted, authoritative sources. However, it is always possible to present your own definition of a term as it is being used in the proposal, with a logical justification or explanation as necessary.

The following example of a definition of special populations, which might be used in a study of the impact of increased fees and charges on such populations, contains both operational and attribute elements.

> As a general definition, *special populations* refers to any subgroup within the community which, either because of disability or impairment of a

physical or mental nature, or because of economic or other social factors, is limited in recreational participation, and therefore requires special programming or adapted activities and facilities. In the proposed study, the preliminary plan will be to identify three special populations: (1) persons with mental or physical disabilities (including visually impaired persons, those with auditory, orthopedic, or neurological impairment, and those with mental retardation or mental illness); (2) economically disadvantaged persons, based on federal poverty guidelines; and (3) those over the age of 65.

Limitations and delimitations of proposed study

These refer to areas of possible weakness in the methodology of the study plan or to exclusions that are deliberately planned. Isaac and Michael comment that an important step in planning research is to ask:

> What are the limitations surrounding your study and within which conclusions must be confined? What limitations exist in your methods or approach—sampling restrictions, uncontrolled variables, faulty instrumentation, and other compromises to internal and external validity?[14]

Limitations. These are certain conditions of the study methodology that you cannot overcome or strengthen, and about which you are warning the reader. For example, it may be a limitation that you are drawing information only from program leaders rather than participants, or that you are exploring events that occurred several years ago, with the likelihood that participants' memories are somewhat faulty.

Another limitation may be that you have not been granted access to a particular facility or source of information, or that you will be unable to check the reliability of a given test procedure. If these are too serious, it may be that members of a study advisory committee might feel that the study design is inadequate or unacceptable and that a new plan must be submitted. Normally, however, statements of limitations are accepted as an honest presentation of possible weaknesses of the study, made in advance, rather than in the form of an apologetic rationalization, at a later point. In some cases, when there are serious limitations in the proposal plan, the researcher may choose to describe it as an "exploratory study," which suggests that he is opening up the subject for research with admittedly crude methods and with the expectation that future researchers will apply more rigorous methods.

Delimitations. These represent decisions made by the researcher in which the study plan *deliberately* excludes certain areas of information or limits the scope or depth of the investigation. For example, setting limits to the population to be examined or the region to be studied would be types of delimitations.

Realistically, many research studies have too broad a scope or complex a problem and try to do too much with inadequate resources. Therefore, it may be desirable to reduce the scope of the study and to carry it out in greater depth and with more rigorous procedures. To illustrate, a study of therapeutic recreation service in mental health centers might deal with the entire nation, a region, a state, or a single community. With limited resources, it might be desirable to delimit it to a narrow geographical focus.

The proposed time frame of the study may impose another type of delimitation on the research. For example, it may be necessary for practical reasons to limit observation of state park visitors to only two seasons of the year, rather than all four seasons, or to operate a short-term rehabilitative camping program on a week-long basis, rather than a longer period of time.

Chapter Two: Literature Review

Although earlier sections of the proposal may include references to the literature, it is at this point that a full-scale review is normally provided. The Literature Review's purpose is to give the proposed study a scholarly background, by discussing it conceptually and by showing the kinds of research that have already been done on the subject, along with their findings. It also has the purpose within an academic setting of assuring the faculty committee guiding the study that the graduate student planning to carry out the research is highly knowledgeable within her area of special interest.

Neuman points out that the literature review is based on the assumption that scientific research is not an activity of isolated "hermits" who ignore one another's work; instead, it recognizes that research findings accumulate over time and build on the work of earlier investigators. He writes:

> [Research] is a collective effort of many researchers who share their results with each other and who pursue knowledge as a community. Although some studies may be especially important and individual researchers may become famous, a specific research project is just a tiny part of the overall process of creating knowledge.[15]

The scope of the research topic should be defined and illustrated in the literature review. In searching the literature, it is important to strike a balance between covering too broad and too narrow a range of subtopics. Too wide a search may result in a lack of focus or in superficial treatment of some issues or research findings. Too narrow a search may mean that potentially important studies or subtopics are not covered at all.

Literature as source of conceptual framework

As indicated earlier, it is desirable whenever possible to place the intended study within a carefully thought out and documented conceptual framework. This means that both the basic principles and the methodology of the research are keyed to a relevant and recognized body of theory within the social or behavioral sciences or developed in applied fields such as recreation and leisure studies. There are numerous examples in the literature of recreation, park, and leisure-studies research projects carried out based on such theoretical underpinnings. Several examples follow.

▼ FOR EXAMPLE

Example 1. Allison and Geiger, in examining the nature of leisure activities among Chinese-American elderly persons, based their research on two competing theoretical orientations with respect to intercultural contact: the *melting pot theory* and the *ethnicity thesis.*[16]

Example 2. In analyzing the motivations and behaviors of adult contract bridge participants, Scott and Godbey examined "social" and "serious" players from the perspective of *symbolic interactionism*—an approach that emphasizes the importance of face-to-face interaction in the "generation and activation of cultural elements."[17]

Example 3. In a study of family involvement in recreational groups, Stokowski and Lee based their rationale and investigative process on *social network* theory, an influential approach to analyzing social behavior and group relationships in community life.[18]

Example 4. Mobily and associates, in a study of the participation of elderly persons in the Midwest in exercise programs, applied two popular models of leisure behavior *(self-determination* and *perceived competence)* rather than the widely accepted assumption that exercise is carried on chiefly for health purposes.[19]

In some cases, such theoretical frameworks may be taken directly from contemporary research approaches or from textbooks in the social and behavioral sciences and applied to recreation, parks, and leisure studies by the individual researcher. In other cases, the researcher may be following up on a line of investigation already initiated by other leisure researchers, applying the concepts to a new problem or research issue.

A considerable number of recently published studies have employed a theoretical framework characterized as a "feminist" perspective. For example, Henderson analyzed selected professional literature dealing with the role of girls and women in recreation, parks, and leisure services from 1907 to 1990, within a gender-related social-role framework.[20]

Literature retrieval process

In the search for relevant sources for the literature review, Salkind suggests that several kinds of materials may be used. These include:

1. *General sources,* which are references of a very general nature on a topic and which provide a useful overview or context for the research effort

2. *Secondary sources,* which are "once removed" from actual studies in the field, consisting of review papers, textbooks, anthologies, or syntheses of other research

3. *Primary sources,* which are direct accounts of research, appearing as journal articles, abstracts, or seminar presentations.

Although the chief sources of useful citations in recreation, parks, and leisure studies research are scholarly journals and other professional publications, the other kinds of references suggested by Salkind are also useful.

In gathering materials for a literature review in the leisure-studies field, it is helpful to use the following techniques:

1. Issue-by-issue examination of the major publications likely to contain relevant articles, usually extending back in time for several years

2. Follow-up of research references found in the bibliographies or footnotes of these articles

3. Examination of textbooks in areas related to the research subject

4. Use of subject indices identifying articles on a wide range of topics in areas such as sociology, psychology, education, urban planning, or environmental education, drawn from many publications and published on an annual or semiannual basis

5. Use of general subject indices, such as the *Reader's Guide to Periodical Literature*

6. Use of annual collections of abstracts of studies reported at research symposia of professional societies

7. Other special bibliographies or reports of research within specialized subject areas in recreation and leisure studies

Increasingly, computer searches are used to locate relevant articles conveniently, although this method may have the disadvantage of producing numerous articles only vaguely related to the topic or in difficult-to-locate publications. The use of "keywords," which identify the major themes found in a research report, is essential in exploring such sources. The literature retrieval process may also be facilitated by the use of interlibrary loans of theses or dissertations in microfilm or microfiche form.

A listing of the most useful journals or professional publications and of a number of subject indices and special databases related to leisure studies appears in the appendix (see page 325). Finally, if you cannot find relevant research that bears directly on the issue that you are planning to investigate, you may cite related studies that provide helpful information, parallel findings, or useful research designs and methods. Rather than indicate that yours is a poor proposal, this might support the need for your research, in that it is directed at a significant *gap* in the available research literature.

Organization of the literature review

In terms of presentation, the literature review usually takes the form of an essay that moves from the general topic or problem area to the more specific issue or question you are researching. It should be carefully organized so that it is not simply a collection of random citations or earlier research findings. Instead, each major topic, subtopic, or line of investigation should be blocked out in a logical sequence (frequently this is done chronologically) with appropriate transitions from area to area. It should conclude with a statement that summarizes the present state of research-based knowledge, identifies areas where there is a need for fresh research, and, ideally, confirms the potential importance of the study you are proposing in terms of what has gone before.

Chapter Three: Methodology

Customarily, the third major section of the proposal includes a detailed description of the methods that will be used to conduct the research.

Study design

This section should specify the nature of the study design (survey, case study, experimental, etc.), and give a brief description of the nature of the investigation. For example, it might state that the study will consist of an experiment carried on with preschool-age children in a playground setting, in which their use of several different kinds of play equipment will be observed and analyzed.

Study variables: subjects and settings

The variables, both dependent and independent, that will be the focus of the investigation will be identified. The methodology section should show how they are to be operationalized; i.e., how they will be described in terms that can be measured.

In research studies where variables will be introduced or controlled by the investigator, as in experimental studies, it may be necessary to describe the different levels at which a given variable may be applied. For example, the responses of players on a team to different coaching techniques may be categorized at different levels, and the coaching methods themselves may be graded in intensity, frequency, or in other ways.

The methodology section should give specific information regarding the subjects who will be involved in the study, including who they are, how they are to be selected, and other relevant information about them (see Chapter 12, which deals with the sampling process in detail). It should also indicate the locations where research will be carried out or the agencies that may be involved.

Data-gathering instruments and procedures

The actual methods that will be used to gather data should be described here, including how the observations, interviews, or surveys will be carried out, or how groups will be organized and tested. The instruments that will be used to gather the data should also be described.

In some cases, the study may require the proposal to include the actual instrument in refined form. In others, it may be acceptable to indicate the nature of the instrument and its subsections or the method that may be used to develop and test it. If the study is to be a historical one, this section might include a description of the sources that will be examined, including an assessment of their availability. If the researcher plans to develop an entirely new instrument, he should indicate how it is to be formulated and tested, with emphasis on determining its validity and reliability.

If the study will require assistant researchers to interview subjects, observe participants, or play other roles in the study, the methodology section should indicate how they will be recruited and trained to ensure consistent performance and objective recording on their part.

Data-analysis plan

The techniques that will be used to analyze the data are presented in this section. If the study is to be primarily quantitative in nature, the statistical tests that will be applied should be presented. Particularly if the research proposal includes a number of statistical hypotheses, appropriate tests must be indicated in terms of the kinds of data that will be analyzed. In the case of a historical study, a preliminary plan for organizing the findings according to a sequence of chronological periods might be presented. In a case study, a system for analyzing the data might be suggested—if appropriate, within a theoretical framework described earlier in the proposal.

If the study has a qualitative design, based on observation of a group or groups involved in leisure activity, a systematic method of recording behaviors or events, categorizing them, and arriving at interpretations should be developed. Merely narrating the flow of group interaction or recounting significant episodes will not satisfy the goals of research.

It is critical that this section be carefully reviewed in terms of the stated purposes or hypotheses of the study proposal. The data analysis *must* be planned to ensure that the study's findings are directly relevant to the major thrust of the research. Otherwise, no matter how interesting the investigation, it will not be a success.

Timetable for the investigation

The methodology section may include a listing of the various steps that are to be taken in carrying out the study, in the appropriate sequence, and with a calendar or "flow chart" of the time frame in which they will be accomplished. While graduate students or other professional researchers are not normally held rigidly to such a precise schedule, when a funded research study is carried out under contract with a sponsoring organization, normally it has a set of deadlines for carrying out each step of the investigation and completing the study. Often these steps may be keyed to payment for the work done, as separate sections of the study are carried out satisfactorily. Figure 10.1 shows how the major steps of a study that involves interviewing a number of subjects at selected leisure-service agencies might be laid out on a flow chart over a one-year period.

Budget plan

Particularly if the proposed study is to be funded by an outside agency or foundation, it will be necessary to provide budgetary information. This should be keyed to each stage of the research and should include estimates of all costs, including staff salaries; use of office space; mailing, duplicating, and computer use; travel; and equipment and supplies. In the case of jointly sponsored research studies, the functions of each of the collaborating agencies should be clearly spelled out, along with the shares of expenses or in-kind services to be provided by each.

Permissions and human subjects' approval

The permissions, authorization, or approval statement that will be needed to carry out the study should be identified here. For example, if the investigator plans to carry out an observational study of patients in a mental hospital, or do an evaluation of the recreation program within a penitentiary, it will obviously be necessary to obtain permission from the director of the institution to be studied—and possibly even from the director of the state mental health department or the department of corrections. Similarly, if the researcher intends to carry out the study in cooperation with a professional organization or government agency, or with their approval and under their letterhead, it will be necessary to have this arrangement formally approved.

In the past, medical, psychological, and sociological researchers tended to have a fairly free hand in experimenting with human subjects. Because of a number of serious abuses of subjects that were later disclosed, the Department of Health, Education, and Welfare published an institutional guide in 1971 on the protection of human subjects, and the National Research Act established a national commission in 1974 for this purpose. Today, educational and other institutions sponsoring research are required to establish Institutional Review Boards (IRBs) to approve projects involving human subjects.

The research proposal should therefore include procedural safeguards intended to prevent human subjects from undergoing physical harm or psychological abuse or placing them under undue stress or in legal jeopardy.

FIGURE 10.1 Time frame for conducting study.

	Jan.	Feb.	Mar.	Apr.	May	June	July	Aug.	Sept.	Oct.	Nov.	Dec.
Planning with research team and cooperating agencies		▯										
Selection or development of study instruments			▯									
Interviewer training and selection of study subjects				▯								
Data-gathering: interviewing and follow-up investigation					▯							
Data-analysis and determination of study findings							▯					
Preparation of final report and submission									▯			

Note: As problems come up during the course of the research, this timetable may be revised, and new research strategies or procedures used. In addition, some tasks may be delayed because of difficulties with earlier steps. In some cases, steps of the research process may overlap with one another, more than is shown here.

Provision must be made for privacy, anonymity of subjects, confidentiality of findings, and "informed consent" agreements for study participants.

Normally, when research proposals are first reviewed by a study committee, such permissions and authorizations need not be in hand. However, before final approval is granted and the research study is authorized to get under way, it is customary to require them.

OPTIONAL ELEMENTS IN THE PROPOSAL

In some situations, the proposal may also be required to include a preliminary breakdown of the chapters that will appear in the final report or the sections that it will include. In masters' theses and doctoral dissertations, a set format may be required by the graduate school or graduate research council. In funded research, the contracting organization may indicate the sections that the report must include, and it is therefore not necessary for the proposal to include this information.

As indicated earlier, proposals for funded research studies will also require a detailed preliminary budget. Customarily, they also require a description of the individuals on the study team, with a detailed resumé of their qualifications and research experience or a summary of other studies that the study team has carried out. Since proposals to do funding research are often submitted on a competitive basis, such information helps the sponsoring or granting organization determine the qualifications of the research groups that are applying for a study grant.

Finally, the research proposal normally includes an appendix, which may contain other background information, preliminary drafts of study instruments, maps, listings of agencies to be examined, or similar elements.

This chapter has focused primarily on scholarly studies that are conducted in academic settings or on research being submitted to funding agencies for formal support and sponsorship. Independent research projects may not require such extensive and detailed proposals. Similarly, qualitative research studies may not require this degree of specificity in their proposals or preliminary plans. However, it is equally important for them to have sound literature reviews, conceptual frameworks, and at least a preliminary statement of the study's methodology.

REVIEWING THE RESEARCH PROPOSAL

As indicated earlier, developing a sound research proposal is a major task. Often, when it has been carried out and approved, half the battle has been won. Therefore, the researcher should ask the following kinds of questions before submitting it for consideration or meeting with a faculty committee for final approval.

Introduction

Does this opening section provide a brief but helpful explanation of the problem area and the essential thrust of the study? Is it easily understood? Is unnecessary or irrelevant information presented?

Statement of the Problem

Is the problem area convincingly presented, and does it appear to be a significant one? Is it placed within a logical context, and is it related to other research efforts and to a meaningful conceptual background? Does it end with a presentation of the key questions that the study will attempt to explore?

Purposes and/or Hypotheses

Do these tell us exactly what we need to know—or what the study intends to discover or test? Are the purposes or hypotheses directly in line with the Statement of the Problem, or do they go off in some new directions? Are they sharply focused, in that they tell us in precise, specific terms what we are going to investigate? Is any significant purpose left out, or are there any purposes that are not necessary and make the study too broad?

Definitions, Limitations, and Delimitations

Do these effectively clarify any ambiguous terms or concepts in the proposal, and do they show possible limitations in the methodology and the reasons these exist? Are the delimitations supported by a logical rationale?

Review of the Literature

Has a comprehensive search been carried out, to uncover all important references on the subject? Has any important source, or type of source, been ignored? While chief emphasis should be given to research reports, have other types of documentation—such as quotations from books, professional articles, newspapers, planning studies, etc.—been used? Are all references correctly footnoted? Does the treatment move logically forward in a chronological way, or from a broad analysis of the subject to a sharper focus on the actual key issues of the proposed study? If adequate references dealing with the exact subject of the study could not be found, were other related research findings cited? Does the Literature Review provide support for carrying out the study?

Methodology

Have all of the necessary elements been described, either in a preliminary or finished form—including the design of the proposed research, the nature of the subjects and settings, the instrumentation, sampling process and method of data analysis, the needed permissions or authorizations, and other relevant information? Most important: Will the study, as presented, gather the kinds of data that will relate directly to the purposes and hypotheses of the investigation? Does it meet high professional standards in terms of being a carefully planned, systematic, and rigorous search for knowledge? Will it contribute meaningfully either to effective professional practice or to theory in the field, or to both?

Finally, will the study be feasible? Will it be possible to carry it out, in terms of its scope and complexity, or will it be too difficult or expensive, given the resources of the investigator or study team? Should it be reduced in scope or redesigned to make it more feasible?

SUMMARY

The proposal represents a key step in the conceptualization and design of any research study. Chapter 10 describes the role and format of proposals of various types and discusses in detail the sections that are typically found in most academic or scholarly research proposals. In each case, illustrations are given of how a section might be approached, using case materials drawn from recreation, parks, or leisure-studies research themes.

The chapter concludes with a set of questions that should be asked before submitting a study proposal for approval.

QUESTIONS AND ACTIVITIES

1. Select and review several proposals for research (thesis or dissertation proposals) by graduate students in the recreation, parks, and leisure-studies department. Critically analyze them for their strengths and possible weaknesses.
2. Select a problem statement or research question that was developed by others in question No. 3 in Chapter 9. Then develop a specific statement of purpose or research hypothesis, based on these questions. Review and critically analyze these as a class.
3. Individuals or small groups of students select a research problem and develop brief outlines of the opening section of a proposal for it, including (1) title; (2) introduction; (3) background of the study; and (4) purposes, hypotheses, and rationale. These outlines are presented to the class for discussion.
4. Prepare a literature review on an assigned topic. The review should be approximately three to five pages in length and must include a minimum number of references, such as eight or ten.

ENDNOTES

1. Lawrence Locke and Waneen Spirduso, *Proposals That Work: A Guide for Planning Research* (New York: Teachers College Press, 1972): x.

2. Earl Babbie, *The Practice of Social Research* (Belmont, CA: Wadsworth Publishing Co., 1992): 111.

3. David Krathwohl, *How to Prepare a Research Proposal* (Syracuse, NY: Syracuse University Bookstore, 1966): 3.

4. Locke and Spirduso, *Proposals That Work,* 1–2.

5. Karla Henderson, *Dimensions of Choice: A Qualitative Approach to Recreation, Parks, and Leisure Research* (State College, PA: Venture Publishing, 1991): 105.

6. Widely used style manuals, in addition to the *Publication Manual of the American Psychological Association* (see footnote 7), include:

   Walter Achtert and Joseph Gibaldi, *The MLA Style Manual* (New York: The Modern Language Association of America, 1985).

   John Grossman, ed., *The Chicago Manual of Style* (Chicago: University of Chicago Press, 1993).

   Kate Turabian, *A Manual for Writers of Term Papers, Theses, and Dissertations* (Chicago: University of Chicago Press, 1987).

7. *Publication Manual of the American Psychological Association* (Washington, DC: American Psychological Association, 1983): 22–23.

8. Ibid., 25.

9. Carol Riddick, Meg DeSchriver, and Ellen Weissinger, "A Methodological Review of Research in the Journal of Leisure Research from 1978 to 1982," *Journal of Leisure Research* 16, no. 4 (1984): 314.

10. Mounir Ragheb, "Leisure and Perceived Wellness: A Field Investigation," *Leisure Sciences* 15, no. 1 (1993): 14.

11. Neil Salkind, *Exploring Research* (New York: Macmillan, 1991): 28.

12. Ibid., 29.

13. Stephen Isaac and William Michael, *Handbook in Research and Evaluation* (San Diego, CA: EDITS Publishers, 1980): 4.

14. Ibid., 6.

15. W. Lawrence Neuman, *Social Research Methods: Qualitative and Quantitative Approaches* (Boston: Allyn and Bacon, 1994): 80.

16. Maria Allison and Charles Geiger, "Nature of Leisure Activities Among the Chinese-American Elderly," *Leisure Sciences* 15, no. 4 (1993): 309–19.

17. David Scott and Geoffrey Godbey, "An Analysis of Adult Play Groups: Social Versus Serious Participation in Contract Bridge," *Leisure Sciences* 14, no. 1 (1992): 47–67.

18. Patricia Stokowski and Robert Lee, "The Influence of Social Network Ties on Recreation and Leisure: An Exploratory Study," *Journal of Leisure Research* 23, no. 2 (1991): 95–113.

19. Kenneth Mobily, John Lemke, Lisa Ostiguy, Rebecca Woodard, Tanya Griffee, and Craig Pickens, "Leisure Repertoire in a Sample of Midwestern Elderly: The Case for Exercise," *Journal of Leisure Research* 25, no. 1 (1993): 84–99.

20. Karla Henderson, "A Feminist Analysis of Selected Professional Recreation Literature about Girls/Women from 1907–1990," *Journal of Leisure Recreation* 25, no. 2 (1993): 165–81.

The Role
of Measurement

Numbers and how they are used [are] the essence of measurement in positivistic research. . . . When research questions are asked, they are composed of variables, *or those concepts which compose the questions. In the research process, those variables must be carefully defined so that they can be measured.* Measurement *of variables implies the assignment of numbers according to an established plan, based on the nature of the variables and the level of sophistication or precision desired in the study.[1]*

Qualitative data are collected in the form of words or pictures rather than numbers. The kinds of data collected in qualitative research include interview transcripts, field notes, photographs, audio recordings, videotapes, diaries . . . and anything else that can convey the actual words or actions of people. In their search for understanding, qualitative researchers do not usually attempt to reduce their data to numerical symbols, but rather seek to portray what they have observed and recorded . . .[2]

INTRODUCTION

At the heart of the research process is the need to gather accurate information that will answer research questions or test the hypotheses that have been advanced. With the exception of qualitative research methods and some conceptually oriented, historical, or analytical study designs, most forms of scholarly investigation require the gathering of data that can be numerically analyzed. The process of gathering and quantifying such data through observation, interviews, questionnaire surveys, and similar methods is known as measurement.

This chapter is chiefly concerned with numeric approaches to measurement as they are typically applied in experiments and several types of descriptive research studies. It illustrates methods of converting different kinds of information, such as values, self-concepts, and similar elements, to numbers that can be statistically analyzed. It briefly describes several methods or instruments that are used to gather research data, such as questionnaires, checklists or rating scales; the actual development of such instruments is described in Chapter 13.

Four levels of measurement, including *nominal, ordinal, interval,* and *ratio-level* kinds of data, are presented, along with essential criteria of research instruments and procedures, such as validity and reliability. The chapter concludes with a discussion of the approaches to measurement that are used in qualitative research.

MEASUREMENT PROCESS: THE IMPORTANCE OF NUMBERS

Measurement in numeric terms is a key element in positivistic research designs that have their origins in the physical and natural sciences, such as chemistry, physics, or biology, and that rely heavily on quantitative analysis. Beyond this, numbers are obviously used in most aspects of contemporary life. The need to measure—that is, to accurately determine the size, weight, frequency, or other characteristics of varied phenomena—appears at every turn.

We characterize our jobs in terms of the hours we work, the salaries we are paid, the sales we make, and a host of similar factors that are expressed as numbers.

We watch ball games that are determined by a final numeric score, and we keep count of a player's hits, fouls, touchdowns, or tackles and of the price we pay for tickets and the number of people attending the game.

In hundreds of other ways, we "keep count" in numeric terms throughout life. Similarly, a systematic review of leading research journals makes it clear that a substantial majority of research studies use quantitative measurement of data and report their findings in numeric terms. For example, an informal tabulation of articles in the *Therapeutic Recreation Journal* during the period from mid-1991 to early 1994 showed that 36 articles relied on numeric analysis and reported their findings in quantitative terms, while 20 did not. Even in the latter group of articles, which included a number of philosophical or conceptual essays, case studies of individuals, and model-building papers, frequent use was made of statistical findings from other research reports, particularly in articles summarizing research in given areas.

METHODS OF MEASUREMENT

What techniques are used to gather quantitative data regarding such variables in community recreation and park programs, therapeutic recreation, and other specialized leisure-service fields? Obviously, measurement of such easily quantified elements as participation or accident rates, funding patterns, or the use of volunteers may be routinely done through internal reporting procedures. In actual research studies, such information may be gathered systematically by investigators using survey methods or through the examination of agency records and reports.

The measurement of less tangible variables or those that do not readily present themselves in numeric terms is a more complex task. For example, studies that attempt to measure values or attitudes about leisure pursuits, effects of recreational involvement on self-concepts or life satisfaction, goals and motivations of recreational professionals, and similar subjects would *not* be readily available in agency reports. Indeed, in many cases, they may represent concepts that must be transformed operationally into elements that *can* be measured in numeric terms.

Typically, this is done through the use of measurement instruments such as questionnaires, indexes, or scales that probe such variables through observing behavior or soliciting responses on a range of issues or points that can then be translated into numeric findings. Often professionally validated, published instruments are used.

Example. In a study of individuals with chronic secondary health problems related to spinal cord injury, Coyle, Shank, Kinney, and Hutchins used two instruments (the Center for Epidemiological Studies Depression Scale and the Satisfaction with Life Scale) to measure depression and life satisfaction among subjects.[3] In a survey of therapeutic recreation specialists to determine their reasons for participation in continuing professional education, Langsner employed the Participation Reasons Scale developed at the University of Illinois.[4] Numerous other examples of the use of instruments intended to measure such nontangible variables appear in research journals.

In many cases, leisure-studies researchers are unable to find appropriate tools to measure important elements in their studies. In such cases, they must devise their own survey instruments, interview schedules, scales, or indexes to gather needed data. Such carefully designed and consistently applied instruments and research procedures provide an essential framework for gathering, classifying, and recording data. To illustrate, if several investigators were asked to examine a number of municipal parks or sports areas and to report on their condition, the resulting reports would be likely to vary greatly—*unless* there was agreement in advance as to the kinds of data that should be gathered, and the standards that would be applied. Such issues are usually determined by the choice or development of a data-gathering instrument which specifies exactly how an investigation is to be carried out and provides the framework for questioning, observing, or otherwise recording data. The development of such data-gathering procedures is described in detail in Chapter 13.

First, however, it is essential to examine the nature of the measurement process in two respects: (1) the four key levels of measurement, in terms of the types of data being gathered, that affect the way in which they are analyzed and (2) the important qualities of investigative instruments and procedures, such as validity, reliability, and objectivity.

LEVELS OF MEASUREMENT

The process of assigning a value or numeric score to any observed phenomenon or research variable is known as measurement. It is done on several different levels, commonly identified as *nominal, ordinal, interval,* and *ratio.* Knowledge of these levels is essential for statistical analysis, because each statistical technique is designed for data measured only at certain levels.

Nominal Scales

Nominal-level scales represent the lowest or least sophisticated level of measurement and apply to data which are classified only by *name* (the word *nominal* is drawn from the Latin word *nomen,* meaning name). Examples of subjects of nominal measurement include: *animals* (horses, cows, goats); *trees* (oak, birch, maple, cherry); or *professions* (doctor, lawyer, architect). The categories and the examples within each category have no numerical value and no assigned order of value or precedence, although one could assign numbers to them purely for identification purposes, by listing them as (1) class, (2) workshop, (3) league, etc. But this would only be for convenience in grouping and referring to them; the numbers would have no other purpose. Any statistical procedure that assumes a meaningful order or distance between the categories should not be used.

The measurement of leisure phenomena may obviously involve nominal measures when respondents are asked to identify the types of pursuits they engage in or similar kinds of categorical information. Nominal measures are not sufficient, however, to describe the degree to which they are motivated, possible outcomes of participation, or similar variables that may appear in greater or lesser quantities.

The measurement of leisure itself illustrates this point. Samdahl points out that some researchers have used basic categorical questions in asking respondents to classify situations as "work" or as "leisure." Others, however, assume that leisure has an incremental nature or that there are degrees of "leisureness." She writes:

> An interesting methodological question rises from these different styles of measurement. Is leisure a categorical phenomenon which is either present or absent, or is leisure more effectively represented as a phenomenon which might be present in degrees. . . . characterized by lower levels of perceived freedom and/or motivation?[5]

Ordinal Scales

This is the next lowest level of measurement. It indicates not only that things differ from each other by belonging in different groups, but that they are recognizedly different in amount or degree and fit into a given *order.*

Ordinal scales are the result of ranking procedures and show the relative positions of individuals within a group, usually based on information about the relative amount of some trait possessed by subjects, such as intelligence or performing skill. For example, tennis players might be ranked in the following sequence: (1) beginner, (2) novice, (3) intermediate, (4) advanced, (5) tournament level. These show the relative level of ability for each rank or category, although they do not provide an exact measurement of the amount of skill or the difference between different ranks or groups. While these categories may be based on quantitative measures of performance, in themselves they have no absolute values or scoring weights, and the differences between adjacent ranks may not be equal. The characteristic of *ordering* (placing in a rank order) is the sole mathematical property of this level.

In many questionnaires, rating scales, or other research instruments, respondents are asked to make judgements along a range of possible reactions. In so-called Likert-type tests (see page 177), replies may range from excellent to very poor or from full agreement to full disagreement. Although the replies to such questions do not have any inherent numeric value, they represent an ordinal type of data and may be transformed into quantitative terms.

Interval Scales

This level of measurement implies that the distances between the categories or intervals of measurement are defined in fixed and equal terms. For example, an examination with fifty questions, each worth two points, would provide an interval scale. Each question answered correctly would raise you two points on the scale; each incorrect answer would lower you by two points. The difference between an 88 and a 90 is the same as between a 62 and a 64. Similarly, a thermometer records temperatures in terms of degrees, and a single degree refers to the same amount of heat, whether the temperature is in the 20s or the 40s.

However, an interval scale does not have a true zero point, at which there is nothing of the element being measured. For example, the zero point on a thermometer does not imply a total absence of heat. Thus, interval-level measurement lets us measure the difference between things but not their proportionate size in terms of ratio. It is not possible to say that an I.Q. score of 120 means that an individual is twice as smart as one with an I.Q. of 60.

Ratio Scales

Ratio scales have all the properties of interval scales, with one added feature— they do have a true zero point, at which it is assumed that there is a complete absence of the element being measured. Physical distance provides a useful example; it can be measured in exactly equal units of distance, such as inches, feet, or yards. Yet, it can have a true zero point; for example, if two objects are exactly side-by-side, with no distance between them, or if a car travels *no* distance. Weight too might constitute ratio-level measurement, with the possibility of absolute weightlessness. Ratio-level measurements have all the properties of actual numbers and may be added, divided, or multiplied or expressed in ratio relationships.

Implications of Levels of Measurement

An important rule of statistical analysis is that statistics that are useful at one level of measurement can always be used with higher-level variables, but not with variables measured at lower levels. In other words, if a type of data is interval in nature, statistics that are useful for it can also be used with ratio-level data. However, they could not be used with ordinal or nominal data. This has important implications for the use of parametric and nonparametric tests, as described in Chapter 14.

QUALITY OF MEASUREMENT PROCESSES

In addition to determining the appropriate level at which research data are to be measured, it is essential that research instruments and procedures meet appropriate standards of rigor. Usually, they are judged in terms of three important qualities: *validity, reliability,* and *objectivity.*

Validity

Validity refers to the accuracy of an instrument or procedure in measuring what it seeks or claims to measure. Selltiz and associates point out that, to be useful, data-collection techniques must produce information that is not only relevant but also correct: "Two crucial aspects of correctness are reliability (that is, the extent to which measures give consistent results) and validity (that is, the extent to which they correspond to the 'true' position of the person or object on the characteristic being measured)."[6]

Berk and Rossi comment that in evaluation, as in other research activities, the overriding goal is to achieve high validity; little is learned from evaluation with low validity. They write: "Broadly stated, validity represents a set of scientific criteria by which the *credibility* of research may be judged. As such, it involves matters of degree; studies are more or less valid."[7]

A test may be a very good test, quite accurate and consistent in its findings, but may simply not measure what it is intended to measure. For example, a supposed test of *intelligence* may accurately measure a subject's reading skill, memory, or fund of information, but may *not* be a valid test of intelligence. Or a test may be correctly focused on a particular element or quality, but may be an incomplete or inconsistent measure of that element. There are three main ways of judging the validity of a test or instrument: content, criterion, and construct.

Content validity

This refers to the degree to which an instrument or test examines the total content of the element or area being measured. For example, in developing a test of fitness, researchers should include all those elements which authorities generally agree are essential parts of physical fitness, such as speed, strength, coordination, endurance, balance, and flexibility. The identification of such elements and the weight they are given in the test may be drawn from the literature or established with the help of a jury of experts. Similarly, expert review is customarily used to judge the content validity of any new instrument or procedure.

Since content validity is not based on the actual performance of subjects or the results of other tests but rather on its content as rationally analyzed, it may also be called *rational* or *logical* validity.

Closely related to content validity is so-called *face* validity, which refers to the relevance of the measuring instrument to what one is trying to measure, based "on the face of it"—or through simple common sense or judgment.

Criterion-related validity

This is determined by whether the results of a test or other data-gathering instrument are in agreement with the findings of other criterion measures. It takes two forms: (1) *concurrent* validity, the degree to which the new instrument agrees with scores of other measurements taken at the same time and under similar conditions that were obtained with the use of an accepted, previously validated test; or (2) *predictive* validity, established by correlating scores with the results of future assessments making use of similar validated measures. For example, the validity of a test of sports conduct might be determined by comparing its findings to those of another test or the ratings of a group of experts who judge participants' behavior in later game situations. Criterion-related validity may also be called *empirical* or *statistical* validity, since it is supported not only by logical analysis, but also by concrete, empirical evidence.

Construct validity

Construct validity is concerned with the underlying construct or theoretical basis for developing a research instrument. It seeks to examine the degree to which given explanatory concepts or constructs may account for the performance of subjects. Determination of construct validity requires both logical or rational analysis and the use of empirical evidence; thus it may be considered to have elements of both content and criterion validity.

In a leisure-related example, one might use other research on satisfaction and apply it to leisure satisfaction or correlate the result on one's new test with those obtained by other instruments that have been shown to have construct validity.

Two other applications of the term *validity* are *internal* and *external,* in relation to experimental research (see page 55). Although related, they should not be confused with the concept of validity that is discussed here.

Many tests that are used in research and reported in the professional literature have had their validity determined in statistical terms as a prerequisite to publication or scholarly acceptance. Tests may be analyzed internally, so that different groups of items are given weights according to their importance within the overall instrument. In some cases, a lengthy test may be given in a "short" form, which uses the most powerful or predictive items (items that correlate most highly with the overall test score or with other criterion scores) as a valid form of the test.

Reliability

Reliability is another important quality of research instruments or testing procedures. It refers to the stability and consistency of the instrument or measure itself. Very simply, it is a question of whether one obtains the same results on repeated administrations of an instrument, given that test conditions remain the same. The repeated measures (test results) would be correlated to obtain a reliability estimate, referred to as a coefficient of stability. A second type of reliability refers to the consistency of various forms of an instrument. The responses to two different forms of the instrument would be correlated to yield a measure referred to as the coefficient of equivalence. Beyond such factors, the reliability of any measurement depends not only on the test itself but on how and when it is applied. Several examples of problems related to making sure that testing procedures or observations are reliable follow:

Measuring speed in a dash might be affected by the type of surface (dirt, grass, cinder, blacktop, or rubber composition), by the weather (wind, rain, or other atmospheric conditions), or by other physical factors affecting the measurement.

If a given test is applied to patients in a hospital or nursing home, they may respond very differently, depending on whether they have just received medication or have had other forms of therapy just before the test. If subjects are shown a test of agility or coordination and are asked to do it one person at a time, the last ones to perform may have a better idea of how it is done (because they have observed it repeatedly). They may therefore perform at a higher level than the first subjects to be tested.

The examples just cited might be regarded as due to poor testing controls and procedures—what Salkind characterizes as *method errors,* or weaknesses in the testing situation.[8] Other threats to reliability may be due to what he describes as *trait errors,* which stem from the characteristics of the persons being observed or taking a test.

Iso-Ahola, Jackson, and others have shown how self-reported data dealing with subjects' motivations for participation and constraints that limit involvement may often be unreliable.[9] Often individuals may not recognize their own leisure needs and sources of satisfaction or the reasons they do not participate in certain activities. Often, too, their responses may reflect culturally influenced stereotypes and expectations. Such factors may be responsible for the differences between what Salkind calls the *observed* or recorded score, based on test results, and the *true* score, which is the actual or correct score that the individual would obtain if the testing procedure were perfectly valid and reliable.

In other types of studies, which use data from government, business, or other "social indicators" sources (see page 89), critical problems of data reliability may arise from the lack of hard evidence of amounts of leisure spending, estimates of outdoor recreation visitations, and similar economic elements. For example, reported data on visitor spending at festivals and other major events is often based on inaccurate application of econometric models, including the assumed "multiplier" effect that magnifies the impact of tourist expenditures.

Whenever possible, the use of instruments whose scientific validity has been established, along with carefully designed procedures to ensure reliable findings and triangulation measurement approaches as well, should help to guarantee accurate measurement outcomes.

Following are two examples of published leisure research that show how investigators have dealt with issues of validity and reliability in their use of study instruments.

Example 1.   In research designed to measure the degree of commitment and ego-involvement of adult participants in recreational tennis, Siegenthaler and Lam adapted a number of instruments that had been used in measuring these constructs in relation to other activities and aspects of consumer research.[10] Typically, the instrument used a six-point Likert scale ranging from *very strongly agree* (6) to *very strongly disagree* (1). It included statements such as "I make important decisions based on how they will affect opportunities to play tennis" or "I would change jobs if it would allow me more time to play tennis."

In addition to using items from previously validated instruments, Siegenthaler and Lam's instruments were subjected to reviews of their wording, clarity, and readability by adult members of a racquet and swim club, university students in a tennis class, and graduate students and then revised on the basis of their comments. After pilot testing, the instruments were revised again before being used in the actual study.

Example 2.   Another example of how instruments are developed to measure leisure-related variables is found in a study of leisure and life satisfaction among aging adults with mental retardation. Hawkins developed the Leisure Assessment Inventory to measure respondents' current leisure involvements, interest in pursuing new activities, and constraints that impeded recreational participation. Consisting of 50 picture-cued leisure activities and 20 leisure constraints, the instrument's content validity was tested in three ways: "(1) cross-referencing the selected set of activities with previous research that examined leisure activities of aging/aged adults; (2) developing a measurement strategy that was consistent with techniques appropriate to persons with mental retardation, and (3) conducting expert panel review of the assessment inventory and interview protocol."[11]

Reliability of the Leisure Assessment Inventory was determined through a test-retest procedure that yielded acceptable levels of agreement based on approved standards for reliability in interest inventories.

Several other methods may be used to test the reliability of research instruments, both in their development and in their actual application. One such method involves *internal consistency* measures, which ask whether findings of different parts of a test are essentially in agreement or whether they are radically different (which would suggest that they are measuring different elements). In another approach, Bocksnick describes the use of matched pairs of elderly persons in a study of the involvement of aging individuals in leisure activities.[12] In each pair, one individual was assigned the task of recording the frequency and duration of activity involvement of the other, who responded to a self-reporting participation form. Thus, the checking of self-reported data by the observer-reporter served as a means of measuring the reliability of the testing procedure.

Objectivity

In quantitatively oriented research, investigator objectivity is considered an essential element. Researchers must be unbiased as they carry out interviews, rate subjects, observe behaviors, or interpret data, if their results are to be trustworthy. This means that they must be consistent in their recording of data and application of standards; often, they must be carefully trained to ensure objectivity and accuracy. Drew writes:

> . . . observation studies often (and should always) include certain precautions that attempt to determine observer reliability. This is typically accomplished by using two or more observers (either continually or on a periodic, spot-check basis) and calculating the degree to which they agree. Such procedures are known as determining interobserver reliability.[13]

It is often helpful to have observers carry out practice sessions, comparing and discussing their ratings, until they can consistently arrive at very similar results.

MEASUREMENT IN QUALITATIVE RESEARCH

As suggested earlier, measurement in qualitative research studies relies much less heavily on gathering numeric kinds of data and analyzing them statistically than it does in quantitative research. This does not mean, however, that no measurement is carried on. Obviously, qualitative researchers must gather data, and they do it in a variety of ways—observing people and events, becoming part of a living situation, and supplementing these approaches with interviews, examination of documents and records, accompanying group members to appropriate settings as they deal with problems of daily life, and so on.

Throughout this process, qualitative researchers must keep records of what occurs in the form of written notes that are often organized systematically and that may use coding systems or other recording methods, tape or video recordings, or other means of documentation. Although these are not customarily translated into numbered values, as in quantitative measurement, the researcher typically assigns them degrees of significance as she begins to develop theories that explain relationships, behaviors, or group structures.

Fraenkel and Wallen comment that analyzing the data in a qualitative study involves synthesizing the material gained from various sources throughout the course of a study, along with interpretations that are developed continuously during the study process. Hypotheses are not tested through statistical procedures, as in experimental or other forms of descriptive research. However, they write:

> . . . some statistics, such as percentages, may be calculated if it appears they can illuminate specific details about the phenomenon under investigation. Data analysis in qualitative research, however, relies heavily on description; even when certain statistics are calculated, they tend to be used in a descriptive rather than an inferential predictive sense.[14]

OTHER KINDS OF ANALYSIS

Some studies that do not use quantitative measurement may nonetheless use other kinds of analysis. For example, Butler and Smale studied several hundred community festivals in the province of Ontario in Canada, examining them as showcases for culture and heritage, as image-building elements, as events promoting community pride and solidarity, and as important in promoting tourism.[15] In their research, they analyzed festivals, subdividing them by major themes and types, seasonal patterns, and regional distribution. Although the data gathered was not treated statistically, geographical plotting of festivals and totals of events of different types provided a more meaningful picture than simple descriptions might have.

In another qualitative research study, Lyng examined the nature of voluntary risk-taking behavior that he called "edgework."[16] Based on his own involvement as a "jump pilot" for a local skydiving center, including a five-year study of a group of experienced skydivers, Lyng made repeated observations that enabled him to identify the key characteristics of this unique group of risk-takers, including their motivations, values, and outcomes from high-risk leisure adventures. Like other qualitative research, this demonstrated how nonquantitative research uses an inductive approach, gathering data that ultimately provide the basis for theory, rather than beginning with hypotheses that must then be tested through the research process.

UNOBTRUSIVE MEASURES

The terms *unobtrusive* or *nonreactive* research were originally coined to describe a number of research techniques that are used to search for clues about social motives and behavior, without directly interviewing or observing subjects. To illustrate, Babbie suggests:

> Want to know which exhibits [in a museum] are popular with little kids? Look for mucus on the glass cases. To get a sense of the most popular radio stations, you could arrange with an auto mechanic to check the radio dial settings for cars brought in for repair. The possibilities are limitless. Like an investigative detective, the social researcher looks for clues, and clues of social behavior are all around you.[17]

In such studies, people being studied are not aware of it, but leave evidence of their behavior naturally. A wide range of subjects may be explored through the use of such data-gathering methods: contrasting types of graffiti in male versus female high school restrooms, the personal descriptions of seniors in high school yearbooks as predictors of future life patterns, or the relation of bumper stickers on cars to observance of traffic laws. While the information gathered through unobtrusive measures is not essentially numeric, it may certainly be examined on a nominal level or may be classified as ordinal data when ranking patterns are observed.

SUMMARY

Measurement is a key ingredient in most research studies, and particularly in quantitative research, where the gathering of numeric forms of data and assigning them to categories defined as nominal, ordinal, interval, and ratio-level leads to appropriate statistical analysis. This chapter describes the approaches to measurement used in recreation, parks, and leisure studies and provides a number of examples of specific studies that use standardized measurement instruments or that involve the development of new instruments.

It describes the need to ensure validity and reliability in the formulation and application of research instruments and shows how these qualities may be achieved and tested. It also discusses researcher objectivity as a means of avoiding threats to validity and reliability. It concludes with a brief examination of measurement in qualitative research that does not usually rely on numeric classifications or analysis, but which does use systematic data gathering and analysis.

QUESTIONS AND ACTIVITIES

1. Individual students select and report on one of the journal articles mentioned in this chapter, identifying (1) the type of data measured in the article, (2) the measurement procedure used, and (3) the level of measurement (such as nominal, ordinal, etc.) used.

2. Students (1) search for articles reporting research in which the investigators developed their own instruments and (2) describe the methods that were used to establish the validity and reliability of these instruments.

3. To illustrate measurement approaches in qualitative research, students develop brief preliminary proposals for nonquantitative research, indicating the kinds of data that would be sought and how it might be systematically recorded and organized.

ENDNOTES

1. Julia Dunn, in Marjorie Malkin and Christine Howe, ed., *Research in Therapeutic Recreation: Concepts and Method* (State College, PA: Venture Publishing, 1993): 162.

2. Jack Fraenkel and Norman Wallen, *Research in Education* (New York: McGraw-Hill, 1993): 381.

3. Catherine Coyle, John Shank, Walter Kinney, and Deborah Hutchins, "Psychosocial Functioning and Changes in Leisure Lifestyle among Individuals with Chronic Health Problems Related to Spinal Cord Injury," *Therapeutic Recreation Journal* 27, no. 4 (1993): 239–52.

4. Stephen Langsner, "Reasons for Participation in Continuing Professional Education: A Survey of the NTRS," *Therapeutic Recreation Journal* 27, no. 4 (1993): 262–73.

5. Diane Samdahl, "Measuring Leisure: Categorical or Interval?" *Journal of Leisure Research* 23, no. 1 (1991): 88.

6. Claire Selltiz, Lawrence Wrightsman, and Stuart Cook, *Research Methods in Social Relations* (New York: Holt, Rinehart and Winston, 1976): 161.

7. Richard Berk and Peter Rossi, *Thinking About Social Evaluation* (London: Sage Publishers, 1990): 16.

8. Neil Salkind, *Exploring Research* (New York: Macmillan, 1991): 81–82.

9. Seppo Iso-Ahola and E. L. Jackson, cited in Roger Mannell and Jiri Zuzanek, "The Nature and Variability of Leisure Constraints in Daily Life: The Case of the Physically Active Leisure of Older Adults," *Leisure Sciences* 13, 4th quarter (1991): 338.

10. K. L. Siegenthaler and T. C. M. Lam, "Commitment and Ego Involvement in Recreational Tennis," *Leisure Sciences* 14, 4th quarter (1992): 303–15.

11. Barbara Hawkins, "An Exploratory Analysis of Leisure and Life Satisfaction of Aging Adults with Mental Retardation," *Therapeutic Recreation Journal* 27, 2nd quarter (1993): 102.

12. Jochen Bocksnick, "Determining How Accurately Older Adults Recall Their Involvement in Leisure Time Activities," *Journal of Applied Recreation Research* 16, no. 3 (1991): 220–33.

13. Clifford Drew, *Introduction to Designing and Conducting Research* (St Louis, MO: C. V. Mosby, 1980): 133.

14. Fraenkel and Wallen, *Research in Education,* 383.

15. Richard Butler and Bryan Smale, "Geographic Perspectives on Festivals in Ontario," *Journal of Applied Recreation Research* 16, no. 1 (1991): 3–23.

16. S. Lyng, "A Social Psychological Analysis of Voluntary Risk-Taking," *American Journal of Sociology* 95, no. 4 (1990): 858.

17. Earl Babbie, *The Practice of Social Research* (Belmont, CA: Wadsworth, 1992): 313.

Selecting Subjects
for Research:
The Sampling Process

. . . the early days of sample surveys produced some notorious failures in terms of false predictions. One of these classics was the 1936 Literary Digest *survey that predicted that Alf Landon would win a landslide victory over Franklin Roosevelt. The* Digest *people used faulty sampling procedures (automobile registration records during the Great Depression, when only wealthy people owned automobiles) that caused the biased findings and erroneous prediction. . . . [Today] we have a wide variety of interesting and effective sampling strategies available to help us do our research as precisely and as accurately as possible.[1]*

INTRODUCTION

A key task in most forms of empirical research that gather data from varied sources is the selection of subjects who are as representative as possible of the overall population being studied. This process is known as sampling. Sampling methods are of two general types: *probability* and *nonprobability.*

This chapter discusses several probability sampling methods that rely on randomization, including systematic, stratified, and cluster sampling. Providing illustrations from the research literature, it also presents examples of nonprobability sampling and examines such issues as the appropriate size of samples, sampling strategies, and sampling error. It concludes with a discussion of sampling in qualitative research.

NEED TO SELECT RESEARCH SUBJECTS

At an early stage in the planning of research studies, investigators must decide not only which variables must be studied, but also which subjects are to be examined. Typically, the term *subjects* refers to people who will be the source of research data through experiments, surveys, case studies, or other forms of investigation. Subjects of research, however, might also involve other types of social units or agencies such as classes, teams, communities, companies, government departments, or other groups.

In some cases, it is possible to study all the members of a given population. For example, if a state recreation and park society had several hundred members, it would not be unreasonable to survey all these individuals. If one wanted to study the leisure interests of all elderly persons in the United States or Canada, however, it would obviously not be feasible to interview, observe, or mail a questionnaire to many millions of individuals. For practical reasons of cost and time, it is usually not possible to measure an entire population. It is customary to select a sample of subjects to work with, who will be more manageable than the entire group would be, in terms of sheer numbers and accessibility. Best defines a sample as:

> . . . a small proportion of a population selected for observation and analysis. By observing the characteristics of the sample, one can make certain inferences about the characteristics of the population from which it is drawn.[2]

On all levels of survey research, heavy reliance is placed on the use of samples. For example, the Gallup Poll typically surveys approximately 1,500 adults across the nation to gain a picture of changing social attitudes, and the Nielsen survey organization monitors television sets in 4,800 homes to draw inferences about all of the television watching in the country.

TYPES OF SAMPLES

There are two general types of samples: *probability* and *nonprobability*. A probability sample is scientifically chosen through random selection and is therefore statistically likely to be representative of the entire population. When this method is used, the probability that any single subject will be chosen in the sample is known.

Although this method is regarded as the preferred approach to sampling, researchers must take into account the realistic factors of time and cost. Backstrom and Hursh write:

> A good . . . probability sample, by practical definition, is one that yields the desired information within expected but tolerable limits of sampling error, for the lowest cost.[3]

In contrast, a nonprobability sample does not use a systematic method that would ensure that all possible subjects have an equal chance of being chosen; the probability that any given subject would be chosen is not known.

STEPS IN THE SAMPLING PROCESS
Determining the Unit of Analysis

The first step in the sampling process is to establish the group of persons or things to be investigated. These objects of study are referred to as the *unit of analysis.* Usually this consists of a number of individual subjects. However, it may also be composed of families, clubs, or other social groups; companies; public or private agencies; or other types of subjects. The sum total of units of analysis represents the *population* or *universe;* each entity in the population is called a *sampling element.*

Defining the Study Population

The next step in the process is to determine the exact nature of the population the sample is to be drawn from. If one plans to survey voters, would it be *all* voters, those in a certain district, or members of one party? Depending on the purpose of the survey and its available resources, different choices might be made. It therefore becomes necessary to define the population exactly, in terms of its personal or demographic characteristics, its geographical or location limits, and similar elements. It also becomes important to recognize that it may simply not be possible to reach *all* individuals within a given population. If one wanted to use all adults living within a city as the overall population from which to draw a sample, it would be necessary to recognize that some people have no telephones or permanent residences, or may be temporarily away from the metropolis, or in institutions or prisons, or other inaccessible settings.

If one seeks to draw a random sample that is representative of all the members of a given population, but if some members of that population cannot possibly be reached, then they are excluded automatically from the possibility of being chosen—and the random sampling process has been faulty. Therefore, the choice of a population to begin with may depend on knowing its accessibility, and may represent one of the delimitations of a study. One might define as a study population all the registered voters within a city, knowing that they constituted only 85 percent of the actual adults in the city, but that at least all of them have recent addresses and are presumably available to be interviewed.

Establishing the Sampling Frame

The sampling frame is a complete list of sampling units from which the sample will be drawn. As stated above, it is often impossible to list every element in a population. The sampling frame is the most comprehensive list one can obtain. Common sources for the sampling frame are voter registration lists, telephone books, city directories, club memberships, utility hook-up lists, school directories, or publication subscriber lists. The sampling frame may use a combination of these sources, with duplicate entries eliminated.

Even using such varied sources, however, may mean that some potential subjects will be excluded from the sampling frame. For example, research has shown that between 8 and 10 percent of U.S. households do not have a telephone and that low-income minority populations, rural people, renters, and poor people generally have fewer telephones per household than other population groups. A more serious problem with the use of telephone directories is that the percentage of unlisted telephones in many cities is close to 20 percent.

PROBABILITY SAMPLING

Subtypes of probability sampling methods include simple random sampling, systematic sampling, stratified sampling; and cluster sampling.

Simple Random Sampling

The most common type of probability sample is the random sample. In this method, subjects are chosen according to a selection process that ensures that all possible subjects have an equal opportunity to be chosen. If a random means of selecting subjects is used, the likelihood is that they will be characteristic of the entire population or universe. The characteristics found in the sample can then be projected to describe the overall population, usually stated with an estimate of the percentage of possible or probable sampling error. For example, in a political poll, a survey may conclude that a given candidate is favored by 60 percent of the voters, with a 3 percent margin, plus or minus, of possible error.

Random sampling may be accomplished by simply placing the complete list of sampling elements in a hat and drawing them out one by one until the desired sample size is reached. Other random sampling methods include the use of a table of random numbers or computer-based selection programs that ensure that the choice of subjects is absolutely arbitrary, without any bias that might exclude some subjects or favor others. Subjects are selected simply on the basis of chance.

Certain factors may distort the accuracy of such random sampling procedures, including location and time elements. The setting in which subjects are questioned and the time at which they are interviewed might influence their representativeness.

For example, people found at a major street intersection in many large cities at 11 o'clock at night would be very different from those who would be there at 11 o'clock in the morning. In a small, readily accessible and homogeneous population, simple random sampling in a limited number of locations and at a few times might be adequate. In a more diversified population, it might be necessary to take a considerable number of locations and times to draw a representative population. To make an analogy from nature, if a chemical pollutant had found its way into a lake, and you wanted to measure the degree of its concentration in the water, a small sample taken at one location might be adequate. However, if the chemical pollutant did not diffuse easily or if the lake was stagnant, with little water movement, different conditions would probably prevail in different parts of the lake. Therefore, it would be necessary to take several tests in different locations.

Systematic Sampling

Systematic sampling is a variation of simple random sampling. In this approach, a starting point is chosen at random in the sampling frame, with every nth person then being chosen for research. For example, if a sample of 60 subjects is required from a population of 3,000 individuals, every 50th person would be chosen—with a random selection of a person between 1 and 50 to start the process.

As an illustration of the use of systematic sampling in conducting visitor surveys, Mills, Um, McWilliams, and Hodgson describe the procedure followed in an evaluation study of the Texas Folklife Festival. It involved a systematic selection

> . . . with a random number start. Every 25th visitor entering the festival through randomly assigned gates during sampling periods was selected. There were five gates and all were randomly assigned to an equal number of one-hour sampling periods. At the time of selection, visitors were tagged with a color-coded sticker and asked to later report to a centrally located survey center to fill out the study questionnaire. Eighty-two percent of the visitors selected in this sample completed the study questionnaire . . .[4]

Specific characteristics of the population must be carefully examined to prevent possible bias. For example, if the plan was to select every tenth house on a given street, it might be found that there were ten houses on each block and therefore the sample consisted only of corner houses, which tend to be larger and more expensive than others. The sample would therefore be faulty. One must be careful to avoid any such inherent bias in the sampling frame when using systematic sampling.

Stratified Sampling

Another variation of the random sampling method is stratification—that is, dividing the overall population into several different subgroups which are homogeneous within themselves, based on such criteria as ethnic identity, age groupings, sex, socioeconomic status, or similar factors. These groups would be given allocations in the sample, with subjects selected from each of them randomly. Ideally, this should be done proportionately, so that each stratum or special group in the sample is represented in numbers keyed to its size in the total population. If all important demographic variables can be blended into a mix in this way—with each individual's age, ethnic, socioeconomic, and other important characteristics factored in—a cross section of subjects will be achieved that suggests a high degree of representativeness.

As an example of stratified sampling, a Clemson University team did a tourism-related study in Myrtle Beach, South Carolina, with a sample stratified based on the type of lodging—hotel room, campground, rental property (home or condominium), and second home.

In general, stratified random samples require fewer cases than simple random samples. However, they may be difficult to obtain, particularly when the effort is made to match several demographic factors within individual subjects. Therefore, although stratified samples are often used in marketing or political polls, they may prove too complex for most research studies in recreation.

Cluster Sampling

This method is most useful when the overall population is very widespread, difficult to identify, or not readily accessible. It involves dividing the sampling frame into groups or clusters of units (such as individuals, families, clubs, and so on). A lesser number of clusters are then randomly selected from the overall universe, and these units are studied. In a multistage form of cluster sampling, one might find that a survey of recreation therapists in all the psychiatric hospitals in the country would represent a difficult sampling problem. Instead, it might be feasible to select a random sample of 10 states from the existing 50 states and then to list all counties in these 10 states and draw a random sample of 100 counties. Within these areas, all existing psychiatric treatment centers would be identified, and a random sample of forty such institutions would be chosen. This method would ensure that the final set of subjects would be chosen in a relatively efficient and inexpensive way.

NONPROBABILITY SAMPLING

Sampling approaches of this type represent a simplified approach that is often used in small-scale, uncomplicated studies that are not intended to provide statistical generalizations for populations beyond those surveyed. They are described as *nonprobability* methods because they do not guarantee that all potential subjects within the sampling frame have an equal opportunity to be selected for the study. As a result, it is not possible to estimate the degree to which the sample that is chosen actually deviates from the overall population being studied; this is referred to as "sampling error."

The term *convenience sampling* is often used to describe nonprobability sampling approaches in which the researcher selects the most accessible subjects or those who are most willing to participate, without a rigorous effort to structure their representativeness. This approach is generally not scientific and does not ensure unbiased or representative findings.

One approach to nonprobability sampling that seeks to achieve a degree of representativeness is *quota sampling*. Here, the population to be studied is divided into mutually exclusive subgroups, based on census data or other sources. The population might be grouped geographically, on an ethnic basis, along age or gender lines, or based on other factors. Based on their proportion within the overall population, members of each designated subgroup are chosen to meet desired totals. For example, field investigators might be assigned to interview 15 white females, 5 African-American females, and 3 Hispanic females all within the same age range. The choice of selecting the individuals in each group is up to the researcher's convenience.

A variation of this approach is *purposive sampling*. Here the researcher focuses on a limited population or small geographic area, for a "pinpoint" approach to sampling. For example, in a study of juvenile gangs in central city areas, a researcher might focus sharply on the neighborhoods where the highest and lowest rates of gang activity are known to take place.

Another type of nonprobability sampling is *snowball sampling*. In this method, the researcher identifies one or more study subjects who meet study needs. After they have been interviewed, they may be used to identify other potential subjects, who then are used to lead to other informants.

OTHER SAMPLING STRATEGIES

Double Sampling

Some studies may require *double sampling*. A double sample is a follow-up survey or retest of a random sample of nonrespondents to a survey, to attempt to determine whether those individuals who did not reply to the initial investigation were, in any major respect, significantly unlike those who did reply. This is a way to check on the reliability of a survey that had a disappointing response rate. The questions may always be raised, "Are those who did not reply significantly different from those who did reply? If this is the case, how much credibility can we give to the findings we have gathered, as representative of the *entire* population?"

In another type of double sampling, the researcher may do an intensive follow-up study of part of the original sample to gather fuller information or test theories or relationships that are beginning to emerge. This smaller group of subjects may be selected randomly or selected according to some of their responses to the first set of questions or study measures.

Time-Sampling Methods

As indicated earlier, the *time* when a survey or other descriptive study is carried out may influence or distort its findings. Efforts must be made to avoid this, if a study is to be valid. From a time perspective, data may be gathered in several different ways:

1. All at once in a single procedure, such as a mailed questionnaire that goes out to all subjects simultaneously.

2. In a period of continuous observation or analysis over a period of time, such as a community planning study over a three-month or one-year period.

3. In a time series, through a set number of observations or data-gathering steps at predetermined intervals (hourly, daily, weekly, etc.) intended to give an accurate picture of subjects under different circumstances.

In any cross-sectional or comparative research, all observations must be done at exactly comparable times, to ensure that the time factor does not distort results. Time-series data gathering is especially useful in showing change; for example, political polling at one-week intervals is commonly done to show shifts in public interest or preference.

SAMPLING ERROR

All the sampling methods or strategies that have been described seek to reduce sampling error. This may be defined simply as the difference between the characteristics of the sample and the characteristics of the population from which the sample was selected. Even with a reasonable sample size and an adequate rate of study response, a degree of built-in error is inevitable because of the chance variations that will occur when a number of randomly selected subjects are examined. For example, if we were to draw 25 samples of 100 subjects from a population of 2,500, the average height within each sample will vary somewhat from the population average, and this sampling error will increase as the heterogeneity of the population increases. The best estimate of sampling error is the standard error of the mean, which will be discussed in Chapter 15.

Estimating or inferring a population characteristic (parameter) based on data drawn from a random sample (statistic) is not an exact process; some level of sampling error will always exist even when rigid sampling procedures are followed. To minimize sampling error, one should adhere to an accepted sampling process as described earlier in this chapter. Further, given all other factors are constant, sampling error can be decreased by increasing the sample size. Beyond this, every effort must be made to prevent nonsampling errors, which may stem from mistakes of recording responses, misunderstanding the meaning of questions, or other mechanical or clerical events. Procedures can be used to estimate the degree of sampling error that will occur, based on the kind of question that is being explored and the size of the sample in relation to the overall population. Usually this is expressed as an estimate of a "degree of confidence" at a 95 or 99 percent level of accuracy. Backstrom and Hursh write:

> ... confidence is expressed as assurance that in 95 (or 99) out of 100 samples like ours the true value is within the estimated range of tolerated

error. So, in a survey where we permit 6 percent error and set 95 percent confidence limits, we are sure that 95 cases out of 100 would contain the population value in an interval within 6 percent in either direction of the estimate.[5]

Size of Sample

A critical question that researchers must therefore resolve is the size of the sample they will use. There is no absolute guideline on this; typically, it becomes a compromise between the ideal of having a large number of cases (or a number that represents a high percentage of the cases in the overall population) and the fact that more cases lead to greater expense. Obviously, the length of time and amount of money required to hire and train interviewers or mail questionnaires and to process study data tend to restrict the size of samples.

From the point of view of statistical analysis needs, Saslow points out that a

. . . problem introduced by too small sample sizes is the difficulty of knowing whether you are sampling normally distributed measures. If you can't decide whether your interval data are normally distributed, you won't know whether you should use tests based on the normal distribution or whether it would be better to rank the interval measures and treat them as ordinal data.[6]

One factor to be considered is the heterogeneity of the population being studied; as indicated earlier, the more diverse subjects on characteristics under study, the larger the sample size should be. Other factors include the nature of the sampling method. Usually, stratified sampling requires the smallest number of cases. Simple random sampling requires a somewhat larger number, and cluster sampling requires a larger number to obtain the same degree of precision. Other factors have to do with the method of analysis that will be used with the study data. For example, in some types of statistical analysis, there must be a minimum of 30 cases for procedures to be applied— depending on whether parametric or nonparametric tests are used. (See page 233.) This, however, does not address the representativeness of the sample.

Bailey illustrates the problem with the example of a research study that has been submitted for publication and that includes variables such as income and education. When the journal editor insists that the variables of race and sex should also be analyzed, the researcher finds that there are only a few male or female black college graduates in the study sample—too few to be reliably analyzed. Bailey concludes:

Thus it is important when deciding upon sample size to estimate how many times the sample may have to be subdivided during data analysis and to ensure an adequate sample size for each subdivision.[7]

He points out also that, regardless of the sample size initially decided on, a substantial number of respondents may refuse to be interviewed, may return illegible or unusable questionnaires (in a survey), or may leave key questions blank for reasons of privacy or inappropriateness. For all these reasons, larger samples may be necessary.

Although several factors have been considered that affect the final determination of the size of a sample, strictly from a statistical perspective, there are some guidelines for sample size. The proper sample size is estimated based upon the size of the sampling error one is willing to accept. Let's take an example using less technical terms and determine the sample size needed. Suppose a researcher was attempting to determine how much money the average spectator would spend in the stadium on food, beverages, souvenirs, and other incidentals at a Carolina Panthers football game. The researcher would have to determine how much error she is willing to tolerate in the estimate of average expenditures for all spectators (the population). For example, does the researcher want the final estimate of average expenditures to be within ±$2.00, ±$4.00, or ±$6.00 of the actual expenditures of all spectators. Let's assume ±$4.00 was selected as the error tolerance. The possible variations in expenditures also needs to be determined. Sometimes this information may be available from previous studies and is expressed in statistical terms as either the variance of the measure or the standard deviation of the measure. These terms will be discussed in detail in Chapter 14. However, in this example, as in most cases, the variation of expenditures is not known, so an educated guess must be made. Obviously, some spectators may spend no money once they are in the stadium, while others may spend $100 or more. Let's assume the range of expenditures is $100. This information is needed to determine an appropriate sample size, and the last necessary decision is the confidence level. Remember that 95 and 99 percent confidence levels were referred to earlier in this chapter. They are the most common confidence levels used in recreation research. Let's assume again, the researcher wants to be 95 percent sure that the estimate of expenditures is within ±$4.00 of the true value of all spectators (population). Now all the information necessary to calculate an appropriate sample size is available. The formula[8] that can be used is:

$$n = \frac{4}{T^2}\left(\frac{R}{6}\right)^2$$

Where: n = the sample size

T = the amount of tolerance one is willing to allow in the estimate

R = the range of potential scores

4 = number used for 95% confidence level

6 = the range is divided by 6 to estimate the variation in scores

Therefore in our example:

$$n = \frac{4}{4^2}\left(\frac{100}{6}\right)^2$$

$$= \frac{4}{16}(278)$$

$$\doteq 69.50 \approx 70$$

The sample size is rounded to the next whole number; thus, the appropriate sample size is 70.

A point of clarification: if the 99 percent confidence level were chosen, then a 9 would have been used in the numerator rather than a 4. These numbers relate to the area under the normal curve, which is a concept that will be explained in Chapter 14. Suffice it to say, these numbers are needed to calculate the appropriate sample size.

This formula can be used in situations where you are utilizing simple random sampling procedures. There are modifications of the procedures when using other sampling processes. It is beyond the scope of this introductory textbook to explore these procedures at this time.

Percentage of Response

A related point is the percentage of the sample that must respond to a survey or a poll for the findings to be valid. For example, one would normally have confidence in a survey with a 98 percent response rate; however, a survey with a 2 percent response rate would obviously lack credibility. At what point between these extremes can one say, "This is an acceptable rate of return"? There are no hard rules as to the minimum percentage rate of return that a survey should have to be acceptable. Usually, surveys with a return rate of more than 50 percent are considered acceptable, although lesser rates of return are frequently reported. Kerlinger writes:

> Responses to mail questionnaires are generally poor. Returns of less than 40 to 50 percent are common. High percentages are rare. At best the researcher must content himself with returns as low as 50 to 60 percent.[9]

Often, the rate of the return is influenced by the nature of the study and by the population to which it is directed. A high rate of return can be expected if respondents are readily accessible to the researcher, if they are members of an organization that is cooperating in the study, or if they have a strong personal or professional interest in the subject of the study. In surveys of the public at large, which includes many individuals who have little interest in the study, much lower rates are likely to occur. A high rate of return is more likely if the survey is as brief as possible, if it is highly professional in makeup and appearance, has precise, clear directions, and if its purpose and significance are explained to respondents in a cover letter or introduction.

Here are some strategies that may be used to increase the response rate to a desirable 60 to 80 percent:

1. Use follow-up mailings, reminder cards, or telephone calls to encourage response, even a late response.

2. Provide letters of support from community leaders or public officials to encourage response.

3. Gain support for the study from relevant organizations, including their sponsorship or direct support, when appropriate.

4. Offer respondents a summary of the findings or other inducements as an inducement to participate.

SAMPLING IN EXPERIMENTAL RESEARCH

Thus far, this chapter has dealt chiefly with the use of sampling in descriptive studies, such as surveys. It also applies, however, to the process of forming experimental and control groups in experimental studies. Such groups should be as comparable as possible so that any differences in outcomes at the end of an experiment can be said to be due to the influence of independent variables rather than to differences in the groups themselves.

The ideal way of assuring such equivalence is to select a large pool of subjects to begin with and then to randomly assign individuals to experimental and control groups. In many situations, however, this is not possible. Even in highly structured, controlled settings such as hospitals or prisons it is difficult to establish such groups and to maintain the necessary experimental controls over them.

The obvious expedient, which experimental researchers frequently use, is to select existing, preestablished groups, such as school classes, units of patients within a hospital, patients residing on different floors in a long-term care facility, or other comparable social units. Through pretesting, it is possible to determine whether the group memberships are comparable in terms of major characteristics (age, socioeconomic class, gender, physical attributes, and so on) so that they may be considered equivalent for study purposes.

SAMPLING IN QUALITATIVE RESEARCH

In general, the use of probability sampling methods is not as prevalent in qualitative research studies as it is in quantitative studies. Even in such research, however, investigators must be concerned about the sampling process to ensure that the observations made or data collected are generally representative of the subjects or settings under study.

Henderson points out that qualitative researchers usually use flexible study designs and rarely specify the number of informants or subjects in advance, although they may have a general idea of the numbers they will need. In general, she writes, qualitative study samples are smaller, more purposive than random study samples and are more subject to change than those in quantitative research. The qualitative strategy

> . . . is concerned with theoretical sampling of constructs rather than the quantitative accrual of large, random sample sizes. . . . Saturation is researched with simultaneous data gathering and analysis, and it occurs when the researcher realizes that the data collected are repetitive and no additional new information is being found.[10]

SAMPLING ATYPICAL OR "SENSITIVE" POPULATIONS

Another difference between qualitative and quantitative research sampling approaches is that in quantitative studies, the investigator is particularly concerned about the sample being representative of a *typical* population. By contrast, qualitative researchers sometimes deliberately focus on unusual settings or populations—for example, individuals with unusual leisure values or patterns of behavior—in order to develop theoretical formulations that may not be apparent in more normal settings or groups. Such groups might include those involved in illegal or controversial forms of leisure activity, such as alcohol or drug abusers, compulsive gamblers, or similar populations.

The task of investigating such "sensitive" subjects presents a unique problem for researchers because sensitive subjects are not usually members of organized groups, their names do not appear in formal lists or directories, and, indeed, they may be extremely cautious about revealing their identities or being studied by outsiders.

Lee points out that research on sensitive topics may be perceived as threatening within three broad areas:

> The first is where the research poses an "intrusive threat," dealing with areas which are private, stressful or sacred. The second is related to the study of deviance and social control and involves the possibility that information may be revealed which is stigmatizing or incriminating in some way. Finally, research is often problematic when it impinges on political alignments, if "political" is taken in its widest sense to refer to the vested interest of powerful persons or institutions, or the exercise of coercion or domination.[11]

In addition to the kinds of sensitive topics just suggested, research in areas related to racial or ethnic values or behaviors, sexual affiliation or involvement in sexual activity, or similar issues may also involve difficulty in developing adequate samples of study subjects or informants. It may even be difficult to estimate the size of hidden, criminal, or so-called deviant populations—such as individuals who have committed sexual offenses against children or youth engaged in delinquent activities. Lee points out that several approaches may be used to develop such estimates: archival or social indicator sources, covert observational methods, or projections from case-based data using "multiplier" methods.

In some cases, it may be possible for investigators to become trusted observers of deviant groups, such as Short and Strodtbeck, who conducted a comparative study of the leisure behaviors of several hundred African-American and white youthful gang members in Chicago.[12] Their approach, however, involved the kind of long-term, intensive contact with groups typical of sociologists or anthropologists and is less likely to be used by recreation and leisure researchers.

Some of these methods of locating difficult-to-reach sample informants include:

Screening, or "sift-sampling," which involves the systematic canvas of a particular location in order to identify members of a sought-for population.

Networking, similar to the "snowball" approach, in which the researcher starts with the initial set of contacts and is passed on by them to others, and so on.

Outcropping, a term taken from geology, in which the researcher finds a site where the members of a rare or deviant population congregate and studies them there.[13]

Still other ways of locating research subjects from a hard-to-reach or deviant subgroup may include advertising—which is often done by medical researchers—offering to provide a service of some kind, or gaining the assistance of professional informants such as police, social workers, probation officers, or similar individuals. Each such group is likely to encounter members of "sensitive" populations in a different way and to be able to offer unique perspectives on them or to assist in recruiting them for research.

SUMMARY

In most research studies, there is a need to identify subgroups of subjects who will provide an accurate representation of a larger population. This process, known as sampling, is of two types: probability and nonprobability. Of the two, the probability approach, which relies on randomized, systematic, stratified, and cluster strategies, is most likely to yield findings representative of the larger population from which the sample is drawn.

Nonprobability or convenience sampling is generally easier to administer and less costly in terms of time and money. At the same time, it yields less trustworthy results with respect to the sample's being representative of the larger population. Specific types of nonprobability samples include quota, purposive, and snowball methods. The chapter continues with a discussion of time-sampling strategies, sample size, and sample error and concludes with an overview of the approach to sampling found in qualitative research and in studying sensitive or controversial topics.

QUESTIONS AND ACTIVITIES

1. Define and explain the differences between probability and nonprobability approaches to sampling.

2. Explain the nature and the special uses or purposes of such sampling methods as systematic, stratified, sampling, quota, purposive, and snowball.

3. Select one or more of the problem areas developed as part of Question 3 at the end of Chapter 9 (page 118). Then carry out the following steps:

   a. Determine the exact population you will investigate and the means of identifying the full list of potential subjects or respondents (the population or university).

   b. Identify alternative approaches to drawing a sample from this population, using both probability and nonprobability methods.

   c. Indicate the approximate size of the sample you would seek to obtain and the percentage of response or completed investigations that you would set as a minimum acceptable figure.

4. Examine several articles in issues of recreation and leisure studies research journals to locate examples of sampling procedures followed in the studies reported. Outline and report to the class the specific methods used in each case, including the numbers involved and the means of selecting and making contact with subjects.

ENDNOTES

1. Richard Hessler, *Social Research Methods* (New York, Los Angeles: Est Publishing, 1992): 114.

2. John W. Best, *Research in Education* (Englewood Cliffs, NJ: Prentice-Hall, 1981): 8–9.

3. Charles Backstrom and Gerald Hursh, *Survey Research* (Evanston, IL: Northwestern University Press, 1963): 24.

4. Allan Mills, Seoho Um, Edward McWilliams, and Ronald Hodgson, "The Importance of Random Sampling When Conducting Visitor Surveys," *Journal of Park and Recreation Administration* 5, no. 2 (1987): 50.

5. Backstrom and Hursh, *Survey Research,* 31–32.

6. Carol Saslow, *Basic Research Methods* (New York: Random House, 1982): 263.

7. Kenneth Bailey, *Methods of Social Research* (New York: Free Press, 1982): 100–1.

8. Gilbert A. Churchill, *Marketing Research: Methodological Foundations,* 4th edition (New York: CBS College Publishing, 1987): 480–82.

9. Fred Kerlinger, *Foundations of Behavioral Research* (New York: Holt, Rinehart and Winston, 1973): 414.

10. Karla Henderson, *Dimensions of Choice: A Qualitative Approach to Recreation, Parks, and Leisure Research* (State College, PA: Venture Publishing, 1991): 133.

11. Raymond Lee, *Researching Sensitive Topics* (Newbury Park, CA: Sage, 1991): 4.

12. James Short, Jr., and Fred Strodtbeck, *Group Process and Gang Delinquency* (Chicago: University of Chicago Press, 1965): 36–53.

13. Lee, *Researching Sensitive Topics,* 64–73.

Implementing the Study: The Data-Gathering Process

Data have no life outside of research. For something to be called data or fact, it must complement or fit into some system of research and explanation. All the comings and goings of the neighbors is not data unless someone has systematically recorded this activity for a specific research purpose. . . .

Data are creations of researchers. The raw materials are the everyday activities of human beings, but data are the end product of research into the why and how of those materials. By their very existence, data are spoken for. Contained within data are categories, even whole theories, representing carefully crafted methodical explanations.[1]

INTRODUCTION

Having explored the process of developing research proposals, formulating questions and hypotheses, creating valid and reliable study instruments and sampling designs, we now embark on the actual research process. This chapter examines general guidelines and specific examples of data-gathering methods used in both descriptive and experimental research. Various types of research instruments are described, with emphasis on the development of survey questionnaires. Surveying and interviewing techniques are analyzed, and guidelines are presented for field observation studies. Study methods in experimental research are also reviewed, with the concluding section of the chapter concerned with data organization and coding schemes.

DEVELOPMENT OF STUDY INSTRUMENTS

Along with the selection of research subjects, a key task in the data-gathering process is selecting or framing study instruments. Such data-gathering tools are of several types. In recreation, parks, and leisure-studies research, they include

(1) questionnaires; (2) rating scales; (3) checklists; (4) observational recording forms; (5) psychological tests; (6) tests of physical attributes or performance; (7) sociometric tests; and (8) other specialized instruments for environmental, economic, or other special research studies.

Questionnaires

These are the most common form of survey research instrument and usually consist of a series of questions or statements to which subjects are asked to respond, as in marketing surveys or political polls. They may deal with items of fact or personal knowledge, with reported behaviors, with attitudes and beliefs, or with professional practices. Customarily, they may be distributed to members of a sample either directly or by mail and filled out, usually on an individual basis, although a test may be administered to a group of individuals simultaneously by an investigator. Questionnaires may also be used in telephone or face-to-face interviews.

Rating Scales

These are quite similar to questionnaires, except that they tend to be narrower in their format and scope and usually involve judgments or ratings on a scale of possible responses. Rating scales are often used to measure or evaluate behavior, the quality of performance, the level of participation, the effectiveness of maintenance or administrative procedures, or such elements. Respondents may be asked to rate their own attitudes or leisure behaviors, usually selecting the most appropriate or correct choice of ratings from a ranked continuum of possible responses.

The term *scale* is frequently used interchangeably with the term *index*. While both are means of ranking people or other subjects of research on given variables, they differ. Indexes are constructed based on a set of scores measuring *individual* attributes that are considered more or less equal in importance. Scales are composite measures of *patterns* of attributes, which may vary in their intensity or importance.

For example, a test of the physical fitness of children and youth might consist of several performance tests involving endurance, agility, flexibility, strength, and coordination—all of which are combined to provide a single score, or *index,* of each subject's fitness.

In contrast, an attitude *rating scale* may measure subjects' self-perceptions in such areas as social participation, job satisfaction, or professional competence with a series of questions and a range of possible scores for different intensities of attitudes or beliefs—either in terms of numbers on a scale or alternative statements to be selected in response. The result may be a profile that indicates different areas of strength or weakness or levels of intensity of beliefs held.

Although scales tend to provide more information than indexes, they are more difficult to construct and apply and therefore are used less frequently. Both illustrate the point that composite measures that examine several aspects of given variables are usually more trustworthy than single measures.

Checklists

These are similar to both questionnaires and rating scales, except that they tend to have lists of items which can be replied to by "yes" or "no" responses or by other concrete pieces of information, rather than opinions or judgments. They are particularly useful in measuring professional practices, facilities, or other types of evaluation studies. For example, in camp accreditation procedures, a number of items regarding camp practices in areas such as food services, safety and health, programming, or facilities might simply require that the director indicate whether or not a particular procedure is carried out. Obviously, in such procedures, the investigator might also require evidence substantiating the director's response and might rely on observation, interviews, or other means of obtaining documentation that supports the use of the checklist.

Observational Recording Forms

These are instruments or forms that are based on direct observation of practices, facilities, behaviors, or other variables. They may be very much like checklists with respect to carrying out routine observations of facilities, as an example, or they may require more subtle judgment. Examples:

Direct observation of behavior; this might involve observation of employees at work, participation of children in a play setting, group interaction in a planning group, or similar activities. The form itself might list a number of typical behaviors, and the observer might note when these occur, who demonstrated them, and with what frequency or duration.

Mechanical recording processes; this might involve the use of film or videotape recording or the use of electronic feedback through computer cards that provide information about those entering facilities or measure the physiological responses of subjects to stimuli.

Psychological Tests

These may involve tests of beliefs, attitudes, personality traits, self-concept, and similar variables. In some cases, they are taken directly, as paper-and-pencil tests, by subjects. In others, they may be filled out by observer/researchers. They may also include projective tests that involve the subject's interpretation of pictures, associations with words or phrases, or other tests of perception, memory, or emotional response to stimuli. Typically, such tests are used to develop descriptive profiles of subjects, rather than numeric ratings as in the case of a rating scale or index.

Measurement of Physical Attributes or Performance

Standardized instruments and recording forms may be used in some research areas involving motor performance or fitness levels. Typically, strength, speed, and similar elements are measured, along with the ability to perform specific athletic skills. These are often referred to as achievement tests.

Sociometric Tests

This is a special form of observation of group behavior in which the researcher notes the relationships and cliques within the group, the leadership/followership roles held by individuals, and similar behaviors or structures. It can also be done through a self-reporting process, in which group members report their feelings toward others, those they would choose to work or associate with, and similar information.

Other Specialized Instruments

In many cases, instruments used in scientific research have been published or otherwise made available for general use. However, as in the case of a number of psychological inventories (tests of personality, intelligence, or self-concept), they may be standardized and protected by copyright. In such cases, they may be used only by permission with a designated commercial fee for use. In other cases, instruments that have been developed for a particular study and that have been carefully validated (tested to determine their scientific accuracy) may be used again by other researchers in new studies, with the permission of the original researchers but without charge. A number of instruments measuring leisure attitudes or behaviors have been used again and again in published research studies, following their initial presentation to the field.

For other studies, there may be no appropriate instruments available, and so the research team or individual investigator must devise their own instruments. This typically involves a process of examining similar instruments in order to identify potentially useful models; selecting the elements or variables that should be in the new form; possibly getting advice or approval from a jury of experts; pilot-testing or field-testing the instrument; and assigning values to given questions or groups of questions. Particularly if a research study is to be used for scholarly or academic purposes, any new instrument that has been developed for it should be tested for validity and reliability (see page 146).

GUIDELINES FOR QUESTIONNAIRE CONSTRUCTION

A questionnaire is essentially a patchwork of concepts that have been operationalized; concepts are defined first at an abstract level and then at a measurement level so that meaningful data can be gathered regarding them.

Although questionnaires may vary greatly in length and complexity, the following guidelines apply generally to their construction.

1. Determine the major areas that are to be covered, based on your proposal. Consult with others and examine the literature carefully, both to ensure that you have identified the key topics and to gather ideas for questions and the overall format of the questionnaire. Make sure that the areas fulfill the stated purposes of your study or relate directly to the hypotheses.

2. Develop a preliminary set of questions for each of these areas. Questions or items (as they are sometimes called) may deal with (a) information about the respondent; (b) matters of fact or knowledge; (c) personal attitudes, values, or opinions; (d) judgments or ratings of others, or of programs, policies, or procedures; (e) rating of priorities; (f) statements of needs and interests; or other types of information.

3. Determine whether the questions should be *closed-end* (with limited, predesignated choice of possible responses) or *open-end* (with unstructured opportunity for response). Closed-end questions in effect restrict the respondent to forced choices or categories of replies; they are very clear and unambiguous and are simple to tally and analyze. Open-end questions provide a fuller range of possible responses, but may be much more difficult to tally.

4. In composing individual questions or items (a question asks for a response and is phrased with terms like "How would you . . .?" or "Are there any . . .?" while an item might state "Please rate the following procedures . . ." or "Indicate the frequency with which . . ."), the following guidelines are helpful:

   a. It is usually best to start with short, easy, or familiar questions that are nonthreatening and encouraging to the respondent to get her started comfortably, rather than with more complicated or challenging questions.

   b. If necessary, define the terms used in individual questions. For example, a question like "How many children live on the average farm in Jones County?" has at least three terms that might be misinterpreted and that should be defined: "children," "live on," and "average farm."

   c. Avoid vague terms. A question like "Do you play sports often?" is ambiguous, because what is "often" for one person might be "infrequent" for another. Such words are best translated into specific categories, like "daily," "weekly," "monthly," etc., or into specific numbers. Similarly, even the word "sports" might have different meanings for different people and possibly should be explained with a phrase like ". . . such as tennis, golf, or racquetball." Also avoid words with which the respondent may not be familiar.

d. Avoid questions that might give incomplete information, like "Are you married?" A negative response will not give you the detailed information you need. Instead, asking respondents to indicate their marital status and giving them all possible or appropriate responses (married, separated, divorced, widowed, single, etc.) will provide an exact answer.

e. In asking for judgments or attitudes, questions should be specific, rather than general. The question, "What do you think of the cafeteria?" will not yield as precise information as one which asks them to rate the cafeteria for cleanliness, service, quality of food, pricing policy, and similar items, and then to provide a general rating. The actual response may be handled several ways: by having respondents check the appropriate point on a numbered scale (from Poor to Excellent), select the correct descriptive adjective, or assign an identified value to the subject.

f. Avoid multiple questions like "Do you go to the movies, theater, or circus?" Each such choice should be presented separately, preferably on a scale that might indicate specific attendance over the past year.

g. Avoid questions that might show any bias or leanings on your part. Respondents will be quick to detect such items and to resent what they may perceive as manipulation or brainwashing, even if you have not consciously framed questions in this way. Questions must be perceived as neutral and should avoid characterizing any element of choice in an unfavorable way.

h. Be cautious with respect to using questions that might be embarrassing or self-incriminating or that may deal with sensitive information, such as the respondent's income, religion, or political affiliation. Consider assuring anonymity to the respondent, although even this may not persuade individuals to reply to such questions. Note: This does not mean that sensitive or personal questions can never be explored in surveys; numerous studies of sexual behavior and attitudes show that this is not so. However, it *does* mean that such questions or issues must be treated very carefully in routine surveys.

5. General guidelines that are useful in composing the overall questionnaire and in ensuring a maximum rate of accurate response include the following:

a. Give complete directions as to how a question should be answered, or how questions that provide for several possible responses should be handled (i.e., "Mark the correct response with an X in the appropriate box," etc.). If possible, provide a rating system that allows for different choices, such as a Likert-type range of responses, unless you deliberately wish to have a "forced choice" format that compels a "yes" or "no," or other sharp "either/or" decisions. Typically, in Likert-type questions, the subject might be asked to respond to a statement by indicating one of five possible opinions: *Agree Strongly; Agree Moderately; Neutral* or *Undecided: Disagree Moderately; Disagree Strongly.*

b. Whenever possible, all questions should be precoded (assigned code numbers or letters) to permit easy transfer to computer disks or tapes for analysis. Some survey questionnaires have attached answer sheets, where the replies should be marked, and in some cases may make use of answer strips attached with perforations to the questionnaire, so they may be electronically tabulated, without the need for a transfer process.

c. Keep the questionnaire as short and simple as possible, to encourage respondents' completing and returning it, particularly if it is going to the general public. More lengthy or difficult forms may be sent to people who have a direct interest in the research or are members of professional groups or organizations related to it and who therefore are likely to be more highly motivated to respond.

d. Make sure the survey form is attractive, readable, and professional in its appearance, while at the same time being careful not to have it too elaborate, ornate, or obviously expensive (set in fancy type, on embossed paper, with several colors, etc.). People who resent surveys or feel that they are a waste of time and money sometimes criticize them because of their cost, or argue that the money could be better spent. The form should not look crowded or confusing; it is important to use white space effectively as a design element. Pastel colors may also be used if there is sufficient contrast between the paper and the print for legibility.

e. Usually, although not always, it is desirable to get specific information about each respondent, in order to be able to break down responses by age, sex, income level, or similar categories. Therefore, questions about such identification factors or other demographic variables should be included, with the assurance that the respondent's name will be kept confidential. While most questionnaires ask for such information in the opening section, some place these questions in the back, feeling that if they appear in the beginning the subject may decide not to answer the survey.

f. Also, make sure to group questions by content areas; for example, place all questions regarding recreation participation together, rather than space them throughout the instrument. When feasible, also group similar question formats together; i.e., all Likert-type questions together, and all open-end questions together. People respond more readily when they do not have to jump back and forth, in terms of either content or format.

6. When the first draft of the questionnaire has been completed, it should be pilot-tested with appropriate subjects, to make sure that it is workable in terms of its clarity, the appropriateness of questions, the simplicity of its language, the length of time it takes to complete it, and similar concerns. It should be carefully reviewed, with a checklist that includes such questions as:

Are you satisfied that the questionnaire is the best method available to obtain the needed information?

Has a workable method for distributing and collecting the questionnaire been devised?

Is the title of the survey accurate and concise? Are the instructions for taking it or applying it also easily understood?

Is the personal information that is requested necessary, and does it run the risk of offending or "turning off" possible respondents?

Are questions arranged in an appropriate sequence, both in terms of grouping subjects and moving generally from simple to more difficult items?

Are there any questions which might "lead" the respondent or might show bias?

Is there sufficient space for responding to open-end questions?

Are questions arranged so that answers can be easily tabulated?

Following the pilot-testing procedure and application of such a checklist, the instrument should be revised as necessary. If it is to be used in a scholarly project, or if it is expected to meet standards of academic rigor, it may also be necessary to determine its validity and reliability as a research instrument (see page 146).

7. If it is a mailed questionnaire, encourage response by providing a self-addressed, stamped envelope for its return. A carefully written cover letter should appeal to the respondent's sense of responsibility or citizenship, professionalism, or other motivations, to encourage response. This letter should establish the credibility of the survey and the researcher by explaining who is conducting the survey and with what purpose; naming individuals or organizations who are supporting it; telling respondents how they were chosen and why the study may be of value to them; assuring confidentiality of responses; providing additional directions for filling out the form; and thanking the respondent in advance for his assistance.

In addition, it may well require additional postcard or telephone reminders or follow-up mailings to achieve an acceptable percentage of response. Studies have shown distinct differences between respondents and nonrespondents (both in terms of their characteristics and their opinions), and therefore it is highly desirable that as high a percentage as possible of the original sample respond, to avoid an inaccurate or biased set of findings.

USE OF QUESTIONNAIRES

Questionnaire surveys may be administered in several ways. Two of the most common are (1) hand-delivering them to respondents or actually administering them in subjects' homes, offices, classrooms, clubs, parks, or other appropriate settings and (2) mailing them, an obviously more convenient approach when survey subjects are scattered geographically.

In both cases, it is advisable to use a variety of methods to interest potential respondents in the survey and to encourage them to participate in it. In a community survey, announcements may be made in local newspapers or on radio or public television. In a membership organization or professional society, newsletters, announcements, or similar media may be used to forecast the study. In mailed surveys, cover letters serve to introduce the questionnaire, giving its purpose and encouraging response. When a survey is presented directly to participants, the researcher may explain its purpose and answer questions about it. In each case, Chadwick and associates write:

> Whatever the level of detail, it is critical that the introduction stress the significance of the study to science, to society, and, if possible, to the individual respondent. . . . The individual respondent's importance to the study should also be clearly stated. This is generally accomplished by noting that the respondent is part of a scientifically selected sample which was chosen to represent a wide variety of opinions and characteristics.[2]

In some cases, respondents may be offered a minor gift if they respond; in others, they may be promised a copy of the completed study's findings. In medical research, they are often offered actual payment for study participation.

Customarily, follow-up efforts are needed to obtain an acceptable rate of return of completed questionnaires. This is less necessary when surveys are hand-delivered to individuals who have indicated their willingness to participate in research or when surveys are administered face-to-face. Mailed surveys, however, frequently yield a response of less than 20 percent, and second or even third rounds of mailing, telephone-call follow-ups, and similar methods may be needed to ensure a fuller response. Reminder postcards and follow-up mailings usually are timed at intervals of from two to four weeks after the initial mailing. Using certified mail has been shown to increase response rates significantly, although it obviously increases the cost of the survey.

Several examples of the use of face-to-face delivery and mailed questionnaire surveys in recreation, parks, and leisure-studies research follow.

Example 1. Lankford, Neal, and Buxton examined work motivators among staff members of public, private/commercial, nonprofit, and armed forces leisure service organizations on the islands of Hawaii and Oahu. Using an instrument based on Herzberg's two-factor motivation/hygiene theory, researchers visited each site (including municipal park and recreation agencies, Boys and Girls Clubs, YMCA and YWCA, hotels, gyms, and U.S. Army and Navy bases), explained the purpose of the research, distributed questionnaires, and collected them immediately after they were filled out. The questionnaire was distributed to 319 professional staff members, and an overall response rate of 55 percent was obtained.[3]

Example 2. Kanters and Botkin conducted a large-scale mailed questionnaire survey of residents of five regions of Illinois that were stratified by population density and geographic location. Intended to measure the economic impact of public leisure services in Illinois, the survey examined specific types of expenditures made during visits to park districts, forest preserves, and conservation district facilities. Initially, 5,579 telephone calls were made to determine if potential respondents had visited such facilities or other designated sites and if they were willing to complete a visitor-expenditure questionnaire. Of this number, 1,749 were eligible and accepted the assignment; 616 actually completed and returned the questionnaire, a 35.2 percent return rate.[4]

Example 3. In some cases, several surveys may be used to gather comprehensive information within an overall research project. For example, Betz and Perdue used three separate surveys to examine the role of amenity resources in rural recreation and tourism development in a southeastern state. These were: (1) a self-administered mail questionnaire sent to a sample of state residents drawn from Motor Vehicle Department registration files; (2) a statewide survey sent to a random sample of residents by the state division of parks and recreation, as part of its Statewide Comprehensive Outdoor Plan (SCORP); and (3) a visitor survey hand-delivered to visitors from other states at interstate highway welcome centers, airports, a visitor center, and popular tourist areas at federally owned parks. Respectively, study returns had 51.5, 45.1, and 55.3 percent response rates.[5]

Problems in the Use of Questionnaires

There are a number of inherent problems in the use of questionnaires that researchers must guard against—both in designing an instrument and in its application. These include the following:

1. Respondents' lack of knowledge about a subject. People may often answer surveys with information that is hazy or insecure in order to "play along" or to appear cooperative. A special problem has to do with the fallibility of memory; it may be wise to advise respondents not to answer questions if they are not sure of their replies. In some cases, it may be helpful to consult records or other sources to support or enrich one's answers.

2. Respondents' failure to understand questions or to mark responses in the correct columns or spaces may result in invalid responses that must be rejected or in some cases incorrect data being tabulated. Careful directions and pretesting of the survey help to prevent such faulty responses. In some cases, the best procedure is to have the survey administered in person, rather than by mail.

3. Cover-up, embarrassment, self-defensiveness, and similar factors may influence respondents to give inaccurate replies—either to make themselves appear in a positive light or because they are influenced by the identity of the interviewer (in the case of an administered questionnaire). Studies have shown, for example, that people will respond differently to a survey depending on the gender or ethnic identity of the person interviewing them.

INTERVIEWING METHODS

A second important data collection technique that is used chiefly in surveys but may also be appropriate in other types of studies is the interview. An interview is a conversation—either face-to-face or over the telephone.

Interviews tend to be of two types: (1) prestructured conversations that use a detailed, printed series of questions that tend to be closed-ended and (2) lengthier and more flexibly structured conversations that often use open-end questions and that may move more freely and spontaneously into different topics.

In open-end questions, the respondent is simply asked the question and is expected to reply in her own words. The interviewer may then follow up by asking for more details or explanations. In either case, the interviewer should use a schedule or an outline to ensure that the same topics are covered with all subjects. If closed-end questions are used, they may be followed by open-end questions to get fuller detail or more subtle nuances of response. In general, quantitatively oriented studies are more likely to use prestructured approaches and closed-end questions; qualitative research tends to use a freer approach and more open-end questions.

The questions themselves may be retrospective (dealing with the past), concerned with present issues or topics, or focused on future expectations. There are essentially six types of questions in terms of subject matter:

1. *Background* or demographic questions, which deal with education, personal characteristics, and similar information.

2. *Experience* or behavior questions, which deal with past or current leisure involvements or practices.

3. *Knowledge* questions, which seek factual information.

4. *Opinion* or values-related questions, which explore what people think about a given issue or question.

5. *Feelings* questions, which explore emotional reactions or responses.

6. *Sensory* questions, which seek to identify basic responses to different stimuli or settings in visual, auditory, or other sensory terms.[6]

GUIDELINES FOR INTERVIEWING

1. The interviewer's appearance should be normal and appropriate to the setting. Interviewers should avoid provocative or unusual clothing and should not wear dark glasses unless it is absolutely essential, since they do not permit subjects to look into their eyes and may create a sense of suspicion.

2. If possible, interviews should be arranged and scheduled in advance, to ensure that subjects will be available and willing to take part. If not, and if an interviewer is hoping to question a group of randomly selected respondents in a recreation setting, it would be advisable to get the approval of the center director and have him or her assist in setting up interviews.

3. In asking questions, make sure they are thoroughly understood. If necessary, restate them, or ask the subject if she is absolutely clear on their meaning. If responses are still uncertain, press to make sure that you are getting an accurate response, and one that the subject really intends to deliver.

4. The interviewer should be careful not to talk too much and dominate the conversation. The chief purpose of the process is to get the respondent's ideas and information. To do this, the interviewer may sometimes deliberately remain silent to encourage a follow-up response or may simply repeat a word or two from the last response to suggest that more information would be helpful. At the same time, the interviewer must maintain control of the session by not letting the respondent ramble on or move into irrelevant topics.

5. At the beginning of the interview, assure the respondent that information given will be held in confidence and that he will not be identified as the source of information or opinions. At the same time, an effort should be made to establish rapport, described as a social relationship marked by mutual feelings of being "in harmony" and working together in an atmosphere of trust and shared purpose.

6. Record responses immediately, using a precoded tally sheet or answer form for closed-end questions (see pages 197–198). This may be reinforced by using a tape recorder with the subject's permission. Take additional written notes as necessary.

7. Do not indicate with any personal expression (humor, disapproval, surprise, disgust, etc.) that you disagree with or disapprove of any of the subject's responses. Never argue with or discuss a point with him or her,

other than through follow-up questions. Subjects should be treated in a respectful, friendly, but impersonal way, and no attempt should be made to influence them in any way.

8. If the interview is a long one, encourage respondents with comments like, "We're doing very well," or "We are halfway through now," if they are getting restless or seem to want to stop.

9. When the interview is completed, thank respondents for their cooperation. Keep detailed notes on when and where the interview was conducted and transcribe your written notes as soon as possible to ensure accuracy and make sure they are not misplaced.

Although most interviews are conducted on a formal, structured basis, with subjects knowing that they are taking part in an actual research study, Moeller and associates argue that formal interviews frequently result in biased or misleading responses. Instead, they suggest that informal interviews, in which the subject is not aware of being purposefully examined but in which responses are still solicited to specific questions, may provide a useful alternative. This approach, they argue, serves as a useful cross check on the validity of data gathered by other methods and avoids some of the sources of bias associated with formal interviews and questionnaires. They write:

> In addition, the relaxed atmosphere of the informal interview may elicit responses that more closely approximate people's private feelings, as opposed to "public" sentiments that they might report on a questionnaire.[7]

Example 1. In some cases, interviews are used as the first stage of a survey, followed up by a mailed, written questionnaire. For example, Dawson, Blahna, and Keith conducted a study of actual and expected economic impacts of Great Basin National Park in three counties in Nevada and Utah. Over an 83-day period, randomly selected visitors participated in short on-site interviews in geographically stratified locations within the park. They were then given a questionnaire to be mailed back when they returned home.[8]

Example 2. Similarly, in a study of alcohol expectancies and leisure, Carruthers interviewed 502 individuals by telephone concerning their leisure involvements, including the frequency and quantity of their alcohol consumption. This procedure was followed by a questionnaire mailed to 151 individuals who had identified themselves as "moderate" to "heavy" drinkers and to 139 "light" drinkers, with a 50 percent response rate overall.[9]

Example 3. Frisby and Brown carried out a qualitative study of women occupying middle and upper management positions in municipal recreation in Ontario, Canada, using an interview approach. Thirty randomly selected individuals were asked a series of preset open-end questions in seven areas dealing with personal background and career development. Frisby and Brown summarized the interview procedure:

Follow-up questions were . . . used to clarify and expand on the information depending on the initial response and the experiences of the subject. For example, the follow-up questions under the family category varied depending on whether or not the subject had children.

The interviews were tape recorded and ranged from 90 minutes to three hours in length. The material was transcribed verbatim, reviewed to uncover themes and sub-themes, and responses were organized accordingly. The content analysis of the data involved a search for patterns that were common to the majority of women, as well as the identification of unique individual experiences that illustrate the diversity of women's career development.[10]

DIRECT OBSERVATION

A third major type of data-gathering in social research consists of direct observation. Actually, all research dealing with human beings in which researchers gather empirical data is a form of observation. Since a central purpose of social research is to understand the actions and behaviors of people, a natural and obvious technique, Robson writes:

> . . . is to watch what they do, to record this in some way and then to describe, analyze and interpret what we have observed. Much research with people involves observation in a general sense. The typical experiment, whether in the laboratory or in the field, is simply a form of controlled observation.[11]

Two distinctly different forms of observation are used in research, however. One is *structured observation,* a quantitatively oriented method which relies on study instruments that provide a framework with which to measure the behaviors of subjects. For example, in a study of the play behavior of children in a carefully designed environment, the observer might watch through a one-way mirror and tabulate different aspects of behavior (see page 189).

The second method is *participant observation,* in which the researcher becomes, to a greater or lesser degree, part of the group she is observing. It is an essentially qualitative approach rooted in the work of anthropologists and sociologists who have examined social behavior in field settings. This method is considered a way to get at "real life" in the "real world."

The participant observer's role may range from one extreme in which he becomes part of the group being studied but remains relatively uninvolved in their interaction, to the other extreme, in which he becomes heavily involved. Both approaches have their disadvantages: The pure observer will be regarded by group members as an outsider; and the heavily involved participant-observer is likely to influence the group significantly and lose a degree of objectivity because he becomes too involved in the group.

Ideally, the researcher should strive for a middle course so that she is close to the action and can see what happens from the perspective of group members. At the same time, she should maintain a degree of distance so that group members continue to be aware of her separate identity and purpose.

Use of Field Notes

As a form of qualitative research, participant observation should be systematic in the sense of requiring accurate and complete field notes. Saslow writes:

> When doing research, observers must answer some questions before making observations. *What* are they looking for? *Whom* are they going to observe? *When* and *where* is the observing to be done? *How* are the observations to be made? *In what form* are the observations to be recorded?[12]

Field notes should include:

1. A narrative account of the researcher's entry into the research setting, including the reasons for selecting it, and the use of "gatekeepers" (individuals with formal or informal authority to control the researcher's access to a setting).

2. An account of the researcher's initial self-disclosure—explanation of his purposes as well as self-presentation and personal style in terms acceptable to group members.

3. Negotiation of social relations with group members.

4. Explanation of methods used in observing group members.

5. Detailed recording of specific events, conversations, or other relevant interactions, with notes of group context, time, and place on each entry.

6. Focusing and sampling, in the sense that the researcher begins by getting a broad picture of the group's character and social interchange and gradually focuses on a selection of experiences or events that illustrate or lead to theory development.

7. Fuller discussion and interpretation of the meaning and implications of data observed, with generalizations that can be transformed into theoretical conclusions.

If field research is quantitatively oriented, it is likely to include other types of data-gathering, such as the use of checklists, rating scales, and frequency counts or duration counts of specific behaviors, to provide material that can be numerically tallied and statistically analyzed.

Mechanical means of recording events may be used, including filming or videotaping, still photographs, or audio recording. They may be used openly or unobtrusively; in either case it may be necessary for researchers to obtain permission from subjects, their parents or guardians, or other authorities. The advantage, Chadwick and associates point out, is that recordings permit continued, in-depth data analysis long after the event.[13]

As the participant observation study continues, it becomes necessary for the researcher to get beyond a preoccupation with the mass of detailed data gathered from ongoing, day-by-day experiences and to begin to sort out the most important issues or perspectives. Hessler calls this stage "hawking," in the sense that the researcher must rise above the forest to see it more clearly, getting away from the individual trees and gaining a broader and clearer perspective of the group under observation.

At the same time, the researcher may begin to take a more probing and detailed set of observations, focusing attention on what appear to be the more critical interactions or processes at work. It is helpful to reread notes periodically and record ideas and speculations prompted by them, both to begin to develop explanatory theories and to guide the continuing study process.

Written notes should be made as promptly as possible after observations and should be kept in a safe place. Often, it is advisable to use pseudonyms for major participants described in records as a way of assuring anonymity and honoring the principle of confidentiality. In some cases, observational field studies may use self-reporting approaches to gather a range of different kinds of data.

Example. In a quantitatively oriented field study, Voelkl and Mathieu examined the daily activity patterns and accompanying affect of a sample of depressed and nondepressed nursing home residents. In addition to using a number of tests to measure the cognitive and functional abilities of subjects and to classify them in terms of degree of depression, the examiners systematically monitored the subjects using electronic paging devices at random times each day to gather accurate information on their involvement and mood at the moment, through self-reporting procedures.

> For each self-report form, subjects responded to a question regarding activity involvement (i.e., "What is the main thing you are doing?"). Responses on activity involvement were categorized into the following groups: daily tasks, eating, television viewing, independent activities, and passive activities. . . . Four 8-point semantic differential items were used to reflect affect (i.e., happy-unhappy, cheerful-irritable, friendly-angry, sociable-lonely . . .).[14]

DATA-GATHERING IN EXPERIMENTAL RESEARCH

The data-gathering procedures used in pre- and posttest stages of experiments may vary greatly, according to the hypothesis being tested. For example, if the study's purpose was to determine whether a given administrative procedure would result in a higher or lower level of staff members' morale, it would be necessary to measure the morale of the members of experimental and control groups both before and after the application of the administrative procedure. This might be done in several ways: through questionnaires, interviews, and observation of on-the-job behavior—or possibly through a combination of these.

If the purpose was to measure the impact of a midnight inner-city basketball league on juvenile delinquent gang activity, the data-gathering process might involve a comparison of police records in a single district of the city over time or a comparison of several districts of the city, served or not served by this program. Or, within a qualitative approach, participant observation might provide more meaningful information about the program's impact than purely quantitative information.

Ensuring Validity and Reliability

Throughout the data-gathering process in experimental studies, it is essential to control the threats to validity and reliability that were described in Chapter 5, such as the effect of pretesting procedures or experimental mortality. It is particularly important to control extraneous or confounding variables that may distort study findings.

For example, the so-called Hawthorne effect, in which subjects in an experiment tend to feel better or perform more effectively simply because they know that they are receiving special attention, can distort the findings of an experimental study. In medical research, when a control group is being given a "placebo," or inert medication, it is common practice to conceal this information from subjects. This is referred to as a "blind" experiment. When both the subjects and the raters are kept ignorant regarding the real treatment, it is known as a "double blind." In social research, it is necessary to maintain similar controls in experimental studies, in order to avoid possible contamination of the findings.

It is difficult to conduct effective experimental research in recreation, parks, and leisure services for two reasons: (1) If the experiment is structured in an artificial, laboratorylike environment, it is difficult to make it realistic for the subjects and to create a truly recreational kind of climate for participation, and (2) if it is carried on in a natural, field setting, it is difficult to maintain effective controls over subjects that would shield them from extraneous variables that might distort the study findings. In addition to those threats, other areas of difficulty include:

1. Investigator bias, either in terms of the experimenter not being totally objective or consistent in his group direction or assessment of study effects or in terms of subjects' response to different types of investigators.

2. Difficulty in maintaining the *ceteris paribus* principle—the Latin phrase that describes the need to keep all factors other than the experimental and control variables constant so that if significantly different outcomes are noted, it can be concluded that the experimental factors had to be responsible for them.

The actual techniques used to gather information in an experimental study may range from the use of self-concept scales or other means of measuring cognitive performance, affective change, or social behavior, to economic analysis or the use of social-indicators.

In experimental research particularly, applying procedures that will not be injurious to study subjects is critically important. Unlike descriptive research, which seeks simply to record and interpret what *is,* experimental research is obtrusive and has a direct impact on people's lives. It is therefore essential that the study design and procedures be carefully planned and monitored to ensure that the experiment is not only valid and reliable in its findings, but that it adheres fully to accepted human subjects guidelines and other principles of ethically guided research.

ORGANIZING DATA AND CODING SCHEMES

In all forms of research, it is necessary to gather data as systematically as possible in terms of both recording it accurately and organizing it so that it can be analyzed efficiently.

Typically, if one were to observe a playground regularly over a period of several weeks, one might see dozens or perhaps hundreds of different kinds of behaviors. These might fall under a number of headings: (1) games, sports, or other activities; (2) different kinds of interpersonal behaviors, such as competition or cooperation, aggression or expressions of friendship; (3) passive and active play; (4) individual and group activity; and (5) risk-taking or cautious use of play equipment.

To record all these possibilities as they occurred might result in a huge incoherent list of notes. Instead, based on the conceptual framework and purposes of the study, it should be possible to identify the key variables, relationships, dimensions of behavior, and other elements that the research is intended to investigate. Based on these, a model might be built that diagrams the major study elements and shows their relationship in terms of setting, roles played, the nature of events, and similar elements. Based on this model, a coding scheme is developed that contains predetermined categories for recording what is observed.

The scheme should identify specific behaviors and should use a time frame that indicates the length of time in which specific behaviors occur. For example, a scheme widely used in the observation of teacher/pupil interaction has 10 categories of interactions; some of those are teacher questions, teacher lectures, teacher gives direction, teacher praises student, student response, silence, and confusion. A typical recording sheet has horizontal rows, each divided into 20 three-second (one minute) intervals. The observer must identify and time the duration of all teacher/student interactions, using the coded numbers for each behavior.[15]

An example of this approach applied to recording the behavior of children in a playground or playschool setting is shown in Figure 13.1. It is designed to record the play behavior of individual children and requires one observer/recorder for each child—or, for less sharply defined observation, each two or three children.

Robson suggests guidelines for developing such coding schemes, based on initial exploratory observation. They should be:

Focused, only looking at carefully selected aspects of what is going on, gathering information relevant to the purposes of the study and excluding irrelevant data

Objective and *Explicitly Defined,* requiring little inference from the observer and clearly defined, with examples showing what belongs within the category and what does not

Exhaustive, covering all possibilities that may occur within the setting that is pertinent to the research

FIGURE 13.1   Recording form for observing play behavior.

Subjects:	Data Category	Time Frame (15 Two-Minute Intervals)														
Susan D.		10:00	10:02	10:04	10:06	10:08	10:10	10:12	10:14	10:16	10:18	10:20	10:22	10:24	10:26	10:28
	Activity or Equipment Use															
	Group Involvement															
	Behavioral Style															

Activity/ Equipment Use	A-1 Slide	A-5 Arts and Crafts
	A-2 Swings	A-6 Wading Pool
	A-3 Sand Box	A-7 Ball Play
	A-4 Play with Toys	A-8 Other (Specify)
Group Involvement	B-1 Individual Play	
	B-2 Play in Dyad	
	B-3 Small-Group Play	
	B-4 Large-Group Play	
Behavioral Style	C-1 Uninvolved/Passive	
	C-2 Aggressive	
	C-3 Creative/Imaginative	
	C-4 Competitive	
	C-5 Cooperative	
	C-6 Other (Specify)	
Coding Method:	Mark code for *predominant* activity/equipment use, group involvement, and behavioral style for subject being observed, during each two-minute time period.	

Mutually Exclusive, so that there is only one category for each element coded and there can be no uncertainty about where to code a given behavior

Easy to Record, by simply checking a box or writing an identification number that classifies behavior automatically.[16]

Obviously, coding makes it easy for an observer to record data systematically and accurately. It also lends itself conveniently to later analysis. It has the weakness of compelling the observer to make instant choices about the nature of given behaviors and in some cases to exclude other relevant data by focusing on only one action during a given time period. Also, while it is a useful tool, it may provide a superficial reading of what is occurring in a given situation that does not probe beneath the surface. Henderson points out that a qualitative researcher with volumes of data may be tempted

> . . . to become mechanistic in organizing the data. One is cautioned, however, not to make the organization of the data too automatic. In other words, coding by reducing data to numbers is not appropriate in keeping with the tenets of interpretive research. Some coding by numbers does help one to reduce the data and may make it more accessible but the researcher must be careful not to replace the rich meaning of words with numbers.[17]

In one form or another, coding may be used in experiments, case studies, documentary or content analysis, or other types of research designs. Normally, questionnaires, indexes, scales, and other types of prestructured instruments requiring responses from subjects or ratings by investigators have their own built-in coding systems that permit ready transfer to numeric totals, percentages, or statistical analysis. A fuller and more detailed discussion of coding methods is provided in Chapter 14.

SUMMARY

Data-gathering is the actual heart of the research enterprise for it is at this point that information is gathered that fulfills the purpose of the study, tests hypotheses, or provides the basis for model-building or theory development. This chapter describes the use of questionnaire surveys, interviews, and participant observation, providing guidelines and giving illustrations of their uses in recreation, parks, and leisure studies research.

The chapter then discusses data-gathering in experimental research, with emphasis on avoiding the difficulties inherent in this type of study. It concludes with an overview of coding methods, both as a means of immediately and systematically recording ongoing events or observations and as a preliminary step leading to efficient statistical analysis of study findings.

QUESTIONS AND ACTIVITIES

The following can be used as in-class workshops.

1. *Instrument Development.* Select one or more of the problems that were developed by class members as assignments for Chapters 9 and 10. Using a small-group approach, develop appropriate instruments for them of the following types, to be presented and reviewed in class:

    a. Questionnaire

    b. Rating scale or checklist

    c. Observational form

    If possible, design these instruments so that different types of studies (surveys, experiments, case studies, etc.) are represented.

2. *Interview Methods.* The instructor prepares an interview schedule for a specific research investigation. Carry out one or more mock interviews in class, using a role-playing approach. Class members may review each performance in turn and develop additional guidelines for effective interviewing.

3. *Coding Scheme.* Students field-test with classmates or other groups of students or in another convenient setting one of the instruments developed in workshop activity 1 above. Based on the range and variety of responses gathered in this procedure, develop a coding scheme to facilitate both the application of the instrument and the later analysis of its findings.

ENDNOTES

1. Richard Hessler, *Social Research Methods* (New York, Los Angeles: West Publishing Co., 1992): 252.

2. Bruce Chadwick, Howard Bahr, and Stan Albrecht, *Social Science Research Methods* (Englewood Cliffs, NJ: Prentice-Hall, 1984): 148.

3. Samuel Lankford, Larry Neal, and Barton Buxton, "An Examination and Comparison of Work Motivators in Public, Private/Commercial, Nonprofit, and Armed Forces Leisure Service Organizations," *Journal of Park and Recreation Administration* 10, no. 4 (1992): 62–63.

4. Michael Kanters and M. Randy Botkin, "The Economic Impact of Public Leisure Services in Illinois," *Journal of Park and Recreation Administration* 10, no. 3 (1992): 3–4.

5. Carter Betz and Richard Perdue, "The Role of Amenity Resources in Recreation and Tourism Development," *Journal of Park and Recreation Administration* 11, no. 4 (1993): 17.

6. Adapted from Hessler, *Social Research Methods,* 336–38.

7. George Moeller, Michael Mescher, Thomas More, and Elwood Shafer, "The Informal Interview as a Technique for Recreation Research," *Journal of Leisure Research* (2d quarter 1992): 155–67.

8. Scott Dawson, Dale Blahna, and John Keith, "Expected and Actual Regional Economic Impacts of Great Basin National Park," *Journal of Park and Recreation Administration* 11, no. 4 (1993): 49.

9. Cynthia Carruthers, "Leisure and Alcohol Expectations," *Journal of Leisure Research* 25, no. 3 (1993): 232–33.

10. Wendy Frisby and Barbara Brown, "Women Leisure Service Managers," *Journal of Applied Recreation Research* 16, no. 4 (1991): 300.

11. Colin Robson, *Real World Research* (Cambridge, MA: Blackwell, 1993): 190.

12. Carol Saslow, *Basic Research Methods* (New York: Random House, 1982): 10.

13. Chadwick, Bahr, and Albrecht, *Social Science Research Methods,* 82.

14. Judith Voelkl and Mary Mathieu, "Differences Between Depressed and Nondepressed Residents of Nursing Homes on Measures of Daily Activity Involvement and Affect," *Therapeutic Recreation Journal* (3d quarter 1993): 148–49.

15. Robson, *Real World Research,* 211.

16. Ibid., 213.

17. Karla Henderson, *Dimensions of Choice: A Qualitative Approach to Recreation, Parks and Leisure Research* (State College, PA: Venture Publishing, 1991): 127.

Data Organization and Descriptive Statistics

The general study of statistics is usually divided into two topical areas: descriptive and inductive statistics. **Descriptive statistics** *or, more accurately, the* descriptive statistical method *is any treatment of numerical data that does not involve making generalizations from a sample to a population. That is, when we are interested in describing a group of elements (people, test scores, etc.), we use descriptive statistics. When we make generalizations, predictions, estimations, or otherwise arrive at decisions in the face of uncertainty, we are using* **inductive statistics** *by a process called* statistical inference.[1]

INTRODUCTION

When all the data in a research study have been collected, they must be organized, analyzed, and interpreted. It is desirable to use quantification to organize and report data whenever possible. *Quantification* has been defined as a numeric method of describing or presenting the events or elements that are part of a study. It provides a valid, precise, and readily understandable means of presenting information and is a useful basis for statistical analysis. Further, the computer, which is the primary tool for analyzing data, deals more efficiently with numeric than with nonnumeric characters. The data values in statistical analysis are represented as numbers in the computer. This chapter introduces the use of statistics in recreation and leisure research and evaluation.

STATISTICS AS AN ESSENTIAL PROCESS

Statistics is the basic process of organizing and interpreting numbers to arrive at their meaning. Using statistics, one can order vast amounts of information in a manner that is easily understood if presented in an appropriate format. The worlds of business, science, the military, education, psychology, and sociology rely upon statistics to clarify life-style trends, patterns of behavior, the effectiveness of products, and similar concerns. Statistics help create order in our lives.

Too often, the claims or conclusions of statistics are poorly understood by the average person—particularly when they are used to support claims by groups or organizations that have vested interests in the outcome. One popular saying has been, "There are three types of liars: plain liars, damn liars, and statisticians." Another saying is that "Researchers too often use statistics the way a drunk uses a lamp post—more as a means of support than for illumination." These claims are unfortunate since, on the whole, statistics are a very common and beneficial tool.

Thus, statistics is an essential means of dealing with research data today, particularly with the help of computers, which make possible extremely rapid and complicated analysis of great bulks of data. We are fortunate to possess the technology that allows us to grasp and understand data that were not readily available to us just a few years ago.

Before we can begin to explore the use of statistics in the research process, we must first understand how we store and prepare the data we have collected for statistical analysis. Data organization is critical to the successful completion of a research project.

METHODS OF DATA ORGANIZATION

This section presents guidelines for preparing and organizing data for analysis, particularly the kinds of data that may be derived from questionnaires or from other data-intensive research studies.

It would be a mistake to think of the data-analysis process as something that happens *after* the study data are gathered. Data analysis should be carefully planned at an early stage in developing the study proposal.

In identifying the study purposes and selecting an appropriate research design, the selection of the variables you intend to identify and measure should have been thought out carefully. Similarly, in designing study instruments, it is desirable to precode all test items and responses so that each potential response is identified by a number and/or letter, with additional space left for other possible replies. This will be explained further in the section on creating a code book.

Planning the Analysis

As you prepare to organize your data, it is helpful to identify in outline form the tables or charts you expect to develop, based on the information you have gathered. This involves restating your research question or hypothesis in a form that lends itself to analysis. There is nothing worse than to determine, after the data is collected, that you need another piece of information. Printing the specific variables across the top and down the side of tables and charts forces you to state the variables explicitly and to decide exactly which totals, percentages, or trends over time you will report or which relationships you may want to explore.

For example, in a survey that reports recreational participation by a diverse sample of community residents in programs sponsored by a public recreation and parks agency, you might decide to develop findings on any of the following:

1. Ranked order of the most popular activities, with the percentage of the overall population that engages in them or with reported frequencies of participation for each activity, by the week, month, or year

2. A breakdown of the most popular groups of activities (such as active sports or creative arts), with respect to participation by different age groups

3. Identification of the major districts of the city, showing patterns of popularity of individual activities or groups of activities within each geographical area

4. Tables showing seasonal participation (for fall, winter, spring, and summer) for overall listing of activities or selected groups

5. Tables showing estimated spending on recreation for different age groups or for areas of the city or types of activities

6. Tables contrasting participation by age, by sex, by race, by socioeconomic status, or by other demographic variables

To develop such analyses, it is necessary to transfer scores from the data-gathering instruments, such as survey questionnaires or survey rating forms, to a form in which they can be systematically analyzed. The construction of a data collection form can be very helpful whether the data are to be hand tabulated or analyzed using a computer.

Data Collection Forms

The *data collection form* provides a means of organizing the data in a manner that allows for easy analysis and interpretation. It is the first step in the analysis process. Usually, it is designed based on the questionnaire or rating sheet itself, with all questions and response items listed in turn, with all possible responses following them. Thus, a data collection form simply reorganizes the information on the questionnaire, which provides space for tallying the responses. To save time and ensure greater accuracy, one person should read the data while another records them on the tabulation sheet. To complete the collection form, a coding system must be in place because only numeric values or symbols will be used on the form. The coding system will be discussed later in the section on developing the code book.

Figure 14.1 is an example of a data collection form for a simple study assessing the level of participation of college students in various sports. Assume that the variables collected were:

*Student ID

*Student age

*Student gender

*Student class

*Days of participation in tennis each year

*Days of participation in golf each year

*Days of participation in volleyball each year

*Days of participation in softball each year

Notice that numeric symbols are used for gender and class. All other variables are represented by their actual numeric values, that is, by age and by days of participation. The days of participation are represented by three-digit numbers, ranging from 001 to 365. This facilitates the data collection forms being used as an intermediary step in transferring the data to a computer for analysis. In most cases, the data must be in a fixed format; that is, all pieces of datum must follow the same form, for computer analysis.

If a very limited number of students was surveyed, the data would probably be hand-tabulated and analyzed. In this case, the data collection form may include TOTAL columns at the bottom of the form for summary information. If several hundred students were involved in the study, the form would be used as an intermediary step to computer data entry.

Consideration of data organization in preplanning a study allows other options that do not involve the creation of a data collection form as described above. The instrument itself could be used as the data collection form if the information is recorded on it in a manner that makes it easily entered into the computer. This may involve placing next to each question or item small numbers that correspond to the possible values of a variable. For example, the question relating to the respondent's gender may be presented as follows, where the appropriate response is checked and the numbers are used for analysis:

Gender: Male____(1) Female____(2)

Another option is to include a column to the right of each question that has appropriate spaces for recording each response. This column would be filled out by the researcher following the completion of the instrument by the respondent. This area of the instrument is bordered in some manner and is labeled appropriately so as not to confuse the respondent. Using gender and student class as examples, the instrument would appear as shown in Figure 14.2.

FIGURE 14.1   Data collection form.

ID	Student age	Student gender 1=male 2=female	Student class 1=freshman 2=sophomore 3=junior 4=senior 5=graduate student	Tennis participation (3 digits)	Golf participation (3 digits)	Volleyball participation (3 digits)	Softball participation (3 digits)

FIGURE 14.2   Sample of a data collection form.

1. Gender: Male _____   Female _____

2. Student Class: Freshman _____

                          Sophomore _____

                          Junior _____

                          Senior _____

                  Graduate Student _____

FOR OFFICE USE ONLY

1. _____

2. _____

As suggested previously, the numeric codes for gender and student class would be written in the designated area (FOR OFFICE USE ONLY) for the appropriate question.

Where resources and technology are available, another means of organizing one's data is through the use of an *optical scoring sheet,* which can be read electronically by an optical scanner. The respondent fills in the scoring sheet that accompanies the study instrument. The scoring sheet has only numeric or alphabetic options for responses; therefore, the study instrument must be designed so that the respondent clearly understands that he must check or mark an appropriate number or letter. These forms are very similar to the ones used for standardized tests such as the SATs or GREs. The advantages of using the optical scoring sheet are that it is very fast and that it eliminates the need to transfer information by hand. The optical scanner does not make mistakes; therefore, there is no concern about the recorder incorrectly transferring the data. On the other hand, optical scanners are quite expensive; one should not assume the use of this method of data organization since it may not be readily available.

Computer Analysis of Data

Increasingly, with the availability of mainframe computers and the increased capabilities of personal computers in terms of hardware and software, electronic data processing has almost completely taken the place of hand tabulation and analysis. Certainly, in more extensive investigations where complex analysis is called for, computers provide the most efficient means of tabulating and analyzing data. A tremendous advantage of computer data analysis is that, once the original findings are on disks, diskettes, or tapes, it is possible to examine them at any level of complexity—from simple totals or percentages to more sophisticated questions involving the relationship of different subgroups or variables in the study population. The investigator may return to the data again and again to test hypotheses or to explore other study findings.

Several computer programs greatly simplify statistical analysis. Two of the most common are Statistical Package for the Social Sciences (SPSS[x]) and Statistical Analysis System (SAS). Versions of these and other packages are available for even the simplest personal computer. Each package is capable of performing a variety of statistical procedures, ranging from simple frequency distributions for descriptive purposes to highly complex statistical analyses. The beauty of these packages is their flexibility—virtually any data set can be analyzed. Each statistical procedure can be adapted to the number of subjects, to the number of variables, and even in some cases to the level of measurement. The same statistical procedure can be run for more than 100 research questions simultaneously. The packages accommodate the transformation of variables, the creation of new variables through arithmetic operations of existing variables, the redefining of variables, and the selection of specific levels of a variable.

Although each package includes a manual that explains the various statistical procedures it can perform, the manual is not a complete textbook on statistical application. One must possess a basic understanding of statistical analysis to utilize these packages effectively. Further, because of the flexibility of the packages, their use becomes quite involved; one must set up the statistical procedure to address the research hypothesis and/or research question and fit the nature of the data set.

To illustrate the use of a statistical package, we will utilize information gathered in a large leisure-services marketing study conducted by the authors of this text. We will illustrate a basic cross tabulation program from the Statistical Package for the Social Sciences (SPSS[x]).[2, 3]

To use a statistical package, a set of control statements and procedure statements must be prepared according to rigidly specified procedures. These statements are organized into a program file contained in the computer where they can be called upon when the researcher desires to conduct a specific statistical analysis. The program file must conform to the data. In addition to the program file, the data must also be entered into the computer so they can be read and analyzed through use of the program file. Sometimes the data are actually contained within the program file, but more often they are organized in a separate file simply called the data file.

Code Book

Normally, when we collect data through any of a variety of mechanisms, we develop a code book. This *code book* specifies how the data should be entered into the data file and also how the program file must be developed to utilize these data. Previously we discussed transferring data into the computer. A file is created in the computer consisting of the data from all respondents and is simply referred to as the data file. The program file refers to the set of statements that relate to the directions (commands) needed to execute a particular statistical analysis the researcher desires. It is also contained within the computer and relates directly to the data file.

A code book is a simple but essential aspect of the research process. Earlier we talked about hand-tabulating our data. Even with this manual procedure, aspects of the code book are needed for ease of tabulation. If we asked 1,000 people to list their favorite leisure activities, they might easily mention hundreds of activities. Rather than writing out the activity each time it is mentioned, we assign it a code. For example, jogging could be the code 0001, swimming could be the code 0002, and so on. Now a number represents an activity. This same principle can be applied to all data we collect; we code the data using numeric symbols. We say numeric symbols because they may not possess any mathematical properties. For example, the number 1 may be the code for male, and the number 2 may be the code for female. These are only symbols for categorical (nominal) data and have no numeric value. However, the number 135 may represent the weight of an individual, and in this case the data do have numeric value with arithmetic properties.

When using the computer for analysis, the code book not only specifies the code for each piece of datum, it indicates the name of each piece of datum to be used for the program file and the placement of the data in the data file. Figure 14.3 presents one page of a code book used for the leisure-services marketing study previously mentioned. The code book has four essential items of information. The first item is the survey question, which indicates the piece of information to be coded, for example the township zone, the age of adult No. 1, and so on. The second item of information is the column in which the data will be placed within the data file. For example, the *I.D. NO.* is the first piece of datum to be placed in the data file.

Therefore, it goes in the first four columns (1–4) of the file. (Traditionally, data files have been set up with 80 columns of information; however, this need not be the case with today's computers and statistical packages.) Because the I.D. NO. can be four digits, it will utilize four columns. The third item of information in the code book is the actual numeric symbol to be used in the data file. In the case of the I.D. NO., the codes will range from 0001 to 1000. This is because there were potentially 1,000 respondents in the study. Notice that, for marital status, the codes are 1 through 4 with a 9 indicating a missing value. The missing value simply tells the computer that the individual didn't respond to this question. The last item of information in the code book is the name of the variable that will be used in the computer program file. Each statistical package has very specific requirements for the "computer names." In this case, we have simply named our variables VAR001 to VAR011. This code book was set up for an SPSS[x] program

FIGURE 14.3   A page from the leisure-services code book.

Survey Question	Column	Code	Computer Name
I.D. No.	1–4	0001–1000	VAR001
Township zone	5	1–5	VAR002
		9=missing value	
Individual information			
Length of residence	6–7	01–96	VAR003
		99=Missing value	
Marital status	8	1=Single	VAR004
		2=Married	
		3=Divorced	
		4=Other	
		9=Missing value	
Adult No. 1 age	9–10	01–98 years	VAR005
		99=Missing value	
Adult No. 1 sex	11	1=Male	VAR006
		2=White	
		9=Missing value	
Adult No. 1 race	12	1=Black	VAR007
		2=White	
		4=Asian	
		5=Other	
		9=Missing value	
Facility maintenance			
Large community center	13	1=Very good	VAR008
		2=Good	
		3=Fair	
		4=Poor	
		9=Missing value	
Neighborhood park	14	Same	VAR009
Tennis courts	15	Same	VAR010
Soft/baseball fields	16	Same	VAR011

file using sequentially named variables, which saves time in writing the program file.

Program File

As stated previously, the program file consists of control statements and procedure statements. Control statements provide information about the variables to be analyzed and general information about the nature of the file itself. The procedure statements address the specific types of statistical analysis the researcher would like to run. Figure 14.4 illustrates the SPSS^x program file used to conduct the cross-tabulation analysis in Table 14.1 (found later in the chapter).

The SPSS^x program file usually has a maximum length of 80 columns but may vary with type of computer and operating system. The name of each control and procedure statement (command keyword) begins in column 1 and continues for as many lines as needed.

The TITLE statement in Figure 14.4 provides a title for the particular analysis the researcher will be performing. The name of the control statement begins in column 1. The title may not exceed 60 characters, and it must be enclosed in apostrophes or quotation marks.

The DATA LIST FILE statement is the most important statement in the program file. It names the variables to be studied and indicates the columns in which the data can be found within the data file. The DATA LIST FILE statement may be continued on several lines with the continuation lines indented at least one column. The name LEISURE refers to the SPSS^x filename for your data file. The term FIXED means the data are placed in the data file in exactly the same way for all respondents. The number after RECORDS indicates the number of lines of data for each respondent. In this case, we could have omitted the number 1 since the default in SPSS^x is one line per respondent. The number following the slash indicates the data line to be read by the computer. Again, since we have only one line of data, we use a 1. However, if there were several data lines per respondent and we desired to only use data from line 3, for example, we would have placed a 3 in this position. Following a blank space, the names of the variables and the columns in which each variable is located

FIGURE 14.4   SPSS^x program file.

```
TITLE 'LEISURE SERVICES MARKETING STUDY'

DATA LIST FILE = LEISURE FIXED RECORDS = 1
   /1     VAR001 --4 VAR002 5 VAR003 6–7 VAR004 8 VAR005 9–10
          VAR006 TO VAR011 11–16
MISSING VALUES VAR007, VAR004, VAR006 TO VAR011 (9) VAR003, VAR005 (99)
VARIABLE LABELS VAR001 'RESPONDENT ID NO' VAR002 'TOWNSHIP ZONE'
          VAR003 'LENGTH OF RESIDENCE' VAR004 'MARITAL STATUS'
          VAR005 'AGE OF ADULT 1' VAR006 'SEX OF ADULT 1' VAR007 'RACE OF ADULT 1'
          VAR008 'MAINTENANCE-COMMUNITY PARK'
          VAR009 'MAINTENANCE NEIGHBORHOOD PARK'
          VAR010 'MAINTENANCE - TENNIS COURT'
          VAR011 'MAINTENANCE - SOFT- BASEBALL FLD'
VALUE LABELS VAR002 1 'ZONE 1' 2 'ZONE 2' 3 'ZONE 3' 4 'ZONE 4' 5 'ZONE 5'/
          VAR004 1 'SINGLE' 2 'MARRIED' 3 'DIVORCED' 4 'OTHER'/
          VAR006 1 'MALE' 2 'FEMALE'/
          VAR007 1 'BLACK' 2 'WHITE' 3 'HISPANIC' 4 'ASIAN' 5 'OTHER'/
          VAR008 TO VAR011 1 'VERY GOOD' 2 'GOOD' 3 'FAIR' 4 'POOR'
CROSSTABS VARIABLES = VAR007 (1,5) VAR008 (1,4)/ TABLES = VAR008 BY VAR007
OPTIONS 3, 4, 5
```

---

in the data file are defined. For example, VAR001 is the first variable in the data file, and its value is contained in columns 1 through 4. This process is continued for each variable. Notice that VAR007 through VAR010 are not explicitly defined in the statement. Since SPSS^x allows implicit definitions using the TO convention, these variables are defined by the term VAR006 TO VAR011. The variables VAR007 through VAR010 are implicit within this term. The term 11–16 indicates the columns in which the values of those variables are located. Six variables and six columns are available; therefore, the SPSS^x program recognizes that each variable is a single digit, each using one column. The variable name can be a maximum of eight alphabetic or numeric characters, but the first character must be alphabetic.

The MISSING VALUES statement provides a means of defining when a respondent does not provide a piece of information. For this case, the digit 9 is used to indicate a missing value of all single-digit variables, and 99 is used for 2-digit variables. Not all variables need a MISSING VALUE definition—only those that are critical to the researcher's analysis. Note the use of the TO convention again in this statement.

The VARIABLE LABELS statement provides a description for each variable. The description may be a maximum of 40 characters. First, the variable name is listed, and, following a blank, the description is provided. Each description is enclosed within apostrophes or quotation marks. For example, VAR001 refers to the respondent's identification number, RESPONDENT ID NO.

The VALUE LABELS statement describes the meaning of each value given to a variable. For example, VAR004 is the marital status of the respondent; a value of 1 indicates that the respondent is single, a value of 2 indicates the respondent is married, and so on. A VALUE LABEL is necessary only for those variables in which the numeric symbols do not have a specific numeric value but rather have some nonnumeric meaning. Note that the numeric symbol immediately follows the variable name, and then the value for each symbol is described enclosed in apostrophes or quotation marks. The description for each variable symbol (value) can be a maximum of 60 characters but may not include a "/" or ")". A slash is used to separate the value label descriptions between variables.

Up to this point, we have control statements only. A program file must also contain procedure statements. In our example, we have only one procedure statement; the CROSSTABS statement allows a very simple analysis of the relationship between two or more variables. In its simplest form, it is a joint-frequency distribution of two categorical variables. Various types of statistical analyses can be conducted with this procedure statement; however, our purpose is only to illustrate the use of a computer package (SPSS^x in this example) and not to explain various statistical procedures.

In our example, the CROSSTABS statement is developed for integer data. In the description section of the statement, the name of all the variables to be analyzed and their limiting values must be stated. The limiting values refer to the numeric symbols used to designate the various categories for each variable; for example, a 1 for VAR007 refers to a black respondent. First, all variables are listed using VARIABLES = followed by the name of each variable and its limiting value in parentheses. All variables to be presented in a table must be listed in this section; then in the TABLES section, the specific tables to be produced are defined. In this example, we are only producing one table, VAR008 by VAR007. The first variable is always the row variable. Several tables may be defined using multiple tables statements; however, we have presented just one table for illustrative purposes. OPTIONS 3, 4, and 5 were selected to print out row percentages, column percentages, and two-way table total percentages, respectively.

Table 14.1 presents the resulting computer printout from the CROSSTABS procedure defined in our program file. Respondents were asked to rate the quality of maintenance of a large community center they were attending. This table presents the cross tabulation of their responses, grouped by race

TABLE 14.1   How respondent rates maintenance of facility: by race.

VAR008	COUNT ROW PCT COL PCT TOTAL PCT	BLACK 1.	WHITE 2.	HISPANIC 3.	ASIAN 4.	OTHER ROW TOTAL 5.	ROW TOTAL
1. Very good		75 36.2 15.1 7.6	131 63.3 28.9 13.3	0 0 0 0	1 .5 100.0 1	0 0 0 0	207 21.1
2. Good		200 52.1 40.3 20.3	167 43.5 36.8 17.0	14 3.6 5.3 1.4	0 0 0 0	3 .8 3.5 .3	384 39.1
3. Fair		147 58 .1 29.6 15.0	95 37.5 20.9 9.7	8 3.2 33.3 .8	0 0 0 0	3 1.2 37.5 .3	253 25.7
4. Poor		74 53.2 14.9 7.5	61 43.9 13.4 6.2	2 1.4 8.3 .2	0 0 0 0	2 1.4 25.0 .2	139 14.1
	Column TOTAL	496 50.5	454 46.2	24 2.4	1 1	8 .8	983 100.0

of the respondent. Tables of this type are common in recreation and park research studies.

The clue to understanding the printout is in the upper left corner in which the four items (COUNT, ROW PCT, COL PCT, and TOT PCT) explain the meaning of the four numbers in each cell of the table.

The first key, COUNT, refers to the first (highest) number in each box. For example, 75 blacks rated maintenance as Very Good; 167 whites rated maintenance as Good; and so on.

The second key, ROW PCT, means Row Percentage and refers to the second number in each cell. *Row* means that the numbers are to be read horizontally, across the rows of cells. It tells each group's percentage of the total number that gave that rating. For example, of the total of 384 respondents who rated maintenance as Good, 52.1 percent were blacks, 43.5 percent were white, 3.6 percent were Hispanic, none were Asian, and 0.8 percent were Other.

The third key, COL PCT, means Column Percentage. It refers to the third number in each cell and indicates the percentage of the total in the column that a particular number represents. For example, of the 496 blacks who took part in the survey, 15.1 percent rated maintenance as Very Good, 40.3 percent as Good, 29.6 as Fair, and 14.9 percent as Poor. In each such case, the row or column percentages must add up to 100.

The fourth key, TOTAL PCT, means Total Percentage. It indicates the percentage that any cell represents, of the total group of respondents. For example, 8 Hispanics of the total of 983 respondents (0.8 percent) rated maintenance as Fair. In another column, 200 blacks out of the total number of 983 respondents, or 20.3 percent, rated maintenance as Good.

The other values to be interpreted are (1) the column on the far right, which shows the absolute number and the percentage for each rating (Very Good, 21.1 percent; Good, 39.1 percent, and so on; and (2) the row on the bottom, which shows the absolute number and percentage of each ethnic group responding to the survey (50.5 percent blacks, 46.2 percent whites, and so on).

DESCRIPTIVE AND INFERENTIAL STATISTICS

Now that we have organized our data and prepared them for analysis, we can begin to explore the use of statistics in the research process. It is helpful to understand its two basic types: *descriptive* and *inferential.*

Descriptive

This branch of statistics is primarily concerned with organizing, displaying, and interpreting data that describe all members of the group under investigation. Typical descriptive statistics include measures of central tendency (mean, mode, median) and measures of dispersion (range and standard deviation) but may include many other measures. Descriptive statistics limits its conclusions to the particular group of individuals observed or tested; no conclusions are extended beyond this group, and any similarity to others outside the group cannot be assumed. *Descriptive statistics* is used to describe a collection of observations, whether of the total population or of a sample from the population; thus, these measures are often used as preliminary forms of interpretation regardless of the nature or intent of the research.

Inferential

This branch of statistics uses data from a sample of individuals to infer one or more characteristics of the entire population. For example, a random sample of adult community residents are studied with respect to their preferences for recreation facilities; the characteristics found in this sample are assumed, within the limits of probable error, to be those of the entire adult community population. The small group is known as the sample; the larger group is the population. The summary value of each such characteristic of a sample is called a statistic, whereas these same measures for a population are referred to as parameters. In this context, a *statistic* is simply a measure (number, figure, and so on) based on observations of the study sample.

STEPS IN STATISTICAL ANALYSIS

Any of the following steps may be used in analyzing research data. The extent and nature of the statistical analysis, however, is tied directly to the problem of the study.

Organizing Data for Analysis

As stated previously, it is necessary to determine which variables or elements are to be measured and to organize them by grouping them into several major categories or sections for tabulation and analysis. At this point, the researcher must decide exactly which comparisons, relationships, time sequences, and other kinds of characteristics of the data she wants to explore. The data analysis relates directly to the original research questions and/or the hypotheses established by the investigation.

Simple Descriptive Measures

This is the most common type of analysis and involves carrying out procedures that describe only the subjects that have been analyzed. This includes measures of central tendency, measures of dispersion, percentage breakdowns, correlations, and similar types of analysis. A comprehensive description of the data is important to gaining an in-depth understanding of the study results and serves as a basis for further interpretation of the results.

Presentation of Descriptive Findings

The findings of such analyses may then be summarized, with interpretations and possible recommendations for action or further research. This should be directly keyed to the stated purposes or hypotheses of the study in precise, definitive statements. In an evaluation study, it may also involve developing a profile of the agency and its programs and comparing it to established norms or standards, as well as identifying areas of strength, weakness, and needed improvement. Frequently, tables, graphs, or charts may be used to visually summarize and present data so that the findings may be readily understood in a simplified, but fairly dramatic form.

Inferential Analysis

If appropriate to the study's purposes and the kinds of data that have been gathered, inferential statistical techniques may be used to explore character-istics of the larger population from which a study sample has been drawn. These methods are used to determine if significant relationships exist among variables, including both correlation and causal (cause-and-effect) relation-ships, and generally to determine whether the study's hypotheses have been accepted or rejected.

IMPLICATIONS OF LEVELS OF MEASUREMENT

In Chapter 11 we discussed the various levels of measurement. The implica-tions of that discussion become important with reference to the statistical pro-cedures one chooses in a study. An important rule of statistical analysis is that statistics that are useful at one level of measurement can always be used with higher-level variables, but not with lower-level variables. In other words, if data are interval-level, statistics that are useful for these data can also be used with ratio-level data. For example, the mean can be used with interval-level data as well as with ratio-level data; the mean cannot be used correctly with ordinal or nominal data. The median and mode are the appropriate measures of central tendency for the ordinal and nominal levels of measurement, respectively.

BASIC CONCEPTS UNDERLYING STATISTICAL ANALYSIS

In addition to levels of measurement, two basic concepts underlying the sta-tistical analysis of data involve the normal distribution of data and probability.

A key to understanding statistical analysis is the normal probability distribution. Early mathematicians found that the distribution of measurements of many phenomena approximated what we now call the normal curve. If one were to plot quantifiable scores of some phenomena (for example, weight, height, IQ) on a graph, the distribution of these measurements fit a bell-shaped curve, with the most frequent occurrences at or near the center. This finding is now commonly used to describe a set of data and predict future investigations. For example, in a graph showing the number of basketball shots that individuals in a youth sports program are able to make within a two-minute period, one might expect to find a pattern like that in Figure 14.5. The most commonly occurring scores are 9, 10, and 11, while higher and lower scores occur less frequently. The farther one moves from the center of the distribution (the mean), the less scores are likely to occur.

Normal Curve

The definition of the *normal curve* says that it is symmetrical around its vertical axis (midpoint), with the scores clustering around the *mean*. If it is fully symmetrical, all measures that mark the center of the scores (mode, median, mean) are in exactly the same location. In real life, however, this would rarely occur, particularly when a relatively few cases are involved.

Theoretically, the curve has no boundaries in either direction and never touches the baseline at its ends. In real distributions, however, scores obvi-

FIGURE 14.5 Example of a normal curve.

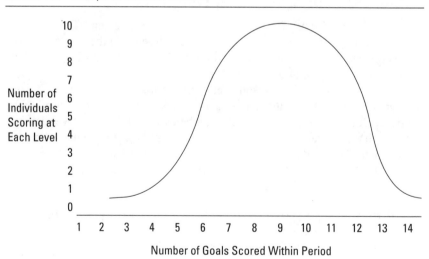

ously do occur very infrequently at either end. The curve is most likely to be symmetrical if the subjects measured are homogeneous in major respects. If they are not, the curve may be distorted. For example, in a population where half the group is active in exercise programs and half the group is not, a test of physical fitness might show a *bimodal* distribution, with two peaks or high points of central tendency and a valley between (see Figure 14.6).

If many participants are active in fitness programs but a small number are inactive or have special problems such as illness or malnutrition, the curve would be *skewed,* with a concentration of scores at one end of the distribution. Figure 14.7 shows a negatively skewed distribution with a preponderance of scores at the upper end of the distribution. A positively skewed distribution would have a preponderance of scores at the lower end of the distribution.

Figure 14.8 shows two distributions that have the same midpoint but a marked difference in the distribution of scores under the curve. This is due to the difference in the variability of the scores across the distributions. Where there is little variability, the normal curve will be peaked; and where scores have large variability, a flattened normal curve would result. This concept of variability will be explored further in the section discussing standard deviation and standard scores.

Probability

Probability has to do with the likelihood—or probability—that given events will occur. As a concept, it is illustrated in many ways in everyday life—for example, when odds are given on a basketball game or when a baseball player's performance is expressed in terms of percentages.

To illustrate, if a baseball player has a batting average of .300, he has hit safely 3 out of 10 times at bat, and the probability is that he will do so his next

FIGURE 14.6   Example of bimodal distribution.

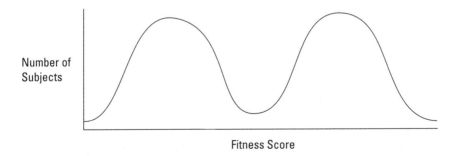

FIGURE 14.7   Example of skewed distribution.

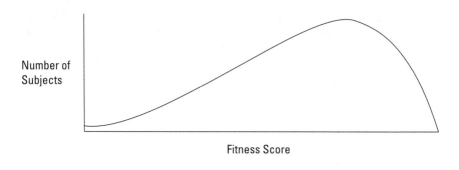

Number of
Subjects

Fitness Score

time at the plate; that is, the odds are 3 out of 10 that he will get a hit. Obviously, other factors may affect the outcome, such as the opposing pitcher's skills or the batter's own confidence or physical health. Thus, the odds may not stand up on a single day or even in a week or two. During a season, however, the likelihood is that the player's performance at the plate will be very close to his past record; a .300 batter will probably be close to that, and a .225 batter will be close to that.

Another example: The forecaster predicts a 30 percent chance of rain. When the current conditions existed in the past, it rained 30 percent of the time. Therefore, the prediction is that there is a 30 percent probability that it will happen again. Chance always influences isolated events. The probability that a tossed coin will come up heads is 50 percent. In a series of a few tosses, the 50/50 heads/tails percentage will probably not prevail; instead, it might be eight heads and two tails, or seven and three. In the long run, however, with hundreds of tosses, the percentage should move toward a 50/50 distribution.

Probability and the normal distribution are directly related. By knowing the characteristics of a distribution, we can estimate the probability of any particular score occurring in the distribution, as well as determine if a specific score is actually a part of the distribution with which we are working. The two dominant characteristics that need to be known to understand a distribution are the mean and standard deviation.

DESCRIPTIVE PROCEDURES

We will continue our discussion of descriptive statistics by examining a set of raw scores that might represent any of hundreds of possibilities in recreation and leisure: (1) figures of attendance at programs or facilities; (2) physical fitness scores of a group of participants; (3) per capita spending of communities on recreation and park budgets; (4) recreation agency employees; or (5) scores on a test of leisure attitudes. If one were to look at such scores in a totally unorganized way, it would be difficult to make sense of them. Therefore, it is nec-

FIGURE 14.8   Example of two distributions with different variability.

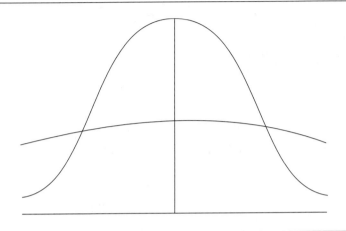

essary to organize them so that they can be conveniently tabulated and analyzed. Customarily this is done by means of frequency distributions.

Use of Frequency Distributions

Frequency distributions are a means of counting the frequency with which each score has been recorded and placing it within a framework that permits easy statistical calculations. The two types of frequency distribution are *simple* and *grouped.*

Simple frequency distribution

Starting with an unorganized set of scores that appear just as they were recorded, all scores would be listed in order of their size or value. A hypothetical set of scores would then appear as:

59	56	52	50	50	47	46	44	44	43	42	42	40
39	38	38	38	37	37	37	36	36	36	36	35	35
34	34	33	32	32	31	31	31	31	30	30	29	29
28	27	27	27	25	26	22	22	21	21	20	19	17

Each score would then be listed in order, with the number of times it occurs in the distribution, as follows:

59-1	58-0	57-0	56-1	55-0	54-0	53-0	52-1
51-0	50-2	49-0	48-0	47-1	46-1	45-0	44-2
43-1	42-2	41-0	40-1	39-1	38-3	37-3	36-4
35-2	34-2	33-1	32-2	31-3	30-2	29-2	28-1
27-3	26-1	25-1	24-1	23-0	22-2	21-2	20-1
19-1	18-0	17-1					

Simple frequency distributions are useful in getting a quick picture of the scores. For example, the range of the scores just shown (meaning the distance between the highest and lowest scores) is from 17 to 59, or 43, when one includes both the top and bottom scores. Simple frequency distributions also make it possible to identify the most common scores. In this case, the mode (the most common score) is quickly identified as 36, with a frequency of 4. Beyond this, it is necessary to group the scores to carry out other calculations.

Grouped frequency distribution

Grouped frequency distribution is a method of grouping data within a series of equal intervals, extending from the highest to the lowest scores. The number of scores occurring within each interval is recorded.

Interval defined. An interval is one of the equal divisions or units of the overall grouped frequency distribution. It is a mutually exclusive subset within the larger set of scores. The upper and lower limits of the interval control the scores that might be tallied within the interval. To design a grouped frequency distribution correctly, it is necessary to understand that individual pieces of data, or scores, may be of two types: *discrete* and *continuous*.

Discrete pieces of data record single, whole events or units. For example, one can shoot a basket 10 times or 11 times, but not 10 1/2 times. There may be 6 people in a room or 7, but not 6½.

Continuous data involve scores with finer measures, as in weight, time, or distance. A person rarely weighs exactly 136 or 163 pounds; instead he is likely to weigh 136.7 or 163.2 pounds—or, with highly sensitive scales, the figure might be extended to several decimal places.

If all scores were single whole numbers—such as 5, 8, or 10—there would be no need to define the limits of the intervals into which they are to be placed other than 4 to 6, 7 to 9, or 10 to 15, as examples. However, when a whole score is accompanied by a fraction or decimal place such as 10.6, where would one place it in a distribution where the intervals are 8 to 10, and then 11 to 13?

Upper and lower real limits. The answer is that intervals are considered to have upper and lower real limits to accommodate continuous data. The real limit is at the midpoint of the bottom integer of an interval and the top integer of the one below. For example, the midpoint between the interval of 8 to 10 and the interval of 11 to 13 is 10.5. To avoid the possibility of getting a score of 10.5 and not knowing where to place it, we will call the upper real limit of the interval of 8 to 10, 10.49, and the lower real limit of the interval 11 to 13, 10.5.

This makes it possible to locate any score that falls within the space between the two intervals. For example, a score of 10.3 would belong to the interval of 8 to 10, because it is below 10.49. A score of 10.6 would belong to the 11 to 13 interval, because it is above 10.5.

Constructing a grouped frequency distribution. To construct a grouped frequency distribution, it is necessary to decide on an appropriate width or size
for each interval. For example, in Table 14.2, the width of the interval is 3
and can be determined by counting up from the beginning of one step to the
beginning of the next (that is, from 16 to 19). It is usually advisable to have
between 10 and 20 intervals in a grouped frequency distribution. One
selects the interval by determining the range and then fitting possible intervals into it.

To illustrate in Table 14.2 the actual range of 43 (59 – 17 + 1) is extended
by adding one number at both the top and the bottom to give a total range of
45 without affecting the distribution. An interval width of 3 can be divided into
this 15 times (which is perfect), yielding the table below. As you view the frequency of each interval, a distribution of scores approximating the normal
curve presents itself; thus, these scores approximate a normal distribution.

By grouping a large number of individual scores into a frequency distribution with a lesser number of intervals, the data have been made much more
compact and easy to work with. The overall shape of the distribution and the
most common scores are easily recognized. A limitation of grouped distributions is that one loses sight of individual scores once they have been placed
within an interval. In fact, for the statistician, they no longer exist as actual
scores and instead are assumed to be spread out evenly along the interval in
which they appear.

TABLE 14.2   Example of grouped frequency distribution.

INTERVAL	TALLIES	FREQUENCY	CF*
58–60	1	1	52
55–57	1	1	51
52–54	1	1	50
49–51	11	2	49
46–48	11	2	47
43–45	111	3	45
40–42	111	3	42
37–39	⦦⦦ 11	7	39
34–36	⦦⦦ 111	8	32
31–33	⦦⦦ 1	6	24
28–30	⦦⦦	5	18
25–27	⦦⦦	5	13
22–24	111	3	8
19–21	111	3	5
16–18	11	2	2

N = (Number) = 52

*Cumulative frequency, added from lowest interval up

Measuring Central Tendency: Mode, Median, Mean

In descriptive statistics, a common beginning procedure is to measure *central tendency,* that is, to see where the center of the scores seems to lie or to identify the most common or typical scores. Measuring central tendency makes it possible to interpret the overall group performance and to compare it with other groups or to see how any single score or performance falls within the group itself. The word *average* (meaning the sum of all the scores divided by the number of scores) is often used to imply central tendency, but it is often applied incorrectly. Actually, the three best-known measures of central tendency are *mode, median,* and *mean.*

Mode

Mode is the single score (either the actual individual score in a simple frequency distribution or the midpoint of the interval that has the highest frequency) that occurs most frequently in a set of scores. In a frequency polygon (see Figure 14.11), the mode is the value along the horizontal axis at which the height of the curve is the highest. The mode provides a quick reference point, and it is the only measure of central tendency that can be appropriately used with nominal data. It can be used with higher-level data, but it does not provide as much insight into the distribution of scores as the other measures of central tendency.

Median

Median is the middle measure, or score, in a series in which all scores have been arranged by order, size, or value. Stated differently, it is the point above which and below which half the scores lie; thus, it divides the top half of the scores from the bottom half. Simply calculated, the median is the middle case (for example, in a series of 31 scores, it would be the 16th score, with 15 scores above it, and 15 scores below). If the number of scores is even, the median is the score midway between the two middle scores even if that score does not exist in the distribution of scores. Calculated statistically, it would be the 50th percentile.

The median is a useful measure, although it does not reflect the actual weight of the scores on either side of it. In other words, in a distorted or skewed distribution, the median would not give a true picture of central tendency. On the other hand, the median honestly shows the midpoint of the scores and is not influenced by a few scores that might otherwise radically affect its position. Data must be at least at the ordinal level of measurement for the appropriate use of the median.

Mean

The mean is the actual arithmetic average, which can simply be determined by adding all the scores and then dividing this sum by the number of scores. The formula for calculating the mean is:

$$\overline{X} = \frac{\Sigma X_i}{N}$$ Where $\overline{X}$ = mean
Σ = sum of
X_i = individual score
N = number of scores

The mean is an effective way to show central tendency for interval- or ratio-level data, although in a skewed distribution a few scores at the extremes can radically affect it out of proportion to their number.

Table 14.3 presents a distribution of scores to illustrate the use of the three measures of central tendency with interval-level data. Assume these scores represent participants' level of satisfaction with a recreation program offered in their community. They answered a series of questions relating to the quality of program offered by the agency. Although it makes no difference in the calculations, assume the satisfaction scores could range from 0 to 50. The mean is 41, whereas the median is 42 and the mode is 43. The similarity of these scores suggests that the distribution closely approximates a normal curve that is symmetrical in nature.

Measures of Dispersion (Scattering of Scores)

In descriptive statistics, it is important to be able to measure the dispersion, or scattering of scores away from the mean, to get a true picture of a distribution. For example, one might select a vacation destination on the basis of what appears to be mild or moderate temperature. Yet, two locations that appear to have exactly the same average temperature, $72°$ Fahrenheit, might

TABLE 14.3   Measures of central tendency.

SCORES (X)	
50	
48	
47	$\overline{X} = \frac{\Sigma X_i}{N}$
45	
43	
43	$\overline{X} = \frac{615}{15} = 41$
43	
Middle score → 42	
38	Mode = 43
38	
37	
36	
33	Median = 42
30	
$\Sigma X_i = 615$	

have radically different climates. In one vacation site, a South Seas island, the temperature over a 24-hour period might vary only from the low 60s to the 80s. In another site, a camping area in the Grand Canyon, the temperature might shift from freezing at night to over $100°$ during the day. Yet both would have the same average temperature. Thus, it is important to know not only the central tendency of scores, but how they are dispersed away from the mean.

The simplest way to measure the spread of scores in any distribution is to examine the *range,* which is the highest score minus the lowest score, plus 1 $(X_{max} - X_{min} + 1 = range).$ This is a quick, rough measure that is useful only to indicate the extreme scores. In the example given in Table 14.3, the range would be: $50 - 30 + 1 = 21.$ While easy to calculate, the range is not reliable and gives no information about how scores may vary within the distribution. Instead, the standard deviation provides a better measure of the variability of scores.

Standard deviation

The standard deviation is an important concept in understanding a distribution of scores when they are measured at the interval- or ratio-level of measurement. *Standard deviation* is a measure of variability that shows how individual scores deviate from the mean of the total distribution, and it permits us to calculate the percentage of scores that fall at various intervals under the normal curve. If the standard deviation of scores is small, most scores will cluster tightly about the mean, and the distribution will be very peaked. If the standard deviation is large, the scores are widely distributed above and below the mean, and the distribution will be quite flat. A conceptual understanding of the standard deviation and its effect on the distribution of scores was presented in Figure 14.8. These two distributions would have markedly different standard deviations.

One method of looking at the variation in scores is to determine how much individual scores (X_i) deviate on the average from the mean of the distribution $(\overline{X}).$ This calculation would theoretically result in zero since the positive scores above the mean would be equivalent to the negative scores below the mean. Therefore, one uses the absolute values of the deviations, without noting the pluses or minuses, to establish the average absolute deviation. Using the previous data on program satisfaction, the following calculation shows how the *average absolute deviation* is determined:

On the average, these 15 scores deviate 4.53 points from the arithmetic mean of this distribution. Although this measure is easily calculated and interpreted, the standard deviation of these scores is preferred because of its utility in other statistical analysis.

In statistical terminology, the standard deviation is the square root of the variance (S^2) where the variance is the average of the squared deviation of scores from the mean. The formula for the standard deviation (S) is:

TABLE 14.4   Raw scores and absolute deviations.

RAW SCORES (X_i)	ABSOLUTE DEVIATIONS $\mid X_i - \overline{X} \mid$ *
50	9
48	7
47 $\overline{X}$ = 41	6
45	4
43	2
43	2
43	2
42	1
42	1
38	3
38	3
37	4
36	5
33	8
30	11
ΣX_i = 615	$\Sigma(X_i - \overline{X})$ = 68

Average absolute deviation (AB) = $\dfrac{\Sigma \mid X_i - X \mid}{N} = \dfrac{68}{15} = 4.53$

*The straight brackets indicate absolute values.

$$S = \sqrt{\frac{\Sigma(X_i - \overline{X})^2}{N}}$$

This formula yields a slight underestimation of the population standard deviation. The underestimate can be corrected by using N – 1 in the denominator of the formula. In most cases the sample size is sufficiently large so that the effect of this correction is negligible.

Using the data from the previous discussion, the calculations of the standard deviation are as shown in Table 14.5.

The standard deviation of this distribution is calculated at 5.46, which is slightly different from the average absolute deviation of 4.53 (see Table 14.4). The value of 5.46 is also referred to as one *standard deviation* unit; 10.92 is considered two standard deviation units, and so on.

Interpretation of Standard Deviation. It is now important to go back to the normal curve we were discussing earlier. Within the normal, bell-shaped curve, about two-thirds (68.2 percent) of the scores will fall within one standard deviation unit (S.D.) of either side of the mean (plus or minus 1 S.D.). About 95 percent of all scores will fall within 2 S.D.s, and almost all scores will fall within 3 S.D.s (see Figure 14.9).

TABLE 14.5   Raw scores/differences/squared differences

RAW SCORES (X_i)	DIFFERENCES $(X_i - \overline{X})$	SQUARED DIFFERENCES $(X_i - \overline{X})^2$
50	9	81
48	7	49
47	6	36
45	4	24
43	2	4
43	2	4
43	2	4
42	1	1
42	1	1
3 8	−3	9
38	−3	9
37	−4	16
36	−5	25
33	−8	64
30	−11	121
$\Sigma X_i = 615$	0	$\Sigma(X_i - \overline{X})^2 = 448$

$$S = \sqrt{\frac{448}{15}} = \sqrt{29.87} = 5.46$$

Applied to the distribution of recreation program satisfaction scores (see Table 14.3), where the standard deviation of this set of scores is 5.46, approximately 68 percent of the scores would fall between 35.54 and 46.46 (5.46 above and below the mean of 41). In fact, 10 scores do fall within this range, and they represent 68 percent of all scores. Keep in mind, the larger the standard deviation in relation to the mean, the wider the spread or dispersion of scores. When different sets of scores are compared, the standard deviation provides useful information. It may also be used to interpret the meaning of any single score. For example, an individual who has a score one standard deviation above the mean is higher than about 84 percent of the entire group (50 percent below and 34 percent above the mean).

Standard scores (z scores)

Comparisons among individual scores within a single distribution or across distributions can be facilitated through the use of *standard scores*. They provide a method of expressing a score in a distribution in terms of its distance from the mean in standard deviation units. For example, in a distribution with a mean of 27 and a standard deviation of 3.5, an individual score of 30.5 would have a standard score of 1. This can be found by using the following formula:

FIGURE 14.9   Interpretation of standard deviation.

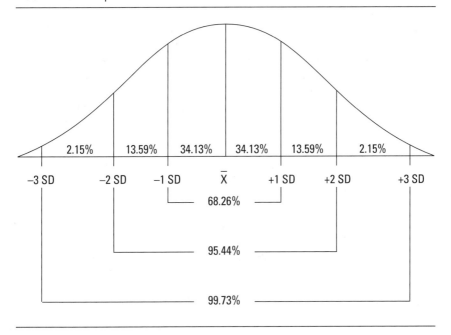

$$z = \frac{(X_i - \overline{X})}{s}$$

$$z = \frac{(30.5 - 27)}{3.5} = \frac{3.5}{3.5}$$

$$z = 1$$

where z = standard score or z score

A score of 1 indicates that the individual score is 1 standard deviation unit above the mean and reveals that 84 percent of the individuals had scores less than or equal to 30.5 (see previous discussion of area under the normal curve). As a second example, an individual with a score of 34 would have a z score of 2 and would lie at approximately the 98th percentile, with only 2 percent of the scores being higher than 34. In our earlier example of recreation program satisfaction, the person with the satisfaction score of 36 would have a z score of − 0.92, which indicates that just less than 84 percent of the participants had scores higher than this individual.

Measures of Association Between Scores

Another important task in descriptive statistics is to measure the degree of association among scores. This involves what are commonly called "proportionate reduction in error" measures, or PRE measures. The PRE measures state the proportion by which one can reduce errors in predicting one's score or value on one variable by using information from a second variable.

Very simply, there are two ways of predicting one's score on a variable. The first involves predicting individual scores by the modal or mean response of the overall study population as a guide. For example, if you know that 200 students played summer softball and 300 did not play, you would arbitrarily predict that each student in the population did not play, since you would have a higher probability of being correct making this prediction. You would be correct 300 times, and incorrect 200 times.

	Softball Participants	
	Yes	*No*
Students	200	300

The second situation involves the use of another characteristic of the population to help categorize individuals. In our example, you now have information regarding the distribution of softball participation by sex. It is as follows:

	Softball Participants		
Students	*Yes*	*No*	
Males	150	75	225
Females	50	225	275

Knowing the sex of the students, one could successfully predict softball participation of individual students 375 times. If the student were a male, you would predict "yes," and if a female, "no." You would be incorrect only 125 times (75 males and 50 females) using the second method. Several PRE measures are available to the researcher, but their use varies depending upon the nature of the data and the purpose of the study. Some common PRE measures for the different levels of data are presented below.

PRE measures for nominal variables

Lambda, and *Goodman* and *Kruskal's tau-y* are two PRE measures suitable for use when both variables are interpreted to be nominal. Both measures are asymmetric; that is, a distinction is made between independent and dependent variables. Normally, two different asymmetric coefficients are computed: the value of predicting *y* from knowledge of variable *x,* and the value of predicting *x* from knowledge of variable *y.* It is up to the discretion of the researcher as to which value to present. Also, both measures vary from 0.0, indicating no reduction in error to +1.0 for perfect reduction. The measures do differ on one dimension, however. Lambda is concerned with prediction of the optimal value of the dependent variable, the mode, while Goodman and Kruskal's tau-y is used to predict the distribution of the dependent variable.

PRE measures for ordinal variables

Kendall's tau-a, Kendall's tau-b, gamma (G), and *Somer's D* are four common PRE measures for ordinal data (rank order data). The first three measures are symmetrical, meaning that there is no distinction between a dependent and an independent variable; while Somer's D is an asymmetric measure. All four measures have a range of -1.0 to $+1.0$. A negative PRE value is associated with a negative or inverse relationship (as one ranking increases, the other ranking decreases), while a positive PRE value involves a direct or positive relationship between the rankings under investigation. Tau-a can be utilized when there are no ties in the rankings on either variable, while tau-b takes into account ties in the rankings on one or the other variable. Gamma, on the other hand, eliminates ties from its calculation; however, it has been criticized on this point because several pairs of observations could potentially be discarded and the measure could actually be based on limited pairs of observations. As stated previously, Somer's D is the only asymmetric measure; two values would be computed, testing both variables as the dependent and independent variable.

PRE measures for interval variables

The most common measure of association found in recreation research is the *product-moment correlation coefficient* (PMCC). The PMCC, r, can be used with two variables measured on interval or ratio levels. The correlation coefficient, r, ranges from $+1$ (perfect positive correlation) to -1 (perfect negative correlation). An r of zero means that there is no relationship at all.

The correlation coefficient provides a quantitative expression of the degree of relationship between two interval variables. In a rating process or test that gives scores on different attributes or performance measures for each subject, it seeks to determine whether these scores are related. If this relationship were assumed to be positive (as in the case of study habits and grades on examinations), one would expect that a high score on one variable would mean that the individual would *tend* to have a high score on the other. This does not mean that every individual would have such a clear positive relationship between the two variables, but rather that it would be a general pattern for the overall group.

If two sets of scores are simply plotted on a chart, a positive correlation will be indicated if the scores tend to fall in a diagonal line from the lower left to the upper right. The higher the degree of positive correlation, the tighter the line in the sense that all scores will tend to be closer to it. If there is little or no correlation, the scores will tend to be randomly scattered. If the correlation is negative (meaning that the higher one is on a given attribute, the more likely one is to be lower on the other), the line will fall in the other direction (from upper left to lower right). Figure 14.10 shows four examples of correlations between variables, with the *r*'s that have been recorded for each of them. The correlation coefficient will be explained further in Chapter 15 in reference to its use as an inferential statistic.

Visual Presentation of Scores: Charts and Graphs

Obviously, the correct calculation of these descriptive measures is the most important aspect of the analysis process. However, the presentation of the result must also be given very serious consideration. In addition to using tables as have been illustrated in this chapter thus far, it is often helpful to present findings in visual form through the use of charts and graphs. Figure 14.11 gives two examples, drawn from the data presented earlier in this chapter (see Table 14.2).

Other types of visual materials include the following.

Pie charts

These show the composition of any subject, such as a budget or program content, by depicting its elements with proportionately sized wedges within a circular, or pie-shaped, chart.

FIGURE 14.10   Different degrees of correlations.

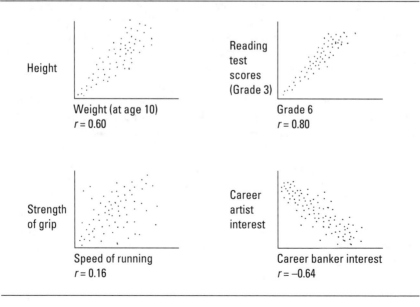

Charts of changes over time

These may show how a particular process or index may rise and fall over a period of time; examples might include participation totals, vandalism occurrences, or revenues.

Charts showing comparisons

These include bar graphs or charts showing change over time, with two or more elements being represented by different textures or by different types of lines on a graph (solid line, punctuated line, line of dots, and so on).

Examination of business reports, annual reports of agencies, and similar sources will reveal several other examples of visual materials designed to present statistical findings concisely.

FIGURE 14.11   Examples of graphs: histogram and frequency polygon.

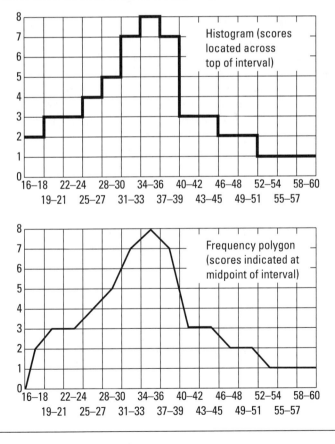

LEVELS OF ANALYSIS: PREPARING RESEARCH REPORTS

In concluding this chapter, it should be stressed that the level of statistical analysis is strongly influenced by the nature of the research itself and by the audience for which it is intended. For example, reports of applied research studies are read primarily by practitioners or the public at large; this audience is largely unfamiliar with statistical concepts and techniques. In addition, it is likely that the research questions that form the focus of the study will call for fairly basic kinds of analysis. Therefore, the methods used and the reporting of the data should be very simple and clear—relying heavily on totals and percentages that are descriptive in nature and on simple tables, charts, or graphs that serve to illustrate the study findings.

In contrast, any research study that is intended to develop or test theory and that is "pure" or abstract in nature is likely to use more sophisticated and difficult methods of statistical analysis. This is often true in academic research and in the research studies that are reported at research symposia and in the scholarly journals in the field. A number of the concepts and methods found in inferential statistics, which are of this nature, are summarized and discussed in Chapter 15.

SUMMARY

This chapter introduces the use of statistics as an essential function in analyzing quantitative research data and describes two major forms of statistics: descriptive and inferential. It discusses the normal distribution curve and principles of probability. It then outlines a number of important concepts of descriptive statistics, including the use of grouped frequency distributions to measure central tendency. The mode, median, and mean are described, along with measures of dispersion. Standard deviation and standard scores are explained.

Measures of association between scores are presented, with illustrations of the coefficient of correlation. Other sections of the chapter suggest approaches to planning data-analysis techniques in designing study instruments, as well as methods of tabulating and organizing study findings, along with a brief presentation of the use of charts and graphs to summarize study findings.

QUESTIONS AND ACTIVITIES

The following can be used as in-class workshops.

1. Individually or in small groups, students prepare a frequency distribution of a set of scores. Then determine the central tendency (mean, median, and mode) and chart the distribution, using a frequency polygon or a histogram. Discuss the results.

2. As an extension of Activity 1 above, have students determine the standard deviation of the scores. Assign several hypothetical scores to them, and have them determine the standard deviations of these scores.

3. Students apply a research instrument (a simple survey would be most convenient) to a selected population. Then estimate the degree of relationship between any two variables using the simple plotting method to show correlation graphically.

4. The instructor provides students with a set of computer printouts, such as the one shown in Table 14.1. Students respond to specific questions to test their ability to read and interpret the printout.

ENDNOTES

1. Sidney M. Stahl and James D. Hennes, *Reading and Understanding Applied Statistics* (St. Louis, MO: C. V. Mosby Co., 1980): 2.

2. SPSS Inc., *SPSS^x: User Guide,* 2nd ed. (New York: McGraw-Hill, 1986).

3. Mark L. Berenson, David M. Levine, and Matthew Goldstein, *Intermediate Statistical Methods and Applications: A Computer Package Approach* (Englewood Cliffs, NJ: Prentice-Hall, Inc., 1983).

Overview of
Inferential Statistics

*A mere quantitative superiority of the experimental group
mean score over the control group mean score is not conclu-
sive proof of its superiority. Since we know that the means of
two groups randomly drawn from the same population were
not necessarily identical, any difference . . . could possibly
be attributed to sampling error or chance. To be statistically
significant, the difference must be greater than that which
can reasonably be attributed to sampling error.[1]*

INTRODUCTION

This chapter summarizes information dealing with a number of the key principles and procedures in inferential statistics. It begins with a discussion of
the central limit theorem, hypothesis development and testing, and the difference between parametric and nonparametric analysis. It continues with the
use of t-tests and one-way analysis of variance (ANOVA) and then discusses
factorial designs, repeated measures designs, and analysis of covariance.

The second section of the chapter deals with measures of association,
including the chi-square test, the product-moment coefficient of correlation,
Spearman–rank-order correlation, and bivariate regression. The concluding
section deals with multivariate procedures, including multiple regression, factor analysis, cluster analysis, discriminant analysis, and canonical correlation.
The reader should take note: Some of this material is quite advanced for an
introductory or basic course on research and evaluation. However, it provides
a valuable explanation of inferential statistics principles and procedures for
those pursuing more advanced courses or seminars in statistical procedures.
Therefore, course instructors must determine how much or how little of it
should be covered.

THE CENTRAL LIMIT THEOREM AND
THE SAMPLING DISTRIBUTION

Descriptive statistics involves describing the characteristics of a set of data,
whether from a sample or a population. Inferential statistics, on the other

hand, involves the procedures for making inferences about a population from sample data. Because it is virtually impossible to measure every element in a population, sample data are used to make inferences about the population based upon estimates of population parameters. Although potential for error always exists in this approach, statisticians have developed mathematic models and established techniques in which the sample mean, x, is an unbiased estimator of the population mean, u. The theory underlying these techniques is based on the central limit theorem as it applies to a sampling distribution.

A *sampling distribution* involves the calculation of means for a large number of samples, all of the same size, from a defined population. Using this approach, one establishes a distribution of sample means with the mean of this distribution (mean of sample means) being the same as the population mean, and the sample means being normally distributed around the mean of the distribution with a standard deviation that equals the population standard deviation divided by the square root of the sample size.[2] These qualities are the foundation of the *central limit theorem,* which states that "if random samples of a fixed N are drawn from any population (regardless of the form of the population distribution), as N becomes larger, the distribution of sample means approaches normality."[3] This suggests that the sampling distribution is a normal distribution and that all properties of the normal curve can be utilized without concern for the actual shape of the population. This is a critical point since we assume the characteristics of the normal curve in conducting our inferential statistical analysis. If we could not make these assumptions, we would not be justified in using sample measures (statistics) to make inferences about population characteristics (parameters).

An important aspect of the central limit theorem relates to the standard deviation of the sampling distribution of means, which is referred to as the *standard error of the mean.* It measures variability of sample means around the population mean. As was stated above, the standard error of the mean is calculated by taking the standard deviation of the population and dividing this standard deviation by the square root of the sample size. In the vast majority of studies, however, the population standard deviation is not known. Therefore, we use the sample standard deviation with a slightly different formula than the one stated above to obtain the standard error of the mean when the population standard deviation is not known. The formula for this estimate is:

$$s_{\bar{x}} = \frac{S}{\sqrt{N-1}}$$

where $s_{\bar{x}}$ = the standard error of the mean

S = the standard deviation of our sample

N = the size of the sample

Note that the above formula calls for the square root of $N - 1$ rather than N. This is to correct for the fact that the sample standard deviation, S, is smaller than the population standard deviation.

The central limit theorem also states that if we base our estimate of population means on a *single* sample drawn from the population, it is likely to be closer to the actual parameter as we increase the size of the sample. However, it is difficult to identify the exact size of a sample required to approximate the population from which it is drawn, because the needed sample size depends on the shape of the population distribution. Again, the standard error of the mean comes into play. As the standard error of the mean becomes larger, the larger the sample needs to be to approach the true population mean; and, of course, as the standard error (sometimes it is just referred to as the standard error) becomes smaller, we can use a smaller sample size.

Attempts have been made to generalize the determination of sample size regardless of the shape of the population. As you recall from Chapter 12, some statisticians have specified 30 as the minimum sample size, while others suggest larger samples. Commonly, one establishes a sample that is within the economic and time constraints of the investigator. Specific sample sizes have been established for various size populations that allow for different degrees of precision as relating to the representativeness of the sample.

Chapter 14 pointed out that under the normal curve about 68 percent of all scores fall between +1 and −1 standard deviation units from the mean, approximately 95 percent of all scores fall between +2 and −2 standard deviation units, and approximately 99 percent of all scores fall between +3 and −3 standard deviation units from the mean. Because of the central limit theorem, these same distributions of scores hold true for sample statistics, and this provides the basis for the estimation of population parameters from sample statistics—the core element in inferential statistics. Thus, 99 percent of all sample means, theoretically, will fall within three standard deviation units from the population mean. Essentially, this is what we do when we assess recreation behavior in a community or an institution; we feel fairly confident in drawing conclusions regarding the larger population from data obtained from a sample of residents because of the strength of the central limit theorem.

The application of inferential statistics may be illustrated in the process of hypothesis testing.

STEPS OF HYPOTHESIS TESTING[4]

Generally, hypothesis testing involves five steps:
- Establishing the hypothesis to be investigated
- Establishing criteria for rejecting the null hypothesis
- Calculating the observed value
- Calculating the critical value
- Accepting or rejecting the null hypothesis

Establishing the Hypothesis to Be Investigated

In Chapter 3, the nature of a hypothesis was explained. It is a proposition that is stated in testable form and predicts a particular relationship between two or more variables. In the actual research effort, the null hypothesis is normally stated. This specifies that no relationship exists between the populations being compared. A statistical test is conducted to determine the probability that the null hypothesis is false and thus rejected. If the null hypothesis is rejected, the alternative hypothesis, which states that there is a relationship between the variables under investigation, is accepted.

Establishing Criteria for Rejecting the Null Hypothesis

Because inferential statistics involves sample data, there is always the possibility of error. For example, two sample means being different may be due to sampling error rather than a true difference in the two populations. The question becomes: At what point are the sample differences observed truly due to differences between the populations under investigation? To assist in answering this question, the researcher must select a level of significance (the Greek letter alpha, α, is used to indicate level of significance). A significance level is based on the degree of probability (p) that these differences are due to sampling error. If the probability is small enough, we reject the null hypothesis and conclude that true differences exist among our results. The significance level is usually set at 0.05 (5 percent of the time) or 0.01 (1 percent of the time). At the first level of significance, we conclude that the differences observed are due to sampling error 5 percent of the time or less, or conversely that they are due to real differences 95 percent of the time or more; thus, we reject the null hypothesis. Recall that these levels of significance relate to the normal distribution and standard deviation units we were discussing earlier in the text.

Although these levels are arbitrarily set, researchers normally feel the chances of differences being due to sampling error are too great to reject the null hypothesis if the probability falls beyond the 0.01 or 0.05 level. In the literature, level of significance is sometimes referred to as the alpha level or level of probability.

Calculating the Observed Value

Each inferential statistical test involves calculation of an *observed value* based upon the data collected. Various formulas have been established for calculating the observed value for appropriate inferential tests. As will be explained later, they may include, for example, the *t*-value, *F*-value, or *r*-value. These values are then compared with a critical value.

Calculating the Critical Value

Each statistical test has an associated critical value, based upon the size of the sample(s) and the level of significance chosen by the researcher. The *critical value* is the criterion that the observed value must meet or exceed for the null hypothesis to be rejected. As a more stringent level of significance is chosen, the critical value will necessarily increase. These criterion values have been established by statisticians and are available in tables in many statistics textbooks. Appendix C presents examples of several tables that are used with various inferential procedures, and they are explained later in this chapter.

Accepting or Rejecting the Null Hypothesis

This final step involves comparing the observed value and the critical value for the appropriate statistical procedure. If the observed value is smaller than the critical value, the researcher accepts the null hypothesis and normally indicates that there is *no* significant difference or relationship between the groups or variables under investigation. On the other hand, if the observed value is larger than the critical value, the researcher rejects the null hypothesis and accepts the alternative hypothesis, indicating that there *is* a significant difference or relationship.

In the literature, the researcher usually reports the probability level at which the null hypothesis was rejected. This is done in symbolic form where, for example, $p \leq 0.05$ indicates that the probability of the differences being due to sampling error was less than or equal to 5 times out of 100.

ERRORS IN HYPOTHESIS TESTING: TYPE I AND TYPE II ERRORS

The decision to accept or reject the null hypothesis always has the possibility of being incorrect because of the use of sample statistics to estimate population parameters. The conjectured differences or lack of differences may be due to sampling errors rather than to the true nature of the populations under investigation. Because of this situation, we can reject the null hypothesis when it is true *(type I error)* or accept the null hypothesis when it is actually false *(type II error)*.

Table 15.1 shows the two types of errors. In addition to the two decision errors, two correct decisions are possible. The upper right quadrant indicates the decision to accept the null hypothesis when, in fact, it is true, and the lower left quadrant indicates the decision to reject the null hypothesis when, in fact, it is false. This last decision is referred to as the *power* of a test. All things being equal, a researcher will choose the statistical test that has the greatest power since in many situations the researcher is seeking to establish significant relationships.

The probability of making a type I error is equal to the level of significance (α) established by the researcher. For example, at a significance level of 0.05, there are 5 chances out of 100 that the sample statistic is large enough to reject the null hypothesis when it is, in fact, true. The researcher may wish to keep the likelihood of type I error as small as possible and may therefore use more stringent levels of significance, such as 0.01 or 0.001.

Unfortunately, there is no simple rule for the probability of making a type II error (this probability is referred to as Beta or B). However, type I and type II errors are inversely related; as the probability of making a type I error increases, the probability of making a type II error decreases. Whether the researcher should be more concerned about a type I or type II error depends on the nature of the investigation. For example, assume you are investigating the effectiveness of a youth program in decreasing juvenile delinquency. You would want to minimize your probability of making a type I error because it would be very costly, financially and politically, to establish a program that, in fact, does not have any affect on juvenile delinquency. Given the concern of making a type I error, the level of significance would be made more stringent. If, on the other hand, the researcher is more concerned about a type II error, the level of significance can be kept lower (for example, from 0.05 to 0.1).

TABLE 15.1   Errors in decisions based on sample statistics.

	REJECT H_0	ACCEPT H_0
H_0 is true in population	type I Error $p = \alpha$	Correct
H_0 is false in population	Correct	Type II Error $p = B$

ONE-TAILED VERSUS TWO-TAILED TESTS

In many research situations, the null hypothesis is stated as: H_0: $u_1 = u_2$ where u_1 is the mean of population 1 and u_2 is the mean of population 2. Therefore, one has the possibility of rejecting the null if u_1 is significantly larger or smaller than u_2. In this case, the hypothesis testing is considered a two-tailed test because it is sensitive to significant differences in either direction. A study comparing males and females on their levels of leisure satisfaction would involve a two-tailed test because we would be looking for differences in either direction (that is, are levels of satisfaction of males greater than or less than those of females?)

At times, however, the nature of the differences is hypothesized more specifically. Rather than look for significant differences in either direction, the researcher may be interested in exploring differences in only one direction. In such a case, the alternative hypothesis is directional (for example, H_a: $u_1 > u_2$), and the null hypothesis states H_0: $u_1 \leq u_2$ (mean 1 is less than or equal to mean 2). When a test concerns only directional differences, it is called a one-tailed test.

For example, if we want to examine the effects of a corporate recreation program on work productivity, we may decide to measure only the positive effects of the program. Thus, the null is H_0: u_1 (control group) $\geq u_2$ (treatment group), and the alternative hypothesis is H_a: $u_1 < u_2$

If the nature of the relationship is unknown, the researcher should use a two-tailed test. The researcher should use a one-tailed test only when relatively certain of the direction of the relationship.

PARAMETRIC AND NONPARAMETRIC STATISTICS

The information presented thus far provides a basis of understanding for the broad area of statistical analysis called *parametric statistics*. Hypotheses that are tested using such procedures must meet certain assumptions. For example, one must assume that the variables being studied are normally distributed in the population from which the sample is drawn. Also, when two or more groups are being investigated, one must assume that these groups have equal variances. Third, although researchers may not be as adamant regarding this criterion, one should normally use parametric procedures only with interval-level data. Within the social and behavioral sciences, however, many investigators use parametric procedures with certain types of ordinal data, including Likert-scaled questions.

Nonparametric statistics, on the other hand, are considered distribution-free procedures. Researchers use such procedures when they feel the data deviate sharply from the above assumptions. Since many parametric procedures are robust with respect to assumptions regarding normal distribution and homogeneity of variances, nonparametric procedures are generally selected only when the sample size is quite small (for example, fewer than 30 subjects) or the data cannot be assumed to be at least at the interval level of measurement.

TESTING HYPOTHESES OF POPULATION MEANS AND VARIANCES

The following section discusses a number of frequently used inferential statistical procedures. Its purpose is to provide a conceptual understanding of these procedures, not the detailed mathematical formulas underlying them. The emphasis is on explaining the uses of these procedures within the overall framework of inferential statistics.

One of the most common uses of hypothesis testing is to determine if a sample mean is significantly different from the population from which it was drawn or if two or more group means arise from different populations or the same population.

One Sample Case for Means

Assume that our purpose is to determine if a particular sample of adults ($N =$ 60) participated in camping to the same extent as the general population within the state of Pennsylvania. From our sample of adults, we find that the average number of participation days per year is: $\bar{x}$ = 9.1 days/year, with a standard deviation of $S = 2.4$. Also, we learn from the 1995 State Recreation Plan that the average number of participation days for all adults in the state is 11.2. To determine if our sample is significantly different from the population, we use the t-test based on the t-distribution. The t-distribution is used in this type of analysis rather than the normal distribution because the population's standard deviation is unknown. The t-distribution approximates the normal distribution with a slightly larger distribution of scores at each end of the curve. We can use the t-test because we meet the general assumption of parametric statistics and our data are interval scale of measurement. Since we will be using a two-tailed t-test (nondirectional), our null hypothesis is H_o: $u = 11.2$, and the alternative hypothesis is H_a: $u \neq 11.2$. The population mean, u, is used in the hypothesis since we are using sample statistics to estimate population parameters. The formula for the t-test is:

$$t = \frac{(\bar{x} - u)}{s_{\bar{x}}}$$

where $\bar{x}$ is the sample mean, u is the population mean, and $s_{\bar{x}}$ is the estimated standard error of the mean. The standard error of the mean for the sample is used because the population standard deviation is unknown, and it is derived using the following formula $s_{\bar{x}} = S/\sqrt{n-1}$ where n is the sample size.

Therefore $s_{\bar{x}} = 2.4 \neq \sqrt{60-1} = 0.31$

Then $t = \dfrac{(\bar{x} - u)}{s_{\bar{x}}} = \dfrac{(9.1 - 11.2)}{0.31} = \dfrac{-2.1}{.31} = -6.77$

This value is referred to as t-observed, or simply the t-value.

Degrees of freedom

The concept of degrees of freedom is critical to the hypothesis-testing process. The term *degrees of freedom* refers to the number of independent observations minus the number of parameters being estimated in the procedure. In this case, there are 60 independent observations, and we are estimating one population parameter, u. Thus, the degrees of freedom is $N - 1$, or 59. Using the appropriate degrees of freedom and the selected level of significance, the researcher is able to determine the t-critical value.

From the table of t-critical values presented in Appendix C, Table C.1, we find the t-critical value for this example to be 2.00 when the $df = 59$ and the level of significance is 0.05. In using the table, you first find the degrees of freedom for your study and then select the t-critical value in the column associated with the level of significance you have chosen. In our case we chose the value for 60 degrees of freedom since that was the closest to our situation. In many cases, however, it is essential to determine the exact t-critical value through interpolation.

Our t-observed (use absolute value) value is larger than the t-critical value; therefore, we reject the null hypothesis and accept the alternative hypothesis, which states that the annual number of camping days for our selected group of 60 adults was significantly different from that of the general adult population in Pennsylvania. In comparing the means, one would conclude that the sample of adults participated significantly less than the general population.

Differences Between the Sample Means (Independent Samples)

In recreation research, we rarely compare sample data to population data. Instead, we tend to compare two groups on selected variables. For example, if we were interested in knowing whether residents' attitudes toward leisure services varied significantly in 2 communities, we might randomly select 2 samples of adults from each community, with each sample consisting of 100 adults. Using a leisure attitude scale, we would determine scores for both groups. Our null hypothesis would be H_0: $u_1 = u_2$. The alternative hypothesis would be H_a: $u_1 \neq u_2$. Because we are looking for possible variations in either direction, this is a two-tailed test. We can use a t-test since our investigation meets the basic requirements for parametric statistics and only two groups are involved (a t-test is not appropriate for more than two groups).

In this analysis, however, we must use a different formula from the previous analysis because we are comparing two independently drawn sample means rather than comparing a sample with the population. The appropriate formula is

$$t = \frac{\overline{X}_1 - \overline{X}_2}{s_{D\overline{x}}}$$

where $\overline{X}_1$ is the mean for community one, $\overline{X}_2$ is the mean for community 2, and $s_{D\overline{x}}$ is the standard error of the difference, which is a variability measure based upon the standard deviations from the two samples.

The formula for the $s_{D\overline{x}}$ is quite simple, although it looks rather involved:

$$s_{D\overline{x}} = \sqrt{\frac{N_1 S_1^2 + N_2 S_2^2}{N_1 + N_2 - 2}\left(\frac{1}{N_1} + \frac{1}{N_2}\right)}$$

In this formula, S_1 is the sample standard deviation for town 1, S_2 is the standard deviation for town 2, N_1, is the sample size for town 1, and N_2 is the sample size for town 2. The appropriate degrees of freedom is $N_1 + N_2 - 2$.

Given $\bar{x}_1 = 8.2$, $\bar{x}_2 = 7.9$, $S_1 = 2.26$, and $S_2 = 2.10$, t-observed is 0.967 and t- critical is 1.96 for 198 degrees of freedom at the .05 level of significance (see Appendix C, Table C.1). Therefore, we retain the null hypothesis and conclude that there is not a significant difference between the residents of the two communities regarding leisure attitudes and that any differences we found were due to sampling error alone.

Difference Between Two Sample Means (Correlated Samples)

In many recreation studies, the t-test is used with correlated samples. For example, one may measure the level of leisure satisfaction of a group of individuals prior to their enrollment in a leisure education program and following their completion of the program to determine if their satisfaction has changed significantly. This is referred to as a "repeated measures" design.

In other situations, a researcher may match two groups of subjects on characteristics that are related to the specific variables under investigation. For example, we want to compare male and female institutionalized mentally retarded adults on their levels of leisure participation. Using an observation procedure, we would match the groups of subjects with respect to length of institutionalization and IQ since these factors are likely to affect their level of participation. This approach is simply referred to as a "matched pairs" design; each male and female pair in the study is matched, based on both factors.

The measurement in both these studies is likely to correlate. For example, if a subject scores the highest on the pretest for leisure satisfaction, she tends to score the highest on the posttest as well. We would therefore use a correlated t-test, such as the "direct difference" method, that takes this condition into account. Applying this method, we use only the differences between the pairs of observations and not the means for the repeated measurement on the matched pairs. This enables us to test the null hypothesis to determine whether there is a significant difference between subjects' pre- and posttest scores on leisure satisfaction and thus to make a statement regarding the effectiveness of the leisure education program. This judgment is limited because we did not use a control group for comparison.

The formula for the correlated t-test is:

$$t = \frac{\overline{D}}{s_{\bar{x}_D}}$$

where $\overline{D}$ is the mean of differences between the pairs of observations and $s_{\bar{x}_D}$ is the standard error of the mean of the differences. The mean of the differences $(\overline{D})$ is found by summing the differences (ΣD) and dividing by the number of pairs, N. The standard error of the mean of the differences $s_{\bar{x}_D}$ can be determined by dividing s_D, the standard deviation of the differences, by the square root of $N - 1$, or $\sqrt{N-1}$. The formula for the standard deviation of the differences is

$$s_D = \sqrt{\frac{\Sigma D^2}{N} - \overline{D}^2}$$

and the formula for the standard error of the mean of the differences is

$$s_{\overline{x}_D} = \frac{s_D}{\sqrt{N-1}}$$

Finally, the degrees of freedom equals $N - 1$. The t-critical value is again found using Table C.1, Appendix C.

Difference Between More than Two Sample Means (ANOVA)

The t-test is an appropriate statistical test for comparing the means of two groups. When more than two groups are involved in the investigation, however, a different statistical test is required. The simplest test for comparing the means among two or more groups is the one-way analysis of variance (ANOVA), a parametric statistic.

A one-way ANOVA involves one independent variable (therefore one-way) and one dependent variable. The independent variable is normally either a nominal or an ordinal scale of measurement involving two or more categories. ANOVA serves the same purpose as a t-test but can be extended for use with more than two groups. (The term *groups* refers to the various categories of the independent variable.) The hypothesis-testing process is similar to the process followed with the t-test, except that the null hypothesis may involve more than two groups. For example, we may investigate the number of times (dependent variable) randomly selected residents from four sections of town (independent variable with four categories) use the town's community park in one year. This type of investigation meets all the assumptions necessary for ANOVA: (1) the dependent variable is measured on the interval or ratio scale of measurement, (2) the residents are randomly selected, (3) the populations from which the residents are selected are normally distributed, and (4) the populations from which the sample is drawn have approximately the same variability (homogeneity of variance). The last two assumptions cannot be directly determined; however, we assume them to be true unless there is strong evidence to the contrary.

The results of a one-way ANOVA are commonly presented in a summary table. Although various formats are used, certain items are normally included, as shown in Table 15.2, which summarizes the investigation just suggested.

The values in this table are fictitious and are used for illustrative purposes. The Source column describes the variation in scores among the residents in the study. Part of the variation in scores is attributed to the section of town in which residents live; this is presented in the Between groups variation. A second part of the variation is attributed to the different responses provided by residents within each group and is referred to in the Within groups variation. The Degree of Freedom column refers to the degrees of freedom for the three sources of

TABLE 15.2   Example of ANOVA: Use of park by four neighborhoods' residents.

SOURCE	DEGREE OF FREEDOM	SS	MS	F-VALUE
Between groups (section of town)	3	90	30	6
Within groups	196	980	5	
Total	199	1070		

variation. The Between groups degree of freedom is calculated by subtracting 1 from the number of groups involved ($4 - 1 = 3$). The Within groups degree of freedom is the total number of subjects (4 groups, each with 50 subjects), minus 4 groups equals 196 degrees of freedom. The total degrees of freedom is merely the sum of the 2 previous degrees of freedom ($3 + 196 = 199$).

The SS (sums of squares) measures variability of scores. A relatively complicated procedure is used to calculate each SS, and it is beyond the scope of this textbook. The MS (mean square) column is a ratio of the SS divided by the degree of freedom for each source. The F-value column contains only one value, which is found by dividing MS between groups by MS within groups. In this case, the resulting F-value is 6. The F-value (also known as F-observed) is the most critical item of information in the table; it is compared with the critical F-value to determine if there are significant differences among the four groups (sections of town). If the comparison shows that F- observed is larger than F-critical, we reject the null hypothesis and conclude that there is a significant difference among the four sections of town. As with the t-critical value, F-critical is found using a table of F values for the associated Between and Within groups degrees of freedom and the selected level of significance (see Table C.2).

The ANOVA procedure tells us only that there is a significant difference somewhere among the four sections of town, but it does not tell us specifically where this difference is. To determine this, one would use any of several post hoc procedures to analyze each possible pair of means to determine which ones were significantly different from the others.

Extended forms of ANOVA

Analysis of variance is a very versatile procedure that can be used for a variety of research designs. In this section, we will describe three of the most common extensions of the basic ANOVA model: *factorial design, repeated measures design,* and *analysis of covariance.*

A *factorial design* involves more than one independent variable (factor). If we were interested in the effects of gender and age on one's attitude toward leisure, we would use a two-way ANOVA procedure. *Two-way* refers to two independent factors: gender and age. Each factor has a specific number of categories, normally referred to as levels. Obviously, gender has two levels, male and female. Age, however, may have several categories; it is up to the researcher to determine these. To illustrate, age might be categorized into three groups: young adults (20 to 35), middle adults (36 to 60), and older adults (60 plus). The two-way ANOVA would be a 2 × 3 ANOVA, with the 2 and the 3 indicating the levels of the factors (gender and age), respectively. The factorial design can be logically extended to more than two factors, but rarely do these designs go beyond three factors in the recreation literature.

A factorial design not only allows the researcher to examine the effect or influence of each factor, it also allows the researcher to analyze the effect of two or more factors in combination. This is referred to as the *interaction effect;* the effects of the individual factors are called the *main effects.* To illustrate the interaction effect of age and gender on leisure attitudes, we have constructed a fictitious set of scores that show group means of scores on a leisure attitudes test (see Table 15.3).

The overall means (means to the far right side and bottom of table) suggest that males and females, as well as the three age groups, all have the same leisure attitude. The individual cells, however, show that males and females differ in two of the age groups and that leisure attitudes are inversely related across age; females' attitudes increase with age while males' attitudes decrease with age. This illustrates the importance of the interaction effect; it allows us to determine the effect of a factor at each level of the other factors. If we had conducted two one-way ANOVA analyses, this potential interaction effect would not have been detected. In research reports, this effect is frequently depicted in graphic format.

In *repeated measures design* studies, subjects are tested or measured more than once. For example, we might test subjects during each of the four seasons to determine if their leisure satisfaction varies with the time of year. In such a case, we would have four repeated measures on the same subject. Or we might compare a group (treatment or experimental group) of subjects who completed a leisure education program with a group (control group) that did not. We would test both groups before the program and at its completion to determine any potential behavioral or attitude change.

The one-way or factorial ANOVAs previously discussed are not appropriate for either of these situations because they do not account for inherent relationships between the individual subject's repeated measures (for example, the fact that one has already taken a given test might influence performance on a retest). The ANOVA for repeated measures is developed specifically to calculate such possible influence, and its summary table is similar to the more basic ANOVA except that it includes a separate "error" term to estimate the effect of the test-retest procedure.

As shown earlier (see page 57), the pre-post-testing procedure with a control group is one of the most common experimental research designs. The ANOVA for repeated measures is an appropriate analysis to use with this design and is commonly referred to as a 2 × 2 ANOVA with repeated measures. In it, there are two factors, each with two levels. Factor one is a grouping factor, with the two levels being the treatment group and the control group. Factor two

TABLE 15.3   Factorial design of leisure attitudes interaction by age and gender.

| | | GENDER | | |
		MALE	FEMALE	
Age	Young adults	x̄ = 38	x̄ = 28	x̄ = 33
	Middle-aged adults	x̄ = 33	x̄ = 33	x̄ = 33
	Older adults	x̄ = 28	x̄ = 38	x̄ = 33
		x̄ = 33	x̄ = 33	

is the testing factor, with the two levels being the pretest and posttest. This analysis also involves an interaction effect, since it is a factorial design and is intended specifically to measure the influence of experimental variables. Theoretically, the researcher hopes to find no difference between the two groups in the pretest procedure, but a substantial difference in the posttest. The interaction effect permits the researcher to make this kind of determination.

Analysis of covariance (ANCOVA) is used with two or more groups of subjects when the researcher wants to control the influence of another variable on the dependent variable. For example, if we are examining the effect of a recreation program on mentally challenged participants from two groups, it is critical to control for the varying levels of retardation across the groups before comparing the results of the recreation program. Since it is not always possible to hand-pick subjects in order to match them exactly, the analysis of covariance procedure is used. A comparison of group means on the dependent variable is conducted after they are adjusted for the influence of the covariate variable.

When using the traditional pre- and posttest, treatment and control group experimental design, for example, the covariate may be the pretest score for the two groups. The posttest scores are adjusted on the basis of the covariate (pretest) scores and then compared to determine if there is a significant difference between the groups. The covariate need not always be the pretest score; it may be any characteristic that the researcher believes may be influencing the study results and may in fact be more than one characteristic. Summary tables are similar to other ANOVA tables except that the results are adjusted for the covariate. This procedure is most useful in determining if the covariate exerts a strong influence on the dependent variable.

TESTS OF ASSOCIATION

Chapter 14 points out that in many situations in recreation research the investigator wants to learn whether two or more variables are related. By determining this, it is possible to achieve a fuller understanding of leisure behavior or other phenomena. The measures of association that are used in descriptive statistics may also be extended to inferential analysis. In this section, we will discuss several measures of association that can be used to make inferences about relationships among variables in recreation research.

Chi-Square Test

Since much of the data collected in recreation research is on the nominal or ordinal scale of measurement, one of the most common statistical tests applied is the *chi-square test* (X^2). It is referred to as a test of independence because the researcher seeks to learn whether the distribution of scores on the variables being investigated are independent of each other or are related in some way. Chi-square is considered a nonparametric test because it need not meet all the assumptions established for parametric statistics. It may be used with data sets that meet the assumptions for parametric statistics, except that the sets are not interval- or ratio-level data. Simple random samples must be used, however, to justify generalizing findings to the population under investigation.

Chi-square analysis is frequently used with analysis of demographic variables. Cheek, for example, conducted a study to determine the use of parks by individuals of different occupational levels.[5] Subjects were queried regarding their use of local parks and were classified as "blue-collar" or "white-collar." Cheek's null hypothesis stated that the two variables (use of parks and occupational level) were independent, that there was no association or relationship between them. The formula for the calculation of chi-square is

$$X^2 = \Sigma \frac{(O - E)^2}{E}$$

where O = the observed frequency in a category

E = the expected frequency in the category

The data fit a 2×2 table, in that there were two levels of each variable; occupation was blue-collar or white-collar, and park attendance was either yes or no. Table 15.4 presents the data and the analysis of the chi square for this study.

The expected value for each cell is calculated by multiplying the column total by the row total for each cell and dividing by the total N. The expected values for each cell in Table 15.4 would be:

$320 \times 225 / 444 = 162$ $124 \times 225 / 444 = 63$
$320 \times 219 / 444 = 158$ $124 \times 219 / 444 = 61$

Cheek's finding was that the chi-square value (X^2) for the data was 0.18. The degrees of freedom for a two-way chi-square analysis is $(r - 1)(c - 1)$ where *r* equals the number of rows and *c* equals the number of columns. In the Cheek study there is one degree of freedom because there are two levels of each variable. Using the chi-square values in Appendix C, Table C.3, for 1 degree of freedom and a 0.05 level of significance, we obtain a critical value of 3.841. Since the observed X^2 did not exceed the critical X^2, we retained the

TABLE 15.4   Differences in park use by occupation.

		Park Use		
Occupation		In Local Park	Not in Local Park	N
	Blue Collar	164	61	225
	White Collar	156	63	269
	Total	320	124	444

O	E	$O - E$	$(O - E)^2$	$(O - E)^2/E$
164	162	+2	4	4/162 = .02
156	158	−2	4	4/158 = .03
61	63	−2	4	4/63 = .06
63	61	+2	4	4/61 = .07
				X^2 = .18

null hypothesis, and therefore park attendance was not related to occupational level.

Chi-square tests may be used with more than two variables and with more than two levels. More than three variables, however, are rarely investigated simultaneously since interpretation becomes much more complex with greater numbers and/or levels of variables. It is suggested that the minimum number of subjects needed for chi-square analysis is the product of the variable levels multiplied by five. For example, if an investigation has three levels of one variable and two levels of a second variable, the number of subjects needed would be $3 \times 2 \times 5 = 30$ subjects.

The chi-square test for independence indicates whether there is a relationship between two or more variables, but does not measure the strength of the relationship. It is possible to obtain a significant X^2 when the strength of the relationship is quite weak; after rejecting the null hypothesis in a chi-square analysis, one would then use other measures such as Cramer's V to determine the actual strength of the relationship. In studies where variables are measured at the ordinal level, Gamma and Kendall's tau are useful procedures, since they are more appropriate for ordinal variables than is chi-square analysis. Both measures are nonparametric and can therefore be used with data that are not normally distributed in the population.

Product-Moment Coefficient of Correlation (r)

This procedure was described as a descriptive statistic in Chapter 14; however, the *product-moment coefficient of correlation* can also be used for inferential tests. When this is done, a test of significance must be conducted to determine if the *r*-observed value is large enough to confirm a relationship between the variables under investigation. A null hypothesis is established and commonly tested at the 0.05 or 0.01 levels of significance. The *r*-observed value is compared with the *r*-critical value, which is identified using a table of critical values.

To use the product-moment coefficient of correlation, interval- or ratio-level data must be used. In some situations, however, when ordinal data have been collected using Likert-type instruments, data have been assumed to meet the criteria of interval data, and the product-moment method has been used. All other assumptions for parametric statistical procedures must be met. It is essential not to interpret a high correlation as a causal relationship between the variables under investigation. The coefficient of correlation merely states that there is a relationship between the variables, but not that one causes the other.

Several formulas are available for calculating the product-moment coefficient of correlation. One of the simplest is the *whole score method,* which deals with pairs of raw scores. Its formula is

$$r = \frac{\frac{\Sigma XY}{N} - \overline{X}\,\overline{Y}}{S_x S_y}$$

where *r*   = correlation coefficient

ΣXY = the sum of the product of each pair of scores

N   = number of pairs of scores

$\overline{X}$ = mean of the *X* distribution

$\overline{Y}$ = mean of the *Y* distribution

S_x = standard deviation of the *X* distribution

S_y = standard deviation of the *Y* distribution

We will use the whole score method of calculating the standard deviation of the two distributions of scores. The formula is

$$S = \sqrt{\frac{\Sigma X^2}{N} - \overline{X}^2}$$

where *S*   = the standard deviation

ΣX^2 = sum of squared scores

$\overline{X}$ = mean of the *X* distribution

N   = number of observations

This formula is also used for the Y distribution of scores by merely substituting the appropriate ΣY^2 and $\overline{Y}$ scores. Table 15.5 presents a set of scores for ten individuals; the X scores refer to individuals' satisfaction with leisure opportunities in their community, and the Y scores refer to individuals' overall satisfaction with their community life. The research question would be to determine if there is a relationship between one's satisfaction with leisure opportunities and one's overall satisfaction with community life.

Table 15.5 shows that the *r observed* is 0.85. To determine if this correlation coefficient is significant, we must compare this value with the *r critical* value found in Appendix C, Table C.4. The degree of freedom used in calculating *r critical* is N – 2. Finding the appropriate score on Table C.4 tells us that *r critical* would be 0.632 at the 0.05 level of significance (probability) or 0.765

TABLE 15.5 Whole score method for calculating correlation coefficient.

SUBJECT	LEISURE SATISFACTION (X)	COMMUNITY SATISFACTION (Y)	X^2	Y^2	XY
A	21	20	441	400	420
B	25	24	625	576	600
C	17	19	289	361	323
D	23	23	529	529	529
E	22	20	484	400	440
F	19	22	361	484	418
G	24	25	576	625	600
H	20	21	400	441	420
I	18	20	324	400	360
J	16	15	256	225	240
	$\Sigma X = 205$	$\Sigma Y = 209$	$\Sigma X^2 = 4285$	$\Sigma Y^2 = 4441$	$\Sigma XY = 4350$

Means: $\overline{X} = \dfrac{\Sigma X}{N} = \dfrac{205}{10} = 20.5$ $\overline{Y} = \dfrac{\Sigma Y}{N} = \dfrac{209}{10} = 20.9$

Standard Deviations: $S_x = \sqrt{\dfrac{\Sigma X^2}{N} - \overline{X}^2} = \sqrt{\dfrac{4285}{10} - \mathbf{420.25}}$ $S_x = \sqrt{8.25} = 2.87$

Standard Deviations: $S_y = \sqrt{\dfrac{\Sigma Y^2}{N} - \overline{Y}^2} = \sqrt{\dfrac{4441}{10} - \mathbf{436.81}}$ $S_y = \sqrt{7.29} = 2.7$

Correlation Coefficient:

$r = \dfrac{\dfrac{\Sigma XY}{N} - \overline{X}\,\overline{Y}}{S_x S_y} = \dfrac{\dfrac{4350}{10} - (20.5)(20.9)}{(2.87)(2.7)} = \dfrac{435 - 428.45}{7.75}$

$r = \dfrac{6.55}{2.25} = .85$

at the 0.01 level of significance. Therefore, since *r observed* exceeds *r critical,* we would say there is a significant relationship between leisure satisfaction and community satisfaction at both levels of significance. In an actual study, we would select our level of significance before we undertook the study, and we would include many more subjects because we would be concerned with the residents being representative of the entire community. We used the subjects here for illustration purposes only.

Spearman Rank-Order Correlation Coefficient

Spearman rank-order correlation coefficient (rho or r_s) is another correlational procedure appropriate for use with ordinal-level data. It is a nonparametric procedure, although it has many similarities to the product-moment coefficient of correlation. Like the product-moment coefficient of correlation, Spearman rho has a range of +1 to −1, with a value of 0 indicating no relationship. Both procedures can be used as descriptive or inferential measures, and tests of significance can be conducted for both. The Spearman rho is used, however, when data represent subjects' rankings on variables under investigation.

To demonstrate, let's assume the sample data in Table 15.5 did not come from a population that is normally distributed with respect to these variables. The researcher then may not be comfortable using a parametric procedure such as the problem-moment coefficient of correlation and therefore chooses to use the Spearman rank-order correlation coefficient, which does not require that the data come from a population that is normally distributed. We will conduct the same study but will use what is known as the Spearman rank-difference method. We selected the 0.05 level of significance for this study. The formula is

$$r_s = 1 - \frac{6\Sigma D^2}{N(N^2 - 1)}$$

where r_s = Spearman coefficient

D^2 = sum of the squared differences between ranks

N = number of pairs of ranks

Table 15.6 presents the data and necessary calculations for the Spearman coefficient. Notice that each score must be converted to a rank to conduct this analysis.

The resulting observed r_s is 0.87. Using Table C.5 in Appendix C, we find that the critical r_s with an N of 10 is 0.648 at the 0.05 level of significance. Since r_s observed exceeds the r_s critical, we would reject the null hypothesis $r_s = 0$, accept the alternative hypothesis $r_s \neq 0$, and state that there is a significant relationship between leisure satisfaction and community satisfaction at the 0.05 level of significance.

TABLE 15.6   Spearman rank difference.

SUBJECT	LEISURE SATISFACTION (X)	COMMUNITY SATISFACTION (Y)	RANK X	RANK Y	D	D^2
A	21	20	5	6.34	1.34	1.80
B	25	24	1	1	1	1
C	17	19	9	9	0	—
D	23	23	3	3	0	—
E	22	20	4	6.34	2.34	5.48
F	19	22	7	4	3	9
G	24	25	2	1	1	1
H	20	21	6	5	1	1
I	18	20	8	6.34	1.66	2.76
J	16	15	10	10	0	0
						$\Sigma D^2 = 22.04$

$$r_s = \frac{6\Sigma D^2}{N(N^2-1)} = 1 - \frac{6(22.04)}{10(100-1)}$$

$$= 1 - \frac{132.24}{990} = 1 - .13$$

$$r_s = .87$$

Bivariate Regression

Beyond exploring the relationship between two variables, the researcher may also use one variable to predict the value of another. *Bivariate regression* is used in this process. For example, you might apply bivariate regression analysis to the task of predicting the number of days that adult members at a private swim club use the pool facilities during the season. Suspecting a relationship between members' ages and their use of the pool, you randomly sample all adult members to learn their ages and frequency of pool visits. Finding a strong positive product-moment correlation *(r)* between these two variables, you use a regression formula to predict how many days present or new members will use the pool, with age serving as the "predictor" variable and pool use serving as the "criterion" variable.

The square of the correlation *(r^2)* between the predictor and criterion variables has significance in regression analysis. This value, known as the coefficient of determination, is the proportion of change in the criterion variable that can be explained by the predictor variable. For example, if we know the correlation between age and pool use is $r = 0.80$, the coefficient of determination is $(0.80)^2$ or 0.64, which means that 64 percent (moving the decimal point two places) of the difference in members' use of the pool can be explained by knowing their age. The coefficient of determination is commonly presented in the literature because it provides some indication of the usefulness of the regression equation. In the above example, one would indicate that age is a good predictor of pool use because a value of 0.64 is a relatively high coefficient in the behavioral and social sciences.

Bivariate regression analysis must meet all the assumptions for parametric procedures, and the variables involved must be at least at the interval level of measurement. As in product-moment correlation procedures, however, ordinal data may be assumed to meet the criterion for interval data when a Likert-type instrument has been used.

OTHER STATISTICAL PROCEDURES

Thus far we have generally focused on procedures involving one independent variable in relation to one dependent variable. Several statistical procedures, however, are used to examine the simultaneous influence of several independent variables on one or more dependent variables. These are usually referred to as multivariate procedures. Some of the most common ones used in recreation research include multiple regression, factor analysis, cluster analysis, discriminant analysis, and canonical correlation. Brief explanations of each follow; for a more detailed description, consult an advanced textbook on statistical procedures.[6, 7]

Multiple Regression

To predict behavior based on more than one predictor variable, *multiple regression* is used. This is an extension of bivariate regression, in which an overall coefficient of determination (R^2) is determined, as well as individual regression coefficients for each of the predictor variables. Multiple regression makes it possible to determine the relative contribution of each predictor variable to the prediction of the criterion variable. This procedure is often used in recreation research when investigators seek to predict future recreation behavior.

Factor Analysis

Factor analysis should be thought of as a reduction technique in which many items are reduced to fewer items based on their underlying dimensions or factors. The interrelationships of a multitude of items are analyzed, and subgroups of variables that reveal a high degree of interrelationship are combined into a single dimension or factor. This process is repeated until all potential relationships have been explored and until the commonalities among related items are established.

Allen used factor analysis to group 51 leisure activities based upon respondents' stated level of interest in each activity.[8] The analysis resulted in grouping the activities under 9 basic headings, according to the common elements within each such subgroup. The 9 headings, or factors, were outdoor activities, sports, hobby-domestic, social interaction, mechanics, cultural-intellectual, swimming, nature, and chance. Activities such as canoeing, motor boating, snow skiing, or tobogganing were most highly related to the outdoor activities factor. The social interaction factor included activities such as dancing, parties, social drinking, and visiting friends. The analysis found that interests in leisure activities were highly interrelated and that generally such activities could be grouped into 9 areas. To enrich the understanding of these factors, one might explore the common elements in the activities within each factor, beyond the superficial analysis that was conducted to identify and label the factors.

Cluster Analysis

This procedure is used to establish groups of highly similar entities. In this sense, it is similar to factor analysis. Factor analysis, however, is usually employed to examine the interrelationship among variables; *cluster analysis* is normally used to classify or group sets of individuals that have a high degree of interrelationship.

Cluster analysis normally begins by gathering a data set of information on a sample of subjects. From this information, the researcher seeks to establish homogeneous groups (clusters) of individuals; those within each cluster have a level of similarity with one another that is higher than that with those in other clusters. The most important step in cluster analysis is selecting variables that best represent the theoretical base of the study. Cluster analysis has been used extensively in market segmentation studies that group individuals into homogeneous subgroups according to their consumer behavior or preference. In the tourism literature, a number of studies have grouped participants according to the types of experiences they are seeking. To illustrate, Mazanea used cluster analysis to segment vacation travelers according to the benefits they sought.[9] He found three clusters: (1) one that exhibited interest in all the varied attractions in a vacation spot, (2) one that had a high interest in swimming and other aquatic activities, and (3) one that was most interested in the natural environment and beautiful landscapes. Once such homogeneous clusters have been established, it is possible to examine the demographic characteristics of each cluster and thus to promote specific vacation destinations to appropriate segments of the potential tourist population.

Discriminant Analysis

Cluster analysis is used to identify homogeneous groups of individuals; *discriminant analysis* is a method of studying the differences between two or more groups of subjects or objects in terms of several variables simultaneously. ANOVA or *t*-tests may be used to look at differences between groups with respect to a single variable or two or more variables independently. These techniques, however, do not take into account the interrelationship among the variables, as discriminant analysis does.

Discriminant analysis is frequently used in recreation research today. For example, Rossman conducted a study that examined differences among five groups of participants, using eight leisure satisfaction dimensions as the discriminating variables.[10] Recreation participants were categorized into one of five groups, based on the type of program format in which they participated most frequently. These formats were leader-directed groups, leagues and tournaments, instructional classes, open facilities, and special events. The eight leisure satisfaction dimensions were achievement, autonomy, environment, family escape, fun, physical fitness, risk, and social enjoyment. Rossman found significant differences among the five format groups in terms of the leisure satisfaction dimensions, with achievement, family escape, environment, and social enjoyment being the most influential elements.

As with other multivariate procedures, an advanced understanding of statistical methods is necessary to conduct and interpret discriminant analysis. Because of its increasing use and the availability of computerized statistical packages, however, it is becoming more readily accessible to those with limited statistical skills.

Canonical Correlation

Canonical correlation can be viewed as an extension of multiple regression analysis, where there is a set of criterion variables rather than a single one. It is possible to investigate a combination of criterion variables in relation to a set of predictor variables. The procedure is quite useful in recreation research since leisure phenomena are rarely related on a one-to-one basis, without other influences playing a part.

For example, Buchanan used canonical-correlation analysis to identify the relationship between "secondary" recreation activities and the satisfaction derived from fishing trips.[11] Secondary activities, the nonfishing experiences encountered on a fishing trip, were investigated for a group of fishermen, along with 20 scores of leisure satisfaction. The extent to which each fisherman participated in a group of secondary activities served as the set of predictor variables; the 20 leisure satisfaction scores constituted the set of criterion variables. Buchanan found a number of significant relationships between predictor and criterion variables. For example, the first such relationship (referred to as a canonical variate) showed that the secondary activities of visiting with others, going for a walk, and sitting around a campfire were highly related to the satisfactions of meeting new people, being with friends, and showing off equipment. He found 3 remaining canonical variates revealing relationships between different sets of secondary activities and leisure satisfactions. This method of analysis is extremely helpful to recreation researchers and planners because it closely approximates human behaviors in which a variety of satisfactions may be sought from different leisure experiences. Canonical-correlation analysis takes into account the interrelationships within each set of information as well as relationships across sets of information.

LIMITS OF QUANTIFICATION

It is worth repeating, in concluding this chapter, that statistics are only as useful as the data provided them. We tend to have an inordinate respect for quantification, as shown in the statement, "If it can't be expressed in figures, it is not science; it is opinion." As a society, we have respected numbers because they are very recognizable and appear to deal with hard, measurable facts as opposed to nonquantifiable elements. Too often, however, numbers themselves may be carelessly gathered and meaningless.

Therefore, it must be stressed that even the most sophisticated forms of statistical analysis cannot compensate for sloppy research work and that quantification is not the *only* form of useful research. Other types of qualitative research, involving historical, philosophical, or other conceptual or model-building but nonempirical studies, can also contribute greatly to our knowledge. At the same time, the fact that we can carry out complex statistical analyses using the methods described in this chapter means that we are able today to gather a wealth of useful information and to understand much more about the nature of leisure motivations and experiences than in the past.

SUMMARY

This chapter describes a number of important principles and methods used in inferential statistics, ranging from sampling distribution and the central limit theorem to hypothesis testing, ANOVA, and several multivariate procedures. It should be stressed again that the descriptions provided here are not intended to *teach* readers to carry out the procedures, but rather to familiarize them with the purposes and general approach of each procedure. Normally, those who seek to become more advanced researchers must take at least two or three courses in statistics—and sometimes several more—to become expert in a variety of specialized methods.

The chapter concludes with a warning about the uncritical acceptance of quantification and statistical analysis as the basis for scholarly research. Other forms of analysis can provide valuable insights to complement those derived from quantitative and statistical investigations.

QUESTIONS AND ACTIVITIES

Students review articles in research journals that make use of the different statistical procedures. Then use their research to show how each procedure is used to handle different types of data or with different research designs. Students may also review and interpret the findings of the statistical analyses.

ENDNOTES

1. John W. Best, *Research in Education* (Englewood Cliffs, NJ: Prentice-Hall, 1981): 269.

2. Joseph E. Healey, *Statistics: A Tool For Social Research,* 3d ed. (Belmont, CA: Wadsworth, 1993).

3. Sidney M. Stahl and James D. Hennes, *Reading and Understanding Applied Statistics* (St. Louis, MO: C. V. Mosby, 1980): 148.

4. Schuyler W. Huck, William H. Cormier, and William G. Burch, Jr., *Readings in Statistics and Research* (New York: Harper and Row, 1974).

5. Neil Cheek, Jr., "Toward a Sociology of Not-Work," *Pacific Sociological Review* (July 1971): 245–58.

6. William W. Cooley and Paul R. Lohnes, *Multivariate Data Analysis* (New York: John Wiley and Sons, 1971); and Richard H. Lindeman, Peter F. Merenda, and Ruth Z. Gold, *Introduction to Bivariate and Multivariate Analysis* (Glenview, IL: Scott, Foresman and Co., 1980).

7. Maurice M. Tatsuoka with contributions by Paul R. Lohnes, *Multivariate Analysis: Techniques for Educational and Psychological Research,* 2d ed. (New York, NY: Macmillan, 1988).

8. Lawrence R. Allen, "The Relationship Between Murray's Personality Needs and Leisure Interests," *Journal of Leisure Research* (1st quarter 1982): 63–76.

9. Josef A. Mazanea, "How to Select Travel Market Segments: A Clustering Approach," *Journal of Travel Research* (summer 1984): 17–21.

10. J. Robert Rossman, "The Influence of Program Format Choice on Participant Satisfaction," *Journal of Park and Recreation Administration* (January 1984): 39–51.

11. Thomas Buchanan, "Toward an Understanding of Variability in Satisfactions Within Activities," *Journal of Leisure Research* (1st quarter 1983): 39–51.

Evaluation as a Professional Function

*An evaluation is a study which has a distinctive purpose;
it is not a new or different research strategy. The purpose
of an evaluation is to assess the effects and effectiveness
of something, typically some innovation or intervention:
policy, practice or service. This can be done using experimental, survey or case study research strategies—or some
appropriate hybrid or combined strategy.[1]*

*The evaluator is looking at value, quality control, impact,
and effects of performance at all stages of program development. Evaluation occurs at the point of input or start-up;
during the process of delivery; and at outcome, result, or
follow-up stages. It is conducted by boards, administrators,
programmers, leaders, and participants, but the responsibility for its conduct is a function of management.[2]*

INTRODUCTION

We now take a more focused look at evaluation, both as a professional function concerned with measuring the quality and effectiveness of leisure-service
agencies and programs and as a specific type of research that systematically
examines the outcomes and benefits of organized recreation services.

In the first context, dealt with in this chapter, evaluation is regarded as an
ongoing professional responsibility and an important element in the "control"
function of recreation and park managers. This chapter describes the purposes
and models of evaluation, examines the process of evaluation, and presents the
specific steps that are followed in conducting systematic evaluations of leisure-
service agencies. It concludes with a discussion of the human-relations and
motivational aspects of evaluation.

MEANING AND PURPOSE OF EVALUATION

Evaluation is a process that judges the worth or value of a particular program, agency, or service. Evaluation uses a variety of research methods but
must be understood as a *purpose* of research, rather than any particular

technique. What distinguishes evaluation from other types of research is the way it deals with what Robson calls the "real worldness" of the enterprise. He continues:

> Issues concerning clearances and permissions, negotiations with "gate-keepers," the political nature of the study, ethics, the type of report, etc., are not in themselves design issues but they set an important context for the choice of design.[3]

As earlier chapters have shown, evaluation research has become a widely used process that seeks to determine the effectiveness of social programs and institutions as a means of guiding public policy, justifying fiscal support, or modifying management practices. During the decades after World War II, numerous innovative social programs related to health, education, social welfare, crime, and other national concerns began to be subjected to mandated program evaluations. Today, evaluation research is used not only for such purposes, but also to contribute to the body of theory and practical knowledge in a wide range of applied fields.

Seen *as* research, evaluation may range from tightly defined, valid, reliable, and statistically sound studies to much more casual or loosely constructed efforts to measure program quality and effectiveness. In simple terms, it is research designed to explore the questions: Is an agency accomplishing its goals? How effective and productive is it?

MAJOR THRUSTS OF EVALUATION

Questions related to meeting goals and determining productivity may be expanded to identify several major thrusts of evaluation in leisure-service programming today:

1. To measure the overall quality of any leisure-service agency or program, in order to document its worth for the public, boards or commissions, trustees, owners, or other funding agencies.
2. To determine how effective it is, or has been, in terms of meeting its goals and objectives—either with respect to total, long-range goals, or the narrower and more short-term objectives of specific programs.
3. To assist agency managers and supervisory personnel in decision making, planning, problem solving, development of policies and procedures, or other ongoing operational tasks.
4. To ensure that public or membership needs and priorities are being met as fully as possible.

From an administrative point of view, evaluation may also be invaluable in terms of providing periodic information about the attainment of agency objectives as a management control mechanism. It may demonstrate the need for new service programs or help to establish priorities among programs in terms of demonstrated needs and outcomes or program elements or strategies that have been proven most effective.

Evaluation may also be employed as a basic tool in two important professional processes: *accreditation* and *systems management.* In accreditation, standards that have been set by recognized professional societies are used to determine agencies' licensing, eligibility for funding, or other important benefits. In systems management, evaluation constitutes a key step in the planning and program development process, with feedback "loops" that lead to further planning, the revision of objectives, or the refinement of program methods.

EVALUATION APPROACHES

Evaluation in recreation, parks, and leisure services may be carried out through several types of approaches.

Professional Judgment

This approach uses a critical review process and the application of professional judgment by one or more experts or authorities who examine an agency or a program. They examine records, manuals, and reports; interview board members, employees on various levels, and participants; observe programs and tour facilities; and gather other needed data. Based on the information they have gathered and their own judgment of the agency's practices in terms of approved professional guidelines, they prepare an evaluation report that identifies its strengths and weaknesses.

Standards and Criteria

A second approach is based on the use of a comprehensive evaluation or rating form that includes a number of approved standards for professional practice, each with its own set of supporting criteria. Customarily, the agency or institution is required to carry out a detailed self-study and prepare a report, using the standards and criteria as an outline of areas or practices to be covered. Typically, a team of outside evaluators comes in and, armed with the self-study report, examines varied aspects of the agency to determine whether the standards and criteria have been met. This method is commonly used in the accreditation of agencies and institutions. Several examples of the standards-and-criteria approach used by major professional organizations are presented in Chapter 17.

Goal Achievement

This approach is based solely on an agency or program's success in achieving specific objectives which have been precisely defined and which have measurable, quantitative outcomes or accomplishments. Such objectives may be stated in terms of populations served, behavioral or affective changes among participants, benefits derived by the community or the sponsoring organization, or similar measures.

A term that has sometimes been applied to this approach to evaluation is the "discrepancy" model. It refers to the possible discrepancy, or gap, between the objectives of the agency and what was actually accomplished.

Participation/Attendance/Income

This is closely related to the goal achievement approach and might be considered a subset of it. It tends to be a limited approach that focuses on statistical reports of participation in an agency's programs, attendance totals, income derived, or similar measures of performance over a given period of time. It is concerned chiefly with profitability and popularity as measures of agency success and does not seek to assess the actual quality of the program or other social or personal benefits that may have been achieved.

An example of the use of participation and attendance as bases for program evaluation is the *cost-benefit* approach to evaluation. At a basic level this approach seeks to analyze the specific costs of different program elements, either in terms of major administrative categories (such as personnel, equipment and supplies, or utilities) or as activity or service units. At a more advanced level, the fiscal costs of programs are determined in terms of the number of individuals served, the totals of participation, or measurable benefits of program elements. Linked to this approach is the *importance-performance* approach that a number of researchers have used to measure both the importance of given elements or services and the degree to which they have been satisfactorily provided.

Staff Ratings or Participant Satisfaction

Frequently evaluation makes use of rating sheets filled out by staff members themselves, who may appraise the success of programs, workshops, or other events, based on a set of guidelines used to judge the quality of programs. Similarly, program participants may also be asked to appraise programs from a user perspective or to rate the effectiveness of leaders or other program arrangements.

Transaction/Observation

A variation of the preceding approach, this method also uses ratings by staff members or program participants who indicate their judgment of program effectiveness. However, it is much more diverse in its documentation, making use of interviews, systematic observation, case studies, or other sources of data. In addition, it tends to focus heavily on the element of human resource management, the use of interpersonal or group dynamics theory, and similar materials that contribute to an integrated case analysis that identifies both strengths and weaknesses of an agency or program. Essentially, it is an approach that is influenced by naturalistic and qualitative approaches to research, making relatively little use of quantitative data and probing more deeply into interpersonal factors and social influences.

Systems-Based Evaluation

In this approach, evaluation is an important tool in such systems-based planning methods as PPBS (Planning-Program-Budgeting Systems) PERT, (Program Evaluation Review Technique), and CPM (Critical Path Method). It provides feedback during the course of program implementation and may also be used to modify goals and strategies, revise program plans, reallocate resources, or initiate fresh planning.

The essential elements of the program system, such as input, process, and outcomes, as well as the environment in which the agency operates, are reviewed. Each element is analyzed, including time and money costs, personnel functions, barriers to successful performance, and policy-making and planning functions. This approach is often based on computer analysis and may use complex formulas to carry out the overall assessment.

OTHER WAYS OF CATEGORIZING EVALUATION

Each approach to evaluation just described may share common elements with other approaches; they represent *emphasis* rather than *unique methods* of conducting evaluations. Often two or more approaches may be used in a single evaluation process. For example, reviewers employing professional judgment may also use standards-and-criteria instruments or staff and participant-rating forms.

In addition, evaluation may also be categorized in several other ways, in terms of the instruments used or the point at which it is applied and used. For example, a distinction is frequently made between *preordinate* and *process* models of evaluation.

Preordinate Models

Most agency evaluations are of this type. They use standards and criteria and other evaluative methods that are structured in advance and that are used to examine or accredit institutions or programs in a uniform way, with similar, objective rating systems.

Process Models

These models make use of evaluation methods that are not firmly fixed or structured in advance, in terms of the procedures that are to be followed, the instruments, the standards that are applied, or similar elements. Instead, the group responsible for carrying out the evaluation may go through a process of determining the need for doing it, its purposes or goals, the methods to be followed, and ways of assigning responsibility—in a continuing, evolving way.

An example of a process model might be a therapeutic recreation program or department in a large psychiatric hospital in which the staff members agree that they wish to review their operation systematically. To accomplish this, they start from the very beginning in reviewing their goals and objectives, and establishing the guidelines or standards through which the program is to be evaluated. In so doing, they must necessarily examine the program based on a fresh outlook and develop a dynamic approach to meeting contemporary needs and conditions.

Evaluation may not necessarily be based on either preordinate or process models, but may employ both methods. Similarly, it may use both *summative* and *formative* orientations to evaluation.

Summative Evaluation

This is the most widely used form of evaluation and generally is applied at the *end* of a project, program, or work period. Although it obviously cannot then be used to improve an existing program (which has already been carried out), it *can* be used to plan effectively for the future.

Formative Evaluation

Formative evaluation is carried on *throughout* a program or project, including its early stages of planning and implementation. Since it provides a constant review and assessment of the effectiveness of what is being done, it yields instant feedback that can be used to develop new strategies or program approaches as necessary.

SCOPE OF EVALUATION: FOCUS AND LEVELS

Like research itself, evaluation may encompass a wide range of subjects for investigation and levels at which it is applied. For example, it may focus on any of the following elements of recreation, parks, and leisure-service management and programming:

1. *Overall agencies* and their administrative subdivisions, including such special units as divisions of maintenance and operations, personnel management, or specific service departments.
2. *Programs,* including total, year-round programs, seasonal programs, special-interest areas, single continuing activities (such as leagues or classes), and special events.

3. *Personnel* on all levels, including full-time supervisors, leaders, special-ists or maintenance employees, and also part-time, session employees and volunteers.

4. *Facilities,* both in terms of overall areas and facilities belonging to a department, and also the adequacy of individual structures or areas for specialized purposes, including safety and accessibility factors.

5. *Participants,* with respect to assessment of their needs and how effective-ly these are being met, as well as to participation patterns and outcomes.

In terms of its application, evaluation may be conducted in any of the fol-lowing ways:

1. As a periodic function through which an agency carries out a self-study of its total operation every three to five years, as in the case of institutions that apply for renewed certification or accreditation

2. As a regular function to be carried out at the end of each indoor or out-door season and after each major activity or program unit

3. As an ongoing daily process in which leaders and supervisors regularly eval-uate program activities and events, staff performance, and other elements

4. As a critical element in an organization's administrative process that reg-ularly feeds information into its management information system and into varied data bases, statistical summaries, and similar records and reports

Evaluation may be voluntarily undertaken, required to meet Civil Service or union contract stipulations, or carried out at the request of a commission, board, or other supervising body. It may also be required as part of a subcon-tracting arrangement or grant, in which an agency is funded to conduct a given program and must then have the program systematically evaluated. Evaluation may be designed as a routine function, carried on without addi-tional staff or funding assistance. However, when it is done on an agency-wide basis, and particularly when it is connected with a large-scale planning effort or with accreditation or certification, it may require a special autho-rization and funding approval.

It should be stressed that the key purpose of evaluation is *not* simply to provide a rating or score. Instead, it is to provide an accurate picture of strengths and weaknesses that can be used to bring about improvement. To the extent that specific standards or objectives are not being met, sound evalua-tion identifies actions that must be taken to improve procedures, change poli-cies, or upgrade professional performance.

STEPS IN EVALUATION

Within any leisure-service agency, the following steps must be carried out if evaluation is to provide meaningful input to the management process:

Assign Responsibility

There is an old cliche that "everybody's business is nobody's business." This implies that saying that everyone is responsible for carrying out agency evaluation is tantamount to accepting that it will not be done in a purposeful and well-coordinated way.

Instead, it is advisable to put the chief responsibility for directing evaluation efforts in the hands of a single individual or—in the case of a larger organization—a small committee or work team that will have this as a direct responsibility. These individuals may then call on others to assist them in planning evaluation processes throughout the agency.

Define Agency Evaluation Needs

The second step is to determine exactly what needs to be evaluated and when. For example, in a therapeutic recreation agency, evaluation may include (1) assessments of patient/client needs and functional abilities, (2) measurement of program outcomes, (3) assessment of staff performance, and (4) adherence of the program to professional standards or guidelines.

Assign Evaluation Tasks

Who actually carries out evaluation in its varied forms? Often, routine observations and ratings are done by regular employees. However, when a large-scale or special agency self-study is to be done, or when an evaluation requires special expertise, one must make the choice of using internal or external evaluators or both.

Internal evaluators are regular employees of an organization, who may be used to gather data, make judgments, or critically analyze programs. Their *advantages* are that they are generally familiar with the situation, have ready access to the facts without being specially briefed, and are available without having to make special arrangements or be paid special fees. Their *disadvantages* are that they may be too close to the situation to be able to view it accurately or may be self-protective or biased in one direction or another. In addition, they may not be fully aware of current trends or standards in the field and may lack the high level of expertise that an outside evaluator might bring.

External evaluators are usually consultants who are regarded as being highly authoritative; they may be assigned by a professional society or accrediting body in a volunteer capacity or may be working for a fee as paid consultants. Their *advantages* are that they may have a high level of knowledge or professional judgment and that they are able to carry out a fully impartial and objective analysis of an agency or program. Their *disadvantages* are that they may need considerable time to get all the needed information and even then may get a partial or distorted picture because of limited evidence and familiarity with the program. In addition, they may be quite costly, both in terms of a professional fee and personal expenses.

Design Instruments and Procedures

Evaluation should make use of systematic, carefully applied data-gathering procedures, just as other forms of research do. Therefore it is necessary to design appropriate questionnaires, observation and rating forms, and similar instruments and to develop precise guidelines for carrying out the investigative process.

In some cases, it is possible to use forms developed by national organizations or accrediting bodies (see pages 269–280) or to modify them for use. However, since agencies vary so greatly in their goals and objectives, regional or community characteristics, and other factors, it is often necessary to develop instruments and procedures that are appropriate for an organization's special needs. Guidelines for developing instruments are suggested in Chapter 13, and examples of instruments are shown in Chapter 17.

Analysis and Conclusions

When observations have been made, interviews carried out, records reviewed, and other data gathered, it is necessary to assemble and analyze the evidence. Some evaluation systems use a quantitative approach to delineate all areas of strength and weakness. An agency or program may be required to achieve a number of points to be regarded as passing, in order to justify future funding or continuing accreditation. In some cases, a profile is drawn, with the stipulation that the agency must meet a minimal standard of performance within each of several categories, such as health practices, public relations, and staffing procedures. In other evaluation models, there is little attempt to quantify the findings. Instead, anecdotal records, narratives, and summaries are used to describe a program or staff member's performance, with emphasis on human relations or group dynamics aspects of program experiences.

It is usually advisable to hold a preliminary conference with those being evaluated—particularly in the case of a program or agency that is being examined by outside consultants. Often, staff members may wish to challenge findings, correct misconceptions, or provide fuller understanding of what has occurred, and they should have the opportunity to do so. In any case, the final step of the process is to prepare a report that includes the actual findings of the evaluation and that presents conclusions and recommendations. Frequently, such recommendations may consist of specific suggestions for steps to be taken to improve agency or staff performance. In the case of programs, they may identify those that should be continued or expanded, as well as those that might well be reduced or terminated.

EVALUATION AS A STAFF PROCESS: HUMAN-RELATIONS IMPLICATIONS

In planning and carrying out evaluation procedures, it is essential to realize that it represents much more than a cut-and-dried, mechanical process that will result in a printed report destined for someone's file cabinet. Instead, evaluation has considerable potential for contributing to the effective functioning of organizations—but also may present a serious threat to many agency personnel.

When evaluation is properly approached, agency managers, supervisors, and leadership personnel in many job categories may join together in a cooperative staff process of developing goals and objectives, setting work or program standards and criteria, and reviewing performance on a continuous basis. Evaluation should be regarded as a process of constructive analysis, intended to improve present and future performance. On a broad scale, entire agencies or consortiums of social-service or health-related organizations may join together to identify community or regional needs, assess present programs, and develop short- and long-range goals and objectives and plans for action.

Threats and Risks

However, evaluation may also represent an area of considerable sensitivity or even fear when it involves threats to job security, promotion, tenure, or the possibility of demotion or dismissal. When negative evaluation ratings are submitted, an organization's weaknesses have been exposed, and its funding may be undercut.

Therefore, many professionals are reluctant to be evaluated. When they are placed in a position of responsibility where they must assess the work of others, research indicates that they may hesitate to be critical or judge others harshly even when the evidence may call for it. There is a tendency to treat other employees or programs blandly and to postpone evaluations, carry them out superficially, or sabotage them by making meaningless or mechanical judgments. In bureaucratic organizations, evaluation forms are often very simple and thus provide no basis for real discrimination, and no serious attempt is made to judge the worth of programs or people. In large cities, labor unions frequently resist serious efforts at personnel evaluation.

It is therefore necessary to recognize the human-relations aspect of evaluation. To develop a positive emotional climate, it is often desirable to separate evaluation from decision-making processes that involve funding decisions or personnel recommendations and to have at least part of the process concerned solely with the goal of improving future performance. Whenever possible, evaluation should involve a two-way sharing of views, rather than consist solely of authoritarian judgments made from above. Ideally, evaluation should be used as a development tool, rather than a punitive or coercive exercise, as Chapter 17 shows.

TODAY'S CLIMATE FOR SCIENTIFIC EVALUATION

Summing up, it should be stressed that evaluation has become an increasingly important aspect of leisure-service agency operations. There is a general trend toward providing fuller scientific documentation and accountability within all human-service fields, including both government and nonprofit organizations.

In all types of organizations, there is much greater use today of systems analysis, computer-based planning methods, and management information systems. Evaluation is an essential element in such processes, as Chapter 1 points out, and is clearly part of a scientific management approach—as compared to "fly-by-the-seat-of-your-pants" approaches. As a result, within each area of leisure-service program management, professional organizations have developed comprehensive standards and guidelines that are used in evaluation.

SUMMARY

This chapter provides an overview of the role of evaluation in leisure-service agencies, beginning with a discussion of its purposes and seven common approaches to evaluation. Many organizations may use more than one approach, sometimes blending several of them in different evaluative processes.

Both summative and formative approaches to evaluation are also discussed, as are process and preordinate models of program assessment. Evaluation may be directed to several aspects of agency management, including programs, personnel, facilities, and participants. It may also be applied at different levels of program operations. Several steps of the evaluation process are identified, and the chapter concludes by discussing the degree to which evaluation is often perceived as a serious threat by practitioners.

QUESTIONS AND ACTIVITIES

1. What are the important purposes of evaluation for recreation, parks, and leisure-service agencies? Particularly in today's economic climate, why is evaluation an important professional function?

2. What makes evaluation a sensitive or controversial kind of process in terms of staff relationships? Given this reality, what kinds of emphases should be stressed in conducting program or personnel evaluations?

The following can be used as in-class workshops.

3. Students divide into small groups and each group is assigned a different type of recreation agency or situation. Each group selects three different approaches to evaluation, using the illustrations given in this chapter. Each group shows how these approaches might be used in the agency they were assigned, either to evaluate the overall agency and/or its program, or

other specific elements of it. Make this a brief, preliminary plan; do not develop actual instruments or procedures.

4. Members of the class plan a comprehensive use of evaluation procedures in a recreation and park curriculum, including the following: (a) evaluation of students by teachers; (b) evaluation of teachers by students; (c) evaluation of courses by students; (d) evaluation of teachers by teachers; (e) evaluation of the overall curriculum by students; (f) evaluation of the entire department by an outside accrediting body; or (g) evaluation of any other aspect of the program, such as student services or job placement, by current or past students. Consider the use of formal models (such as actual accreditation manuals) in this process.

ENDNOTES

1. Colin Robson, *Real World Research* (Cambridge, MA: Blackwell, 1993): 170.
2. Herberta Lundegren and Patricia Farrell, *Evaluation for Leisure Service Managers: A Dynamic Approach* (Philadelphia: Saunders College, 1984): 1.
3. Robson, *Real World Research.*

Agency-Centered Evaluation: Programs and Practices

How are we doing? Do we "measure up"? The standards provide a tool for "benchmarking." Benchmarking is a systematic and rigorous examination of an agency's work processes, services, and products, measured against what professionals believe to be desirable practices and policies. . . . Accreditation through self-evaluation can lead to increased efficiency and effectiveness of operations, enhanced quality of service to a local constituency, and provide the public with evidence of agency accountability.[1]

INTRODUCTION

As Chapter 16 points out, evaluation in recreation, park, and leisure-service agencies is intended to assess both the quality and the effectiveness of professional services and programs. This chapter focuses on the measurement of agency quality by applying approved standards and criteria to its operations as part of self-study or accreditation procedures. It also provides examples of participation/attendance/income models of agency evaluation and describes methods of evaluating personnel, areas and facilities, strategies, and special projects.

THE MEANING OF "AGENCIES" AND "PROGRAMS"

The two terms "agencies" and "programs" are often used synonymously to refer to the overall operation of recreation and park organizations. One might comment colloquially about a given public or voluntary recreation agency with the phrase, "That's an excellent program."

More precisely defined, the term "agency" refers to the organization itself as an operating entity, including its legal status and governing boards or commissions, its managers on various levels, its structural units and physical resources, and—beyond all these—its essential character or identity as a social institution.

In contrast, the term "program" refers to the work of the agency in terms of service delivery. While it involves the organization's resources and operational procedures, it is *chiefly* concerned with goals, objectives, activities, services, and outcomes.

This chapter outlines contemporary approaches to evaluating both agencies and their programs, recognizing that in practice the structure and management approaches of an organization are closely intertwined with its program practices and may indeed be evaluated at the same time. It illustrates the point made by Howe that there are

> . . . several practical reasons for program evaluation. Services must be improved; resources must be allocated or reallocated based on rational decision making; the support of the grass roots consumer must be expanded; the ethic and value of a meaningful recreational lifestyle must be instilled; two-way communication between agencies and their public must be fostered; and a sensitivity to the impact of the leisure experience upon the individual must be maintained. What all this means is that we must use evaluation to critically examine our effectiveness.[2]

EVALUATION OF PUBLIC LEISURE-SERVICE AGENCIES

A comprehensive evaluation plan for a public recreation and park agency may include three important elements to ensure a detailed, objective set of conclusions: (1) an administrative evaluation plan; (2) public assessment of program impact and quality; and (3) use of an external evaluation team.[3]

Administrative Plan

The agency's director and key management personnel work with members of a staff advisory team and possibly community representatives and/or advisory council members to lay the groundwork for carrying out the evaluation. They must:

1. Make decisions regarding the form of the evaluation
   a. Who needs it?
   b. What purposes will it serve? What decisions must be made?
   c. What questions must be asked? What information will be needed to answer these?
   d. At what stage of agency operations or program implementation should questions be asked?
   e. What resources are available to do the evaluation?
   f. How are results to be reported and to whom?
   g. Who should do the evaluation?

2. Determine what areas are to be reviewed, including the following:
   a. Philosophy and goals.
   b. Long-range planning process.
   c. Agency resources: areas, facilities, and equipment.
   d. Program effectiveness.
   e. Personnel performance.
   f. Community relations and input in policy development and program planning.
   g. Effectiveness of interagency planning and utilization of existing community resources.

All the elements described in this administrative plan may be incorporated in or lead to a comprehensive *internal audit*—essentially a detailed self-assessment of the agency's quality and effectiveness, conducted by members of the professional staff. To be most meaningful, this internal evaluation should use systematic *public assessment* of the program and may also include an examination by an *outside evaluation team.*

Public Assessment of Program Impact

The staff team develops a questionnaire to be used with different groups of citizens: participants, parents, representatives of schools and other community agencies, and other professionals. Administered internally (by agency staff members), this survey examines:

1. Program variety and breadth.
2. Scheduling factors and suitability to different community needs.
3. Leadership effectiveness, including use of volunteers.
4. Use of available facilities, and varying locations in terms of needs of special populations in community.
5. Program costs and revenues, possibly using a cost/benefit analysis.
6. Public relations practices and community relations.
7. Community relations efforts, including cosponsorship with other community agencies.

In addition to use of a survey questionnaire, the public assessment may also include input from special town meetings, focus groups, neighborhood or recreation center councils, and similar sources.

External Evaluation Process

As an option, the overall evaluation may include a site visit and study by an external evaluation team. Composed of representatives of a professional society, other government agencies, or consultants, this team might have two emphases: product evaluation and process evaluation.

1. Product evaluation focuses on the program's effectiveness, utilizing:
   a. Review of documents and reports developed by internal review team.
   b. Examination of goals statements and evidence of their accomplishment.
   c. Interviews with staff members and participants.
   d. Application of professional standards and criteria, as basis for judgments.
2. Process evaluation examines the "how" of program operations:
   a. Review of agency program-planning process.
   b. Examination of staff reports for major program elements.
   c. Review of operations manuals, including leadership, maintenance, and programming for special populations.
   d. Records dealing with community participation, interagency cooperation, and volunteer involvement.

Beyond this "product" and "process" focus on programming, the external evaluation should also analyze the agency's administrative operations, structure or organization, fiscal practices, personnel procedures, and other elements of effective management.

The three-phase plan just described provides a framework in which each agency—whatever its type—can develop its own approach to evaluation, depending on its special needs and resources. Typically, many leisure-service organizations are likely to rely heavily on a combination of the professional judgment and standards-and-criteria approaches described in Chapter 16. Often, the evaluation team makes use of self-study rating forms that contain recommended standards for practice.

THE NATURE OF STANDARDS

The standards used in the standards-and-criteria approach to agency evaluation are desirable guidelines or descriptions of recommended professional practices, which have been formulated by respected professionals in the field. They provide a means of measuring the quality of programs—not as optimal or maximal goals, but rather minimal levels of quality or performance that are to be met. As an example, the National Institute of Senior Centers developed detailed standards over a five-year period based on the following assumptions:

Quality is best achieved from *within* a field through standards—guidelines to operating a successful program—rather than from outside through licensure and government regulations.

Standards should be realistic and flexible, adaptable to centers with a wide variety of structures, resources, and settings; they are *not* a list of components making up a model program.

Standards are not "cast in concrete," but should be continually monitored to respond to changing needs, resources, and knowledge.[4]

Several examples of the use of standards and criteria in the evaluation of leisure-service agencies follow. They include instruments and processes that have been developed by professional societies in such specialized fields as public recreation and park departments, therapeutic recreation, and armed forces recreation.

NRPA Community Recreation Evaluation Manual

In the early 1970s, the National Recreation and Park Association published a manual, *Evaluation and Self-Study of Public Recreation and Park Agencies: A Guide with Standards and Evaluative Criteria.*[5] This instrument was the revised and updated version of an earlier manual that had been developed by the Great Lakes Standards Committee, based on numerous evaluation guidelines used by professional associations and voluntary organizations.

The primary use of the NRPA evaluation and self-study manual was to assist departments or local public agencies in examining and improving their own programs by providing a systematic instrument through which their practices could be compared with statements of recommended practices.

The self-study manual had 35 standards in the following 6 categories: (1) philosophy and goals; (2) administration; (3) programming; (4) personnel; (5) areas, facilities, and equipment; and (6) evaluation. Each standard was followed by one or more criteria that consisted of a specific statement of recommended procedures or operational practices and thus provided a means of judging whether the overall standard was met. The agency's self-study team was asked to respond to each criterion on a 5-point scale ranging from Yes (5) to No (0). Average scores of the criteria were compiled for each standard, and the results were plotted on a Standards Profile chart (see Figure 17.1).

Accreditation Process for Public Agencies

In the mid-1990s a new manual was developed to serve local public recreation and park agencies for self-assessment procedures leading to accreditation. As part of the drive to improve quality operation of such agencies, the National Committee on Accreditation sponsored by the American Academy for Park and Recreation Administration and the National Recreation and Park Association developed guidelines and a self-assessment manual.[7] Constituting a revision of the earlier standards, this new process was based on 152 standards divided into 10 major categories as follows:

1. *Agency Authority, Role, and Responsibility*
   Example of Standard: The source of authority of and powers for the local public recreation and park managing authority shall be clearly set forth by legal document.

FIGURE 17.1   Standards profile for NRPA community recreation evaluation manual.[6]

For each standard, plot the Standard Profile value as computed on the work sheet; then join the dots with a red line—shown as a broken line of this example—to give a graphic picture of the standards profile.

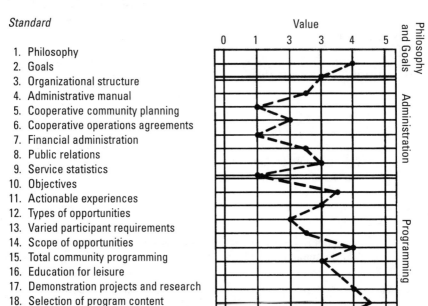

Standard

1. Philosophy
2. Goals
3. Organizational structure
4. Administrative manual
5. Cooperative community planning
6. Cooperative operations agreements
7. Financial administration
8. Public relations
9. Service statistics
10. Objectives
11. Actionable experiences
12. Types of opportunities
13. Varied participant requirements
14. Scope of opportunities
15. Total community programming
16. Education for leisure
17. Demonstration projects and research
18. Selection of program content
19, Participant involvement

Note: This illustrates the first three categories of standards.

2. *Planning*
   Example of Standard: There shall be a comprehensive park and recreation system plan, which is basically an inventory of existing conditions and recommendations for future programs and services, acquisition and development of areas and facilities, and administration. The plan shall be officially adopted by the appropriate governing body, updated regularly, and be linked with a capital improvement budget and a phased development.

3. *Organization and Administration*
   Example of Standard: The Agency shall establish an organizational structure, specifying in detail the interrelationships of the system from the highest authority to all staff positions.

4. *Human Resources*
   Example of Standard: There shall be written policies which govern the administration of personnel procedures for both professional and non-professional employees and are reviewed annually.

5. *Finance (Fiscal Policy and Management)*
   Example of Standard: There shall be annual operating and capital improvement budgets, including both revenues and expenditures.

6. *Program and Services Management*
   Example of Standard: The program and services provided shall be based on conceptual foundations of play, recreation, and leisure that enhance positive leisure lifestyles; constituent needs; community opportunities; Agency philosophy and goals; experiences desirable for clientele.

7. *Facility and Land Use Management*
   Example of Standard: There shall be written environmentally sound standards and procedures for development and maintenance of the Agency's natural resources, with particular attention to protection and preservation of especially-sensitive land and water areas.

8. *Safety and Security*
   Example of Standard: There shall be a law enforcement in-service training program conducted either by the Agency or in conjunction with the jurisdictional police or other agency.

9. *Risk Management*
   Example of Standard: There shall be a risk management plan reviewed annually and updated to reflect new information, operational techniques, and services.

10. *Evaluation and Research (Evaluative Research)*
    Example of Standard: There shall be a systematic evaluation plan to assess outcomes and the operational efficiency and effectiveness of the Agency.[8]

In two detailed documents prepared by the National Committee on Accreditation, the purpose of the accreditation process and the specific standards and procedures for agencies applying for accreditation are fully discussed. As an example of the degree to which accreditation—which represents a formal, comprehensive approach to evaluation—has become a high priority of national organizations in this field, a 17-step procedural sequence has been developed that requires a major commitment of agency effort and the cooperation of a visitation team and other key professionals (see Figure 17.2).

RECOMMENDED STANDARDS OF PRACTICE

Beyond such comprehensive systems for the accreditation and evaluation of agencies, a number of professional societies or study groups have formulated guidelines for the operation of specific types of programs.

NTRS Standards of Practice

One example of recommended guidelines for professional practice was developed by the National Therapeutic Recreation Society in the early 1980s,

FIGURE 17.2   Procedural sequence: accreditation process.[9]

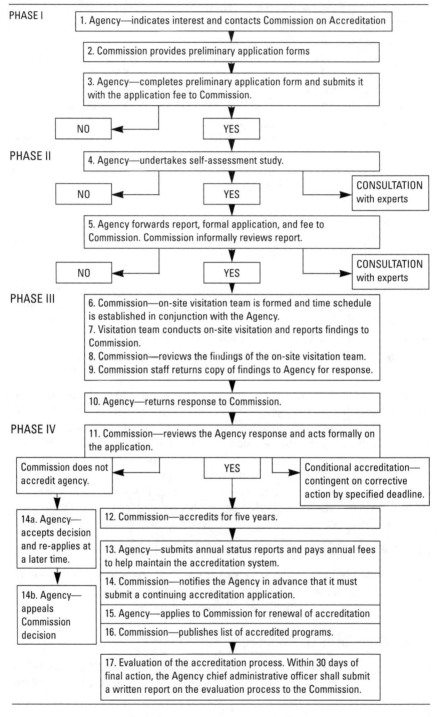

reflecting an increased emphasis on clinical approaches in the provision of treatment services.[10]

The NTRS manual was not designed specifically to be an evaluation instrument. However, each of its six major standards (covering the *Scope of Services, Agency or Department Objectives, Individual Treatment/Program Plans, Documentation, Scheduling of Services* and *Ethical Practices*) may be used as the basis for examining and rating a therapeutic recreation program. An example of one such standard and the criteria used to determine whether it is met follows.

Standard III. Individual Treatment/Program Plan

The therapeutic recreation staff develop an individualized treatment/program plan for each client referred to the unit/agency/department.

CRITERIA

A. The plan is based on complete and relevant diagnostic/assessment data.

 1. The plan reflects the client's physical, social, mental, and emotional aptitudes and skills and current level of leisure functioning.

 2. The plan indicates precautions, restrictions, or limitations related to an individual's participation as determined by the diagnosis/assessment.

B. The plan is stated in behavioral terms that permit the progress of the individual to be assessed.

C. The plan is periodically reviewed, evaluated and modified as necessary to meet the changing needs of the client.

D. The plan differentiates among short-term, long-term, and discharge/transition goals.

E. The plan is documented in the personal record of the client.

F. The plan reflects an integrated approach.

 1. The plan is consistent with interdisciplinary treatment goals for the client.

 2. When feasible, the client and/or his/her family assist in developing and implementing the therapeutic recreation treatment plan.

 3. The plan reflects the client's goals and expectation of benefits to be derived from the therapeutic recreation program.

Program Evaluation in National Youth Sports Program

Another example of evaluation systems that focuses on examining program practices may be found in the process used by the National Youth Sports Program (NYSP). Through this program, funded by the United States Congress and administered by the National Collegiate Athletic Association, many urban colleges and universities have sponsored summer day-camp programs emphasizing sport and designed primarily for disadvantaged children and youth in inner-city neighborhoods.

Each camp must have its program evaluated through a site visit by qualified evaluators who visit sponsoring colleges and universities, observe activities and facilities, interview staff members and participants, and examine records. Using a manual with 106 standards, they must rate the program in terms of whether or not each standard is fully or partially met. The standards fall under the following headings: *Institution, Participants, Activities, Enrichment Program, Project Schedule, Nutrition, Medical Services, Staff, Project Organization,* and *Coordination.* Several of these are illustrated in Figure 17.3.

Evaluators must be carefully prepared to carry out the site visit. To assist them, the NYSP national organization has prepared a detailed set of instructions, including interpretations of each item and suggestions for applying them.

A maximum number of 180 points may be awarded to any program. Depending on its total score, an institution may be approved fully for Youth

FIGURE 17.3   NYSP evaluation form.

	Points	Item	
Institution:	2	[1].	Institutional facilities are provided for an effective project
	1	2.	Cooperation afforded by several departments in the University or College
Total—13	1–2	3.	Lockers used daily by each participant
	1–2	4.	Playing fields are marked off and equipped to accommodate all field activities offered
	1–2	5.	Court areas are marked off and equipped to accommodate all court activities offered
	2	[6].	Adequate equipment was readily available for each activity
	2	[7].	NYSP shirts provided to participants
Participants:	2	[1].	Roster available
	2	[2].	Project meets minimum of 90% disadvantaged participants
	1–2	3.	If actual enrollment equals or exceeds projected enrollment
Total—23	2	[4].	If average daily attendance equals at least 80% projected enrollment
	1	5.	If average daily attendance equals at least 90% projected enrollment
	1–2	6.	Daily attendance recorded by name and filed
	2	[7].	Evidence of efforts made to maintain high average daily attendance
	1–3	8.	Data collected on (1) physical fitness, (2) performance records, and (3) behavior inventories
	1–2	9.	Observable evidence that participants are enjoying the experiences
	2	10.	At least 50 per cent of enrollees are returnees
	1	11.	Returnees exceed 60 per cent of enrollees
	2	[12].	All participants are within the age range of 10–18

Note: This figure includes two of the form's ten sections.

Sports Camp funding in the following year, approved conditionally (with required actions that must be taken to improve the program), or disapproved.

ILLUSTRATIONS OF PROGRAM EVALUATION METHODS

Several specific approaches to evaluation in recreation, park, and leisure-service agencies were listed in Chapter 16. These are now described in fuller detail, with examples drawn from a number of community agencies.

Participation/Attendance/Income Model

This represents one of the most common ways of evaluating program success. Typically, public, voluntary-agency, armed forces, and other types of recreation sponsors tend to set attendance or registration goals for programs. If these are met, and if the number of those involved continues to grow, it is assumed that the program is meeting the needs of the public or the organization's membership. In addition, healthy attendance levels usually mean that programs are yielding needed income. While commercial recreation businesses are the only type of sponsor with the primary aim of making a financial profit, all types of agencies today rely on fees and charges to some degree to pay for operational costs.

Cost-benefit analysis

Statistics of attendance and income from recreation facilities and programs may also be used in cost-benefit analysis. This is a method of measuring the relative costs and positive outcomes of programs to determine those that are most successful and worthy of continued support. It involves identifying all program costs, in terms of direct charges for space, leadership, equipment, and similar elements, and also taking into account a portion of the overhead costs of the organization. It is also used to assess the benefits, in terms of the numbers served and their level of recreational need, as well as other kinds of criteria which may be used to judge the value of a program activity.

For example, should a sports program that serves 200 children at a total cost of $1,000 be given a higher priority than one that serves 50 senior citizens at a similar cost? Is a creative arts program more valuable than an environmental studies workshop? Such issues must be considered in developing a cost-benefit approach. Beyond this, it should be recognized that many of the benefits of recreation are very difficult to measure quantitatively and that program impacts often extend over a period of time into the future. Posavac and Carey write:

> A sophisticated cost analysis will include benefits occurring at times in the future. Successful rehabilitation or therapy will enable a person to live

with less need of special services in future years. Improvements in work skills, psychological adjustment, and physical health may well have benefits for the children of people served or cared for. The worth of these long-term benefits is, not surprisingly, hard to estimate.[11]

Attendance/income quotas

In some cases, attendance and income may be used to develop a productivity formula covering all the specialized facilities or programs within a large agency. In one YWCA which was evaluated by a coauthor of this text, the practice was to assign each of the different areas of the agency's building (including auditoriums, multipurpose or exercise rooms, arts and crafts rooms, pool, and gymnasiums) an actual quota that stated the revenue it was required to "earn." This was defined as an average hourly income during the period of active programming throughout the week. Each area or specialized facility was programmed to achieve its target income with a variety of revenue-producing activities. Attendance and income were used directly to assess the success of programming in this Y.

In some cases, a comprehensive systems-based analysis of program operations may include measurement of the department's success in achieving objectives set for the coming year with respect to numbers of community residents enrolled in classes, workshops, or other programs, as shown in Figure 17.4.

Staff Ratings and Participant-Satisfaction Approach

Particularly in terms of evaluating specific program activities and events, this is one of the most common evaluation techniques. Staff members often are required to submit evaluation reports of programs they have directed. Their supervisors may also carry out evaluations of activities led by subordinates. Similarly, participants may be asked to fill out evaluation sheets about programs they have taken part in, dealing with such questions as the level of the activity, the adequacy of the facility, the leadership, the fee or charge, the schedule, and similar information. Often, such evaluations may be combined with questions about the future, asking whether they would enroll in a similar activity if it were offered again or asking them to indicate their preferences for new programs that might be offered by the agency.

The measurement of participant satisfaction may be carried out at different levels of complexity or research rigor in terms of the instruments used, sampling procedures, or nature of statistical analysis of findings. For example, some agencies use a relatively simple means of evaluating members' satisfaction with program activities, as shown in Figure 17.5, which asks Y members to rate various elements of the agency, including facilities, program activities, or services. When cross-checked with the ages of respondents, their

FIGURE 17.4   Sunnyvale, California: Evaluation of customer activity and retention.[12]

Objectives: To provide Division class/workshop programs at a satisfactory level with 17% of Sunnyvale residents registering, 87% of registrants being residents, 50% of registrants returning a consecutive quarter, 96% of registrations with no customer generated refunds, 85% of classes offered conducted, and 75% of customers placed in their first choice class.

	1993/94 Planned	1993/94 Achieved
1. Number of Sunnyvale resident registrations and percentage to Sunnyvale population.	20,010 17%	
2. Number of Sunnyvale resident registrations and percentage to total registrations.	20,010 87%	
3. Number of customers who register in any class/ workshop program two consecutive quarters and percentage to total registrations in a quarter.	2,875 50%	
4. Number of registrations where there were no customer generated refunds and percentage to total registrations.	22,080 96%	
5. Number of customers who participated in class/workshop programs, and percentage of total registrations.	19,550 85%	
6. Number of Customers completing and returning surveys who were placed in first choice requested program, and percentage to returned surveys.	45 75%	

---

membership categories, their frequency of Y visitation, and the way in which they learned about the Y, this type of membership survey can provide useful marketing information.

In another example of patron evaluation forms, a numbered rating of overall satisfaction with the program is combined with several open-end questions as in Kamloops, British Columbia, Canada (see Figure 17.6).

Increasingly, as more and more leisure-service agencies adopt an aggressive marketing orientation, efforts are being made to achieve a high level of consumer or participant satisfaction through what has been called Total Quality Management (TQM). Methods of assessing agency success in this area have become more sophisticated and are frequently reported today in the research literature—a clear indication of the link between research and evaluation.

Example. Vaske, Donnelly, and Williamson describe the use of report cards distributed each year to thousands of visitors to more than 30 New Hampshire state park units, including historic sites, day use areas, campgrounds, and beaches.[13] Respondents were asked to rate the area they visited on a 5-point scale, in terms of 11 variables, including helpfulness of staff, cleanliness of restrooms, safety and security, ease of access, hours of operation, and overall satisfaction. When used annually, it was concluded that the report card pro-

FIGURE 17.5   Ambler, Pennsylvania, YMCA membership survey (1994).

Ambler Area YMCA Facility Usage/Member Satisfaction Survey

The Ambler Area YMCA is here to serve you with quality programs, services and facilities. By providing us with this information, you will assist us in our quest to deliver the highest level of program and facility satisfaction possible.

1. What membership type are you?

Check one		Check one	
____ Full Facility	____ Fitness Center	____ Youth	____ Couple
____ Swim	____ Basic	____ Adult	____ Family

2. Rate the facilities used by you and/or your family over the past year.

1-Excellent   2-Good   3- Fair   4-Poor

Circle one				Circle one				
Pool	1	2	3	4	Nursery School Building	1	2	3	4
Fitness Center	1	2	3	4	Preschool Center	1	2	3	4
Steam/Sauna	1	2	3	4	Annex Building	1	2	3	4
Gymnasium	1	2	3	4	Parking	1	2	3	4
Locker Rooms	1	2	3	4	Whirlpool	1	2	3	4

3. Please check the approximate number of times you utilize YMCA facilities per week:

____ less than one ____ one ____ two ____ three ____ four or more

4. How did you hear about the YMCA?

____ Newspaper   ____ Brochure   ____ Word of Mouth/Friend   ____ Other

5. Please rate our services.   1-Excellent   2-Good   3-Fair   4- Poor

Circle one				Circle one				
Registration process	1	2	3	4	Maintenance of equipment	1	2	3	4
Staff and instructors	1	2	3	4	Communication with members	1	2	3	4
Building cleanliness	1	2	3	4	Facility hours	1	2	3	4
Maintenance of building	1	2	3	4	Scope and variety of programs	1	2	3	4
Babysitting service	1	2	3	4					

6. Other comments and/or suggestions_____

_____

FIGURE 17.6   City of Kamloops Parks and Recreation Services.

We value your opinion about our programs—are we meeting your needs? No names are necessary.

Instructor: _____

Location: _____

1. Please indicate: Name of program: _____

   Day: _____

2. How did you hear about this program?

Flyer _____   Friend _____   Radio/TV _____   Newspaper _____   Other _____
(Specify)

3. Level of satisfaction with this program:

1	2	3	4	5
Not very Much		Moderately Pleased		Very Much

4. What did you like about this program?

5. Were your expectations of the program met?

6. What additional programs would you like to see offered?

7. Any other comments or suggestions?

vided a useful management tool for identifying both the areas where services were meeting user expectations and those where improvements were needed.

Importance-Performance Measures in Program Evaluation

Another trend in program evaluation that uses visitor or staff ratings has been the application of instruments measuring both the importance of given variables or program elements and the degree to which they are satisfactorily provided.

Example. Hollenhorst, Olson, and Fortney describe the use of Importance-Performance (I-P) analysis in evaluating park cabins operated by the West Virginia state park system.[14] Using a mail-questionnaire survey addressed to past cabin users, they determined which aspects of park cabin usage were more important (including such elements as cleanliness, reservation system, furniture and appliances, seclusion, scenic views, and access to park recreational features) and how well they were being provided. Quantitative analysis of findings revealed high- and low-priority items, including both areas that were in need of improvement and those providing strong user satisfaction.

OTHER AGENCY-CENTERED USES OF EVALUATION

Beyond those already described, the research literature contains a number of other examples of the applications of evaluation methods in recreation agency operations in such areas as personnel management, areas and facilities, and the effectiveness of innovative management strategies.

Personnel Evaluation

The evaluation of personnel performance represents another key area of administrative responsibility in leisure-service agencies. Frequently it is mandated by Civil Service regulations, or the procedures for carrying it out may be stipulated by labor union contracts.

There are essentially three purposes for carrying out personnel evaluations:

1. To provide an objective and documented basis for personnel decisions and actions related to approval or regular job status (after a probationary period), transfer to another position, promotion eligibility, bonuses, job upgrading, or similar actions. This may include records of both positive and negative examples of the employee's performance, including warnings, disciplinary actions, or citations for superior on-the-job performance.

2. To provide a systematic method for gathering information about the employee's work and for assessing it in order to help the individual recognize strengths and weaknesses and upgrade future performance. A key purpose of evaluation must be not simply to appraise or rate what has happened in the past, but to provide direction to the employee by recognizing past successes and identifying areas in which improvement is needed.

3. Personnel evaluation may also be used to obtain an accurate picture of the utilization of staff members within the organization. In this sense it may include an analysis of work assignments and schedules, problems of work commitment and motivation, or other factors in the job situation that encourage or inhibit fully productive staff functioning.

While measurement of personal traits and qualities used to receive considerable emphasis in personnel evaluation, today they tend to be considered too subjective a basis for accurate judgments. In addition, they are not as relevant to job performance as a more objective measure of the individual's actual behavior and accomplishments. In measuring the latter, various techniques may be used, including scales used to rate employees on various job functions; recording of critical incidents or specific actions; the use of descriptive essays or anecdotal descriptions of work performance; and comparison of actual results with predetermined objectives. Information can be gained from various sources, including ratings by the employee's immediate supervisor, fellow-workers, participants, or even the individual employee.

Personnel evaluation must be examined within the context of the philosophy of supervision that prevails within an organization. If the management approach is an old-line, authoritarian approach to having a clearly defined chain of command, with orders passed down in an autocratic way from supervisors to subordinates and with sharply defined and rigidly enforced work assignments, evaluation is usually designed to enforce this approach. Its purpose essentially will be to measure whether staff members are adhering to agency policy and performing as required, with resultant rewards or punishments part of a "carrot-or-stick" supervisory process.

If, however, the management philosophy is marked by open communication, shared decision making, and delegation of authority within a participative management approach, staff evaluation must assume a different style. It becomes more of a two-way process, with an open, trust-based effort to analyze the work situation and the individual's performance in it. Performance standards are more flexible, with creativity being encouraged and a readiness to accept temporary failures as part of a larger effort to enrich and strengthen agency productivity.

Evaluation methods and instruments

Personnel may be evaluated in a number of ways, including (1) casual daily or weekly observation by supervisors, with informal feedback; (2) staff meetings that review program activities and staff performance; (3) supervisory coaching or counseling sessions with staff members; or (4) program reports submitted at the end of events or seasons.

A common procedure is to require a formal, written evaluation report, frequently linked to a supervisor-subordinate conference that is held at regular intervals. Typically, such reports are based on a detailed evaluation of the employee's work, which the employee is required to read and sign. The employee may enter a statement in the form, which may include a response to criticism or justification for actions taken. The forms that are used vary greatly, ranging from extremely simple, impersonal assessments of the individual's work to a much more complex and probing analysis.

There are three kinds of information that may be assessed to judge an employee. These are: (1) the personal traits or qualities of the individual that are relevant to the job; (2) specific work performance and on-the-job behaviors; and (3) outcomes or results, as measured by the accomplishment of predetermined objectives.

Several examples of personnel evaluation instruments follow, drawn from those used in a number of public recreation and park departments.

Examples of instruments

Many widely used instruments appraise employees on a number of personal and work-related traits, such as cooperation, initiative, leadership, dependability, good human relations, and skill in varied activities or administrative tasks. One problem with such evaluation instruments is that they are subjective and may be interpreted differently by different supervisors. Some forms avoid this problem by providing a range of descriptive statements that characterize behavior in specific terms. This is illustrated in Figure 17.7, which shows the rating system developed by the Nassau County, New York, Department of Recreation and Parks. It is to be filled out by the employee's direct supervisor.

Emphasis on improving performance. Some agencies stress the need to make concrete recommendations for improving the individual's work. For example, in the Long Beach, California, Department of Parks, Recreation and Marine, each employee is asked to identify several challenging, specific objectives to be accomplished during the next rating period. Such objectives should involve both regularly assigned job responsibilities and new projects to be undertaken. When feasible, estimated dates of completion should be given with detailed measures of successful performance.

An interesting feature of the Long Beach evaluation approach is that employees are asked to evaluate their supervisors anonymously and to forward the confidential statements to the supervisors for their personal use. Questions such as the following are asked:

In your opinion, what kind of job is this supervisor doing? Consider both his or her good points and weaknesses needing improvement.

Were you in his or her position, what would you do to improve and to bring about improvement in your employees?

Detailed job analysis methods. A last example of personnel appraisal methods is found in the Edmonton, Alberta, Canada Parks and Recreation Department. Here, both leaders and supervisors play an active role.

Leaders are required to analyze their job responsibilities and to identify all significant functions, estimating the amount of time given to each responsibility during the week. They must then describe their work in detail, including (1) statements about those who supervise them and with whom they work in the department; (2) responsibility for management functions; (3) policy-related functions; (4) personal schedule and role in supervising other employees; and (5) difficult or abnormal working conditions and similar information.

In turn, supervisors must list each leader's key responsibilities and analyze how well they are carrying them out, with specific statements regarding planning, organizing, communicating, problem solving, and other areas of performance. Supervisors must then suggest ways to improve performance in each of these areas, suggesting a priority order for each method and providing a timetable for carrying them out. These include such methods as:

1. Directed self-development (reading, self-study, and so on).
2. Formal training program in in-service courses within department.
3. Outside educational programs, such as courses or seminars.
4. Counseling or coaching assistance by the supervisor.
5. Other on-the-job training.

FIGURE 17.7 Nassau County, N.Y. Department of Recreation and Parks, personnel rating form (selected items).

(continued)

PLEASE PRINT:

Employee _____

Last Name _____   First Name _____

Civil Service Title _____

Duties (working title) _____

Park or Unit _____   Division _____

Period of Supervision From _____   to _____

Reason for Report _____

1. JOB CAPABILITY

☐ Not observed.

☐ Has gaps in fundamental knowledge and skills of the job.

☐ Has a satisfactory knowledge and skill for the routine phases of the job.

☐ Has excellent knowledge and is well skilled on all phases of the job.

☐ Has an exceptional understanding and skill on all phases of the job.

2. PLANNING ABILITY

☐ Not observed.

☐ Relies on others to bring up problems. Often fails to see ahead.

☐ Plans ahead just enough to get by in his present job.

☐ Is a careful effective planner. Anticipates and takes action to solve problems.

☐ Capable of planning beyond requirements of the present job. Sees the big picture.

3. LEADERSHIP

☐ Not observed.

☐ Often weak in command situations. At times unable to exert control.

☐ Normally develops fairly adequate control and teamwork.

☐ Consistently a good leader. Commands respect of his subordinates.

☐ Exceptional skill in directing others to great effort.

FIGURE 17.7 Continued.

4. EXECUTIVE JUDGMENT

☐ Not observed.	☐ Decisions and recommendations are sometimes unsound or ineffective.	☐ Judgment is usually sound and reasonable, with occasional errors.	☐ Displays good judgment, resulting from sound evaluation; is effective.	☐ An exceptionally sound, logical thinker in situations which occur on the job.	☐ Has a knack for arriving at the right decision, even on highly complex matters.

5. HUMAN RELATIONS

☐ Not observed.	☐ Does not get along well with people. Definitely hinders his effectiveness.	☐ Has difficulty in getting along with associates.	☐ Gets along with people adequately. Has average skill at maintaining good human relations.	☐ Has above average skills in human relations are an asset.	☐ Outstanding skills in human relations increases effectiveness.

6. JOB ACCOMPLISHMENT

☐ Not observed.	☐ Quality or quantity of work does not always meet job requirements.	☐ Performance is barely adequate to meet job requirements.	☐ Quality and quantity of work are very satisfactory.	☐ Performance is above normal expectations for meeting job requirements.	☐ Quality and quantity of work are clearly superior.

Note: In addition to a number of other personal traits, the second page of this rating form calls for an overall evaluation of the staff member, with documentation required if he/she is rated in an extremely high or low category. It also asks for a recommendation with respect to "promotion potential."

The plan must be discussed and signed by both the supervisor and the subordinate employee. In addition to a systematic appraisal of the employee's personal qualities, a final confidential section describes the "promotional potential" of the employee and the supervisor's recommendation as to the best ways in which the employee can be used in the department.

Focus on overall staff development and performance. Tedrick suggests several possible measures that might be used to evaluate the effectiveness of staff performance as a whole.

> . . . (1) a cost-effectiveness ratio between staff required and hours open or numbers served; (2) accident statistics showing low rates per participant; or (3) praise or a lack of complaints by attenders or parents of attenders. Rather than focus on a negative standard . . . managers may find it helpful to develop measures of performance oriented toward positive situations . . . .[15]

The point that evaluation represents one type or purpose of research is illustrated by a number of research studies that deal with issues that may also be examined in evaluation procedures.

Example. McKinney and Chandler conducted a comprehensive, empirically based study of the job tasks performed by part-time versus full-time recreation leaders.[16] In addition to the obvious finding that part-time personnel had significantly fewer and less important tasks than full-time leaders, they also found that part-time personnel required more and closer supervision than regular staff members. In another personnel-related research study, Yen and McKinney examined the relationship between satisfaction with compensation and job characteristics among representative public and private leisure-service professionals.[17] They found that public and private managers differed significantly in their perceptions of their jobs and compensation and in their levels of satisfaction with salaries, benefits, and other job characteristics.

Although such studies are not examples of personnel evaluation as such, they are helpful in developing personnel policies for effective staff management that may then be tested through ongoing evaluation procedures.

Areas and Facilities

Another major area of agency operations that requires evaluation, either as a separate function or as part of overall agency appraisal, involves areas and facilities. Within public recreation and park agencies in particular, the provision and maintenance of parks, ballfields, aquatic areas, centers, and numerous other specialized facilities represent a major responsibility. Therefore, within all models of agency and program evaluation are major sections that have to do with the adequacy of physical places for recreative activity—including their availability, diversity, appropriate design, accessibility, safety, and quality of maintenance.

Over the past several decades, major professional organizations have developed standards that recommend both the amount of open space or parkland available for community leisure uses and the specific provision of different types of facilities to meet neighborhood needs. Although their applicability may vary according to the nature of the community, they provide general guidelines that are useful in recreation and park agencies' self-assessments.

Linked to the standards approach is a classification system that defines the specific number of persons that facilities of different types may be expected to serve and that thus provides the basis for a set of standards for individual sports areas, as an example. To illustrate:

Ice hockey requires an area of 22,000 square feet, including support areas; one such indoor rink should be provided for each 100,000 in population and may be expected to serve people within a $\frac{1}{2}$ to 1 hour of travel time.

Tennis requires an area of 7,200 square feet for a singles court; one court should be provided for each 2,000 in population and should serve people with a service radius of $\frac{1}{4}$ to $\frac{1}{2}$ mile.

Football requires a minimum of 1.5 acres; a football field should be provided for each 20,000 in population and should serve people with a service radius of $\frac{1}{4}$ to $\frac{1}{2}$ hour of travel time.[18]

Similar standards have been developed and published for different categories of parks. For example:

Mini-parks of 1 acre or less should have a service area with a less than $\frac{1}{4}$ mile radius, to meet the needs of a concentrated population or special groups such as tots or senior citizens in close proximity to apartment complexes, townhouse developments, or housing for the elderly.

Neighborhood park/playground areas should consist of 15 or more acres, with service radiuses of $\frac{1}{4}$ to $\frac{1}{2}$ miles to meet neighborhood needs for populations of up to 5,000.

Community parks, which may include varied athletic, aquatic, or natural areas, should serve several neighborhoods, with a 1- to 2-mile service radius.[19]

Supply–Demand Approach

Based on such factors, the Standards Revision Task Force of the National Recreation and Park Association developed a model through which each community may measure its own needs for specific recreation and park facilities and acreage. This is a supply–demand model based on the following key concepts:

Participation Rate (PR): The percentage of a given population that will participate in a specific activity.

Participation Days (PD): The average number of times each individual user will participate in a recreation activity during a year.

Demand (D): The number of people who can reasonably be expected to attend or participate in a particular recreation activity during a year.

Design Day (DD): An average weekend day during a peak season of use for a particular activity.

Design Capacity (DC): The percentage of participation days that can be expected to occur in a specific activity on a design day.

Spatial Standards (SS): Reasonable capacities of recreation facilities or areas by spatial unit at any given time.

Turnover Rates (TR): The number of times a recreation activity spatial unit can be used during a single day.

Facility Need (FN): The number of spatial units required to accommodate a particular activity.[20]

To apply this model, it is necessary to gather scientifically valid information about the population to be served. Surveys are carried out to determine the preference or demand for each type of facility or activity. The participation rate multiplied by the base population and an estimate of the number of participation days yields the total number of preference days that will occur during a year, or "preference."

The model then employs the following formula:

$$\frac{\text{Preference} \times \text{Design Capacity}}{\text{Spatial Standard} \times \text{Turnover Rate}} = \text{Facility Need}$$

Facility need is an expression of the activity preferences translated into specific facility requirements. In it, the spatial requirement for a given activity or facility use is multiplied by the turnover rate to establish the total number of participation events each unit can accommodate on a given day. Multiplying preference by design capacity determines the number of participation events accommodated for each activity. Dividing this number by the product of the standard and turnover rate results in the basic facility need, including both active and passive events. The facility need should be measured against the currently available supply of facilities in the community, in order to determine the number of new facilities that would be needed to accommodate projected demand.

Other guidelines today govern management concerns such as accessibility and barrier removal to ensure that persons with disabilities can make maximum use of public facilities and safety and risk management in the design and operation of facilities.

For example, Adaptive Environments Center, Inc., and Barrier-Free Environments were authorized by the National Institute on Disability and Rehabilitation Research to provide information, materials, and technical assistance to agencies, based on regulations set by the Americans with Disabilities Act. In a detailed checklist covering the operation of recreation and park facilities, public accommodations are defined, and guidelines are presented for dealing with "path of travel," "ramps," "entrance," "rooms and spaces," "elevators," "lifts," "restrooms," "telephones" and "drinking fountains."[21]

Similarly, numerous professional organizations have developed operational guidelines to promote participant safety. Again, the link between research as such and evaluation as an applied management function is shown by numerous studies that examine varied types of recreation-related injuries and accidents, their causes, and the effectiveness of risk-management strategies.

Evaluation of Strategies and Projects

A final application of evaluation in agency management consists of its use in assessing the effectiveness of agency policies, strategies or special projects, and innovative programs. For example, Chapter 5 describes a category of quasiexperimental research that is usually referred to as *action research.* Typically, such studies are carried out in fields such as social work, education, health services, and law enforcement, where they are used to evaluate the results of new programs or local projects.

Example. Selin and Chavez conducted a study of the impact of the United States Department of Agriculture's Forest Service's National Recreation Strategy, which sought to develop partnerships between units of the Forest Service and private groups or nonprofit organizations concerned with outdoor recreation.[22] A survey of several hundred district, regional, and forest employees confirmed that this strategy's effort to vigorously promote partnership projects had positively influenced recreation policy and management operations in the Forest Service.

SUMMARY

A major thrust in the evaluation of recreation, park, and leisure-service agencies involves the systematic analysis of operational practices and programs for purposes of general self-improvement, documenting outcomes, or accreditation. This chapter describes varied approaches to such agency evaluation and self-study efforts, with emphasis on the use of standards and criteria within several major areas of management responsibility. In addition to public recreation, park, and leisure-service agencies, it presents examples of evaluation practices in therapeutic recreation and youth sports programs. Cost-benefit and participant/attendance/income models of evaluation are presented, along with examples of participant-satisfaction rating instruments. The chapter concludes with an overview of the evaluation of personnel, areas and facilities, and agency strategies and special projects, with examples of the latter drawn from the recent literature.

QUESTIONS AND ACTIVITIES

The following can be used as in-class workshops.

1. The instructor obtains the full evaluation or accreditation instrument or operational guidelines published by any of the organizations cited in this

chapter, such as the National Council on Accreditation (AAPRA/NRPA), the National Youth Sports Program, or the National Therapeutic Recreation Society, or any similar manual. Students review it for comprehensiveness, appropriateness of the items, usefulness of the rating system, effectiveness of the instructions, and similar elements. Students prepare specific recommendations for updating or improving the manual.

2. Refer to Activities 3 or 4 in Chapter 16. Students develop more detailed instruments and procedures for carrying out evaluations in settings or situations that were identified in these processes. For example, students might develop an instrument for evaluating a specific course or a more detailed plan for evaluating a recreation agency. Review and analyze these instruments and procedures in class, and identify their strengths and weaknesses.

3. The instructor contrasts the traditional approach to personnel evaluation in recreation and park agencies with the newer approaches that are based on current participative-management theories. Then individuals or small groups develop personnel evaluation forms specifically designed for use in armed forces, voluntary agency, campus recreation, or other types of recreation agencies. Review and critically analyze them in class.

ENDNOTES

1. *Overview of Local Public Park and Recreation Agency Accreditation* (Arlington, VA: National Committee on Accreditation, American Academy for Park and Recreation Administration, and National Recreation and Park Association, 1994): 3.

2. Christine Howe, "Evaluation of Leisure Programs," *Journal of Physical Education, Recreation and Dance* (Oct. 1980): 25.

3. Based on a model by David Santellanes, modified by Dr. Lawrence Allen, University of Wyoming, 1983.

4. See *Senior Center Standards: Guidelines for Practice* (Washington, DC: National Council on the Aging and National Institute of Senior Centers, 1978): 13.

5. Betty van der Smissen, ed., *Evaluation and Self-Study of Public Recreation and Park Agencies: A Guide with Standards and Evaluative Criteria* (Arlington, VA: National Recreation and Park Association, 1972).

6. Ibid., 57.

7. *Self-Assessment Manual for Quality Operation of Local Public Park and Recreation Agencies: A Guide to Standards for National Accreditation* (Arlington, VA: National Committee on Accreditation, Sept. 1993).

8. Ibid.

9. Ibid.

10. For a description of the process from which these standards evolved, see Glen E. Van Andel, "Professional Standards: Improving the Quality of Services," *Therapeutic Recreation Journal* (2d quarter 1981): 23–26.

11. Emil Posavac and Raymond Carey, *Program Evaluation: Methods and Case Studies* (Englewood Cliffs, NJ: Prentice-Hall, 1985): 268.

12. This table is drawn from *Tools for Measuring Quality of Programming, Service and Satisfaction: Performance Indicators* (Sunnyvale, CA: Department of Parks and Recreation, Sept. 1993).

13. Jerry Vaske, Maureen Donnelly, and Bradford Williamson, "Monitoring for Quality Control in State Park Management," *Journal of Park and Recreation Administration* 9, no. 2 (1991): 59–71.

14. Steve Hollenhorst, David Olson, and Ronald Fortney, "Use of Importance-Performance Analysis to Evaluate State Park Cabins: The Case of the West Virginia State Park System," *Journal of Park and Recreation Administration* 10, no. 1 (1992): 1–11.

15. Ted Tedrick, "Personnel Evaluation: In Search of Valid Performance Standards," *Journal of Park and Recreation Administration* 1, no. 2 (1983): 38–39.

16. William McKinney and Carrie Chandler, "A Comparative Assessment of Duties Between Full-Time and Part-Time Recreation Leaders," *Journal of Park and Recreation Administration* 9, no. 1 (1991): 13–29.

17. Tsu-Hong Yen and William McKinney, "The Relationship Between Compensation Satisfaction and Job Characteristics: A Comparative Study of Public and Private Leisure Service Professionals," *Journal of Park and Recreation Administration* 10, no. 4 (1992): 15–56.

18. Adapted from Roger Lancaster, ed., *Recreation, Park and Open Space Standards and Guidelines* (Alexandria, VA: National Recreation and Park Association, 1983): 60–61.

19. Ibid., 56.

20. Ibid., 46.

21. *Checklist for Existing Facilities: The Americans with Disabilities Act* (Washington, DC: National Institute on Disability and Rehabilitation Research, Adaptive Environments Center, Inc. and Barrier-Free Environments, Inc., 1992).

22. Steven Selin and Debbie Chavez, "Recreation Partnerships and the USDA Forest Service: Managers' Perceptions of the Impact of the National Recreation Strategy," *Journal of Park and Recreation Administration* 11, no. 1 (1993): 1–8.

18

Evaluation Research: The Goal-Oriented Model

Interest in evaluation research has been greatly stimulated by a . . . . demand for more productive and efficient intervention programs. Searching questions have been raised about the adequacy of organized programs in such institutional sectors as health, justice, education, employment, housing, transportation, and welfare . . . . reformers have urged that the quest for more effective institutions be orderly and cumulative. They have argued that careful program evaluation is needed as a basis for continued planning and have recommended that the methods of social research be utilized in the evaluation of reform programs.[1]

INTRODUCTION

We turn now to a second important aspect of evaluation in recreation, parks, and leisure services—the *goal-oriented model,* which is designed to systematically assess program effectiveness in achieving agency goals and objectives.

In contrast to the standards-and-criteria approach or relying on the testimony of program participants or staff members, the goal-oriented model focuses sharply on the issue of efficacy and accountability. Using the established methods of research, it seeks to determine whether an agency's goals and objectives are being met, with respect to desired outcomes or benefits for participants or the community at large. The goal-oriented model is called *evaluation research* because it employs accepted research methods, and its findings are often reported in recognized research journals.

Rather than being initiated by agency staff members for applied purposes, it is frequently conducted by university educators or other professional researchers as part of the overall stream of scientific investigation in leisure studies. Because it usually is carried on in field settings, it signifies an important and growing form of cooperation between researchers and practitioners in recreation and park agencies.

NEED FOR AGENCY ACCOUNTABILITY

In the recreation, park, and leisure-service field, most public and voluntary agencies tended in the past to justify their operations in terms of widely accepted beliefs and traditions. It was assumed—and often supported anecdotally or by statements of law-enforcement officials, for example—that youth programs such as organized sports, playgrounds, and recreation centers helped to prevent juvenile delinquency.

We have increasingly come to recognize, however, that subjective judgments or opinion-based testimonials do not provide adequate proof of a leisure service's value or effectiveness. Particularly as fiscal cutbacks affected government expenditures on all levels, it became clear that leisure services—along with other cultural, social, or human services—would have to demonstrate accountability. Connolly emphasized the need for such programs to convincingly document their value, writing:

> Accountability is a relative term that describes the capability of a service delivery system to justify or explain the activities and services it provides. Program accountability reflects the extent to which program expenditures, activities, and processes effectively and efficiently accomplish (their) purposes. Evaluation methods are employed to determine program accomplishments. . . .[2]

BENEFITS OF ORGANIZED RECREATION SERVICE

A number of arguments have traditionally supported public, organized recreation, parks, and leisure programs. Typically, beyond the obvious purpose of providing fun and creative challenge for community residents, recreation and parks have been expected to:

1. *Improve the overall quality of life for residents* by helping them use leisure in creative and fulfilling ways;
2. *Promote mental and physical fitness* through a broad range of sports, outdoor recreation, and other free-time pursuits;
3. *Encourage positive social and moral values* that are keyed to the dominant values held by the community at large, and to present desirable adult role models for children and youth;
4. *Help prevent and control juvenile delinquency* and other forms of youthful deviant behavior by working closely with "at-risk" youth and offering them alternative, constructive forms of play;
5. *Strengthen family and neighborhood cohesiveness* by encouraging or sponsoring events and volunteer-based programs that build pride and a sense of community belonging;

6. *Serve mentally and physically disabled persons* either directly in recreation programs for special populations or by working with organizations, residences, or treatment centers that meet their leisure needs;

7. *Sponsor and assist programs and institutions in the arts* to promote community awareness and support and to enrich cultural life for all ages and social classes;

8. *Protect and improve the natural environment* by maintaining parks, nature centers, zoos, and ecologically fragile sites and by offering educational programs and services to promote environmental awareness;

9. *Strengthen the community's economic base* by making it a more pleasant and more attractive place to live and by attracting tourists and others to sports events, historic celebrations, and other programs and institutions that contribute to the local economy and to employment;

10. *Build better understanding and cooperative relationships* among those of different races, ethnic and national backgrounds, religions, socioeconomic classes, and generations; and

11. *Blend all of these values or benefits together holistically,* so that leisure becomes a positive force in daily life for individuals, families, neighborhoods, or the community at large.[3]

A number of recent studies have sought to define these benefits more precisely and to gather evidence that would validate them. For example, in a recently published text, Driver, Brown, and Peterson suggest that the goals and benefits of leisure services should be summarized under a number of major headings: *physiological* and *psychophysiological, psychological, social, economic,* and *environmental.*[4]

In 1992, the Parks and Recreation Federation of the Province of Ontario, Canada, published a major report that reflected and extended this analysis.[5] In addition to listing what it considers the key benefits, the report cites hundreds of research references that document the positive outcomes of recreation under four major headings: *personal, social, economic,* and *environmental.*

Although these stated benefits provide a persuasive rationale for the support of publicly sponsored recreation and park programs and services, the reality is that the documentary support for them is of mixed quality. In a number of cases—as in the research showing the physical and health-related values of physical recreation and exercise—the documentation is impressive. In others, such as "building strong communities," "promoting ethnic and cultural harmony," or "building strong families," the evidence supporting the benefits of public recreation and parks is less convincing.[6]

MEASURING PROGRAM OUTCOMES

Research designed to measure leisure-service program outcomes and benefits may take many forms. Empirically based studies in this area may involve actual field research with agencies that are conducting ongoing programs or programs that are deliberately planned and carried out under controlled conditions to test hypotheses or for other research purposes. In general, the following guidelines should govern evaluation conducted under the goal-oriented model:

1. Goals and objectives must be concisely stated and must be capable of being measured—either in terms of achieving social or community-related benefits or in terms of behavioral change.

2. The controls that are customarily used in social research—such as valid and reliable instruments and study procedures, appropriate sampling procedures, and data-gathering controls—must also be used in benefits-based evaluation.

3. Study designs such as experimental, quasiexperimental, or case-study methods provide the best means of evaluating program outcomes, and quantitative data are generally regarded as providing the most convincing evidence of success.

DEFINING ORGANIZATIONAL GOALS

Within this context, it is important to recognize the exact nature of goals and objectives. Goals are the essential purposes of an organization and must be based on its underlying philosophy or mission statement. Daft and Steers write:

> An organizational goal is a desired future state of affairs that the organization attempts to realize. Goals pertain to the future, but they influence current activities. Goals are important because organizations are goal-attainment devices. Organizations exist for a purpose, and goals define and state that purpose.[7]

Goals themselves may be divided logically into two types: *internal* or *operational* goals and *external* or *outcome* goals. The first type is based on an organization's effort to define its role and to function as effectively as possible. Several such *internal* goals might include the need to use available resources widely, make effective decisions in problem areas, adapt to changing environmental conditions, or gain community support. In general, internal goals are concerned chiefly with how an agency mobilizes itself to perform effectively and maintain a high level of credibility and support.

In contrast, an agency's *external* goals consist of the outcomes it seeks to achieve by offering programs. Generally, they have to do with the kinds of benefits listed earlier, relating to the improvement of personal health, intergroup relationships, community economic and social betterment, services to special populations, or environmental protection.

Viewed from the perspective of practitioners, goals may also be defined on three levels: (1) *official* goals, which are formally stated or approved by top management and which relate to public or community needs and purposes; (2) *operative* goals, which are middle-management concerns having to do with the overall success of the organization in terms of marketing, acquiring needed resources, productivity, profitability, or staff functioning; and (3) *operational* goals, which are a lower-level responsibility, having to do with day-to-day operations and are concerned with specific performance objectives and outcomes.[8]

Goals of Leisure-Service Agencies

Goals may vary considerably according to the type of leisure-service agency, its resources, and its community setting.

For example, in a voluntary agency—such as a YMCA, YWCA, YM-YWHA, CYO, Boys or Girls Club, or Scout group—goals are likely to center around developing participants' personality, social skills, values, and citizenship traits.

The goals of company-sponsored employee programs generally seek to maintain health and fitness as an important element in job performance and productivity and to promote positive staff morale and cohesiveness.

The goals of military recreation center around building a high level of physical fitness and team morale, meeting the needs of families and dependents of military personnel, and reducing negative or antisocial uses of leisure.

In therapeutic recreation, goals have to do with helping clients or patients overcome the effects of disability or illness, develop healthy and socially rewarding lifestyles, and become integrated to the fullest possible extent in community life.

Program Objectives

In general, goals represent rather broad philosophical intentions or values. By contrast, objectives are statements of intent that *are* attainable and measurable. In effect, they are goals that are transformed into a program of intended actions, usually of a short-range nature.

Objectives often express desired *behavioral change* for participants, particularly in therapeutic or human-service programs that seek to improve the emotional health, physical fitness, or social functioning of participants. For example, Peterson and Gunn describe the development of therapeutic recreation treatment plans as a three-stage process: (1) the identification of *terminal program objectives,* which represent the major thrusts of the individual's treatment or rehabilitation; (2) specific *enabling objectives,* indicating units of knowledge or skill that the patient or client is expected to achieve; and (3) *performance measures,* which are statements of the exact behaviors that will provide evidence that the enabling objectives have been reached.[9]

Objectives may also be expressed as forms of *program implementation,* such as the intention to initiate new projects or activities, attract a given number of participants, or develop new forms of services that meet important community needs. Examples of program implementation objectives might include:

1. To successfully establish 6 multiservice senior centers, one in each district of the city, with average memberships of 150 men and women over the age of 65

2. To provide day care programs serving a minimum of 200 children of service personnel on a military base

3. To expand club membership nationally by 56 percent over a 5-year period to a total of 700,000 more disadvantaged young people

Programs can best be evaluated when such statements of objectives *are* operationally measurable, specific, scheduled to be achieved within a stated time-frame, and quantifiable. Ideally, objectives should not be formulated at a top management level and imposed on line personnel arbitrarily. Instead, they are usually formulated by program planners and leaders and serve to provide a basis for monitoring programs as they are carried on and to evaluate them systematically at their conclusion.

MANAGEMENT BY OBJECTIVES AND BENEFITS-BASED MANAGEMENT

They may also be an integral part of a department's planning and staff development process, as in the Management by Objectives (MBO) approach, which involves all agency personnel in the development of objectives. Clegg and Chambliss describe such a process, as it was carried out by the Recreation Division of the Dallas, Texas, Parks and Recreation Department. It began with a series of seminars and training sessions to gain competence in developing and evaluating objectives:

> After the training sessions, the difficult job of writing specific objectives began. First, recreation leaders at each center developed a personal set of objectives. Once approved by the center director, these objectives were combined with the center director's to create a set of objectives for that particular recreation center. This process was used at each management level, following the chain of command up the hierarchy until final approval was given each sub-division head by [the] division director. . . . objectives included: enrolling in a training course, improving public relations skills, developing certain new management skills, and becoming more involved in a civic activity.[10]

Today, a strong thrust in many public recreation and park agencies consists of benefits-based management, which emphasizes the need to define meaningful goals and objectives at every level of program planning and operations—with the primary emphasis on achieving important benefits for participants. As outlined at the 1994 National Recreation and Park Congress, this approach incorporates a benefits-identification phase as an essential part of its overall implementation strategy, with the following steps:

1. Analyze agency mission, goals, and management plan.
2. Identify potential benefits sought by users.
3. Determine core group of benefits that users seek and management can realistically provide.
4. Modify agency mission and goals, if necessary, to reflect target agency benefits.
5. Determine linkage between identified benefits and potential opportunities offered by agency.
6. Identify structural elements for each recreation opportunity that are essential to benefit achievement. Elements include: social, environmental, physical, temporal properties, etc.
7. Identify needed managerial changes for benefits achievement.[11]

Following the implementation of programs designed to achieve the benefits that have been identified as needed, the last step of the process is to measure the degree to which they have been accomplished. Reports of success or failure in meeting stated objectives should be prepared, disseminated to appropriate agency or other officials or publics, and used as the basis for making policy or procedural goals in agency programming practices.

Examples of Benefits-Based Evaluation

We now examine a number of examples of benefits-based evaluation that measure the success of leisure-service programs in achieving goals and objectives. The bulk of these examples are drawn from the research literature and reflect carefully designed studies based on systematic data-gathering and analytical procedures.

The categories of recreation benefits that follow are grouped under six major headings: (1) *physical* and *health-related* benefits of sports, exercise, and physical recreation; (2) *cognitive* and other *developmental* benefits of play for children; (3) *psychophysiological* benefits of recreation, particularly related to *quality of life* and *stress management;* (4) effects of recreation-related programs on *juvenile delinquency;* (5) *economic* outcomes of recreation, parks, and leisure services; and (6) benefits of *therapeutic recreation* for population groups with varied forms of disability.

Physical and health-related benefits of recreation

Over the last three decades, abundant evidence has been gathered of the important health-related values of recreation. An early study of 17,000

Harvard alumni found that there were significantly fewer heart attacks among those who engaged regularly in strenuous sports activities such as jogging, swimming, tennis, and mountain climbing than among those who were less active. Numerous later studies confirmed that regular exercise is useful not only in maintaining cardiovascular fitness and helping to prevent heart attacks or strokes, but in promoting neuromuscular fitness and endurance and preventing arthritis and degenerative bone conditions among older persons.[12] Regular exercise has been linked to the prevention of cancer. Men with active jobs are less likely to develop colon cancer than less active men, and athletic women cut their risk of breast and uterine cancer in half and their risk of diabetes by two-thirds.[13] Although exercise may, of course, be taken as a prescribed health-related regimen, it is far more likely to be enjoyable and continued regularly when it has social and recreational components.[14]

Example. A considerable number of studies in Canada support these findings and document the benefits of physical recreation for different population groups. Stevenson and Topp found that moderate and low-intensity long- term exercise improved fitness levels of older adults, prolonged independent functioning, and promoted positive perceptions of well-being.[15] Santiago, Coyle, and Troup found that adults with physical disabilities had significant improvements in cardiovascular and metabolic functional capacity and cholesterol levels following 12 weeks of aerobic exercise, compared with a matched group of nonexercisers.[16]

The acceptance of these findings is illustrated by the many major corporations that have initiated employee recreation and fitness programs. For example, the Canada Life Insurance Company showed a 22 percent reduction in absenteeism for employees participating regularly in a fitness program, compared with nonparticipants and employees from a similar company. Productivity increased by 7 percent, and employee turnover significantly decreased.[17] Similar findings have been reported by many corporations and groups of employees in the United States.

Developmental benefits of play for children

A number of major authorities on child development have documented the value of play experience in the psychomotor, affective, and cognitive growth of children. Harvard psychologist Jerome Bruner concluded that play serves as a valuable environment for children's conceptual development, learning skills, and sense of autonomy. Similarly, in a summary of research studies on children's play, Barnett concluded that play provided children with a flexible approach to exploring their environments and contributed to their cognitive and problem-solving skills.[18]

Example. Research has documented the importance of physical activity in the intellectual and academic development of children. One study comparing 4-year-olds who had been exposed to swimming after their 2nd month of life to others who were involved in swimming after their 28th month found that the "swimming babies" were better adjusted, more independent, and better able to make decisions and performed higher on standardized intelligence tests than the nonswimmers.[19] Other studies confirmed a strong relationship between regular physical fitness activities and superior performance in reading and arithmetic. Still other studies have documented the value of early creative play experience in helping young children develop qualities of inventiveness and later exploratory, creative behavior.[20]

Research studies in areas such as camping and outdoor recreation have shown significant positive outcomes in a wide range of developmental areas for children and youth. For example, Ewert compiled a summary of findings of the benefits of outdoor adventure recreation with respect to improved self-concept, self-efficacy and confidence, self-actualization and well-being, group cooperation skills and respect for the law, and improved academic abilities linked to problem-solving and values-clarification.[21]

Psychophysiological benefits of recreation

Another substantial group of research and evaluation studies has documented the important values of recreation in terms of emotional well-being, life satisfaction, and the ability to overcome stress-related pressures. Iso-Ahola and Weissinger conclude that:

> Empirical research leaves little doubt that intrinsically motivated leisure is positively and significantly related to psychological/mental health. That is, those who are in control of their leisure lives/experiences and have feelings of engagement in and commitment to leisure activities/experiences are psychologically healthier than those who are not in control of their leisure lives and do not have feelings of engagement and commitment.[22]

▼ FOR EXAMPLE

A number of studies have shown specifically that satisfying leisure involvements help to reduce symptoms of depression, provide important sources of life satisfaction and social support, and strengthen the ability to resist stress. Studies by Katz, Szentagothai, Greenwood, Weiss, and Jamieson found that such activities as physical exercise, tennis, and water play effectively reduced symptoms of depression.[23] Research by Kelly and Steinkamp confirmed the value of recreation in contributing to the life satisfaction, social integration, and feelings of competence and self-worth of older adults.[24]

Recreation and delinquency

As earlier chapters have shown, much of the support for early developments in public recreation and parks came from the conviction that organized play did much to reduce juvenile delinquency. Numerous statements by judges, probation officers, and police officials during the beginning decades of the twentieth century expressed the view that organized recreation was an effective deterrent to youthful gang activity.

▼ FOR EXAMPLE

Most such reports lacked convincing research controls, however, and the few actual studies of recreation's effectiveness in combatting youth crime—such as the post–World War II study of the impact of a Boys' Club program in Louisville, Kentucky—had only limited credibility, as forms of *ex post facto* analysis.[25] A number of more recent reports have documented the effectiveness of sports in reducing delinquent behavior. In one study of several Midwestern high schools, Donnelly found that only 7 percent of male students who had participated for at least a full year in an interscholastic sport had been apprehended for delinquent behavior, compared with 17 percent of nonathletes.[26] Searle documented the effects of community sports programs in northern Manitoba in reducing crime, compared with communities that had not initiated such programs.[27] Kelly and Baer found that juvenile delinquents who had taken part in Outward Bound programs had a substantially lower recidivism rate than young offenders who had not been involved in this outdoor program.[28]

Today, it is generally accepted that recreation by itself cannot prevent or significantly reduce delinquency or crime. Instead, recreation must be linked with other significant youth services. A number of U.S. and Canadian cities have sponsored such multiservice programs. In Phoenix, Arizona, the Parks, Recreation and Library Department has initiated expanded summer outreach programs in recreation centers and schools, involving sports, teen councils, arts and special events, linked to a juvenile curfew program, counseling services, and late-night structured recreation in target areas. Comparative police statistics for neighborhoods involved over a three-year period showed a reduction in crime calls by as much as 52 percent.[29]

Similarly, John Crompton describes a three-year, carefully monitored study in several English cities that linked sports and other leisure activities, along with health and first-aid courses, counseling, and other probationary services, with high-risk juvenile offenders. The final report of the British Sports Council, a national body that evaluated the project, was that, while British confidentiality laws limited the ability to publish actual recidivism rates, the overall impact was positive.[30]

Economic benefits of recreation

A fifth major benefit derived from organized recreation is economic in nature. Much of the research in this field has to do with building conceptual models of the nature of economic value, equity in public access to recreation, costs and benefits, and similar concerns. A more direct approach consists of estimating the amounts of public expenditure on varied forms of recreation at the municipal, state, regional, or national level.

▼ FOR EXAMPLE

In terms of specific contributions to national or regional economies, numerous estimates have been made regarding the impact of specific types of recreation activities. For example, tourism in the mid-1980s was estimated to be a $234 billion industry and has been climbing steadily since that time. The purchase of sporting goods and equipment was estimated at $45 billion annually in the early 1990s. Recreational boating is an immensely popular activity; in a single recent year, the boating industry employed more than 10,000 people in Texas, with annual revenues in excess of $600 million.

The benefits to individual states or cities stemming from recreation spending are impressive. In Baltimore, Maryland, the creation of a critical mass of attractions in the city's Inner Harbor increased the amount of tourist spending to $400 million and sharply upgraded the psychological attitude of Baltimore residents toward their city.[31] It was estimated that 650,000 visitors a year to Kansas City generated about 35,000 convention-related jobs, and cruise industry tourism at the Port of Miami, Florida, totaled about $546 million annually and generated more than 21,000 jobs.[32]

The economic contribution made by recreation and park programs is greater and more diversified than simply the money spent on recreation. Crompton has identified six aspects of economic benefit:

1. Recreation and park events and facilities that bring pleasure travelers to the community or region
2. The importance attached to "quality-of-life" amenities by "footloose" corporations that make relocation decisions based in part on the recreation opportunities for their employees in different settings
3. The appeal of communities, in terms of public leisure facilities and opportunities, for elderly persons who are retiring
4. The role of recreation and parks in the rejuvenation of older, major cities that rehabilitate their physical environments and upgrade their image nationally
5. The enhanced value of residential property in the vicinity of attractive parks and other cultural facilities

6. The volume of retail equipment sales that are dependent on nearby public recreation facilities, such as marinas, golf courses, ice rinks, and similar resources.[33]

At the same time, it should be recognized that many estimates of recreation's economic benefits may be flawed, in the sense that spending "multipliers" are often exaggerated or analysts fail to recognize the negative aspects of certain activities. For example, proponents of gambling as a source of government revenues for desirable social purposes usually fail to consider the negative outcomes of gambling in terms of its impact on other leisure attractions, the social cost of addictive gambling on families and personal businesses, or the costs of law enforcement and increased crime that have been shown to accompany legalized casino gambling.

Outcomes of therapeutic recreation service

Until the 1980s, it was generally agreed that the field of therapeutic recreation service lacked a body of systematic, rigorous research in terms of testing program outcomes. Before that time, it tended to be justified chiefly on philosophical grounds or on subjective assessment of program outcomes.

Over the past 15 years, however, considerable progress has been made in the area of *efficacy research*—that is, studies designed to objectively measure the outcomes of therapeutic recreation service. Perhaps the best evidence of this progress came in a three-year research project co-sponsored by the U.S. Department of Education and the Program in Therapeutic Recreation at Temple University.[34] Initiated in 1988, this study's purpose was to determine the efficacy of therapeutic recreation rehabilitation. Since the chief funding source of the grant was the Medical Sciences Division of National Institute on Disability and Rehabilitation Research, its primary purpose was to focus on rehabilitation benefits that could be closely related to medical treatment and outcomes. As such, it sought evidence of therapeutic recreation's goals, objectives, and treatment outcomes within six major areas of illness or disability.

Within each study area, the study explored the nature of settings and diagnostic groups, theoretical perspectives, impact of disability on the individual, the outcomes sought through therapeutic recreation, and findings of research in the field. Study teams were assigned to each of six major population groups involving important categories of disability and their related medical disciplines. Based on extensive literature searches, they identified benefits derived from therapeutic recreation within the following areas of patient or client outcomes: (1) physical health and health maintenance; (2) cognitive functioning; (3) psychosocial health; (4) growth and development; (5) personal and life satisfaction; and (6) societal and health care systems benefits.

Documenting these benefits, they cited numerous published research reports, such as the following two studies.

Study 1. Rawson and McIntosh conducted a study to test the effectiveness of therapeutic camping programs on a sample of children between the ages of 10 and 12 enrolled in a 10-day residential camping session for children with severe behavior problems.[35] Findings of a Self-Esteem Inventory for Children (SEI), administered as pre- and posttests, disclosed statistically significant improvements in overall self-esteem and were repeated in a follow-up study of a sample drawn randomly from the same camp population. Since low self-esteem is characteristic of such groups, it was concluded that the behavior modification methods used in the study were an important treatment approach and might be useful also with other types of special populations.

Study 2. Mactavish and Searle randomly assigned 26 older men and women with mental retardation to experimental and control groups in a study to determine the effect of a physical activity program designed to facilitate choice and responsibility on their perceptions of competence, locus of control, and self-esteem.[36] The program, utilizing a variety of community facilities—based on several scales for leisure competence, leisure control, and self-esteem—demonstrated significant and positive changes on these measures for elderly persons in the experimental group. In addition to statistical findings, anecdotal records of subjects' comments on their experiences provided a qualitative dimension to the study.

A number of other therapeutic recreation studies have sought to measure the impact of new management or leadership approaches. For example, Bullock, Mahon, and Welch conducted a detailed investigation of the effects of changing the Easter Seals camping and leisure services programs in North Carolina from traditionally segregated approaches to a progressive mainstreaming model.[37] Both children and adults with serious physical disabilities—and often with multiple impairments—reported a high level of satisfaction and improvement in leisure skills and often found new friendships through such mainstreaming experiences.

Acceptance of Benefits-Based Management

Prompted by such evaluation research findings in a wide range of organized recreation program services, many leisure-service agencies are now making benefits-based management the keynote of their operations. This approach uses several steps shown on page 297 and concludes with a benefits-assessment phase:

Evaluation and Documentation Phase

1. Analyze data to determine effects of recreation participation on benefit achievement
2. Review formative evaluations for content or structural changes
3. Determine if unanticipated benefits were achieved

4. Prepare final reports documenting benefit achievement and implementation process

5. Disseminate findings to appropriate local, state and national audiences.[38]

Increasingly, public recreation and park authorities, along with other leisure-service sponsors in commercial, voluntary nonprofit, armed forces, and other types of agencies, are adopting such management priorities to maintain public support and involvement in an era of increasing financial stringency. At the same time, it has become evident that leisure-service practitioners—particularly on the management level—must have sophisticated research and evaluation skills if they are to provide successful leadership within a highly competitive and rapidly changing society.

SUMMARY

Evaluation research is concerned chiefly with measuring the outcomes and benefits of recreational services or experiences. As such, it is a crucial link between research itself and evaluation as an applied form of investigation. In this chapter, the social goals of public, local leisure-service agencies are presented, supplemented by a recent Canadian report that documents the varied benefits of recreation under four headings: personal, social, economic, and environmental. The remaining section of the chapter reviews evaluation research exploring these and other areas of outcome of organized recreation service, with examples of recently published studies documenting specific findings of carefully designed studies.

QUESTIONS AND ACTIVITIES

1. Why is the evaluation of program outcomes particularly important in today's society? Explain how the goal-oriented evaluation approach illustrates the strong link between research and evaluation in recreation, parks, and leisure services.

2. This chapter describes several major areas in which the benefits of leisure services have been documented through evaluation research. Select any three of these, such as developmental, economic, or therapeutic benefits, and discuss the kinds of outcomes that have been found as well as the need for additional research efforts.

3. Select a single hypothetical agency with community-oriented goals, such as a municipal recreation and park department or a nonprofit youth-serving organization. Outline its appropriate goals and objectives, and identify several specific, measurable objectives to be assessed during the course of the year. Describe and give examples of the types of instruments or procedures that would be used to measure program benefits.

ENDNOTES

1. Francis Caro, *Readings in Evaluation Research* (New York: Russell Sage Foundation, 1977): xi.

2. Peg Connolly, "Evaluation's Critical Role in Agency Accountability," *Parks and Recreation* (Feb. 1982): 34.

3. See Richard Kraus, *Recreation and Leisure in Modern Society* (Glenview, IL: Scott, Foresman and Co., 1990): 378–95.

4. B. L. Driver, Perry Brown, and George Peterson, ed., *Benefits of Leisure* (State College, PA: Venture Publishing, 1991).

5. *The Benefits of Parks and Recreation* (Gloucester, Ontario, Can.: Parks and Recreation Federation of Ontario, 1992).

6. Ibid., 9–15.

7. Richard Daft and Richard Steers, *Organizations: A Micro/Macro Approach* (Glenview, IL: Scott, Foresman and Co., 1986): 319–20.

8. Ibid., 321, 325.

9. Carol Peterson and Scott Gunn, *Therapeutic Recreation Program Design: Principles and Procedures* (Englewood Cliffs, NJ: Prentice-Hall, 1984): 90–112.

10. Charles Clegg and George Chambliss, "Management by Objectives: A Case Study," *Journal of Physical Education, Recreation and Dance* (April 1982): 4.

11. Presentation by Lawrence Allen, "Time to Measure Outcomes," at National Recreation and Park Congress in Minneapolis, October 1994.

12. "Keeping Fit: America Tries to Shape Up," *Newsweek* (May 23, 1977): 78–86.

13. "Sweat Cure: Exercise May Prevent Cancer," *Time* (Feb. 29, 1988): 68.

14. L. Wankel, "Personal and Situational Factors Affecting Exercise Involvement," *Research Quarterly for Exercise and Sport* 56, no. 3 (1985): 281.

15. J. S. Stevenson and R. Topp, "Effects of Moderate and Low Intensity Long Term Exercise by Older Adults," *Research in Nursing and Health* 13 (1990): 209–18.

16. M. C. Santiago, C. P. Coyle, and J. T. Troup, "Effects of Twelve Weeks of Aerobic Exercise in Individuals with Physical Disabilities," Paper presented at 8th International Symposium on Adapted Physical Activity, Miami, FL (Nov. 1991).

17. See *Benefits of Parks and Recreation,* 64.

18. Lynn Barnett, "Developmental Benefits of Play for Children," *Journal of Leisure Research* 22, no. 2 (1990): 138–53.

19. Liselott Diem, "Early Motor Stimulation and Personal Development," *Journal of Physical Education, Recreation, and Dance* (Nov./Dec. 1982): 25.

20. Barnett, "Developmental Benefits of Play."

21. Alan Ewert, "Values, Benefits and Consequences of Participation in Outdoor Adventure Recreation," *A Literature Review: The President's Commission on Americans Outdoors* (Washington, DC: U.S. Government Printing Office, 1986): Values, 71.

22. Seppo Iso-Ahola and Ellen Weissinger, "Leisure and Well-Being: Is There a Connection?" *Parks and Recreation* (June 1984): 41.

23. See *Benefits of Parks and Recreation,* 27.

24. J. R. Kelly and M. W. Steinkamp, "Later Life Leisure: How They Play in Peoria," *The Gerontologist* 26 (1986): 531–37.

25. Roscoe Brown, Jr., and Dan Dodson, "The Effectiveness of Boys' Clubs in Reducing Delinquency," *The Annals of the American Academy of Political Science* (1956): 47–52.

26. Peter Donnelly, "Athletes and Juvenile Delinquents: A Comparative Analysis Based on a Review of the Literature," *Adolescence* (summer 1981): 415.

27. M. S. Searle, *Synthesis of the Research Literature on the Benefits of Recreation: A Technical Report* (Winnipeg, Manitoba: University of Manitoba, 1989).

28. See Stacey McKay, "Research Findings Related to the Potential of Recreation in Delinquency Prevention," *Trends* 30, no. 4 (1993): 27.

29. Phoenix Parks, Recreation and Library Staff, "Recreation Fights Crime," *Parks and Recreation* (Mar. 1994): 44–46.

30. John Crompton, "Rescuing Young Offenders with Recreation Programs," *Trends* 30, no. 4 (1993): 23–26.

31. M. L. Millspaugh, "Leisure and Tourism: Economy Strategy," *World Leisure and Recreation* (summer 1990): 13.

32. Timothy Mascon and George Vozikis, "The Economic Impact of Tourism at the Port of Miami," *Annals of Tourism Research* 12 (1985): 515–28.

33. See Lisa Love and John Crompton for a detailed discussion of the second benefit in "A Profile of Companies that Considered Recreation and Park Amenities in their (Re)location Decisions," *Trends* 30, no. 4 (1993): 14–18.

34. Catherine Coyle, W. B. (Terry) Kinney, Bob Riley, and John Shank, eds., *Benefits of Therapeutic Recreation: A Consensus View* (Philadelphia, PA: Temple University, 1991).

35. Harve Rawson and David McIntosh, "The Effects of Therapeutic Camping on the Self-Esteem of Children with Severe Behavior Problems," *Therapeutic Recreation Journal* (4th quarter 1991): 39–49.

36. Jennifer Mactavish and Mark Searle, "Older Individuals with Mental Retardation and the Effect of a Physical Activity Intervention on Selected Social Psychological Variables," *Therapeutic Recreation Journal* (1st quarter 1992): 38–47.

37. Charles Bullock, Michael Mahon, and LuAnne Welch, "Easter Seals' Progressive Mainstreaming Model: Options and Choices in Camping and Leisure Services for Children and Adults with Disabilities," *Therapeutic Recreation Journal* (4th quarter 1992): 61–70.

38. Lawrence Allen, "Time to Measure Outcomes."

Research and Evaluation Reports and Presentations

The research task is not completed until the report has been written. The most brilliant hypothesis, the most carefully designed and conducted study, the most striking findings, are of little import unless they are communicated to others. Many social scientists seem to regard the writing of a report as an unpleasant chore tacked on to the end of the research process but not really an inherent part of it . . . Nevertheless, communication of the results so that they become part of the general store of knowledge is an essential part of investigators' responsibilities; such communication should receive the same careful attention that earlier stages do.[1]

There's really no point in doing research unless you report your results. Until other people get a chance to review and use the information produced by your work, your experiment, survey, or evaluative study is not complete. To maximize benefits from research, you need to have in mind when you plan your study how you are going to organize and communicate your findings.[2]

INTRODUCTION

The full value of any piece of research or evaluation has not been achieved until its results have been carefully compiled and interpreted and made available to all appropriate audiences. This chapter examines the process of preparing research reports of various types, ranging from full scholarly dissertations or theses to brief summaries of research addressed to professional or lay readers. It outlines the content of typical research reports and presents guidelines with respect to organizing and developing materials, as well as other elements of style and format. It also presents guidelines for reporting research at professional conferences or in other settings or through channels useful in reaching a broader audience. Finally, it discusses the use of research or evaluation in contributing to effective policy-making or operational practices in leisure-service agencies.

The obligation of the researcher or evaluator to present full, accurate, and honest findings is stressed; in some cases, published reports of research tend to emphasize only favorable findings or to distort results in unacceptable ways. In keeping with sound scientific values, this chapter suggests principles underlying the publication of findings that will contribute to scholarship and improved practices in the field and to the professional career of the researcher.

THE ROLE OF REPORTS

Chapter 9 points out that the final stage of the research process involves preparing a report that sums up the entire investigation and presents a detailed account of its findings. Why is such a report necessary?

The obvious answer is that research may be carried out for many reasons—but that none of them are likely to be fulfilled unless study findings are carefully compiled and made available to appropriate audiences. If a graduate student has undertaken a research study to meet degree requirements, she must write a thesis or dissertation report that is defended before a graduate faculty examining committee. Beyond this, there is the obligation to submit what has been learned to the scrutiny of one's academic peers and to contribute new knowledge to the body of scholarship that supports the professional field of parks, recreation, and leisure services.

When research or evaluation studies are carried out to test the effectiveness of a form of professional service or the work of a leisure-service agency, it is obviously important for the findings to be precisely reported and communicated to appropriate audiences. Clearly, research is of value not only to scholars but also to practitioners in leisure-service agencies. Thus, study findings that document the benefits of recreation and park facilities and programs or that contribute to sound programming and marketing of leisure services must be utilized in management information systems and ongoing planning activities.

For these reasons, it is essential that reports be prepared at the conclusion of research or evaluation studies and addressed to one or more of the following audiences: (1) the scholarly community, including both faculty members responsible for supervising research and the broader group of one's academic peers; (2) professionals in the field who may be interested in the subject of the research or evaluation study; (3) the public at large, assuming that the topic is meaningful to them; (4) organizations that may have commissioned the research or supported it financially; and (5) practitioners in the agencies that may have cooperated in the research or evaluation effort.

TYPES OF REPORTS

Too often, it is assumed that the only kind of report that is meaningful is the typical blackbound thesis or dissertation report or the shorter version of it that appears in scholarly research journals. To reach varied audiences, however, one can identify a much fuller range of possibilities for disseminating research findings.

Traditional Academic Research Reports

This is the formal academic thesis or dissertation, often hundreds of pages long, which is normally read by members of the student's committee and then filed in the university library, although it may then become available through interlibrary loan or microfilm or microfiche exchange. Normally, it is expected that such reports meet accepted criteria of academic scholarship in terms of content, format, and writing style.

Independent Publications

Many nonacademic studies, particularly planning reports or those funded by foundation grants or other sponsors, are summed up in separately published monographs. Often they are attractively produced and illustrated and may be widely distributed. Customarily, they are less technical and scholarly and designed for a broader audience than academic reports.

This type of report may also take the form of a technical paper, a monograph, or a summary that appears in newsletters or annual reports published by the agencies conducting research studies. Such reports may be used internally and may also be disseminated to a wider audience through professional societies or regional associations.

Articles in Scholarly Journals

Many academic research studies are summed up in articles in refereed journals (meaning that they must be reviewed by a jury of qualified scholars before they can be accepted for publication). These studies tend to be similar to theses or dissertations, although they are necessarily much briefer.

Articles in Professional or Popular Magazines

Research studies that have a more applied focus may be reported in articles in magazines published by professional societies or even in appropriate popular publications. They may also be summarized in research "briefs," or concise statements of findings, in such magazines.

Presentations to Sponsoring Organizations

Sponsored study findings frequently are summarized directly in presentations to trustees, boards, membership meetings, town councils, and similar groups. The verbal presentation may be accompanied by printed summaries of findings.

Presentations at Professional Meetings

Recreation and leisure-studies research is frequently presented at professional society meetings in two forms: (1) technical reports focusing solely on research, at research symposia, and (2) part of the content at educational sessions dealing with current issues and trends.

Use of Mass Media

In addition to these forms of publication, some research studies may also reach the public broadly through news reports or special programs on network or local television, on radio "talk shows," or through newspaper articles. Particularly if a research study deals with a timely or controversial theme, it may be picked up by the wire services or the news media and receive widespread dissemination, usually in a simplified form.

The researcher who is interested in reaching as broad an audience as possible may use more than one of these channels for disseminating study findings. Obviously, reports or articles intended for a scholarly audience are likely to be more theoretical in nature and to present more technical analyses of data than those directed to a professional or popular audience.

CONTENT OF ACADEMIC RESEARCH REPORTS

There is no single prescribed format that all research reports are expected to follow.

In academic research reports, however, a typical pattern is to require a thesis or dissertation to include five chapters. The first three are essentially an extension of the study proposal, with Chapter 1 being the *introduction, statement of the problem, and the purposes or hypotheses* of the study, Chapter 2 being the *literature review,* and Chapter 3 being a *report of the methodology* as it actually occurred. In each case, the chapter is likely to expand from the version in the proposal. The literature review should be a full-scale survey of the relevant research on the problem as it provided useful background for the study that was carried out. The methodology chapter should go beyond the initial plan that was advanced at the time the proposal was approved and should describe what actually occurred. Often, studies are not fully crystallized at the time the study plan is approved. If a fuller statement of the problem has been developed or if new hypotheses have emerged or different investigative procedures have been followed, these should be explained in full at this time.

Chapter 4 customarily gives a detailed presentation of the actual *findings of the study*. If the study involved a survey, each of the major sections of the questionnaire returns should be reported, with the key topics assembled in sequential sections of the chapter. Normally, data are summarized in tables, followed by interpretation or explanations of their meaning. If the study was an experimental one, customarily the data would be reported as they relate to the study hypotheses, with statistical treatment indicating whether there were significant findings accepting or rejecting the hypotheses.

Dane suggests that this chapter should be divided into two sections: (1) *preliminary* results, and (2) *main* results. The preliminary section would serve as an introduction to the major findings of the study and would include brief summaries of the data-gathering and analytical procedures, with statements justifying the effectiveness of the instruments or manipulations that were used or other research steps. He continues:

> Other material in the preliminary results might include analyses of inter-rater reliability, descriptive statistics about the participants, information about data eliminated from the analyses, and any other results that move the reader toward your main results. How much information you include in a preliminary results subsection depends on the specific nature of your study and your data.[3]

The main results section presents the overall study findings systematically and in detail, with each major issue, hypothesis, or other subtopic dealt with both in descriptive prose form and through statistical analysis. Customarily, tables that present quantitative findings or figures, such as graphs, pictures, or drawings, are used to summarize data in compact or concise form or to depict study results vividly.

While it is essential to include all important details in this chapter, the author may choose to be selective by presenting the most critical findings directly and including other sections of materials in the appendix of the report. However, this must *not* distort the actual findings or implications of the research, which must be presented fully and clearly. Since data may be presented in varied ways, this text will not attempt to present any single model; instead, the reader is advised to examine a number of theses, dissertations, or other scholarly reports to see how findings are typically analyzed and summarized.

Chapter 5 *summarizes the conclusions* reached by the study. Without repeating the data and their meaning at length, it draws out and presents the highlights of the research. It also interprets them in the light of the theoretical or conceptual framework presented in the first two chapters and shows how they may support or challenge the findings of other studies. Finally, Chapter 5 should conclude with a statement of the meaning of the overall study for the field. The researcher may suggest recommendations for future research that will extend the boundaries of knowledge in the problem area. The researcher may also suggest direct applications for professional practice.

Particularly in an applied research study, such as a comprehensive agency evaluation or master-planning study, the recommendations may include specific statements of ranked priorities, in terms of land to be acquired, facilities to be constructed, or population groups to be served. In a study of volunteerism in Philadelphia that was conducted by the authors of this text, the final report provided guidelines for the recruitment and use of citizen volunteers and gave a number of examples of successful volunteerism projects conducted within the city's recreation and park system.[4]

GUIDELINES FOR PREPARING THE RESEARCH REPORT

The researcher should not wait until the full investigative process has been completed before beginning to write the report. Instead, it is advisable to think in terms of organizing and writing the final report from the very beginning. Careful notes should have been kept at all stages of the study, with preliminary copies of major sections of the report developed at an early stage—particularly in terms of the data-gathering process—while the investigator's memory is fresh. All materials, forms, or administrative actions or summaries should be carefully organized and filed so that they are readily accessible at the time of report writing.

Work from an Outline

It is helpful to prepare a detailed outline of each chapter of the report in advance, with a clear indication of topics, subtopics, and other subdivisions of content. This makes it possible to determine that all important points are being covered, that duplication is avoided, and that elements are introduced in the proper order, and it helps to reduce the anxiety that often makes it difficult for researchers to *begin* the final task of writing the report.

Academic reports of theses or dissertations normally follow the five- chapter breakdown that has just been described; other types of reports may use a simpler format. Saslow suggests, for example, that a general outline of a research report should include four sections: *Introduction, Methods, Results,* and *Discussion.* While the length, emphasis, and ordering of these sections may differ for articles, talks, or other nonacademic presentations, Saslow's suggestions provide a useful general framework for developing report outlines.[5]

In addition, journal articles will typically require an abstract (see page 123) and a listing of references cited in the paper itself, as well as a bibliography section that identifies other useful background sources that may not have been directly used in the article. As part of preparation for writing the final report, such materials should have been gathered or prepared in preliminary form during the conduct of the study.

Writing Style

The writing style should be clear and accurate. Although the material may be scholarly and technical, every effort should be made to have all passages understandable, with a minimum of jargon, convoluted writing, or excessively pretentious words. Typically, shorter sentences are more effective than long, rambling sentences. It is helpful to have fairly brief paragraphs, with a liberal use of headings to set off major sections of each chapter. In general, writing should be impersonal and written in the third person. While humor may be permissible at points, a scholarly work should be fairly reserved and should avoid the use of slang or extremely informal writing.

It is essential to recognize that many readers of articles or other nonacademic reports may *not* be knowledgeable in the subject field and that they may have relatively little time to "puzzle out" the meaning of a paper or an article. Saslow points out that consumers of research information often must read and attempt to make sense of articles in a number of journals or magazines. She continues:

> If they are attending a talk, it may be one of several to which they'll be listening on the same day. Your research results will go relatively unnoticed if they are presented in an unorganized, repetitive, obscure, and lengthy fashion. It takes careful writing to prepare a good, clear scientific report.[6]

In general, it is desirable to use active, rather than passive voice forms, and to write in the third person, although infrequent first-person statements may be acceptable, particularly in studies involving participant-observation methods. Past tense is normally used to describe all procedures or events in the study, although the present tense may be used to offer general conclusions about the data, recommendations for future research, or needed agency priorities. Finally, it is important to avoid stereotypes with respect to age, gender, ethnicity, or other demographic factors and to use appropriate ways of referring to individuals with disabilities.

Follow Manual for Style and Format

Most dissertation committees require the use of a recognized manual that describes or presents an approved format for each section of the report and that is the source for authoritative treatment of such details as punctuation, spelling, capitalizations, italics, abbreviations, use of quotations, design of tables and figures, and footnotes and bibliographic references.

As an example, the *Publication Manual of the American Psychological Association* gives detailed directions for the preparation of papers for publication, that defines different types of articles, and describes in detail each of the elements that go into them.[7] It gives helpful suggestions with respect to writing style and other key elements of the report. Many universities rely on this and similar manuals for authoritative rules for the preparation of research reports. In some areas of professional or academic writing, other manuals, such as Chicago, Turabian, or American Standard may be used.[8] Many publishers or university presses prepare their own style manuals; journals often print two or three pages of *Notes for the Contributor*, usually in the first or last issue of the year.

Customarily, other sources are not quoted extensively in research reports or journal articles. Instead, they can be summarized in the author's own words, with credit given to the original author or other source. Short quotations are usually included in the regular text, with double quotation marks, while longer quotations, if they are used at all, should be single-spaced and indented without quotation marks.

The most common approach to citing references involves giving the source (author and date) in parentheses, directly in the body of the text, with an alphabetic listing of all sources in the back of an article, with full reference information. Many book publishers and some journals follow the format used in this text, however, with all references numbered and listed at the end of chapters in consecutive order.

Style manuals usually include guidelines for the use of tables and figures. Customarily, tables consist of lists of numbers and are useful in summarizing different elements and their values concisely. Figures, which provide illustrations of equipment, settings, relationships, or other information in diagrammatic or picture form, are helpful in showing change over time or other types of contrasts in a vivid way.

Evaluate Report Carefully

When a first draft of the research report has been written, it is advisable to review it carefully. Of primary concern is the actual content of the report; such questions must be asked as:

- Is the research question significant, and is the work original and relevant to scholarly or professional concerns?
- Have the instruments been shown to have adequate reliability and validity?
- Does the research design fully test the stated hypotheses or meet the other purposes of the investigation?
- Are the study subjects representative of the larger population about which generalizations are made?
- Were ethical standards observed in the treatment of human subjects?[9]

While such questions should have been asked at earlier stages of the investigation, they must again be raised at the point of preparing the final report. If any weaknesses are disclosed at this stage, they must be forthrightly discussed in the report itself. In addition, other questions must be raised regarding the quality of the presentation itself. For example, the American Psychological Association's *Publication Manual* asks the following questions with respect to research reports that are submitted to scholarly journals:

- Is the topic appropriate for the publication to which the article is being submitted?
- Is the paper's introduction clear and complete, and does its statement of purpose fully orient the reader to the thrust of the research?
- Is the literature adequately reviewed, with appropriate and complete citations?
- Are the conceptualization and rationale of the research clearly presented?
- Is the methodology adequately described; could the study be replicated from the description given in the paper?
- Are the data analysis techniques appropriate, with sound assumptions underlying the statistical procedures which were chosen? Are the study results and conclusions unambiguous and meaningful?
- Does the manuscript meet the style and format criteria of the APA, as outlined in the Manual's checklist?[10]

PREPARATION OF NONACADEMIC, INDEPENDENT REPORTS

Research reports that are published by nonacademic agencies or professional societies are likely to be much more flexible in their format and writing style. Typically, planning reports published by government agencies tend to avoid formal hypotheses and complex statistical analyses. Instead, they are likely to stress the applied purpose of the research and to present findings in simple clear language, with a generous use of tables, diagrams, and other illustrative materials.

Often such reports, when published by professional societies, represent factual presentations describing current practices in the field or analyses of trends or problems relating to professional development. They have relatively little conceptual content and do not usually present a detailed literature review as background. However, assuming that their methodology has been sound, they do provide an important body of information helpful to practitioners in advancing the work in their field.

▼ FOR EXAMPLE

A number of such reports were referred to earlier in this text, including (1) the *Municipal and County Park and Recreation Study (MACPARS);* (2) the *Report of the President's Commission on Americans Outdoors;* and (3) the *Benefits of Therapeutic Recreation: A Consensus View.* In some cases, a single organization may publish several such reports around a single theme or problem. For example, in the City of Ottawa, Ontario, Canada, a Citizen's Task Force on Culture published a group of major reports on culture and the arts in the late 1980s and early 1990s.[11]

Some federal outdoor recreation and park agencies in the United States, such as the U.S. Forest Service, maintain major research stations that regularly publish independent reports of their study findings.[12]

Articles in Professional or General Magazines

Most magazines of a professional or general nature, like *Parks and Recreation, Journal of Physical Education, Recreation and Dance,* or *Recreation Canada,* do not normally include reports of recreation research in full-fledged articles. However, they frequently include articles dealing with problems or trends in research and evaluation and may also accept articles dealing with issues of professional concern that are based heavily on research studies.

The researcher who seeks to prepare such articles for publication should carefully study the magazine to which she intends to submit material. Probably she will find that it is necessary to key the research findings to an issue or problem of important professional concern. While many articles in the publication are likely to represent "thought pieces" (meaning simply the point of view or opinion of the authors), others use research findings as a basis for their conclusions or analyses. In preparing the article, one normally would *not* include an abstract, a literature review, a detailed statement of hypotheses and purposes, or the study's data-gathering procedures and statistical analysis techniques.

Often it is helpful to write the editor of the magazine *before* submitting an article and perhaps even before writing it. The purpose of such an inquiry is to solicit the editor's interest in the topic of the proposed article, hopefully to gain his encouragement in advance, and possibly also to get suggestions about the content that might be helpful in preparing the article. Not infrequently, the editor may point out that a special issue of the magazine is being planned and that this article would fit well into it, if it were given a certain emphasis and written at a given length.

Unlike scholarly research reports that are sent to academic journals, which frequently have a lengthy waiting period during which they are being reviewed and which also may require extensive revisions, most articles sent to more general publications receive a prompt reading and may not require any significant rewriting.

Presentations at Professional and Scholarly Meetings

Often, in addition to writing full research reports or submitting brief articles to journals, investigators also make presentations at research symposia or other sessions of professional societies. Customarily these take two forms:

(1) an individual presentation, often lasting about 20 minutes to half an hour, as part of a series of research presentations by other scholars; and (2) a general educational session, presented to a broader professional audience, not particularly interested in research, but open to its inclusion as part of a discussion of a significant current issue or trend.

While the presentation itself is a verbal one, often making use of audiovisual materials, it may also involve giving copies of an abstract or research summary to the audience. Sometimes these may appear in printed proceedings of conference presentations or in annually published collections of presentations at research symposia.

By taking advantage of all such opportunities for disseminating research findings, the investigator will have made certain that the original reasons for undertaking the study have been achieved. Instead of gathering dust on a library's shelves, her research will have reached one or more appropriate audiences and may, in fact, provide direction for future investigations.

Internal Dissemination and Use

In many cases, research study findings are published in the form of internal memoranda, newsletter summaries, staff directives, or other documents that may be reviewed within agencies and result in recommended changes in policies, priorities, or operational procedures. Often, they may provide useful information that helps shape strategy employed in carrying out a specific project.

▼ FOR EXAMPLE

Fletcher and King describe the use of voter surveys to plan effective bond campaigns for recreation and park acquisition efforts in the East Bay Regional Park District in California.[13] Wicks, Backman, Allen, and Van Blaricom show how geographic information systems (GIS) may be used internally by urban recreation and park agencies to integrate spatial and demographic data, help manage growth, and assure fair service allocations.[14] Ken Kutska describes the use of detailed accident reporting and auditing systems to improve safety conditions in public playgrounds.[15] Similarly, Jeff Witman suggests approaches to measuring outcomes in therapeutic recreation settings, both to help improve service programs and to document their worth for other treatment disciplines or administrators in the agency setting.[16]

Evaluation Reports

Although agency or program evaluation reports are rarely published for the profession or public at large, they should be as carefully prepared as other types of research reports.

When they deal with specific areas of agency performance or with such concerns as personnel, facility usage, or program outcomes, they should be used directly to guide staff practices. They may also be used to define new agency priorities or to plan future program events and services. In some cases, action research projects such as those described in Chapter 5 may result in detailed reports to funding sponsors, governing boards, or similar bodies. Typically, such evaluation reports focus on the project's success in achieving stated goals and objectives, as determined by outside evaluators.

Management Information Systems

Such examples illustrate the importance of research and evaluation techniques in agency planning and marketing efforts. Increasingly, leisure-service agencies are relying on systematically gathered data that are part of "management information systems." Perlman writes:

> The term Management Information System (MIS) refers to the processes and procedures by which raw data are organized into information useful for administrative decision making. Management information systems are commonly computer-based since the repetitive task of tabulating and aggregating large quantities of detailed information can be handled most efficiently by data-processing machines . . . .[17]

What characterizes a true management information system is the quality, accessibility, compatibility, and comprehensive nature of the data and the way in which they have been organized to serve important management needs. He concludes, "An integrated management information system is necessary to implement other new administrative techniques and strategies."

In large organizations, the task of developing effective information systems is carried out by a combined team of systems analysts or data-management specialists, working together with representatives of the agency who are familiar with its programs, maintenance operations, personnel practices, and fiscal structure. Together, they determine exactly what kinds of information must be gathered and the uses to which it will be put.

Program codes are developed and software acquired to permit efficient processing of the data, using programs that are compatible with the computer hardware being used. Such a system makes it possible to analyze costs and conduct inventories with much greater speed and specificity than is possible under other approaches. For example, Lange and Mescher describe a management information system developed for the Pittsburgh, Pennsylvania, Department of Parks and Recreation and housed within the department itself, rather than in a centralized office of city government:

> Department managers now have the ability to compare actual program costs against planned program costs. Facilities were inventoried, and facil-

ity codes were developed so that cost information can be retrieved by operating division, primary site, or by a sublocation . . . . An additional benefit of the system is a "computer mystique" which has encouraged compliance with program and facility coding . . . . Historical information is produced for code account, subaccount, facility, and program codes for up to three years on-line, and for as many years as needed through batch reporting.[18]

ACCURACY, HONESTY, AND ETHICAL STANDARDS

A final important consideration is the need for all published research reports to maintain the highest possible degree of scientific accuracy. Although researchers may be tempted to exclude negative or uncertain findings, a cardinal rule of scientific reporting is to give all the evidence relevant to the research questions asked; scientific authors are not free to choose what they will include and exclude in terms of the effects they wish to create.

Beyond this, it is important to recognize that scientific research is carried on by human beings who are subject to the same temptations that people in other professions face. An individual researcher may have a stake in exaggerating or suppressing data because a particular outcome may confirm his theory, be consistent with his ideological biases, or may make him famous and successful. In some cases, practitioners may be tempted to distort evaluation data to make their programs appear more successful than they really are. Graduate students may take "shortcuts" in the effort to get their theses or dissertations completed or approved as easily or rapidly as possible.

Each year, examples of such misuses of research are reported in the nation's press. Simon cites a number of outstanding examples of scientific dishonesty, some resulting in frauds and mistaken beliefs in the scholarly world that lasted for long periods of time.[19] Similarly, Blakely, Poling, and Cross write of "fraud, fakery, and fudging" in the world of science, including a famous case of two researchers who claimed that they had successfully trained a number of chronic alcoholics to drink moderately—findings revealed by later investigations to have been based on "careless" if not "fraudulent" study methods and reporting.[20]

Anthropologists, medical researchers, chemists, and sociologists have all been guilty of significantly distorting research findings and in some cases perpetuating major, dishonest claims that ultimately destroyed their careers. Simon gives advice to the young researcher:

> Doctoring the data can ruin your reputation and it can cause you great suffering from pangs of conscience. On the positive side, some of the world's great discoveries have come from researchers who took apparently conflicting data seriously and pursued the discrepancy, rather than sweeping it under the rug, thereby leading to great new findings.[21]

It is important to recognize that even a study that achieves negative results or that fails to confirm a researcher's pet hypothesis makes a contribution to knowledge. All knowledge is valuable and part of the growing tide of scholarship that provides validity to the recreation and leisure-studies field—whether or not it provides dramatic new insights or proofs of valuable outcomes.

Ethical Concerns

As Chapter 10 points out (see page 135), it is essential that all research proposals that involve human subjects adhere to formal guidelines and be approved by Institutional Review Boards, in order to prevent possible physical or mental abuses. These concerns extend to such procedures or practices as (1) obtaining "informed consent," meaning that subjects are fully aware of the purposes of a study, its possible dangers, and the credentials of the researchers; (2) assurance of privacy or anonymity of subjects, to prevent their embarrassment or other negative outcomes; and (3) avoidance of deception during the course of the study that might be harmful to subjects.[22]

Within specific professional fields, such as sociology, psychology, or therapeutic recreation service, national societies have established codes of ethics that outline the moral and legal framework within which practitioners and researchers must function. Research reports must show how these principles were observed during the course of a study and must be consistent with them in terms of reporting data and providing anonymity for subjects.

Another important ethical concern has to do with acknowledging and sharing credit fairly with individuals who assisted in the research effort. Authorship of published works, which is a key element in promoting academic careers, should be properly apportioned to those responsible for the work. Finally, researchers must keep careful records of all their analytical and investigative procedures and data files, both to share with other researchers as necessary and to meet possible challenges to their work.

SUMMARY

Preparing detailed, accurate research reports is a final critical step in the research process. This may take a number of different forms, ranging from scholarly theses or dissertations to articles in professional magazines or presentations at research symposia.

This chapter describes the task of writing research reports, including the typical content of scholarly publications and a number of guidelines related to writing style, using respected manuals to ensure correct usages, and similar functions. It gives suggestions to assist researchers in finding outlets for reports of their findings on different levels and concludes with a reminder of the need for highly ethical behavior in conducting studies and reporting outcomes. Suppression of negative findings and unwelcome data or exaggeration of research successes occur in many fields, and researchers must be aware of the need to maintain rigorous standards of personal honesty and scientific accuracy.

QUESTIONS AND ACTIVITIES

1. Become familiar with the presentation of scholarly research studies to the academic community by:

   a. Attending a professional society meeting and sitting in on research presentations; preparing summaries of these sessions and reporting on them in class.

   b. Reviewing annual collections of presentations at research symposiums published by the National Recreation and Park Association and classifying reports according to subjects, methods or designs, and types (applied, pure, etc.).

2. Examine research reports that are published by government agencies, nonprofit organizations, or similar groups. These should not be academic in nature but rather they should be written to provide information to a general professional or public audience. Contrast these reports with more academic reports in terms of both style and content.

3. Review several issues of general newspapers (*USA Today* is a useful example), or weekly news magazines, trade publications, etc., to identify summary reports of research in the social sciences, business field, etc. Summarize and report what you read to the class.

ENDNOTES

1. Claire Selltiz, Lawrence Wrightsman, and Stuart Cook, *Research Methods in Social Relations* (New York: Rinehart and Winston, 1976): 500.

2. Carol Saslow, *Basic Research Methods* (New York: Random House, 1982): 323.

3. Francis Dane, *Research Methods* (Pacific Grove, CA: Brooks/Cole, 1990): 222.

4. Lawrence Allen, Richard Kraus, and Delores Williams-Andy, *Philadelphia Recreation Volunteerism Project: Final Report* (Philadelphia: Temple University, City of Philadelphia and American Academy for Park and Recreation Administration, 1986).

5. Saslow, *Basic Research Methods*, 324–25.

6. Ibid.

7. *Publication Manual of the American Psychological Association* (Washington, D.C.: American Psychological Association, 1983): 21–22.

8. See endnote 6, page 140.

9. Adapted from APA Manual, 19–20.

10. Ibid., 29.

11. See for example: *Final Report, Citizens' Task Force on Culture* (Ottawa, Ontario, Canada: Department of Recreation and Culture, 1992).

12. Typically, a number of U.S. Forest Service studies have been initiated or funded by the Wildland Recreation and Urban Culture Research Work Unit of the Pacific Southwest Research Station, Riverside, California.

13. James Fletcher and Michael King, "Use of Voter Surveys to Plan Bond Campaigns for Parks and Recreation," *Journal of Park and Recreation Administration* 11, no. 2 (1993): 17–27.

14. Bruce Wicks, Kenneth Backman, Jeffrey Allen, and Donald Van Blaricom, "Geographic Information Systems (GIS): A Tool for Marketing, Managing, and Planning Municipal Park Systems," *Journal of Park and Recreation Administration* 11, no. 1 (1993): 9–23.

15. Ken Kutska, "Public Playground Safety: Paradigm or Paradox," *Parks and Recreation* (April 1994): 47.

16. Jeff Witman, "Demonstrating Treatment Outcomes in Therapeutic Recreation," *Parks and Recreation* (April 1994): 84–89.

17. Daniel Perlman, in Diane Borst and Patrick Montana, ed., *Managing Nonprofit Organizations* (New York: American Management Association, 1979): 61.

18. Alice Lange and Dolores Mescher, "Development of a Management Information System," *Journal of Park and Recreation Administration* (3d quarter 1985): 15–19.

19. Julian Simon, *Basic Research Methods in Social Sciences: The Art of Empirical Investigation* (New York: Random House, 1978): 25.

20. Elbert Blakely, Alan Poling, and Jeffrey Cross, "Fraud, Fakery, and Fudging," in Alan Poling and R. Wayne Fuqua, ed., *Research Methods in Applied Behavior Analysis* (New York: Plenum, 1986): 322.

21. Simon, *Basic Research Methods,* 26.

22. For a fuller discussion, see Kenneth Bailey, *Methods of Social Research* (New York: The Free Press, Collier-Macmillan, 1982): 431–46.

Appendix A

RESEARCH PERIODICALS

A number of the following journals are exclusively devoted to publishing research articles in recreation, parks, and leisure studies. Others are of a more general nature, but frequently publish research reviews or articles that summarize research findings.

Annals of Tourism Research. Department of Habitational Resources, University of Wisconsin-Stout. Menomonie, Wisconsin

Journal of Applied Recreation Research. Ontario Research Council on Leisure. Wilfrid Laurier University Press. Waterloo, Ontario, Canada N2L 3C5

Journal of Festival Management and Event Tourism. Cognizant Communication Corp. Elmsford, New York

Journal of Leisurability. Leisurability Publications, Inc. Box 507, Station Q. Toronto, Ontario, Canada M4T 2M5

Journal of Leisure Research. National Recreation and Park Association. 2775 So. Quincy St., Suite 300. Arlington, Virginia, 22206

Journal of Park and Recreation Administration. American Academy for Park and Recreation Administration. Sagamore Publishing. P.O. Box 647. Champaign, Illinois, 61824

Journal of Physical Education, Recreation and Dance. American Alliance for Health, Physical Education, Recreation and Dance. 1900 Association Drive, Reston, Virginia 22091

Journal of Sport Management. North American Society for Sport Management. Human Kinetics Publishers. Box 5076, Champaign, Illinois 61825

Journal of Travel Research. Travel and Tourism Research Association. Box 420, University of Colorado. Boulder, Colorado 80309

Journal of Travel and Tourism Marketing. The Haworth Press, Inc. Binghamton, New York 13904-1580

Leisure Sciences. Taylor and Francis. 1101 Vermont Ave., Suite 200. Washington, DC 20005

Leisure Studies. E. and F. N. Spon. 2-6 Boundary Row, London SE1 8HN, United Kingdom

Parks and Recreation. National Recreation and Park Association. 2775 So. Quincy St., Suite 300. Arlington, Virginia 22208

Recreation Canada. Canadian Parks/Recreation Association. 1600 Promenade James Naismith Dr. Gloucester, Ontario, Canada K1B 5N4

Tourism Management. Elsevier Science LTD. Kidlington, Oxford OX5 1GB United Kingdom

Travel and Tourism Analyst. Economist Intelligence Unit. 15 Regent St., London SW1 4LR United Kingdom

Trends. Park Practice Program. National Park Service and National Recreation and Park Association. P.O. Box 37127, Washington, DC 20013

World Leisure and Recreation. World Leisure and Recreation Association. Sharbot Lake, Ontario, Canada K0H 2P0

Appendix B

LITERATURE RETRIEVAL SOURCES

To conduct literature searches as background for research proposals, the following electronic databases are useful. In most college and university libraries, reference librarians or scholars' information centers can provide additional resources.

1990 Census of Population and Housing. Offers a wide variety of statistical data describing U.S. population and housing characteristics.

ABI/INFORM. Provides comprehensive, current information on human resources, international trade, real estate, advertising, marketing, and management from more than 800 journals.

Dissertation Abstracts. Comprehensive access to doctoral dissertations and masters theses from more than 500 universities throughout the world.

ECONLIT. Comprehensive indexed/bibliography with selected abstracts of worldwide literature on economics from more than 300 major economic journals and books.

ERIC. Most widely used database for educational literature, with abstracts and bibliographic citations for journal literature from more than 775 periodicals and thousands of reports.

Ethnic Newswatch. Full-text articles from ethnic and minority press in America, including African American, Asian American, Middle Eastern, European, and other sources.

GPO. Data contains more than 275,000 references to books, reports, studies, periodicals, maps, and other publications issued by government agencies from 1976 to the present.

Philosopher's Index. Indexes and abstracts on aesthetic, epistemology, ethics, logic and metaphysics, and philosophy of related disciplines such as history, law, religion, and science.

Psyclit. Citations and abstracts from more than 1,300 journals, including topics on all aspects of psychology and related elements of education, medicine, sociology, and other fields.

Social Work Abstracts Plus. Cites references from two databases dealing with social work practices and professional trends.

Sociofile. Comprehensive coverage of world literature on theoretical and applied aspects of sociology, drawn from 1,800 journals and relevant dissertations.

Sport Discus. International sports database, covering fields of exercise, medicine, biomechanics, coaching, and sports medicine.

Other sources specifically on recreation, parks, and leisure studies include:

A Literature Review. Comprehensive review of literature on recreation and leisure trends and demands, values and benefits, natural resources management, special populations, activity participation trends, urban recreation, tourism and financing, published as appendix to the *Report of the President's Commission on Americans Outdoors* in January 1987.

Abstracts from the Symposium on Leisure Research. Held in conjunction with the National Congress for Recreation and Parks, published annually by the National Recreation and Park Association.

Note: Other collections of research abstracts are published by the Ontario Research Council on Leisure, or following special conferences on therapeutic recreation, environmental issues, management practices, and similar topics.

A useful article on literature searches and reference tools in the interdisciplinary fields of health, physical education, and recreation, by Elaine Clever and David Dillard, was published in *The Reference Librarian* (New York: Haworth Press, 1991): 143–50.

The Leisure, Recreation and Tourism Abstracts. Abstracts of research reports, articles, and other literature dealing with recreation, leisure, and tourism on the world scene; published by the World Leisure and Recreation Association.

Appendix C

STATISTICAL TABLES

TABLE C.1   Critical values of t.

LEVEL OF SIGNIFICANCE FOR ONE-TAILED TEST			LEVEL OF SIGNIFICANCE FOR TWO-TAILED TEST		
df	.05	.01	df	.05	.01
1	6.314	31.821	1	12.706	63.657
2	2.920	6.965	2	4.303	9.925
3	2.353	4.541	3	3.182	5.841
4	2.132	3.747	4	2.776	4.604
5	2.015	3.365	5	2.571	4.032
6	1.943	3.143	6	2.447	3.707
7	1.895	2.998	7	2.365	3.499
8	1.860	2.896	8	2.306	3.355
9	1.833	2.821	9	2.262	3.250
10	1.812	2.764	10	2.228	3.169
11	1.796	2.718	11	2.201	3.106
12	1.782	2.681	12	2.179	3.055
13	1.771	2.650	13	2.160	3.012
14	1.761	2.624	14	2.145	2.977
15	1.753	2.602	15	2.131	2.947
16	1.746	2.583	16	2.120	2.921
17	1.740	2.567	17	2.110	2.898
18	1.734	2.552	18	2.101	2.878
19	1.729	2.539	19	2.093	2.861
20	1.725	2.528	20	2.086	2.845
21	1.721	2.518	21	1.080	2.831
22	1.717	2.508	22	2.074	2.819
23	1.714	2.500	23	2.069	2.807
24	1.711	2.492	24	2.064	2.797
25	1.708	2.485	25	2.060	2.787
26	1.706	2.479	26	2.056	2.779
27	1.703	2.473	27	2.052	2.771
28	1.701	2.467	28	2.048	2.763
29	1.699	2.462	29	2.045	2.756
30	1.697	2.457	30	2.042	2.750
40	1.684	2.423	40	2.021	2.704
60	1.671	2.390	60	2.000	2.660
120	1.658	2.358	120	1.980	2.617
—	1.645	2.326	—	1.960	2.576

Source: Runyon, R.P. and Harber, A. (1972) *Fundamentals of behavioral statistics*. Reading, MA: Addison-Wesley.

TABLE C.2   Values of F at the 5% and 1% levels of significance.

df ASSOCIATED WITH THE DENOMINATOR		*df ASSOCIATED WITH THE NUMERATOR*								
		1	2	3	4	5	6	7	8	9
1	5%	161	200	216	225	230	234	237	239	241
	1%	4052	5000	5403	5625	5764	5859	5928	5982	6022
2	5%	18.5	19.0	19.2	19.2	19.3	19.3	19.4	19.4	19.4
	1%	98.5	99.0	99.2	99.2	99.3	99.3	99.4	99.4	99.4
3	5%	10.1	9.55	9.28	9.12	9.01	8.94	8.89	8.85	8.81
	1%	34.1	30.8	29.5	28.7	28.2	27.9	27.7	27.5	27.3
4	5%	7.71	6.94	6.59	6.39	6.26	6.16	6.09	6.04	6.00
	1%	21.2	18.0	16.7	16.0	15.5	15.2	15.0	14.8	14.7
5	5%	6.61	5.79	5.41	5.19	5.05	4.95	4.88	4.82	4.77
	1%	16.3	13.3	12.1	11.4	11.0	10.7	10.5	10.3	10.2
6	5%	5.99	5.14	4.76	4.53	4.39	4.28	4.21	4.15	4.10
	1%	13.7	10.9	9.78	9.15	8.75	8.47	8.26	8.10	7.98
7	5%	5.59	4.74	4.35	4.12	3.97	3.87	3.79	3.73	3.68
	1%	12.2	9.55	8.45	7.85	7.46	7.19	6.99	6.84	6.72
8	5%	5.32	4.46	4.07	3.84	3.69	3.58	3.50	3.44	3.39
	1%	11.3	8.65	7.59	7.01	6.63	6.37	6.18	6.03	5.91
9	5%	5.12	4.26	3.86	3.63	3.48	3.29	3.29	3.23	3.18
	1%	10.6	8.02	6.99	6.42	6.06	5.61	5.61	5.47	5.35
10	5%	4.96	4.10	3.71	3.48	3.33	3.22	3.14	3.07	3.02
	1%	10.0	7.56	6.55	5.99	5.64	5.39	5.20	5.06	4.94
11	5%	4.84	3.98	3.59	3.36	3.20	3.09	3.01	2.95	2.90
	1%	9.65	7.21	6.22	5.67	5.32	5.07	4.89	4.74	4.63
12	5%	4.75	3.89	3.49	3.26	3.11	3.00	2.91	2.85	2.80
	1%	9.33	6.93	5.95	5.41	5.06	4.82	4.64	4.50	4.39
13	5%	4.67	3.81	3.41	3.18	3.03	2.92	2.83	2.77	2.71
	1%	9.07	6.70	5.74	5.21	4.86	4.62	4.44	4.30	4.19
14	5%	4.60	3.74	3.34	3.11	2.96	2.85	2.76	2.70	2.65
	1%	8.86	6.51	5.56	5.04	4.70	4.46	4.46	4.14	4.03
15	5%	4.54	3.68	3.29	3.06	2.90	2.79	2.71	2.64	2.59
	1%	8.68	6.36	5.42	4.89	4.56	4.32	4.14	4.00	3.89
16	5%	4.49	3.63	3.24	3.01	2.85	2.74	2.66	2.59	2.54
	1%	8.53	6.23	5.29	4.77	4.44	4.20	4.03	3.89	3.78
17	5%	4.45	3.59	3.20	2.96	2.81	2.70	2.61	2.55	2.49
	1%	8.40	6.11	5.18	4.67	4.34	4.10	3.93	3.79	3.68
18	5%	4.41	3.55	3.16	2.93	2.77	2.66	2.58	2.51	2.46
	1%	8.29	6.01	5.09	4.58	4.25	4.01	3.84	3.71	3.60
19	5%	4.38	3.52	3.13	2.90	2.74	2.63	2.54	2.48	2.42
	1%	8.18	5.93	5.01	4.50	4.17	3.94	3.77	3.63	3.52
20	5%	4.35	3.49	3.10	2.87	2.71	2.60	2.51	2.45	2.39
	1%	8.10	5.85	4.94	4.43	4.10	3.87	3.70	3.56	3.46
21	5%	4.32	3.47	3.07	2.84	2.68	2.57	2.49	2.42	2.37
	1%	8.02	5.78	4.87	4.37	4.04	3.81	3.64	3.51	3.40

TABLE C.2   (cont.)

df ASSOCIATED WITH THE DENOMINATOR		df ASSOCIATED WITH THE NUMERATOR								
22	5%	4.30	3.44	3.05	2.82	2.66	2.55	2.46	2.40	2.34
	1%	7.95	5.72	4.82	4.31	3.99	3.76	3.59	3.45	3.35
23	5%	4.28	3.42	3.03	2.80	2.64	2.53	2.44	2.37	2.32
	1%	7.88	5.66	4.76	4.26	3.94	3.71	3.54	3.41	3.30
24	5%	4.26	3.40	3.01	2.78	2.62	2.51	2.42	2.36	2.30
	1%	7.82	5.61	4.72	4.22	3.90	3.67	3.50	3.36	3.26
25	5%	4.24	3.39	2.99	2.76	2.60	2.49	2.40	2.34	2.28
	1%	7.77	5.57	4.68	4.18	3.86	3.63	3.46	3.32	3.22
26	5%	4.23	3.37	2.98	2.74	2.59	2.47	2.39	2.32	2.27
	1%	7.72	5.53	4.64	4.14	3.82	3.59	3.42	3.29	3.18
27	5%	4.21	3.35	2.96	3.73	2.57	2.46	2.37	2.31	2.25
	1%	7.68	5.49	4.60	4.11	3.78	3.56	3.39	3.26	3.15
28	5%	4.20	3.34	2.95	2.71	2.56	2.45	2.36	2.29	2.24
	1%	7.64	5.54	4.57	4.07	3.75	3.53	3.36	3.23	3.12
29	5%	4.18	3.33	2.93	2.70	2.55	2.43	2.35	2.28	2.22
	1%	7.60	5.42	4.54	4.04	3.73	3.50	3.33	3.20	3.09
30	5%	4.17	3.32	2.92	2.69	2.53	2.42	2.33	2.27	2.21
	1%	7.56	5.39	4.51	4.02	3.70	3.47	3.30	3.17	3.07
40	5%	4.08	3.23	2.84	2.61	2.45	2.34	2.25	2.18	2.12
	1%	7.31	5.18	4.31	3.83	3.51	3.29	3.12	2.99	2.89
60	5%	4.00	3.15	2.76	2.53	2.37	2.25	2.17	2.10	2.04
	1%	7.08	4.98	4.13	3.65	3.34	3.12	2.95	2.82	2.72
120	5%	3.92	3.07	2.68	2.45	2.29	2.18	2.09	2.02	1.96
	1%	6.85	4.79	3.95	3.48	3.17	2.96	2.79	2.66	2.56

From M. Merrington and C. M. Thompson, Tables of percentage points of the inverted beta (F) distribution, *Biometrika* 33: 73–88 (1943). Copyright 1943 by the Biometrika Trust, London.

TABLE C.3   Critical values of chi-square.

df $(r-1)(c-1)$	PROBABILITY	
	.05	.01
1	3.84	6.64
2	5.99	9.21
3	7.82	11.34
4	9.49	13.28
5	11.07	15.09
6	12.59	16.81
7	14.07	18.48
8	15.51	20.09
9	16.92	21.67
10	18.31	23.21
11	19.68	24.72
12	21.03	26.22
13	22.36	27.69
14	23.68	29.14
15	25.00	30.58
16	26.30	32.00
17	27.59	33.41
18	28.87	34.80
19	30.14	36.19
20	31.41	37.57
21	32.67	38.93
22	33.92	40.29
23	35.17	41.64
24	36.42	42.98
25	37.65	44.31
26	38.88	45.64
27	40.11	46.96
28	41.34	48.28
29	42.56	49.59
30	43.77	50.89

Source: Fisher, R. A. and Yates, F. (1963). *Statistical tables for biological, agricultural, and medical research* (6th edition). New York: Hafner Publishing Co.

Table C.4 Table of critical values for r.

DEGREE OF FREEDOM	PROBABILITY	
(n − 2)	.05	.01
1	.997	1.00
2	.950	.990
3	.878	.959
4	.811	.917
5	.754	.874
6	.707	.834
7	.666	.798
8	.632	.765
9	.602	.735
10	.576	.708
11	.553	.684
12	.532	.661
13	.514	.641
14	.497	.623
15	.482	.606
16	.468	.590
17	.456	.575
18	.444	.561
19	.433	.549
20	.423	.537
21	.413	.526
22	.404	.515
23	.396	.505
24	.388	.496
25	.381	.487
26	.374	.478
27	.367	.470
28	.361	.463
29	.355	.456
30	.349	.449
35	.325	.418
40	.304	.393
45	.288	.372
50	.273	.354
60	.250	.325
70	.232	.302
80	.217	.283
90	.205	.267
100	.195	.254
125	.174	.228
150	.159	.208
200	.138	.181
300	.113	.148
400	.098	.128
500	.088	.115
1000	.062	.081

Source: Fisher, R. A. and Yates, F. (1963). *Statistical tables for biological, agricultural, and medical research* (6th edition). New York: Hafner Publishing Co.

TABLE C.5   Values of Spearman r_s for the 0.5 and .01 levels of significance.

N	.05	.01	N	.05	.01
6	.886	—	19	.462	.608
7	.786	—	20	.450	.591
8	.738	.881	21	.438	.576
9	.683	.833	22	.428	.562
10	.648	.818	23	.418	.549
11	.623	.794	24	.409	.537
12	.591	.780	25	.400	.526
13	.566	.745	26	.392	.515
14	.545	.716	27	.385	.505
15	.525	.689	28	.377	.496
16	.507	.666	29	.370	.487
17	.490	.645	30	.364	.478
18	.476	.625			

From E.G. Olds, Distribution of sums of squares of rank differences for small numbers of individuals, *Annals of Mathematical Statistics 9:* 133–48 (1938), and E.G. Olds, The 5% significance levels for sums of squares of rank differences and a correction, *Annals of Mathematical Statistics 20:* 117–18 (1949). Copyright 1949 by the Institute of Mathematical Statistics, San Francisco, Calif.

Author Index

Subject Index